British Economic Growth, 1270–1870

This is a definitive new account of Britain's economic evolution from a backwater of Europe in 1270 to the hub of the global economy in 1870. A team of leading economic historians reconstruct Britain's national accounts for the first time right back into the thirteenth century to show what really happened quantitatively during the centuries leading up to the Industrial Revolution. Contrary to traditional views of the earlier period as one of Malthusian stagnation, they reveal how the transition to modern economic growth built on the earlier foundations of a persistent upward trend in GDP per capita which doubled between 1270 and 1700. Featuring comprehensive estimates of population, land use, agricultural production, industrial and service-sector production and GDP per capita, as well as analysis of their implications, this will be an essential reference for anyone interested in British economic history and the origins of modern economic growth more generally.

STEPHEN BROADBERRY is Professor of Economic History at the London School of Economics, Research Theme Leader at CAGE and Director of the Economic History Programme at CEPR.

BRUCE M. S. CAMPBELL is Emeritus Professor of Medieval Economic History at the Queen's University of Belfast.

ALEXANDER KLEIN is an Assistant Professor at the School of Economics, University of Kent.

MARK OVERTON is Professor of Economic and Social History at the University of Exeter.

BAS VAN LEEUWEN is a postdoc researcher in economic history at Utrecht University.

British Economic Growth, 1270–1870

STEPHEN BROADBERRY
London School of Economics

BRUCE M. S. CAMPBELL
The Queen's University of Belfast

ALEXANDER KLEIN
University of Kent

MARK OVERTON
University of Exeter

and

BAS VAN LEEUWEN
Utrecht University

CAMBRIDGE
UNIVERSITY PRESS

CAMBRIDGE
UNIVERSITY PRESS

University Printing House, Cambridge CB2 8BS, United Kingdom

Cambridge University Press is part of the University of Cambridge.

It furthers the University's mission by disseminating knowledge in the pursuit of education, learning and research at the highest international levels of excellence.

www.cambridge.org
Information on this title: www.cambridge.org/9781107070783

First published 2015

A catalogue record for this publication is available from the British Library

Library of Congress Cataloguing in Publication data
British economic growth, 1270–1870 / Stephen Broadberry, London School of Economics and 4 others.
    pages   cm
ISBN 978-1-107-07078-3 (Hardback) – ISBN 978-1-107-67649-7 (Paperback)
1. Great Britain – Economic conditions.   2. Economic history.
I. Broadberry, S. N., editor.
HC253.B85   2015
330.941–dc23

                                                            2014026528

ISBN 978-1-107-07078-3 Hardback

Contents

Tables

Figures

Appendices

Preface and acknowledgements

Publication in 1962 of Phyllis Deane and Max Cole's *British economic growth, 1688–1959* marked a watershed in historical analysis of economic growth. Simon Kuznets and his colleagues at the National Bureau of Economic Research had already applied the relatively new techniques of national income accounting to the measurement of economic growth since the late nineteenth century, when the modern statistical age effectively began. Deane and Cole's innovation was to extend national accounting methods to investigation of a period spanning 272 years and beginning long before statistical agencies produced long time-series of data on consistently defined variables. To achieve this they assembled their own datasets, made ingenious use of proxy measures when direct evidence was lacking, and modelled what was missing altogether. Their book is a mine of information and a model of clarity and logic.

It is fair to say that this new approach to economic history before the mid-nineteenth century was not welcomed by all economic historians, and some reviewers focused their attention on the shortcomings of the data series constructed by Deane and Cole, which they saw as undermining the credibility of the conclusions being drawn about the processes of British economic development. Other economic historians, inspired by Deane and Cole's novel approach but sceptical of the authors' findings, responded by refining and extending the available datasets, seeking better ways of combining them into robust estimates of national income, and ensuring that all assumptions made were empirically well grounded. After 50 years of work in this vein, Deane and Cole's basic analysis has been fairly comprehensively revised and understanding of the processes of economic growth during the world's first industrial revolution has been elevated to a new plane.

Among the most important revisions is that of Nicholas Crafts and Knick Harley, who argue that the rate of economic growth during the period 1700–1830 was much slower than Deane and Cole had suggested and, by implication, that Britain was altogether richer and more developed on the eve of the industrial revolution than had previously been thought. That finding raises an important challenge for economic historians who wish to understand fully the processes by which a poor agrarian country off the coast of mainland Europe made the transition to become the workshop of the world. In particular, it invites further extension of historical national income analysis back in time as far as available data sources permit, which means notionally as far back as the remarkable Domesday Survey of 1086. This book is a response to that challenge. Like Deane and Cole before us, we both hope and expect that the data assembled, methods employed, assumptions made and estimates derived will prompt debate and provoke and stimulate others to undertake more work and in due course come up with a more robust set of results.

It is the historian's inevitable regret that had more time and resources been available more archives might have been searched and extra data collected and processed. Nevertheless, sufficient data have already been gathered by generations of scholars to facilitate this preliminary attempt at describing quantitatively what happened in Britain during the centuries leading up to, as well as during, the industrial revolution. Government income and expenditure are recorded from the twelfth century, price series extend back to the late twelfth century, wage series to the first half of the thirteenth century, annual customs statistics of dutiable exports begin in the 1270s and good runs of farm-level agricultural output data at about the same time. Tin output is known from the early fourteenth century, there are estimates of iron output from the fifteenth century and coal production from the late sixteenth century, and library catalogues capture publication of printed books from William Caxton's first printing in 1476 of Chaucer's *Canterbury tales*. England's demographic history has been reconstructed in detail back to 1541 and more tentatively back to 1086, and thanks to the curiosity of William I, Gregory King, Joseph Massie and Patrick Colquhoun there are social tables for 1086, 1688, 1759 and 1801/03. Many gaps remain, not least because some topics and archives have attracted far more historical attention than others, but enough material is now available to justify the current enterprise.

We are by no means the first to be tempted to fashion national income estimates from this substantial body of evidence. Historians have long been engaged in advancing estimates for individual components of the national economy – population, urbanisation, land use, kilocalorie food output and much else – and a few have taken the additional step and assembled these into estimates of GDP. Some of these earlier attempts at national income estimation merely focus upon individual benchmark years, others either lack transparency in their methods and assumptions or rely too heavily on real-wage-rates. They have nevertheless emboldened us to try and come up with a better set of results that avoid these shortcomings. In Part I of this book, 'Measuring economic growth', established methods of national accounting are applied on an annual basis to data spanning the 600 years from 1270 to 1870, with the 170 years from 1700 overlapping the estimates of Crafts and Harley (and, before them, Deane and Cole). Results obtained for the period after 1700 therefore serve as a cross-check of our method. Further, an input–output table for 1841 reconstructed by Sara Horrell, Jane Humphries and Martin Weale likewise provides the anchor point for calibrating these results. These are constructed from the output side and built up sector by sector, taking full account of inconsistencies in spatial and chronological coverage, before being combined into a single weighted estimate of national economic output which, when divided by the estimates of national population, yields GDP per head. These estimates naturally make extensive use of information on prices and wages and are informed by urbanisation ratios, but are not overly dependent upon them. In fact, the results highlight several striking divergences between GDP per head and the real-wage-rates of agricultural and building labourers and building craftsmen.

Because results of this level of generality should not be taken on trust, much space is devoted in Part I to documenting sources, describing methods and setting out the assumptions that generate the component estimates of population, agricultural output, industrial output and service sector output, which then combine together into overall estimates of GDP and GDP per head. Within the allowance of space available to us, we have endeavoured to be explicit about what we have done so that others may improve upon it. Part II of the book then offers a critical reflection on these estimates of GDP, population and GDP per head and explores some of their implications. These include the alternative chronology of real-wage-rates, levels and patterns of food and non-food consumption, income inequality and the changing social distribution of wealth, the productivity of labour and Britain's growth performance relative to that of other countries in both Europe and Asia. Effectively, therefore, the second part offers a fresh perspective on the broad sweep of British economic history from the high middle ages to the late nineteenth century. As far as possible conventional historiographic periodisations are ignored so that the chronological continuities and discontinuities that emerge are those intrinsic to the evidence.

Whatever shortcomings these estimates undoubtedly have, they have one redeeming merit: they are internally consistent, insofar as the component estimates of population, sectoral output and total output really fit together. Here it is helpful to draw an analogy with the construction of a table, where it is crucially important that the four legs are all of the same length, of an appropriate height and ideally of matching materials and design. This will not result if the legs are made independently of each other. Our national income table does not have this fault, since its four legs of population, agricultural output, industrial output and service-sector output have all been fashioned according to an overarching national accounting template. At various points in this book, attention is drawn to alternative estimates for particular parts of the economy which are difficult to reconcile with each other. Identifying and eliminating these types of mismatch are one way of reducing the margins of error by which all historical output estimates are inevitably bounded. Moreover, since all component elements of a national economy are interrelated, a change in the value of any one variable must necessarily entail adjustments to all the others. Changes to some values make little difference; alterations to a few have potentially big repercussions. For instance, any change in the estimated area under arable cultivation affects the dependent estimates of agricultural output and kilocalorie food output and, thus, the size of the population that could potentially be fed. Likewise, the size of the national sheep flock bears upon the value of agricultural output, export earnings, national wool-textile production and the kilocalorie supply of mutton. Getting all the estimates in this study to align with each other has been one of the greatest challenges of the undertaking, but also one of the most satisfying.

This project has its origins in a session at the 14th World Economic History Congress held in Helsinki in 2006. The session, on 'Progress, stasis, and crisis: demographic and economic developments in England and beyond AD c.1000–c.1800', contained papers by Bruce Campbell and Mark Overton on England's long-run agricultural productivity performance and by Stephen Broadberry and Bishnupriya Gupta on long-run real-wage developments in Europe and Asia. During the conference, Broadberry, Campbell and Overton discussed the feasibility of reconstructing British national income over the late-medieval, early modern and modern periods and continued to advance these plans when they met at the annual conference of the Economic History Society. Others interested in the quantification of long-run economic development also attended these meetings, including Jan-Luiten van Zanden, who was developing a similar project for Holland.

During 2007, with funding provided by the European Commission's Research Training Network 'Unifying the European experience: historical lessons of pan-European development' (FP6–512439), Broadberry hired two of Zanden's recent doctoral students, Bas van Leeuwen and Peter Földvari, to work for six months as postdoctoral researchers at the University of Warwick. During this period a feasibility study was undertaken and then a grant application written, bringing together the proposed British and Dutch projects. This culminated in the award of a Leverhulme Trust grant for the period 2007–2010 for the project 'Reconstructing the national incomes of Britain and Holland, c.1270/1500 to 1800' (Reference Number F/00215AR). With this funding two postdoctoral researchers were hired. Bas van Leeuwen joined the project immediately and remained a vital part of the team throughout, from the feasibility study in 2007 to delivery of the final manuscript in 2014. The second research position was initially filled by Alexander Apostolides, but in 2008, after his early withdrawal from the project, Alexander Klein took over and he, too, remained with the team until delivery of the final manuscript. The project's work was further enhanced when Broadberry, in collaboration with Kevin O'Rourke, secured additional funding via the European Commission's 7th Framework Programme for Research (Contract Number SSH7-CT-2008–225342), for the project 'Historical patterns of development' (HI-POD). This brought together researchers working on historical national accounting for other economies in Europe and beyond, thus broadening significantly the international comparative aspects of the British and Dutch project.

From the outset the project had available to it the two major agricultural datasets assembled by Campbell from manorial accounts for the late-medieval period, and by Overton from probate inventories for the early modern period. Without these datasets the agricultural output estimates presented in Chapter 3 could not have been constructed. Each was put together over many years with funding assistance from a number of bodies. Campbell's work on the manorial accounts database was begun in 1983–4 during tenure of a Personal Research Fellowship from the Economic and Social Research Council (ESRC). Additional data for ten counties around London were collected as part of the two 'Feeding the City' projects funded between 1988 and 1994 by the Leverhulme Trust and ESRC and undertaken in collaboration with Derek Keene, Jim Galloway and Margaret Murphy. In 2005–7 further funding was obtained from the ESRC for the project

'Crops yields, environmental conditions, and historical change, 1270–1430' (RES-000–23-0645). It allowed more data to be gathered, including those relating to the estates of the bishops of Winchester and Westminster Abbey extracted from the original rolls by Jan Titow and David Farmer and now deposited with their respective papers at the Hampshire Record Office and University of Saskatchewan Archives. Thanks are due to Dr Titow for permission to use his materials, to the staff of both archives for expediting this task and to David Hardy for visiting Saskatoon and making scanned copies of Professor Farmer's notes. In 2005 a British Academy small grant financed work on the rich archive of Canterbury Cathedral Priory, where Marilyn Livingstone helped with transcription, and the next year a Margery Grant from the Sussex Archaeological Society paid for Christopher Whittick and Anne Drewery to undertake similar work on major runs of accounts relating to manors belonging to Battle Abbey and Glastonbury Abbey. Much of this material was input to a database by staff of the Centre for Data Digitisation and Analysis at The Queen's University of Belfast, under the expert supervision of Elaine Yates. Further information on these archives and the manors included in the database, together with all the crop yield calculations, is available on the website: B. M. S. Campbell (2007), *Three centuries of English crop yields, 1211–1491* (www.cropyields.ac.uk). Hard-copy transcriptions of most of this material are also now on deposit at the Public Record Office of Northern Ireland.

Mark Overton began collecting probate inventories during work for his doctoral thesis on Norfolk and Suffolk which was funded by the Social Science Research Council from 1972 to 1974. These were augmented by a further sample from Hertfordshire, Lincolnshire, Worcestershire and County Durham collected by Bridget Taylor, Linda Crust, Brenda Webster, Meemee Wong and Joanna Laidlaw during 1987–9 as part of an ESRC-funded project on 'Prices from probate inventories in England, 1550–1750' (B00232211). The Leverhulme Trust funded a two-year project during 1996–8 on 'Household economies in southern England, 1600–1850' during which the inventories from Kent and Cornwall were transcribed by Darron Dean and Andrew Hann and further Kent inventories were collected by Darron Dean during an ESRC-funded project on 'Contextualising consumption: a study of Kentish households 1600–1750' (R000222733). Much of the software for manipulating inventories was developed during Mark Overton's Visiting Fellowship at All Souls College Oxford in 1992–3, but considerably refined by Mark Allen during the Leverhulme project in 1996–7.

In addition to these agricultural datasets, Larry Poos gave access to materials he had gathered on local population counts from manorial tenancy and tithing sources, while Leigh Shaw-Taylor and Tony Wrigley provided us with their data on the occupational structure of England and Wales, which is indispensable for the analyses of sectoral labour productivity in Chapter 9. Many other scholars within the wider economic history research community have given generously of their advice and encouragement and allowed us access to unpublished data. Here, specific thanks are due to the late Richard Britnell, Nick Crafts, Ben Dodds, Martin Ecclestone, John Hatcher, Leigh Shaw-Taylor, Philip Slavin, Richard Smith, Jan de Vries and Tony Wrigley. We have also received useful feedback during seminar and conference presentations at Bocconi, Cambridge, Durham, Evanston, LSE, Reading, Tokyo, Utrecht, Venice, Warwick and Yale. Finally, comments from two anonymous readers of the original proposal for this volume have been helpful in preparing the final text and Michael Watson and the production team at Cambridge University Press have done a sterling job at getting a complex manuscript into print.

Weights, measures and money

Imperial measures and their metric equivalents

Length
1 mile (ml.)	= 1,760 yards	= 1.6093 kilometres

Area
1 acre (ac.)	= 4,840 square yards	= 0.4047 hectare (ha)
1 square mile (ml.²)	= 259 hectares	= 2.590 square kilometres

Liquid volume
1 pint		= 0.5683 litres
1 gallon	= 8 pints	= 4.546 litres

Dry volume
1 bushel (bus.)	= 8 gallons	= 35.238 litres
1 quarter (qtr)	= 8 bushels	= 281.904 litres
		= 2.819 hectolitres

Volume by area (a measure of yield)
1 bushel per acre (bus./ac.)	= 86.072 litres per ha	= 0.8607 hectolitres per ha
1.1485 bushels per acre (bus./ac.)		= 1 hl. per ha

Weight (based on the pound avoirdupois)
1 pound (lb.)	= 16 ounces	= 0.4536 kilograms
1 stone	= 14 lbs	= 6.3504 kilograms
1 quarter (qtr)	= 2 stone	= 12.7008 kilograms
1 hundredweight (cwt)	= 4 qtrs	= 50.8032 kilograms
1 ton	= 20 cwts	= 1.016 tonne

Money
1 penny (d.)		
1 shilling (s.)	= 12d.	
1 pound (£)	= 20s.	= 240d.

Prologue: Historical national income accounting

Gross Domestic Product (GDP) is the single most widely employed measure of the value of a country's market-based economic activity, as GDP per head is of relative and absolute levels of prosperity, and annual rates of change in GDP per head are of the pace of economic growth. GDP has its flaws (it omits non-market activity and leisure, and captures changes and differences in quality, especially of services, imperfectly) but has the merit of being widely understood and respected (Leunig, 2011: 358). There is no alternative single measure that does the same job more effectively. That is why today many governments make their own estimates of GDP per head based upon official statistics of economic output and population and why the United Nations, World Bank and other organisations publish annual estimates of GDP and GDP per head for most of the world's economies, including many for which only the most rudimentary economic and demographic data are available. It is these estimates that inform contemporary debates about the pace of economic growth, widening gap between rich and poor countries, and progression of countries from underdevelopment to development. Obtaining a proper historical perspective on these issues is more problematic, for governments took little interest in the gathering of official statistics before the nineteenth century and the first attempts to measure GDP followed some time later. It has therefore devolved upon historians to rectify this deficiency, drawing upon a range of mostly unofficial data sources.

No attempt to provide historical GDP figures has been more ambitious than that of the late Angus Maddison, who generated national income estimates for most of the world's economies over the last two millennia, persevering with this ambitious project even when appropriate historical data were largely lacking (Maddison, 2001,

2003, 2007, 2010; Bolt and van Zanden, 2014). Other more cautious economic historians have concentrated upon reconstructing the historical national accounts of individual well-documented countries for which good quantitative data series are available prior to the advent of official statistics in the mid-nineteenth century. Deane and Cole (1967) led the way with their reconstruction of British economic growth from 1688 to 1959, although the project to reconstruct robust series of key economic variables had begun a hundred years earlier with the tabulations of prices and wages from 1259 to 1793 made by J. E. Thorold Rogers (1866–1902). Systematic work on England's uniquely copious public and private archives has since yielded data series on government revenues and expenditures, dutiable overseas trade, money supply, interest rates, rents, agricultural production and productivity, the outputs of key industries, the size and structure of the population, the occupational structure, and the share of the population living in towns, all mostly commencing long before Deane and Cole's start date of 1688 (see Part I, 'Measuring economic growth', for details). More recently, subsets of these data have been combined to shed light on core components of the economy – agriculture, urbanisation, population – and the first attempts have been made to estimate the total value-added output of the entire economy (Wrigley, 1985, 2006b; Wrigley and Schofield, 1989; Mayhew, 1995a; Snooks, 1995; Overton and Campbell, 1996; Campbell, 2000; Clark, 2010a). Meanwhile, the pioneering GDP estimates of Deane and Cole have been revised by Crafts and Harley (1992) and GDP estimates extending back to at least the sixteenth century have been reconstructed for Holland, Italy, Spain and Sweden (van Zanden and van Leeuwen, 2012; Malanima, 2011; Álvarez-Nogal and Prados de la Escosura, 2013; Schön and Krantz, 2012).

Within the methodological framework provided by national income accounting, the estimation of GDP can be approached in three different ways, via income, expenditure and output, all of which ought to yield broadly similar results. From the income side, GDP is estimated as the sum of wages paid to workers, profits accruing to the owners of capital and rents received by landowners:

> *GDP = (daily wage-rates × days worked) + (return on capital ×
> capital stock) + (rent × land area)*

Although nominal and real daily wage rates have been available on an annual basis for England back to the mid-thirteenth century since the pioneering work of Phelps Brown and Hopkins (1956), to convert these into reliable estimates of annual labour income requires information on the total number of days worked. That in turn hinges on the share of the population working and the average number of days worked by each person in a year, neither of which is easy to establish. Since labour income accounts for some two-thirds to three-quarters of national income, this is an important limitation to any strategy of estimating GDP from the income side alone. As Chapter 6 demonstrates, there is a real risk that GDP per head thus estimated will merely replicate trends in real wage rates.

An alternative approach is to estimate GDP from the expenditure side by summing the various categories of expenditure, using the famous Keynesian identity:

> *GDP = consumption + investment + government spending +
> net exports*

Historical data on consumption and investment, which together make up the lion's share of expenditure, are, however, limited and without them the expenditure approach cannot be used as more than a rough cross-check on the other approaches to the estimation of GDP. This is frustrating, for systematic accounts of government expenditure and revenue reach back to the late-medieval period, as do data on exports and imports generated by government taxation of international trade. Instead, these data are more usefully incorporated into an output-based estimate of GDP.

In terms of output, GDP is estimated as the sum of outputs produced in the three main sectors of the economy: agriculture, industry and services:

> *GDP = agricultural value added + industrial value added +
> services value added.*

It is important here to work in terms of value added in each sector, to eliminate double-counting. So, in the case of woollen cloth sold by a merchant operating in the service sector, the final selling price of the cloth includes the values added in (i) the agricultural sector (the tending of sheep to produce raw wool), (ii) the industrial sector (the spinning and weaving of the raw wool into woollen cloth) and (iii) distribution (the margin between the price the merchant paid for the cloth and the price at which he sold it). It would be fair to say that in historical national accounting, available information on agricultural and industrial outputs is better than that on the service sector, partly because the last has received the least historical attention. This is a real limitation in the recent past but is less of a problem in the remoter past when services remained the smallest sector and economic activity was dominated first by agriculture, then by industry.

One approach to output-based reconstruction of GDP is to divide the economy between agricultural and other activities. Output of the agricultural sector is then estimated via a demand function, drawing upon data on population, real wage rates and the relative price of food, and employing elasticities derived from the experience of other economies at comparable levels of development but in later periods. Allowance is also made for external trade in food. For the industrial and service sectors, the urban (non-agricultural) population is used as a proxy for trends in output, but with some allowance made for rural industry. This is a short-cut approach, heavily reliant for its results upon evidence of wages, prices and the urban and non-urban populations, and has been developed and applied with particular effect by Álvarez-Nogal and Prados de la Escosura (2013).

Alternatively, available historical evidence can be deployed to estimate the output of each sector directly. The sum of these results, weighted by each sector's output share, then yields total output. This is the approach adopted in Part I of this book. Thus, in the case of agriculture (Chapter 3), it has entailed, first, estimating the amounts of land under different agricultural land uses (Chapter 2) and, then, deriving valid national trends from spatially weighted farm-specific output information on cropped areas and crop yields and livestock numbers and livestock yields (Chapter 3). The latter task is further complicated by the need to correct for data biases towards particular regions, periods and classes of producer. The physical outputs of crops and livestock products are then converted into value-added outputs at constant prices using corresponding price information. Availability of comprehensive price series at annual resolution is therefore a sine qua non of this method (Appendices 5.1 and 5.2).

Inevitably, direct evidence of output is rarely available for all economic activities. In these situations historical national accountants typically employ proxy measures to model the activity in question. For several key industries the scales of their raw-material inputs provide the relevant proxies (Chapter 4, Section 4.2). In the case of woollen textiles, for example, there are no contemporary estimates of the volume of cloth output. Instead, estimates of the volume of wool produced by the agricultural sector can be obtained from available information on the number of sheep, the proportion of sheep producing wool and average fleece weights. There are also reliable data on exports of raw wool, which declined substantially as England was transformed during the fourteenth century from an exporter of raw wool to an exporter of woollen textiles. Subtracting raw wool exports from total domestic production thus yields a time-series of the major raw-material input used by the woollen textiles industry. Knowledge of the industry's cost structure can then be used to convert this measure of gross output into a value-added series. A similar approach is used for the leather industry, where the major input was raw hides. Relevant agricultural outputs likewise provide a basis for estimating value added in food processing. Output of the construction industry, on the other hand, is assumed to have varied with the size of the population but qualified by data on major prestige building projects and the growth of towns.

In the case of services, the major use of proxy measures is in distribution and domestic service (Chapter 4, Section 4.3). Thus, the combined outputs of the agricultural and industrial sectors serve as the

relevant proxy for distribution, weighted to take account of the growing proportion marketed, as measured by an index of the number of
markets during the medieval period and the share of the population
living in towns during the early modern period. Domestic service, on
the other hand, is taken to have grown in line with the population,
following Deane and Cole (1962), who assumed that there was no
labour productivity growth in this sector, so that output grew in line
with the labour-force, which in turn is assumed to have grown in line
with the population.

Summing the value-added outputs of agriculture, industry and
services to yield the GDP of the entire national economy (England
1270–1700, Great Britain 1700–1870) presents a further methodological challenge, since their respective shares of value-added output were
neither equal nor fixed over time. Much of Chapter 5 is devoted to this
issue, whose resolution hinges upon establishing an appropriate set of
sectoral weights that capture the changing structure of the economy.
The real value-added output series of agriculture, industry and services
provide the starting point. These are then converted to nominal or
current-price output series (thereby taking account of the effects of
relative prices upon each sector's contribution to total value added)
and linked to a nominal input–output table for 1841 reconstructed by
Sara Horrell and others (1994), with nominal price output shares for the
benchmark years 1381, 1522, 1600, 1700, 1759 and 1801 providing
additional anchor points. GDP is then the sum of these price-weighted
and benchmarked sectoral output series. Again, the availability of
detailed price information for each output component of each sector
is fundamental to the entire exercise.

The last variable requiring estimation is, of course, population,
since it is the denominator of the GDP per head equation. It also serves
as the proxy for domestic service output and as a partial proxy for
output of the construction industry. As a rule, the more people there
were the more output there was. Thanks to the work of Wrigley and
Schofield (1989), estimates of English population 1541–1870 are
uncontroversial; corresponding estimates for the period 1270–1541

are, however, less certain and are the subject of Chapter 1. Debate has tended to focus more on the size than the trend of the late-medieval population but an upper limit to credible estimates is set by the estimated kilocalorie output of the agricultural sector net of exports, since 2,000 kilocalories per head per day was the minimum required to enable a population to work and reproduce itself (Livi-Bacci, 1991). These population estimates, in their turn, when linked to benchmark information on sectoral shares of the labour-force (taking account of the differential occupational participation rates of men and women), provide the basis for estimating sectoral labour productivity (Chapter 9). Disaggregated by socio-economic class they also allow estimation of the proportions of households and individuals living above and below the poverty line in 1290, 1381, 1522, 1688, 1759 and 1801 (Chapter 8).

One of the aims of extending national income analysis back to well before the industrial revolution is to investigate whether, as Malthus claimed, increases in economic output merely allowed larger populations to be supported with no material gain in living standards. This, after all, is the implication of the inverse relationship between trends in the real wage rates of building and agricultural labourers and trends in population that prevailed until the very end of the nineteenth century. There has been a tendency to assume that trends in wage-rates equate to trends in earnings and living standards, without taking account of changes in the lengths of the working day and year. Yet households clearly varied how hard they worked according to their need to maintain incomes and the demands of the labour market. Comparison between real wage rates and GDP per head reveal several periods when the two diverged (Angeles, 2008), either because, as in the fifteenth century, high real wage rates enabled labourers to work less hard, or because, as in the sixteenth century and during an era of industrial expansion, it was only by working more industriously that they could maintain their living standards (Chapter 6). Hence the paradox that real wage rates stagnated whereas GDP per head slowly improved. Investigation of this important issue naturally requires

consideration of both the output and income approaches to the estimation of GDP. The same applies to discussion of the social distribution of income in Chapter 8, while issues of expenditure feature in
discussion of food and non-food consumption in Chapter 7.

The more countries to which historical national income analysis
is applied, the more robust the results, since these should be consistent
between economies at similar stages of development. Any differences
in levels of GDP per head should also be consistent with other measures of economic development, such as urbanisation ratios. Where
common patterns emerge between countries, as in the case of divergences between real wage rates and GDP per head, there is good reason
to believe that they are genuine rather than artefacts of the estimation
process or evidence used. For that reason this reconstruction of the
British historical national accounts has been conducted as part of a
joint project comparing Britain with its southern North Sea neighbour,
Holland (van Zanden and van Leeuwen, 2012). It has also taken place in
parallel with studies of other countries using the historical national
accounting framework, including Italy and Spain within Europe, and
India, China and Japan within Asia (Malanima, 2011; Bassino and
others, 2012; Álvarez-Nogal and Prados de la Escosura, 2013;
Broadberry and others, 2014a, 2014b). This has enabled Britain's
growth to be evaluated within the context of developments taking
place elsewhere in Eurasia, including the most developed economies
of the pre-industrial era: China under the Northern Song Dynasty
(960–1127), Renaissance Italy and Holland during its sixteenth- and
early-seventeenth-century Golden Age.

The historical national accounts reconstructed in Part I of this
book indicate that GDP per head doubled in England between 1270 and
1700 and then, in the enlarged context of Great Britain, doubled again
between 1700 and 1850. In the process, Britain was transformed from a
poor and predominantly primary producing economy on the periphery
of Europe, which in the twelfth century even in its most developed
regions lagged behind Song China, to the most dynamic economy in
Europe from the late seventeenth century during its own commercial

revolution, when trade and industry were growing strongly and agriculture improving in productivity (Chapters 5 and 10). This pre-industrial growth made possible the industrial revolution which placed Britain at the hub of the global economy in the nineteenth century. Until the industrial revolution Britain's slow but cumulative rise is nevertheless part of a wider story, for, from the sixteenth century, the more dynamic parts of Europe were forging ahead of their Asian counterparts in what has become known as the Great Divergence and, at the same time, a Little Divergence was opening within Europe, as its own economic centre of gravity shifted from the Mediterranean to the countries bordering the southern North Sea, led in turn by the southern Low Countries, Brabant, Holland and, eventually, Britain. Throughout this process Britain gradually improved its economic position relative to other countries but had to compete hard against smaller but richer and more successful Holland, whose impressive GDP per head – by the seventeenth century the world's highest – Britain only finally overtook during the industrial revolution. Plainly, this is not a story of Malthusian stagnation, rather, it is one of the progressive escape from Malthusian constraints and transition to a post-Malthusian economy in which, from 1700, prosperity and population rose together. This analysis leaves it at the point, in the 1870s, when, with onset of the demographic transition, population growth declined but GDP per head climbed ever higher.

PART I
Measuring economic growth

I   Population

I.I   INTRODUCTION

Economic growth can be either extensive or intensive. Extensive growth arises where more output is produced in line with a growing population but living standards remain constant, while intensive growth arises where more output is produced by each person. In the former case, there is no economic development, as the economy simply reproduces itself on a larger scale: in the latter, living standards rise as the economy goes through a process of economic development. To understand the long-run growth of the British economy reaching back to the thirteenth century therefore requires knowledge of the trajectories followed by both population and GDP. Of particular interest is whether periods of intensive growth, distinguished by rising GDP per head, were accompanied by expanding or contracting population. For it is one thing for living standards to rise during a period of population decline, such as that induced by the recurrent plagues of the second half of the fourteenth century, when survivors found themselves able to add the land and capital of those who had perished to their own stocks, but quite another for living standards and population to rise together, particularly given the emphasis of Malthus [1798] on diminishing returns. Indeed, Kuznets (1966: 34–85) identified simultaneous growth of population and income per head (i.e. the concurrence of intensive and extensive growth) as one of the key features that distinguished modern from pre-industrial economic growth.

    A full discussion of these issues surrounding the transition to modern economic growth will have to wait until after the estimates of GDP per head have been established in Part I of this book. Meanwhile, the first task is to reconstruct population numbers. The reason for giving this priority is not just because of its importance in estimating GDP per head, nor even because extensive growth is also of interest in its own right. Rather, it is because, following a long tradition started by Deane and Cole (1962) in their pioneering study of British historical national accounting, estimation of some of the component parts of GDP requires knowledge of the size of the population. Indeed, as will become clearer later, the scale of the population feeds directly into the estimation of the output of parts of the service sector. Aggregate development of England's population since 1541 is now firmly established, and there is little disagreement respecting the population of the rest of Great Britain after 1700. This chapter will therefore focus its attention on reconstructing English population before 1541, where there is some controversy.

The pioneering work on English medieval population by Russell (1948) established benchmark levels of population for 1086 and 1377 and deployed time-series evidence to link these to each other and to estimates for the early modern period. Russell paid particular attention to the consistency of his estimates over this long sweep of history and arrived at the conclusion that the peak level of medieval population before the Black Death was around 3.7 million. This view was challenged by Postan (1966), who criticised both of Russell's benchmarks as unrealistically low. He advocated a much higher level of population throughout the medieval period, and a peak level before the Great Famine of around 6 million, but did not consider the difficulties of reconciling such high figures with the early modern estimates, which have subsequently been established more firmly by Wrigley and Schofield (1989). Furthermore, it must be noted that Postan (1966: 561) regarded any such quantitative exercise with a high degree of scepticism, reflected in his phrase 'the lure of aggregates'.

Postan's view of medieval population has proved influential, with Smith (1988: 191) concluding that 'there is every reason to accept an English population in 1300 of over 6 million'. Yet not all have been convinced. In particular, Blanchard (1996) points to the lack of substantive evidence offered by Postan (1966) and subsequent writers for their criticisms of the main assumptions underpinning Russell's 1086 and 1377 benchmark estimates, and endorses a lower rather than higher estimate of the population at its pre Black Death peak. In like vein, Campbell (2000) questions whether domestic agriculture could have provided enough food for more than 5 million people. It is worth noting that by the 1650s, when the economy was more developed and technology more advanced, the population still numbered barely 5.4 million. Also at issue are whether the Great Famine of 1315–22 or Black Death of 1348–9 constituted the key demographic turning point, the scale and duration of the fifteenth-century downturn in numbers, and when the upturn began that was clearly in full swing by the 1540s when the first parish registers come on stream.

The chapter proceeds as follows. Russell's (1948) benchmark estimates of population levels and evidence on rates of population change during the medieval period are critically reviewed in Section 1.2. Section 1.3 then derives a new time-series for aggregate population from manor-level data on tenant numbers using an appropriate regional weighting scheme. The absolute level of the population in the medieval period is pinned down by linking the estimated time-series to the revised benchmark for 1377, with the need for consistency with the benchmarks for 1086, 1522 and 1541 limiting the degrees of freedom. Russell's benchmarks for 1086 and 1377 are shown to have been too low, but not by as much as suggested by Postan (1966), so that the medieval population peaks at less than 5 million. How the national total was distributed across counties and how that distribution evolved over time is then considered in Section 1.4. Sections 1.5 and 1.6 set out the much less controversial trends in population for, respectively, England from 1541 to 1700 and Great Britain from 1700 to 1870.

1.2 THE BUILDING BLOCKS OF MEDIEVAL POPULATION ESTIMATES

To be convincing, estimates of English medieval population must be able to encompass both the macro cross-sectional evidence for a number of benchmark years, including most obviously that from

Domesday Book for 1086 and the poll tax returns of 1377, as well as the time-series evidence amassed by scholars over the years from diverse mostly micro-level sources. The time-series must be able to link up the medieval benchmarks as well as connect to the more reliable population estimates for the early modern period, starting in 1541. Although the quality, quantity and range of the available evidence are superior to those extant for most other countries at this early period in time, reconciling the cross-sectional and time-series data with each other and with the more firmly grounded estimates available from 1541 is far from unproblematic.

1.2.1   A benchmark for 1086

A benchmark estimate of the population in 1086 can be derived from Domesday Book. The pioneering study was by Russell (1948) and his assumptions are set out in the first column of Table 1.01. The starting point is the total of rural households recorded in Domesday Book, to which must be added tenants-in-chief and under-tenants, as well as an allowance for the omitted four northern counties. Russell applied an average household multiplier of 3.5 to arrive at total rural population. Finally, he made an allowance for urban population, since towns were largely omitted from William I's great survey. Darby (1977: 89) presented a number of alternative estimates. One issue is whether slaves should be included as household heads, as in Russell (1948), or individuals. Nevertheless, as there were only 28,100 slaves, this does not make a very large difference and is not pursued here. Of more significance is the effect of increasing the household multiplier. Darby (1977: 88) claimed that later medieval evidence suggests a multiplier of 4.5 to 5.0, and that the figure for 1086 is unlikely to have been much less. Using Russell's assumption results in a total population of 1.11 million, while Darby's approach yields a population of between 1.45 and 1.60 million.

Although Harvey (1988: 48–9) did not present any underlying calculations, she claimed that the Domesday population could well have approached 2 million. Rather than arguing for a higher household multiplier, Harvey (1988) proposed a much greater scale of omissions

Table 1.01 *Alternative estimates of English population in 1086 (thousands except where otherwise specified)*

	Russell's estimate	Darby's estimate (I)	Darby's estimate (II)	Harvey's estimate
Recorded rural households	268.3	268.3	268.3	268.3
Omissions rate (%)	0.0	5.0	5.0	25.0
Allowance for omissions	0.0	13.4	13.4	67.1
Tenants-in-chief	1.1	1.1	1.1	1.1
Under-tenants	6.0	6.0	6.0	6.0
Northern counties	6.8	6.8	6.8	6.8
Total rural households	282.2	295.6	295.6	349.3
Household multiplier (persons)	3.5	4.5	5.0	5.0
Total rural population	987.7	1,330.2	1,478.0	1,746.5
Urban population	117.4	120.0	120.0	120.0
TOTAL POPULATION	1,105.1	1,450.2	1,598.0	1,866.5

Sources and notes: Derived from Russell (1948: 54); Darby (1977: 63, 89); Harvey (1988: 48–9). For ease of comparison, there are two very small adjustments to the original estimates. First, there is a slight discrepancy with Darby (I) because Darby did not allow his total for northern counties to vary with the household multiplier. Here, the number of households in the northern counties is held constant across the different estimates, so that the population in those counties increases with the household multiplier. Second, Russell's urban population includes clergy.

than the 5 per cent allowance made by Darby (1977), on the grounds that Domesday Book was more concerned with the landed wealth of the tenants-in-chief and their head tenants, and hence tended to under-record or omit independent smallholders, sub-tenants and those who were landless. The final column of Table 1.01 presents an estimate of the English population in 1086 in the spirit of Harvey's assumptions. This involves increasing the rate of omissions from 5 per cent to 25 per cent – the maximal scale of omissions claimed by Postan (1966: 562) for the poll tax of 1377 – which results in a population of 1.87 million. Note that for the population to exceed 2 million, which Harvey (1988: 49) claims should not be ruled out, would require an omissions rate of the order of 40 per cent.

1.2.2   A benchmark for 1377

It is also possible to obtain a benchmark estimate of population from the returns to the poll tax of 1377, which was levied at a fixed rate on adult males and females. The key assumptions made by Russell (1948: 146) to derive a population total for England are the proportion of children in the population and the rate of under-enumeration. Russell's assumptions and results are set out in the first column of Table 1.02. Postan (1966: 562) suggested alternative assumptions, leading to the results set out in the second column of Table 1.02. Whereas Russell

Table 1.02 *Alternative estimates of English population in 1377*

	Russell's estimate	Postan's estimate	'Best estimate'
Laity	1,355,555	1,355,555	1,355,555
Clergy	30,641	30,641	30,641
Allowance for Cheshire, Durham and mendicant friars	31,994	31,994	31,994
Adult total	1,417,380	1,417,380	1,417,380
% share of population under 15 years	*33.3%*	*45.0%*	*37.5%*
Allowance for children	708,690	1,159,675	850,428
Total including children	2,126,070	2,577,055	2,267,808
Assumed % rate of under-enumeration	*5%*	*25%*	*10%*
Allowance for under-enumeration	106,303	644,264	226,781
TOTAL POPULATION	2,232,373	3,221,319	2,494,589

Sources: Russell (1948: 146); Postan (1966: 562).

assumed that children under the age of 15 accounted for 33.3 per cent of the population, Postan suggested that the ratio may have been as high as 40 to 45 per cent. For the period after 1541, when reliable data become available, the percentage of under-15s in the population never rose above 40 per cent, which surely represents the upper limit for 1377 (Wrigley and Schofield, 1989: Table A3.1). As Blanchard (1996) points out, such a high ratio tended to occur in periods of rapid population growth driven by high fertility. Since population was declining in the aftermath of the Black Death, a ratio as high as 40 to 45 per cent in the 1370s is improbable and a lower ratio more likely.

The second assumption of Russell that was challenged by Postan concerns the assumed rate of under-enumeration. Russell's figure of 5 per cent is based on an examination of the distribution of terminal numbers of local tax returns for evidence of excessive rounding, together with an allowance for 'indigent and untaxed persons'. Postan suggests a much higher rate of 25 per cent, which he justifies with reference to discrepancies between the poll tax returns and unspecified manorial sources. Poos (1991), however, supports Russell's ratio on the basis of a comparison of the poll tax returns and tithing evidence for a sample of Essex parishes. For a later period, Campbell (1981: 150) uses the discrepancy between the tax returns of 1524–5 and the muster rolls of 1522 to infer an evasion rate of males varying from a minimum of 5 per cent to a maximum of 20 per cent, arguing for an average figure of the order of 10 per cent. The poll taxes, of course, taxed both adult males and females, and although the latter may have been less visible to the taxers than the former, Goldberg (1990: 200) concludes that 'the under-enumeration of women cannot have been a serious fault of the earlier [i.e. 1377] returns'.

Russell's assumptions of a children's share of 33.3 per cent and a 5 per cent under-enumeration rate yield a population total for 1377 of 2.23 million, while Postan's assumptions of a children's share of 45 per cent and a 25 per cent under-enumeration rate lead to an esti-mate of 3.22 million. The third column of Table 1.02 presents a 'best estimate' of 2.50 million, based on a children's share of 37.5 per cent and an under-enumeration rate of 10 per cent, which is more in line with Wrigley and Schofield's demographic evidence and the evidence of tax evasion from Poos and Campbell.

1.2.3   Population trends, 1086–1317

The next step is to establish population trends between the two benchmarks and link them up to the early modern estimates of Wrigley and Schofield (1989), as amended in Wrigley and others (1997). The starting point is the time-series evidence of tenant numbers assembled by Hallam (1988) for the period 1086–1317. Hallam's methodology was to find population estimates for individual manors at benchmark years from diverse sources and compare them with the population for the same manors given in Domesday Book. Index numbers of population were then constructed for up to eight regions and for the country as a whole, taking account of regional diversity. The composition of the eight regions used by Hallam is indicated in the notes to Table 1.03. To obtain a reliable index of population for England as a whole, it is important to ensure a balance between the relatively high-density core regions to the south and east of a line running roughly from the Wash to the Severn Estuary, and the lower-density peripheral regions to the north and west of this line, including southwest England.

Hallam's (1988) estimates (Table 1.03) suggest that population in the country as a whole roughly tripled between 1086 and 1262, before stagnating to 1317. Unfortunately, there are a number of problems with these estimates, which become apparent upon close inspection of the data. First, dividing the dataset into eight regions means that the number of observations for any particular region is quite small, making it difficult to place much faith in the regional breakdown, even if the aggregate picture is reasonably plausible. Thus, for example, it seems inconceivable that the population of northern England could have behaved in the wildly volatile fashion suggested by Table 1.03. Second, when the underlying data presented by Hallam (1988) are examined in more detail, it becomes apparent that although the estimates are presented for particular years, they often cover an extremely wide range

Table 1.03 *Hallam's estimated English population trends, 1086–1317 (1086 = 100)*

	1086	1149	1230	1262	1292	1317
Eastern England	100.0	165.7	299.3	368.3	416.2	433.7
Southeast England	100.0	–	–	259.5	260.3	382.0
East midlands	100.0	160.5	272.7	272.7	211.6	255.4
Southern England	100.0	168.8	218.5	255.1	316.2	305.7
West midlands	100.0	209.2	211.6	252.8	233.7	317.7
Southwest England	100.0	–	–	–	–	190.3
Northern England	100.0	–	–	781.1	1,380.8	575.9
The Welsh Marches	100.0	–	–	–	378.2	266.5
TOTAL ENGLAND	100.0	171.2	248.0	309.9	326.0	315.1

Sources and notes: Hallam (1988: 591–3). Eastern England = Lincs., Norfolk, Suffolk, Essex, Cambs. Southeast England = Middx, Surrey, Sussex, Kent. East midlands = Notts., Leics., Rutland, Northants., Hunts., Beds., Herts., Bucks. Southern England = Berks., Hants., Wilts., Dorset, Somerset. West midlands = Derby., Staffs., Warks., Worcs., Glos., Oxon. Southwest England = Devon, Cornwall. Northern England = Yorks. The Welsh Marches = Hereford, Salop, Cheshire.

of surrounding years. The most extreme case is 1149, which actually covers most of the twelfth century, spanning the period 1114–93.

Hallam's (1988) dataset, checked, corrected and augmented with additional material, has therefore been reworked to produce a revised set of population estimates for the period 1086–1315, and the same approach then extended to the period after 1315. Table 1.04A presents these estimates for the period 1086–1315 on a national basis only, since, although the data are sufficient to establish the national trend, they are too thinly spread to derive reliable sub-trends for individual regions. Hallam's method of weighting individual manors by the importance of the counties in which they were based is nevertheless followed. A full listing of the manors is provided in Appendix 1.1, while the population of individual counties is discussed in Section 1.4. Compared with Hallam (1988), a slightly smaller population increase

Table 1.04 English population trends and annual growth rates, 1086–1450

A. *1086–1315 (1086 = 100)*

Year	Indexed population level	Period	*% annual growth rate*
1086	100.0	1086–1190	*0.58*
1190	181.6	1190–1220	*0.83*
1220	232.7	1220–1250	*0.21*
1250	247.9	1250–1279	*0.16*
1279	259.4	1279–1290	*0.65*
1290	278.5	1290–1315	*–0.05*
1315	274.8		

B. *1300–1377 (1300 = 100)*

Year	Indexed population level	Period	*% annual growth rate*
1300	100.0	1300–1315	*0.52*
1315	108.1	1315–1325	*–1.30*
1325	94.9	1325–1348	*0.68*
1348	111.0	1348–1351	*–18.53*
1351	60.0	1351–1377	*–0.16*
1377	57.5		

C. *1377–1541 (1377 = 100)*

Year	Indexed population level	Period	*% annual growth rate*
1377	100.0	1377–1400	*–0.79*
1400	83.3	1400–1430	*–0.10*
1430	80.8	1430–1450	*–0.29*
1450	76.2	1450–1522	*0.29*
1522	94.0	1522–1541	*1.02*
1541	112.8		

Sources: Derived from data on manorial trends as described in the text, apart from estimates for 1522 from Cornwall (1970: 39) and for 1541 from Wrigley and others (1997).

is found between 1086 and the late thirteenth century, but a similar pattern of faster growth in the twelfth than in the thirteenth century. Note that the annual population growth rates presented in the table provide a check on the credibility of the estimates by demonstrating that successive benchmark estimates do not require implausible rates of change. Significantly, during the periods of population expansion, the annual growth rates do not exceed the firmly established rates seen over sustained periods between the mid-sixteenth and mid-eighteenth centuries, and are well below the rates observed from the second half of the eighteenth century (Wrigley and Schofield, 1989).

1.2.4 Population trends, 1300–1377

Next, Hallam's (1988) methodology is extended to the period after 1315, again using estimates of manorial population from diverse sources (Table 1.04B). Although there are fewer manors with data than for the pre-1315 period, there is a clear improvement in another dimension, since use can now be made of runs of observations for particular manors taken from a single source, rather than comparing one-off estimates from different sources. This is illustrated by Figure 1.01, derived from data assembled by Poos (1991) and charted by Smith (1988: 193), which tracks trends in numbers of adult males on four Essex manors. Note, even within this one county the divergence in trends between High Easter and Great Waltham on one hand and Margaret Roding and Chatham Hall on the other. To capture national trends it is therefore important to ensure as wide a geographical spread of manors as possible, weighted by the relative population share of the counties in which the manors were located.

Linking up with the time series for the period 1086–1315 requires extending the chronology back to 1300 so as to capture the growth of population to its peak in 1315 on the eve of the Great Famine. The estimates given in Table 1.04B confirm that the famine led to a substantial drop in the population and endorse Russell's (1948) belief and the evidence assembled by Campbell (2010: 295–7) that in aggregate the population bounced back strongly after 1322 and continued, with

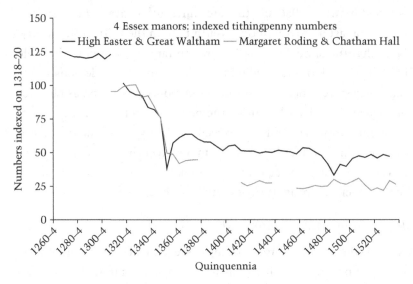

FIGURE 1.01 Trends in numbers of adult males on four Essex manors, 1260s–1530s (1318–20 = 100). *Source:* Derived from data underlying Poos (1991: 96–103).

certain notable exceptions, to rise until the first outbreak of plague in 1348–9. This contrasts with the substantially greater famine losses on the four Essex manors charted in Figure 1.01 and the absence of any post-famine bounceback on these same manors, possibly due to net out-migration of young adult males to London. This is a further reminder of the need to take account of divergent trends in different regions and between countryside and town.

The first outbreak of the Black Death in 1348–9, exacerbated by inclement weather and serious harvest failure, had a catastrophic effect, reducing the population by around 46 per cent within the space of just three years. This is consistent with estimates which reckon the excess mortality of these years at 40 per cent or greater (Hatcher, 1994: 8–9). Although such a catastrophic decline was almost certainly followed by an immediate rebound, further national outbreaks of plague in 1361–2, 1369 and 1375 progressively eroded the population's capacity to replace itself and ensured that by 1377 nearly half of the population had been wiped out (Table 1.04B; Hatcher, 1977: 25).

Furthermore, it is widely accepted that the population decline was fairly evenly spread across the country, affecting both core and periphery alike, as successive plagues penetrated the furthest reaches of the realm and migration redistributed the survivors.

1.2.5   Population trends, 1377–1541

Table 1.04C tracks the path of population from 1377 to 1541. The manorial evidence suggests that numbers continued to fall between 1377 and 1400 and that decline was not finally arrested until the middle years of the fifteenth century when the pronounced post-Black Death inflation of the real wage rates of building and farm labourers finally abated (Figure 1.02). One way of understanding this trend would be if the later plague outbreaks, in conjunction with other diseases, disproportionately affected younger age groups so that heightened infant and child mortality rates offset any gains in fertility (Hatcher, 1977: 58–62; Razi, 1980: 134–5, 150–1). This punitive demographic regime seems to have maintained the population in a low-pressure equilibrium for several successive generations, preventing any sustained recovery despite the

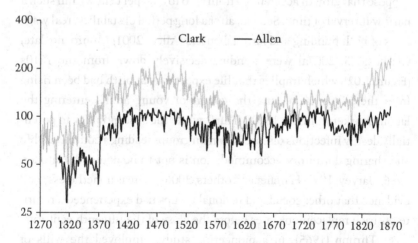

FIGURE 1.02 Indexed daily real wage rates of unskilled building and farm workers, 1270–1870 (1700 = 100, log scale). *Sources:* Allen (2001); Clark (2005).

powerful Malthusian incentives of resource abundance and unprecedentedly high real wage rates.

The period from the 1450s to the advent of parish registration of baptisms, marriages and burials in 1538 is very much a demographic Dark Age. The manorial sources ossify and cease to be of much value and trust therefore has to be placed in the record of specific groups that are well recorded but neither socially nor geographically representative: tenants-in-chief of the Crown, certain monastic communities, scholars at Winchester School, and the growing numbers of will makers. Although Smith (2012) argues that bouts of high mortality depressed adult life expectancy and thwarted any return to positive replacement rates until well into the reign of Henry VIII (r. 1509–47), there are some serious problems with this line of argument. First, population needed to recover at some point to reach Wrigley and Schofield's (1989) firmly grounded estimate of 2.83 million by 1541, by which time the population was growing rapidly at 0.64 per cent per annum. If demographic recovery was postponed until the second quarter of the sixteenth century, then the rate of population growth required to reach a total of 2.83 million by 1541 becomes implausibly high. Nor is it realistic to suppose that growth accelerated from zero to 0.64 per cent within such a narrow interval of time. Second, after a long period of stability, real wage rates of both building and farm labourers (Allen, 2001; Munro, no date; Clark, 2005, 2007a) were trending decisively down from the 1510s (Figure 1.02), which implies that life expectancy at birth had been rising from the 1490s, increasing the cohort of young adults entering the labour market from the 1510s. Third, while the susceptibility to potentially deadly infectious diseases of urban groups leading a communal life and sharing dormitory accommodation is not to be doubted (Hatcher, 1986; Harvey, 1993; Hatcher and others, 2006), there is nonetheless good evidence that other social and regional groups had experienced a return to positive replacement rates before the close of the fifteenth century.

Thrupp (1965), in a pioneering study, employed the wills of relatively humble people to chart trends in male replacement rates during the latter part of the fifteenth century when she believed 'replacement rates may have begun to stay on an upward curve' (1965: 114). In the two archdeaconries of Essex and St Albans she identified steadily rising numbers of sons per male testator from the mid fifteenth century, which, by the 1460s in Barnet and 1480s in Essex, had become clearly positive. Wills proved in the consistory court of Norwich reveal a similar improvement in replacement rates in the 1470s and more marked rise in the 1480s, which was especially pronounced among better-off testators (Gottfried, 1978: 204–13). These results chime with the shift in the 1470s to consistently positive replacement rates among a national sample of tenants-in-chief of the Crown, as calculated by Hollingsworth (1969) from information on death and inheritance contained in *inquisitiones post mortem* (Table 1.05). Lag effects between birth and inheritance mean that the improvement in survival rates had probably begun some years earlier. Quinquennial population growth rates derived from these replacement rates became persistently positive the early 1460s, with positive growth clearly outweighing negative growth during the 1440s and 1450s.

Although materially privileged tenants-in-chief clearly constitute a skewed sample of the population as a whole, they are demographically less unrepresentative than cloistered communities of Benedictine monks in Durham, Canterbury and Westminster or schoolboys at Winchester. Consequently, it is difficult to interpret the upturn in replacement rates for tenants-in-chief and some other social groups as anything other than a clear signal that the negative demographic pressures which had prevailed for a century following the Black Death were at last easing. Combined with the indirect evidence of real wage rates and the high growth rates needed for the population to reach its 1541 population level, the case for a return to population growth from the 1470s, and maybe earlier, is strong. Plainly recovery was not uninterrupted, and in 1457, 1471, 1485 and the early 1500s death rates undoubtedly soared (Smith, 2012: 61–2), as they would do again later in the sixteenth century when the momentum of growth had become firmly established. In this transition from stagnation to growth some regions led and others lagged, although more is currently

Table 1.05 *Hollingsworth's replacement rates (and derived annual growth rates) of male tenants-in-chief in fifteenth-century England*

Period	Replacement rate	Period	% annual growth rate
1401–05	0.887	1385–89	−0.374
1406–10	0.869	1390–94	−0.438
1411–15	0.758	1395–99	−0.862
1416–20	0.805	1400–04	0.676
1421–25	0.697	1405–09	−1.122
1426–30	0.818	1410–14	−0.622
1431–35	0.832	1415–19	−0.573
1436–40	0.944	1420–24	−0.180
1441–45	0.986	1425–29	−0.044
1446–50	1.250	1430–34	0.700
1451–55	1.250	1435–39	0.700
1456–60	0.946	1440–44	−0.173
1461–65	1.118	1445–49	0.349
1466–70	1.418	1450–54	1.097
1471–75	0.958	1455–59	−0.134
1476–80	1.370	1460–64	0.989
1481–85	1.038	1465–69	0.117
1486–90	1.217	1470–74	0.616
1491–95	1.603	1475–79	1.484
1496–1500	1.423	1480–84	1.108

Sources and notes: Hollingsworth (1969: 379). The replacement rate is the ratio between the estimated number of sons and the deceased male tenants-in-chief recorded in the *inquisitiones post mortem* (IPM) preserved in The National Archives (formerly Public Record Office), London. The annual growth rate is calculated from the replacement rate by assuming that the increase took place over a generation lasting 32 years, with each observation lagged half a generation (Hollingsworth, 1969: 376).

known about regions, places and communities of demographic deficit than those of surplus. The southwest, west midlands, northwest and immediate Home Counties were all economically and demo-graphically more dynamic than eastern England and the east midlands (Table 1.09 and Figure 1.03D below). The countryside was also

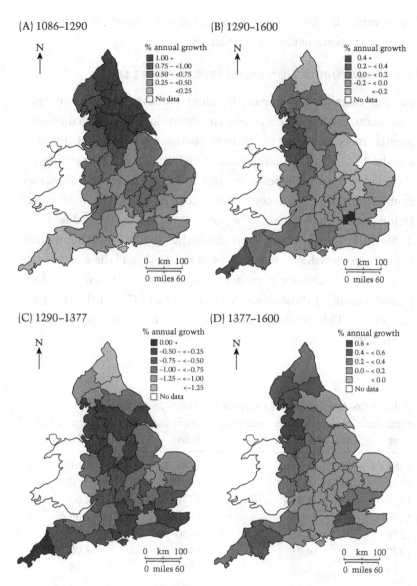

(A) 1086–1290

N

% annual growth
- 1.00 +
- 0.75 – <1.00
- 0.50 – <0.75
- 0.25 – <0.50
- <0.25
- No data

(B) 1290–1600

N

% annual growth
- 0.4 +
- 0.2 – < 0.4
- 0.0 – < 0.2
- –0.2 – < 0.0
- <–0.2
- No data

(C) 1290–1377

N

% annual growth
- 0.00 +
- –0.50 – <–0.25
- –0.75 – <–0.50
- –1.00 – <–0.75
- –1.25 – <–1.00
- <–1.25
- No data

(D) 1377–1600

N

% annual growth
- 0.6 +
- 0.4 – < 0.6
- 0.2 – < 0.4
- 0.0 – < 0.2
- < 0.0
- No data

0   km   100
0   miles 60

FIGURE 1.03 English county population annual growth rates, 1086–1600. *Source:* Derived from Tables 1.08 and 1.09.

significantly healthier than towns and already London's growth was dependent upon a net inflow of migrants.

I.3 NEW POPULATION ESTIMATES, 1086–1541

Having assembled the main building blocks, they are now put together to produce a new consistent chronology of English medieval population covering the period from 1086 to 1541. The first step is to use the 1377 'best estimate' benchmark from Table 1.02 to calibrate the level of population between 1086 and 1450 using the time-series from Table 1.04. The second step is then to check the 1086 population value thus obtained against the benchmark value from Table 1.01. The third step is to check the credibility of the implied population growth rate between 1450 and 1541, and the consistency with other benchmark population estimates for the early modern period, including those of Cornwall (1970) and Campbell (1981) for the 1520s. This produces the population estimates presented in Table 1.06.

Table 1.06 *English population totals, 1086–1541 (millions)*

Year	Total population (m.)	Year	Total population (m.)
1086	1.71	1348	4.81
1190	3.10	1351	2.60
1220	3.97	1377	2.50
1250	4.23	1400	2.08
1279	4.43	1430	2.02
1290	4.75	1450	1.90
1315	4.69	1522	2.35
1325	4.12	1541	2.83

Sources: Benchmark years 1086–1450 from Table 1.04, with absolute level determined by the 'best estimate' for 1377 from Table 1.02. Benchmarks for 1522 from Cornwall (1970: 39) and for 1541 from Wrigley and others (1997).

The 'best estimate' of population in 1377 from Table 1.02 is 2.50 million. Projecting backwards with the time series from Table 1.04B produces a peak medieval population of 4.81 million in 1348, and a slightly lower value of 4.69 million in 1315. The Great Famine shows up as a notable negative shock, with the population falling by 12 per cent to 4.12 million by 1325. The decline during and following the Black Death was even more catastrophic: the population shrank from 4.81 million in 1348 to 2.60 million by 1351 and then to 2.50 million by 1377, a reduction of 48 per cent. Projecting back further in time by splicing the series from Table 1.04A to the 1315 benchmark from Table 1.04B yields a population level of 1.71 million in 1086 as shown in the first column of Table 1.06. The net increment between 1086 and 1315 was thus 2.74-fold, which is consistent with the growth of at most threefold noted earlier. Note that the time-series projection of 1.71 million for 1086 falls between the Darby II estimate of 1.60 million and the Harvey benchmark of 1.87 million given in Table 1.01, but is 54 per cent greater than the 1.11 million proposed by Russell (1948). Projecting forwards from 1377 reveals a further fall in the population to a level of just 1.90 million by 1450 (11 per cent greater than the estimated Domesday total and 60 per cent below the pre-Black Death maximum), after which it recovered to the level of 2.83 million in 1541 established by Wrigley and others (1997).

Also included in Table 1.06 is Cornwall's (1970: 39) benchmark for 1522 of 2.35 million, which is also broadly consistent with the figure of 1.90 million for 1450 and the Wrigley and others (1997) estimate of 2.83 million for 1541. Growth from, say, 2.00 million in 1475 to 2.35 million by 1522 would have required a rate of 0.34 per cent a year, trebling to almost 1.00 per cent between 1522 and 1541. Cornwall's estimate was based on the 1522 muster rolls with additional information from the 1524 and 1525 lay subsidies. Although it is above Campbell's (1981) more carefully considered central figure of 1.84 million (requiring an unrealistically high annual growth rate of 2.3 per cent to reach 2.83 million by 1541), it is well below his maximum figure of 2.92 million. Additionally, Cornwall (1970: 33) provided a benchmark figure for 1545 based on a comparison between the chantry certificates and the 1377 poll tax returns. The idea was taken from Russell (1948), and by disregarding the least reliable parish estimates, Cornwall arrived at a figure of 2.80 million in 1545, which is very close to the Wrigley and others (1997) figure of 2.91 million. Notwithstanding that significant margins of error surround all these figures, including that of Wrigley and others (1997), all imply a marked upturn in the rate of English population growth around 1520 for reasons that remain obscure.

I.4   THE DISTRIBUTION OF THE POPULATION BY COUNTY

For national population trends to be credible implied county-level growth rates between the key benchmark years of 1086, 1290, 1377 and 1600 must also be credible. This can be checked using the data set out in Tables 1.07, 1.08 and 1.09 and Figure 1.03. The county population shares given in Table 1.07 provide a starting point. These are then applied to the corresponding benchmark estimates of the national population given in Table 1.06 to produce the county populations given in Table 1.08. Finally, from these population totals are derived the county population annual growth rates given in Table 1.09, from which Figure 1.03 is drawn.

Looking first at the period 1086–1290, in Figure 1.03A, the population growth rate was slightly above 1.0 per cent for some northern counties, but this is not unreasonable during the recovery from the very low levels in the aftermath of the post-Conquest Norman reprisals in this region. Note that other parts of the geographical periphery, particularly the southwest, grew more slowly during this period. Growth was significantly stronger in a wedge of more populous counties in eastern England and the east midlands. Turning to the period 1290–1377 in Figure 1.03C, population declined in all core counties and in all peripheral counties apart from Cornwall, which, even after allowance for the omission of tin miners in 1290, uniquely appears to have continued to expand its population. The northern counties,

Table 1.07 *County shares of English population,*
1086, 1290, 1377 and 1600

County	1086 (%)	1290 (%)	1377 (%)	1600 (%)
Bedfordshire	1.27	1.35	1.47	1.05
Berkshire	2.24	1.29	1.64	1.38
Buckinghamshire	1.77	1.87	1.78	1.36
Cambridgeshire	1.82	2.89	2.12	1.76
Cheshire	0.56	0.76	1.07	1.80
Cornwall	1.73	*0.73	2.48	2.50
Cumberland	0.54	1.27	0.91	1.84
Derbyshire	0.95	1.79	1.76	1.70
Devon	5.70	3.11	3.45	6.28
Dorset	2.72	2.06	2.48	1.82
Durham	0.45	1.59	0.98	1.86
Essex	5.10	3.53	3.68	3.76
Gloucestershire	3.08	3.20	3.28	2.46
Hampshire	3.85	1.98	2.83	2.53
Herefordshire	1.87	1.53	1.21	1.51
Hertfordshire	1.45	1.78	1.44	1.41
Huntingdonshire	0.94	1.39	1.02	0.67
Kent	4.42	3.44	4.30	3.69
Lancashire	0.67	1.28	1.73	4.41
Leicestershire	2.24	1.48	2.45	1.53
Lincolnshire	8.21	8.13	6.88	4.21
Middlesex	2.34	1.63	2.50	6.81
Norfolk	8.68	10.25	7.07	4.16
Northamptonshire	2.73	3.06	3.02	2.21
Northumberland	0.72	3.12	1.22	1.77
Nottinghamshire	1.84	1.48	2.09	1.90
Oxfordshire	2.29	1.91	1.98	1.63
Rutland	0.27	0.50	0.43	0.28
Shropshire	1.63	2.41	1.94	1.92
Somerset	4.57	3.18	4.06	4.11
Staffordshire	1.06	1.19	1.63	1.88
Suffolk	6.65	4.75	4.52	3.36
Surrey	1.45	1.72	1.30	2.06
Sussex	3.88	2.60	2.62	2.48

Table 1.07 (*cont.*)

County	1086 (%)	1290 (%)	1377 (%)	1600 (%)
Warwickshire	2.17	1.83	2.19	1.59
Westmorland	0.28	0.71	0.53	1.03
Wiltshire	3.72	3.36	3.31	2.80
Worcestershire	1.55	1.27	1.16	1.59
Yorkshire, E.R.	–	2.44	3.07	1.62
Yorkshire, N.R.	–	3.44	2.92	2.47
Yorkshire, W.R.	–	2.68	3.48	4.80
Yorkshire	2.60	(8.56)	(9.47)	(8.89)
ENGLAND	100.00	100.00	100.00	100.00

Sources and notes: * Probably an under-estimate because stannary workers (i.e. tin miners) are excluded. County population shares for 1086 from Russell (1948: 53–4). Note that the shares from Darby (1977: 336, 364–8) would be identical, since they are based on the same underlying data but with different household multipliers. County population shares for 1290 and 1377 from Campbell (2008: 926) and for 1600 from Wrigley (2009: 721).

which had shown the fastest growth between 1086 and 1290, displayed the greatest rate of decline between 1290 and 1377 partly due to the region's exposure to the prolonged military conflict between England and Scotland, with its raids and counter-raids. Otherwise, it was often the most populous counties that sustained the greatest relative losses. From 1377 to 1600, the geographical periphery once again tended to show faster growth than the core, this time in the southwest as well as the north, as can be seen in Figure 1.03D. The counties around London also displayed above average demographic dynamism. To a significant extent it was the expanding populations of these emergent regions that drove the sixteenth-century demographic recovery (Figure 1.03B). Comparing 1600 with 1290 (Tables 1.08 and 1.09 and Figure 1.03B) reveals, unsurprisingly, that recovery and growth were strongest in counties which had been most thinly peopled at the earlier date, including those closest to, and furthest from, London.

Table 1.08 *Total populations of English counties,*
1086, 1290, 1377 and 1600

County	1086	1290	1377	1600
Bedfordshire	21,695	64,194	36,771	43,059
Berkshire	38,232	61,498	41,081	56,889
Buckinghamshire	30,162	88,631	44,604	56,059
Cambridgeshire	31,123	137,373	52,885	72,492
Cheshire	9,589	36,035	26,757	73,896
Cornwall	29,532	*34,914	61,964	102,892
Cumberland	9,265	60,567	22,633	75,687
Derbyshire	16,249	84,852	43,912	69,791
Devon	97,221	147,860	86,239	258,587
Dorset	46,375	98,113	61,904	74,961
Durham	7,732	75,490	24,587	76,483
Essex	87,005	167,660	92,053	154,882
Gloucestershire	52,565	152,058	81,923	101,256
Hampshire	65,702	94,062	70,736	104,197
Herefordshire	31,861	72,502	30,230	62,054
Hertfordshire	24,742	84,529	36,113	58,104
Huntingdonshire	16,004	66,186	25,616	27,627
Kent	75,388	163,636	107,482	151,713
Lancashire	11,459	60,962	43,172	181,622
Leicestershire	38,167	70,356	61,163	63,140
Lincolnshire	140,176	386,202	171,965	173,199
Middlesex	39,851	77,399	62,476	280,063
Norfolk	148,085	486,920	176,844	171,163
Northamptonshire	46,611	145,582	75,393	91,075
Northumberland	12,300	148,084	30,389	72,923
Nottinghamshire	31,390	70,520	52,221	78,148
Oxfordshire	39,003	90,759	49,424	66,909
Rutland	4,642	23,655	10,837	11,371
Shropshire	27,895	114,640	48,502	78,958
Somerset	78,022	151,003	101,376	168,984
Staffordshire	18,030	56,715	40,658	77,559
Suffolk	113,452	225,770	113,106	138,295
Surrey	24,710	81,629	32,613	84,804
Sussex	66,135	123,415	65,437	102,003

Table 1.08 (*cont.*)

County	1086	1290	1377	1600
Warwickshire	37,107	86,829	54,714	65,455
Westmorland	4,807	33,777	13,358	42,199
Wiltshire	63,470	159,857	82,847	115,163
Worcestershire	26,376	60,470	29,105	65,614
Yorkshire, E.R.	–	115,777	76,760	66,520
Yorkshire, N.R.	–	163,634	73,099	101,596
Yorkshire, W.R.	–	127,371	87,049	197,498
Yorkshire	44,304	(406,782)	(236,907)	(365,615)
ENGLAND	1,706,436	4,751,489	2,500,000	4,114,891

Sources and notes: *Probably an under-estimate because stannary workers (i.e. tin miners) are excluded. County population totals obtained by applying the shares given in Table 1.07 to the national population totals given in Table 1.06.

Table 1.09 *Annual growth rates of English county populations, 1086–1290, 1290–1377 and 1377–1600*

County	1086–1290 (%)	1290–1377 (%)	1377–1600 (%)
Bedfordshire	0.53	−0.64	0.07
Berkshire	0.23	−0.46	0.15
Buckinghamshire	0.53	−0.79	0.10
Cambridgeshire	0.73	−1.09	0.14
Cheshire	0.65	−0.34	0.46
Cornwall	*0.08	**0.66	0.23
Cumberland	0.92	−1.13	0.54
Derbyshire	0.81	−0.75	0.21
Devon	0.21	−0.62	0.49
Dorset	0.37	−0.53	0.09
Durham	1.12	−1.28	0.51
Essex	0.32	−0.69	0.23
Gloucestershire	0.52	−0.71	0.10
Hampshire	0.18	−0.33	0.17
Herefordshire	0.40	−1.00	0.32

Table 1.09 (cont.)

County	1086–1290 (%)	1290–1377 (%)	1377–1600 (%)
Hertfordshire	0.60	–0.97	0.21
Huntingdonshire	0.70	–1.09	0.03
Kent	0.38	–0.48	0.15
Lancashire	0.82	–0.40	0.65
Leicestershire	0.30	–0.16	0.01
Lincolnshire	0.50	–0.93	0.00
Middlesex	0.33	–0.25	0.68
Norfolk	0.59	–1.16	–0.01
Northamptonshire	0.56	–0.75	0.08
Northumberland	1.23	–1.80	0.39
Nottinghamshire	0.40	–0.34	0.18
Oxfordshire	0.41	–0.70	0.14
Rutland	0.80	–0.89	0.02
Shropshire	0.70	–0.98	0.22
Somerset	0.32	–0.46	0.23
Staffordshire	0.56	–0.38	0.29
Suffolk	0.34	–0.79	0.09
Surrey	0.59	–1.05	0.43
Sussex	0.31	–0.73	0.20
Warwickshire	0.42	–0.53	0.08
Westmorland	0.96	–1.06	0.52
Wiltshire	0.45	–0.75	0.15
Worcestershire	0.41	–0.84	0.37
Yorkshire, E.R.	–	–0.47	–0.06
Yorkshire, N.R.	–	–0.92	0.15
Yorkshire, W.R.	–	–0.44	0.37
Yorkshire	1.09	–0.62	0.19
ENGLAND	0.50	–0.74	0.22

Sources and notes: *Probably an under-estimate because stannary workers (i.e. tin miners) are excluded in 1290; ** probably an over-estimate because stannary workers (i.e. tin miners) are excluded in 1290. Growth rates calculated on a logarithmic basis from the estimated county population totals given in Table 1.08.

1.5   ENGLISH POPULATION, 1541–1700

On 5 September 1538, Henry VIII's vicar general, Thomas Cromwell, ordered all Anglican parishes to maintain a register of baptisms, marriages and burials, thereby creating an invaluable demographic record of the nation's population. These are the data used by the Cambridge Group for the History of Population and Social Structure to reconstruct the population history of England from 1541 until 1840, when civil registration became effective (Wrigley and Schofield, 1989: 15). The Cambridge Group's study used local volunteers to gather data from a large sample of 404 parishes. Priority was given to the best maintained, longest and earliest surviving registers but care was also taken to ensure the sample was geographically representative and included a full range of agricultural, industrial and commercial parishes (Wrigley and Schofield, 1989: 40, 47). The sample was found to be biased towards large parishes, but this was redressed by dividing it into size classes and weighting them in line with the national proportions of those classes (Wrigley and Schofield, 1989: 49–50). Correction was made for two sources of under-registration. First, unregistered deaths of unbaptised infants were estimated from family reconstitution studies. Second, an allowance was made for Nonconformity, which is known with accuracy for the nineteenth century, and more speculatively before 1800 from trends in Nonconformist registers (Wrigley and Schofield, 1989: 89–102).

The Cambridge Group developed the technique of back-projection to interpolate new national population totals at quinquennial intervals spanning the period 1541–1871 from the parish register information. The known population and age structure given in the 1871 census is taken as the starting point. Working back from 1871 to 1866, for example, each cohort in the 1871 census was 5 years younger in 1866, and its size in 1866 is found by adding back an estimate of the number who died, based on age-specific mortality rates taken from life tables. In a closed population, the procedure would be relatively straightforward, but the existence of substantial migration flows complicates the analysis. The method deduces migration flows from inconsistencies between the age structure of the population and the recorded flows of births and deaths. For the period back to 1801, census totals are available every decade, but for earlier years the method is totally reliant on the projections and any errors become retrospectively cumulative. Although the back-projection procedure was criticised by Lee (1985) as a method of deriving reliable population totals, sensitivity analysis subsequently conducted by Oeppen (1993) suggests that the estimates of Wrigley and Schofield (1989) are robust. Some relatively minor modifications were, however, made in Wrigley and others (1997) following completion of the Cambridge Group's family reconstitution studies. These revised 1997 quinquennial estimates have now acquired the status of orthodoxy and have here been interpolated using Wrigley and Schofield (1989: 531–5) to obtain annual totals.

Table 1.10 presents estimates of English population for five benchmark years from 1541 to 1700. The recovery of the population which had begun in the final decades of the fifteenth century was maintained until the mid-seventeenth century, by which time the population had risen to a new peak of almost 5.4 million. Growth was fastest in the middle years of the sixteenth century but then

Table 1.10 *English and British populations totals, 1541–1700 and 1700–1870 (millions)*

Year	Total English population (m.)	Year	Total British population (m.)
1541	2.83	1700	6.21
1560	3.02	1750	7.22
1600	4.11	1800	10.61
1650	5.31	1850	20.65
1700	5.20	1870	25.84

Sources: Wrigley and others (1997); Wrigley and Schofield (1989); Mitchell (1988).

slowed to less than 0.5 per cent per year during the first half of the seventeenth century (Table 1.11 below). Thereafter, as mortality rose, emigration increased and fertility declined, numbers drifted gently downwards for the remainder of the century, to 5.2 million at its close, thereby giving the economy much-needed demographic breathing space.

1.6   BRITISH POPULATION, 1700–1870

For the period 1700–1870, the territory under consideration is the whole of Great Britain including Wales and Scotland, but excluding Ireland, which did not become part of the United Kingdom until 1801. From 1801 onwards, annual data on the population of England, Wales and Scotland are available from Mitchell (1988: 9). Prior to 1801, as noted earlier, the population of England has been reconstructed firmly by Wrigley and Schofield (1989) and Wrigley and others (1997). Although annual estimates are not available for Scotland and Wales, there is scattered information to fill in the gaps. For Scotland, population estimates for 1700, 1750 and 1801 have been interpolated using the population of England (Schofield, 1994: 93). Corresponding estimates for Wales have been extrapolated from the 1801 ratio of the population of Wales to that of England. The resulting aggregate estimates for Great Britain are reported in Table 1.10.

The first half of the eighteenth century (following union with Scotland in 1707) saw a return to population growth, which gathered pace during the second half of the century. Growth peaked at around 1.5 per cent per year during the first three decades of the nineteenth century, before slowing down as Britain entered its demographic transition, as falling birth rates followed falling death rates and life expectancy at birth steadily improved. By 1871 England's population had risen to 21.3 million and that of Great Britain to 25.84 million and both were still rising. England was almost four times more populous than in 1650 and over four times more populous than in 1315/1348.

1.7   CONCLUSIONS

Table 1.11 provides a summary of population growth rates in England from 1270 to 1700 and in Great Britain from 1700 to 1870. Growth rates are presented between decadal averages, reflecting a periodisation that will be useful later in analysing economic growth, as well as capturing the main turning points in population trends. At the outset of the series England supported a population of approximately 4.37 million and the great demographic boom that had brought about an increase of more than two-and-a-half-fold since 1086 was almost at an end. England's population was already stagnating by the time the Great Famine struck in 1315–22, although it was the Black Death a generation later that proved to be the decisive demographic turning point. Four successive plague epidemics reduced the population by

Table 1.11 *Annual population growth rates, 1270–1870*

Period	England (%)	Great Britain (%)
1270/79 – 1300/09	0.23	
1300/09 – 1340/48	−0.02	
1340/48 – 1400/09	−1.33	
1400/09 – 1450/59	−0.14	
1450/59 – 1553/59	0.48	
1553/59 – 1600/09	0.67	
1600/09 – 1650/59	0.45	
1650/59 – 1691/1700	−0.08	
1700/09 – 1760/69		0.34
1760/69 – 1780/89		0.74
1780/89 – 1801/10		1.09
1801/10 – 1830/39		1.44
1830/39 – 1861/70		1.17
1270/79 – 1691/1700	0.04	
1700/09 – 1830/39		0.76
1700/09 – 1861/70		0.84

Sources and notes: Derived from data underlying Tables 1.06, 1.08 and 1.09.

almost half between 1348 and 1377, shrinking it to a relatively securely documented 2.5 million. Numbers continued to dwindle until the mid-fifteenth century when decline finally bottomed out and hitherto rising real wage rates reached a plateau and stabilised for the next 60 years. The low-level equilibrium thereby established persisted until the final decades of the fifteenth century when, in defiance of periodic surges in disease mortality, signs of incipient recovery become apparent.

From early in the sixteenth century, as real wage rates trended downwards once again, numbers were clearly rising strongly and in the second quarter of the century annual growth rates may have reached 1 per cent. For the next 100 years, although disease and dearth continued to levy a periodic toll on the population, positive growth of at least 0.5 per cent a year persisted. By 1625 the medieval peak of 4.8 million had been exceeded and in the 1650s, when growth finally ceased, the population had risen to almost 5.4 million. For the next half century the population stagnated and by 1700 England's population had dwindled slightly to 5.2 million with a further million in Wales and Scotland. The eighteenth century brought a return to positive growth and acceleration to hitherto unprecedented rates of increase. These reached a historical maximum of around 1.5 per cent in the first three decades of the nineteenth century by which time the population of Great Britain was fast approaching 20 million. Although growth then again slowed, the scale of subsequent absolute gains in numbers remained substantial, elevating the population of Great Britain to 37 million by the close of the century.

There is little about this chronology after 1541 that is controversial. The eighteenth-century Welsh and Scottish estimates are capable of refinement but any revisions are unlikely to have a significant impact on the aggregate estimates for Great Britain. For England, the post-Commonwealth parish register dataset is fuller and more reliable than the pre-Civil War dataset and the evidential basis of the Cambridge Group's estimates narrows as it goes back in time. Margins of error on their back-projection results similarly widen. Nevertheless, the broad contours of their population reconstruction remain undisputed and as yet there are no alternative estimates that carry greater conviction. For the time being, therefore, the post-1541 population estimates stand unchallenged.

Before 1541 there is no such consensus. This chapter has therefore constructed new estimates of English medieval population from the available time-series and cross-sectional evidence, based upon realistic and transparent assumptions and taking account of geographical inconsistencies of coverage and variations in trends. These estimates have the merits that they are consistent across time, geographically representative, chronologically reconcilable with the Cambridge Group's post-1541 estimates, compatible with the course of real wage rates, and historically credible. Undoubtedly some historians will claim that their absolute level is consistently too low. Yet the case for a substantially larger medieval population at peak before the Black Death founders on the difficulty, without resort to special pleading (Stone, 2006) or unrealistic assumptions (Clark, 2007a: 118–27), of demonstrating how a population in excess of 4.8 million could have been fed, given what is known about prevailing patterns of land use, crop and livestock mixes, grain yields, rates of food extraction and the country's socio-economic profile as reconstructed in Chapters 2, 3 and 8. The strength of the pre-Black Death population estimate advanced here is that the numbers proposed were supportable, just, by the estimated output capacity of the economy. All other estimates then follow from this within the constraints set by the available evidence and the need to link up with the post-1541 estimates established by Wrigley and others (1997). There are undoubtedly a great deal more data that might be gathered or more rigorously analysed that would improve and refine this picture. This applies above all to the demographic Dark Age between c.1450 when the manorial records effectively end and 1540 when the parish records commence. It was across this documentary watershed that one demographic cycle dominated by decline ended and a new cycle characterised by growth began.

APPENDIX 1.1

List of manors included in the population estimates

A. 1086–1190 (17 MANORS)

County	Manors
Berks.	Ashbury
Dorset	Sturminster Newton
Essex	Beauchamp
Glos.	Adlestrop, Bishop's Cleve, Broadwell, Pucklechurch, Willersey
Northants.	Badby
Warks.	Abbot's Salford, Sambourn
Wilts.	Badbury, Christmalford, Grittleton, Doverham, Nettleton, Winterbourne Monkton

B. 1086–1220 (46 MANORS)

County	Manors
Beds.	Caddington
Cambs.	Balsham, Ditton with Horningsea, Doddington with March, Downham, Gransden, Hardwick, Linden End, Littleport, Shelford, Stretham, Thriplow, Wilburton, Wisbech
Essex	Barking, Beauchamp, Chingford, Hadstock, Littlebury, Runwell, Tidwoldingham, Tillingham, Wickam
Herts.	Luffenhall, Sandon
Hunts.	Bluntisham, Colne, Somersham
Middx	Drayton
Norfolk	Dereham, Feltwell, Northwold, Pulham, Shipdam, Upwell with Outwell, Walsoken, Walton
Northants.	Harlestone
Suffolk	Barking, Brandon, Glemsford, Hartest, Hitcham, Rattlesden, Wetheringsett
Surrey	Barnes

C. 1086–1250 (105 MANORS)

County	Manors
Beds.	Barton, Cranfield, Shillington with Pegsdon
Cambs.	Balsham, Burwell, Chatteris, Ditton with Horningsea, Downham, Ely, Girton, Gransden, Hardwick, Linden End, Littleport, Shelford, Stretham, Thriplow, Wilburton, Willingham
Essex	Hadstock, Havering, Littlebury, Rettendon
Hunts.	Bluntisham, Brington, Broughton, Colne, Hemingford Abbots, Holywell, Old Weston, Slepe, Somersham, Upwood, Warboys, Wistow
Lincs.	Spalding
Norfolk	Brancaster with Burnham Deepdale, Dereham, Feltwell, Northwold, Pulham, Ringstead with Holm, Upwell with Outwell, Walsoken, Walton
Oxon.	Adderbury, Baldon, Crowmarsh, Rousham, Salford
Som.	Ashcott, Baltonsborough, Butleigh, Ditcheat, Doulting, East Pennard, High Ham, Marksbury, Mells, Mere, Othery, Pilton, Shapwick, Street, Walton, Wrington
Staffs.	Alrewas
Suffolk	Barking, Bramford, Brandon, Glemsford, Hartest, Hitcham, Rattlesden, Wetheringsett
Sussex	Aldingbourne, Bishopstone, Boxgrove, Denton, Ferring, Mundham with Kipson Bank and Hunston, Preston, Selsey, Sidlesham, Walberton with Barnham and Abington
Worcs.	Alston and Packington, Blackwell, Cleeve, Cropthorne, Grimley with Knightwick, Hallow, Harvington, Overbury, Phepson, Shipston, Stoke, Wolverley cum Eymore
Yorks.	Asenby, Leeds, Linton, Pocklington, Rowley, Skirpenbeck, Spofforth, Tadcaster

D. 1086–1279 (168 MANORS)

County	Manors
Beds.	Biggleswade, Bletsoe, Clapham, Easton, Felmersham, Oakley, Odell, Pavenham, Podington, Stagsden, Stevington, Symington, Thurleigh, Woburn

D. 1086–1279 (168 MANORS) (*cont.*)

County	Manors
Bucks.	Dodford, Edgcott, Foxcott, Gayhurst, Haversham, Lamport, Lathbury, Leckhampstead Magna, Leckhampstead Parva, Maids Moreton, Marlow, Ravenstone, Stewkley, Thornborough, Thornton, Turweston, Water Stratford, Westbury, Weston Turville
Cambs.	Bottisham, Chippenham, Comberton, Conington, Elsworth, Eversden, Gamlingay, Girton, Great Abington with Little Abington, Hildersham, Histon, Horseheath, Knapwell, Lolworth, Orwell, Rampton, Silverley, Swavesey, Thriplow, Waterbeach with Landbeach
Devon	Axminster
Glos.	Badgeworth, Brimpsfield, Campden, Hatherop, Prestbury, Sevenhampton, Bagworth
Herts.	Little Hadham
Hunts.	Barham, Broughton, Buckden, Bythorn, Catworth, Dillington, Ellington, Fleeton, Giddings, Hemingford Abbots, Hemingford Grey, Holywell, Horton cum Whitton, Old Weston, Sawtry, Slepe, Stukeley, Warboys
Leics.	Knighton, Leicester, Thurmaston
Lincs.	Dunholme, Howell, Louth, Marton, Nettleham, Normanby, Norton, Sleaford, Spalding, Stow St Mary
Norfolk	Banham, Hindolveston
Northants.	Kilsby
Notts.	Barnby-in-the-Willows, Coddington, Collingham, Newark-upon-Trent
Oxon.	Alwoldesberie, Baldon, Banbury, Begbrook, Bladon, Bucknell, Checkendon, Chinnor, Chislehampton, Cropredy, Crowmarsh Gifford, Cuddesdon, Dorchester-on-Thames, Draycott, Drayton, Easington, Fritwell, Fulbrook, Grafton, Heyford Warren, Horsepath, Ipsden, Lillingstone Lovell, Mapledurham Chauzy, Mixbury, Pyrton, Rousham, Salford, Taynton, Thame, Warpsgrove
Rutland	Liddington

D. 1086–1279 (168 MANORS) (cont.)

County	Manors
Salop	Cheswardine
Staffs.	Harbourne with Smethwick, Winnington
Warks.	Ashow, Brandon, Burton Dassett, Coundon, Honington, Kenilworth, Oxhill, Priors Hardwick, Ratley and Upton, Stoneleigh, Walsgrave on Sowe, Wormleighton
Wilts.	Bishopstrow, Brigmerston, Calstone Wellington, Compton Chamberlayne, Stratton St Margaret, Sutton Mandeville, Swallowcliffe, Whadden, Widhill with Groundwell, Winterslow
Worcs.	Fladbury, Hanbury, Hartlebury, Ripple
Yorks.	Aldbrough, Barnby, Danby-in-Cleveland, Gilling, Hutton Mulgrave, Lythe, Skelton

E. 1086–1290 (28 MANORS)

County	Manors
Essex	Feering, Kelvedon Churchall
Glos.	Haresecombe
Hunts.	Broughton
Lincs.	Digby, Frieston, Pinchbeck Town, Ruskington, Spalding Town, Stowe
Norfolk	Martham
Notts.	Radcliffe-on-Soar with Kingston-on-Soar, Tuxford
Som.	Compton Dundon, Stoke under Hamdon
Staffs.	Betley, Cradley
Sussex	East Lavant, Tangmere, West Tarring, Willingham
Warks.	Middleton
Wilts.	Elcombe
Worcs.	Halesowen
Yorks.	Bridge Hewick, Danby, Garton on the Wolds, Gilling

F. 1086–1315 (59 MANORS)

County	Manors
Berks.	Englefield, Swallowfield
Bucks.	Ardington, Avington, Chilton, Ilsley, South Moreton, Speen
Cornwall	Braddock
Devon	Carswell Regis, Deptford, Sutton Walerland
Essex	Chickney
Glos.	Chedworth, Dean, Dyrham, Hull and Nympfield, Thornbury
Herts.	Ashwell
Hunts.	Broughton
Middx	Hendon
Norfolk	Barney, Binham
Northants.	Titchmarsh
Oxon.	Caversham, Ducklington, Emington, Garsington, Hardwick, Mapledurham Chauzy, Rutherford
Rutland	Ridlington
Salop	Acton Burnell, Euden Burnell
Som.	Baltonsborough
Staffs.	Wigginton
Sussex	Bignor
Warks.	Claverdon, Coldfield, Kingsbury, Middleton, Sherborne
Wilts.	Grimstead, Newton Toney, Stourton, Stratford Toney, Wardour, Wilsford with Lake, Wootton Rivers
Worcs.	Acton Beauchamp, Comberton, Elmley, Inkberrow, Naunton Beauchamp, Pirton, Salwarpe, Tenbury, Wadborough, Newynton

G. 1300–1315 (11 MANORS)

County	Manors
Bucks.	Great Horwood
Essex	Chatham, Great Waltham, High Easter

G. 1300–1315 (11 MANORS) *(cont.)*

County	Manors
Hunts.	Broughton, Godmanchester
Leics.	Kibworth Harcourt
Northants.	Brigstock
Som.	Taunton
Wilts.	Cherhill
Worcs.	Halesowen

H. 1300–1325 (12 MANORS)

County	Manors
Bucks.	Great Horwood, Newton Longville
Essex	Chatham, High Easter
Hunts.	Broughton, Godmanchester, Holywell, Warboys
Leics.	Kibworth Harcourt
Northants.	Brigstock
Som.	Taunton
Worcs.	Halesowen

I. 1300–1348 (12 MANORS)

County	Manors
Bucks.	Great Horwood, Newton Longville
Essex	Chatham, Great Waltham, High Easter
Hunts.	Godmanchester, Holywell
Leics.	Kibworth Harcourt
Norfolk	Coltishall
Northants.	Brigstock
Som.	Taunton
Worcs.	Halesowen

J. 1300–1351 (8 MANORS)

County	Manors
Bucks.	Great Horwood, Newton Longville
Essex	Chatham, Great Waltham, High Easter
Hunts.	Godmanchester
Leics.	Kibworth Harcourt
Worcs.	Halesowen

K. 1300–1377 (11 MANORS)

County	Manors
Bucks.	Akeley, Great Horwood, Newton Longville
Essex	Chatham, Great Waltham, High Easter
Hunts.	Godmanchester, Holywell, Warboys
Leics.	Kibworth Harcourt
Worcs.	Halesowen

L. 1377–1400 (13 MANORS)

County	Manors
Bucks.	Akeley, Great Horwood, Newton Longville
Essex	Berden, Chatham, Great Waltham, High Easter, Writtle
Hunts.	Godmanchester, Holywell, Warboys
Leics.	Kibworth Harcourt
Worcs.	Halesowen

M. 1377–1430 (8 MANORS)

County	Manors
Bucks.	Great Horwood, Newton Longville
Essex	Great Waltham, Hatfield Broadoak, High Easter, Writtle
Hunts.	Holywell, Warboys

N. 1377–1450 (7 MANORS)

County	Manors
Bucks.	Great Horwood, Newton Longville
Essex	Great Waltham, High Easter, Writtle
Hunts.	Holywell, Warboys

APPENDIX 1.2

List of sources for the manors included in the population estimates and additional to those listed by Hallam (1988)

A. 1086–1250

County	Manor	Source
Essex	Havering	McIntosh (1986)
Oxon.	Adderburry	Russell (1948)

B. 1086–1279

County	Manor	Source
Devon	Axminster	Russell (1948)
Herts.	Little Hadham	Russell (1948)
Notts.	Collingham	Russell (1948)
Oxon.	Crowmarsh Gifford, Drayton	Russell (1948)
Salop	Cheswardine	Russell (1948)

C. 1086–1290

County	Manor	Source
Lincs.	Stowe	Russell (1948)
Norfolk	Martham	Campbell (1980)
Warks.	Middleton	Russell (1948)

D. 1086–1315

County	Manor	Source
Berks.	Englefield	Russell (1948)
Bucks.	Ardington, Avington, Ilsley, Speen	Russell (1948)
Cornwall	Braddock	Russell (1948)
Devon	Carswell Regis, Deptford, Sutton Walerland	Russell (1948)
Glos.	Dean, Thornbury	Russell (1948)
Oxon.	Mapledurham Chauzy, Rutherford	Russell (1948)
Salop	Acton Burnell, Euden Burnell	Russell (1948)
Warks.	Claverdon, Coldfield, Kingsbury, Middleton	Russell (1948)
Worcs.	Newynton	Russell (1948)

E. 1300–1315

County	Manor	Source
Bucks.	Great Horwood	Poos (personal communication)
Essex	Chatham, Great Waltham, High Easter	Poos (1991)
Hunts.	Broughton	Britton (1977)
	Godmanchester	Raftis (1990)
Leics.	Kibworth Harcourt	Poos (personal communication)
Northants.	Brigstock	Bennett (1987)
Som.	Taunton	Titow (1961)

F. 1300–1325

County	Manor	Source
Bucks.	Great Horwood, Newton Longville	Poos (personal communication)
Essex	Chatham, High Easter	Poos (1991)

F. 1300–1325 (cont.)

County	Manor	Source
Hunts.	Broughton	Britton (1977)
	Godmanchester	Raftis (1990)
	Hollywell	DeWindt (1972)
	Warboys	Raftis (1974)
Leics.	Kibworth Harcourt	Poos (personal communication)
Northants.	Brigstock	Bennett (1987)
Som.	Taunton	Titow (1961)

G. 1300–1348

County	Manor	Source
Bucks.	Great Horwood, Newton Longville	Poos (personal communication)
Essex	Chatham, Great Waltham, High Easter	Poos (1991)
Hunts.	Godmanchester	Raftis (1990)
	Holywell	DeWindt (1972)
Leics.	Kibworth Harcourt	Poos (personal communication)
Norfolk	Coltishall	Campbell (1984)
Northants.	Brigstock	Bennett (1987)
Som.	Taunton	Poos (personal communication)

H. 1300–1351

County	Manor	Source
Bucks.	Great Horwood, Newton Longville	Poos (personal communication)
Essex	Chatham, Great Waltham, High Easter	Poos (1991)

H. 1300–1351 (cont.)

County	Manor	Source
Hunts.	Godmanchester	Raftis (1990)
Leics.	Kibworth Harcourt	Poos (personal communication)

I. 1300–1377

County	Manor	Source
Bucks.	Akeley, Great Horwood, Newton Longville	Poos (personal communication)
Essex	Chatham, Great Waltham, High Easter	Poos (1991)
Hunts.	Godmanchester	Raftis (1990)
	Holywell	DeWindt (1972)
	Warboys	Raftis (1974)
Leics.	Kibworth Harcourt	Poos (personal communication)

J. 1377–1400

County	Manor	Source
Bucks.	Akeley, Great Horwood, Newton Longville	Poos (personal communication)
Essex	Berden, Chatham, Great Waltham, High Easter, Writtle	Poos (1991)
Hunts.	Godmanchester	Raftis (1990)
	Holywell	DeWindt (1972)
	Warboys	Raftis (1974)
Leics.	Kibworth Harcourt	Poos (personal communication)

K. 1377-1430

County	Manor	Source
Bucks.	Great Horwood, Newton Longville	Poos (personal communication)
Essex	Great Waltham, Hatfield Broadoak, High Easter, Writtle	Poos (1991)
Hunts.	Hollywell	DeWindt (1972)
	Warboys	Raftis (1974)

L. 1377-1450

County	Manor	Source
Bucks.	Great Horwood, Newton Longville	Poos (personal communication)
Essex	Great Waltham, High Easter, Writtle	Poos (1991)
Hunts.	Holywell	DeWindt (1972)
	Warboys	Raftis (1974)

2   Agricultural land use

2.1   INTRODUCTION

Agriculture was for long the single largest component of the English and British economies, both in terms of its share of employment and the value of its output. The latter was a function of the amount of land under cultivation, the uses to which it was put, the productivities of crops and animals and their respective prices. The main purpose of this chapter is to describe the methods used to derive the areas under arable and grass and, in particular, the total sown acreage. The crops produced and animals stocked are the subjects of the following chapter. Along the way, it will be demonstrated that claims that the peak arable area in the medieval period may have exceeded 20 million acres (Clark, 2007a: 124) are unrealistic, since, on the best available evidence, the combined total under field crops and fallow could not have been more than 12.75 million acres. In the absence of significant food imports, this limited both the population that could be supported and the supply of kilocalories per head needed for survival. It also shaped the production choices made by agricultural producers.

Comprehensive national agricultural statistics were collected annually from 1866 and provide the starting point for calculating the acreages of arable and grass (Anon, 1968; Coppock, 1984). Together with the tithe files, which provide a precise but incomplete guide to the share of land in each county devoted to arable production during the 1830s (Kain, 1986; Overton, 1986), they are used to provide a nineteenth-century benchmark. The chapter proceeds as follows. After a discussion of the potential agricultural area of England in Section 2.2, Section 2.3 reviews the arable acreage by county from the tithe files of the 1830s and from the agricultural statistics of 1871. Section 2.4 then examines changes in land use between 1290 and 1871, while Section 2.5 presents county-level estimates of the arable acreage in 1290. Section 2.6 provides a further cross-check by examining changes in land use between 1086 and 1290. Finally, Section 2.7 provides estimates of land use for a number of benchmark years between 1270 and 1871.

2.2 THE POTENTIAL AGRICULTURAL AREA OF ENGLAND

Only a proportion of England's 32.3 million acres of land is potentially suited to and available for agricultural use. In 1871, following the first systematic national survey of farmland and farm output, the total area under crops of all kinds, bare fallow and temporary and permanent grass was 23.5 million acres: 73 per cent of the total (Table 2.01). Of the remaining 27 per cent, woodland, on the evidence of the tithe files, probably accounted for at least 5 per cent (Table 2.02). Unfarmable moorlands and mountains (the latter accounting for over half of the county of Westmorland), ornamental parks, surface water,

Table 2.01 *The regional distributions of grassland and agricultural land in 1871*

Region	Total acreage 1871	Agricultural area as % total acreage	Permanent grass as % agricultural area	All grass as % agricultural area
NE midlands	2,433,209	83.5	53.1	61.0
W midlands	2,404,899	82.1	48.9	58.8
E counties	4,848,111	81.5	22.7	34.6
SW midlands	3,360,492	78.4	50.2	61.2
SE counties	6,866,189	73.6	30.4	41.6
NE counties	5,721,160	64.7	47.3	58.4
NW counties	4,155,139	62.3	60.8	73.7
SW counties	2,539,132	61.2	33.6	52.3
ENGLAND	32,328,331	72.7	41.1	52.6

Source: Agricultural Returns for Great Britain for 1871.

Table 2.02 *The composition of agricultural land use in the 1830s*

Land use	No.of counties represented	Minimum % of total area	Mean % of total area	Maximum % of total area
Arable[a]	35	21.5	44.1	72.4
Grass[a]	35	15.5	41.3	70.4
Commons[b]	30	0.9	4.6	23.3
Grass + commons[b]	30	16.6	45.9	71.9
Woodland[c]	32	1.4	5.5	15.1
Arable as % (arable + grass + commons)[b]	30	23.0	49.5	79.4

[a] The unrepresented counties are: Cumberland, Leicestershire, Northamptonshire, Nottinghamshire, Westmorland.
[b] The unrepresented counties are the same as (a) plus: Bedfordshire, Derbyshire, Huntingdonshire, Lancashire, Northumberland.
[c] The unrepresented counties are the same as (a) plus: Cheshire, Gloucestershire, Lancashire.
Sources and notes: Kain (1986).

communications and settlements made up the rest. Discounting wood-land as an agricultural land use, it is doubtful, therefore, whether it has ever been possible to farm more than three-quarters of England's surface area, and even to achieve that has involved extensive land drainage, soil underdrainage, stone clearance and liming. Whereas in earlier centuries communications and settlements occupied less space, woodland (for utility and amenity) undoubtedly took up more, especially before the land-saving substitutions of coal for wood and charcoal and iron for timber. Additionally, during the middle ages large areas had been subject to forest law, which privileged amenity over agricultural uses (Young, 1979). By 1871, although parks now landscaped for amenity and man-aged for grazing remained an integral feature of the landscape (Prince, 1980), pursuing foxes over farmland had largely replaced hunting deer and wild boars through forests and chases.

The agricultural area always comprised a combination of arable and grassland, with some overlap between them. In practice, distinguishing between 'permanent' pasture and 'temporary' grassland can be difficult since some pasture was occasionally ploughed. In 1871 arable (i.e. land that was regularly ploughed) of all sorts occupied 59 per cent, and permanent grassland (i.e. unploughed hay meadows and pastures) 41 per cent of the agricultural area. By this date sown grasses had become a feature of many arable rotations, as crop and livestock production became increasingly integrated on the same land. Permanent and temporary grassland together accounted for just over half – 53 per cent – of the agricultural area (Table 2.01). Similarly, in the 1830s, on the evidence of the partial geographical coverage of the tithe files, arable and pastoral land uses (grassland and common pastures) existed in almost equal proportions (Table 2.02). Grassland was the default agricultural land use wherever slopes were too steep, soils too heavy, thin, dry, rocky, acidic or infertile, and water tables too high, rainfall too heavy, altitudes too great and growing seasons too short for arable cultivation. It was also the default agricultural land use wherever the institutional barriers of common rights and forest law prevented land from being ploughed. By 1871 private and parliamentary enclosure agreements and the disafforestation of most areas once subject to forest law had shrunk but not quite eliminated these institutional obstacles, which had reached their maximum extent under England's Norman and Plantagenet kings (Young, 1979; Campbell and Bartley, 2006: 55–68, 150–7).

Maintaining a proportion of all land as grass was also indispensable to the organic mixed farming which had long been the prevailing husbandry type throughout England. Tillage could not be maintained on the scale it was without the deployment of several million draft animals for ploughing and carting and additional animals to breed replacement stock and produce the manure so vital to on-the-farm recycling of nutrients. No arable farmer could yet manage without some permanent grassland, so arable farming at its most arable was in fact mixed farming (Overton, 1996: 10–15). Animals and their products also made a vital contribution to diets (Chapter 7) and supplied a range of raw materials to the manufacturing sector (Chapter 4). Of course, the precise balance struck between arable and permanent grass varied a good deal. In 1871 in the heartland of intensive arable production in the eastern counties, permanent grass accounted for less than a quarter of all farmland, but in the hillier and rainier western and northwestern counties with a comparative advantage in pastoral production this proportion rose to half and sometimes substantially more. By this date temporary grass leys were widely incorporated into arable rotations, so that nationally over half of all farmland was devoted to grass of one sort or another. Inclusion of sown grasses into arable rotations had been a key innovation of the agricultural revolution, enabling the arable area to expand at the expense of permanent pasture so that at this climax of Victorian 'high farming', following repeal of the Corn Laws but prior to the American grain invasion, in most of the predominantly arable parts of England more land was tilled and under arable rotations than ever before.

As a rule of thumb, therefore, it can be assumed that England had a potential agricultural area of 24 million acres, divided roughly equally between arable and grass, with more tillage than pasture in the south and east and vice versa in the north and west. Even after partial substitution of temporary grass for permanent pastures, around 40 per cent of the agricultural area remained under permanent grass (Table 2.01), so that the country's potential arable area was at most 15 million acres, equivalent to 46 per cent of the national land area. Extrapolating from the tithe files indicates that 13.9 million acres were under all kinds of grain, green and root crops, bare fallow, clover, sainfoin and grasses under rotation, amounting to 43 per cent of the total national land area. In fact, this was close to the maximum that was agriculturally feasible given England's soils, terrain, climate, mixed-farming needs, and property rights and the competition for land from woodland, settlements, communications, extractive industries, recreational activities and much else.

2.3   LAND USE IN THE 1830S AND 1871

The year 1871 marks the culmination of the era of 'high farming' (so named because of the high inputs used to obtain high outputs), when the intensity of organic methods of agricultural production attained its fullest development and the area under agricultural land uses of one sort or another was pushed close to its natural limits. With 21.3 million people to feed, much wet and ill-drained land had been brought into arable production for the first time using techniques not previously available. Nevertheless, for reasons of comparative advantage, considerable tracts of land which had been worked as arable during the high middle ages but subsequently converted to pastoral production (creating the phenomenon of deserted villages) remained under permanent grass. To quantify the net effect of these and other changes in land use, it is necessary to track the changing distribution of arable acreage by county, starting with the distribution of the arable acreage in England at the time of its peak usage during the nineteenth century (Table 2.03).

Table 2.03 *The percentage of land under arable in English counties, c.1836 and 1871*

County	Acreage	1836 (%)	1871 (%)	Mean of c.1836 and 1871 (%)
Bedfordshire	303,360	60.1	61.5	60.8
Berkshire	481,920	58.5	57.3	57.9
Buckinghamshire	475,520	55.8	45.8	50.8
Cambridgeshire	558,080	70.1	75.6	72.8
Cheshire	613,120	25.5	27.6	26.6
Cornwall	889,600	23.8	43.0	33.4
Cumberland	979,200		27.5	27.5
Derbyshire	646,400	25.3	23.8	24.5
Devon	1,672,320	22.5	39.6	31.0
Dorset	661,760	21.5	37.8	29.6
Durham	635,520	54.9	35.2	45.0
Essex	983,680	72.4	60.4	66.4

Table 2.03 (*cont.*)

County	Acreage	1836 (%)	1871 (%)	Mean of c.1836 and 1871 (%)
Gloucestershire	800,640	32.0	43.8	37.9
Hampshire	1,030,400	64.3	50.2	57.2
Herefordshire	539,520	39.7	38.5	39.1
Hertfordshire	399,360	66.6	63.5	65.1
Huntingdonshire	236,800	49.8	65.8	57.8
Kent	1,000,320	48.5	52.3	50.4
Lancashire	1,234,560	27.1	20.6	23.8
Leicestershire	532,480		35.3	35.3
Lincolnshire	1,707,520	48.7	59.2	54.0
Middlesex	189,440		22.5	22.5
Norfolk	1,317,760	63.8	62.1	62.9
Northamptonshire	638,720		44.7	44.7
Northumberland	1,297,920	46.5	26.1	36.3
Nottinghamshire	532,480		54.8	54.8
Oxfordshire	473,600	55.8	58.1	57.0
Rutland	96,640	38.2	46.3	42.3
Shropshire	860,160	47.0	41.4	44.2
Somerset	1,044,480	24.4	28.3	26.4
Staffordshire	740,480	44.8	32.3	38.6
Suffolk	957,440	70.3	65.0	67.7
Surrey	485,120	48.8	39.9	44.3
Sussex	935,040	43.8	41.3	42.5
Warwickshire	620,800	47.5	43.7	45.6
Westmorland	506,240		12.2	12.2
Wiltshire	849,920	35.1	49.0	42.0
Worcestershire	451,200	42.7	45.1	43.9
Yorkshire, E.R.	755,200	65.6	64.7	65.2
Yorkshire, N.R.	1,378,560	32.2	31.3	31.8
Yorkshire, W.R.	1,815,040	30.0	28.3	29.2
ENGLAND	32,328,320			42.9

Sources: Kain (1986); *Agricultural Returns for Great Britain for 1871.*

The second column of Table 2.03 sets out the total acreage of land in each county, while the third and fourth columns show the arable acreage reported in the tithe files and the 1871 Agricultural Returns as percentages of the county area. The fifth column takes the mean of these two ratios, which is taken as the most realistic indicator of the amount and proportion of arable land use in each county and in the country as a whole. At this time, arable accounted for more than 60 per cent of all land use in just seven counties, all in eastern England (Essex, Suffolk, Norfolk, Cambridgeshire, Bedfordshire, Hertfordshire and the East Riding of Yorkshire). Only in the recently drained and reclaimed Cambridgeshire did the proportion exceed 70 per cent. At the other extreme, arable comprised less than a quarter of all land use in Lancashire, Derbyshire and metropolitan Middlesex, and less than one eighth in hilly and mountainous Westmorland. These maximum and minimum proportions suggest that in earlier centuries, when no farming region could do without at least some tillage and some grassland, no county is likely to have had less than one-eighth or more than two-thirds of its land area in arable production.

Nationally, 42.9 per cent of England's surface area was devoted to arable in the mid-nineteenth century, comprising 13.9 million acres. At that time, England's population was three-and-a-half times its level in 1290, the country was still heavily dependent on domestic grain production, and arable and livestock production were more closely integrated than ever before through the incorporation of fodder crops and sown grasses into arable rotations and the near universal adoption of fodder-fed horses for farm work (Table 2.01 and Figure 2.01). It is therefore improbable that the amount of arable land in 1290 could have been greater than this. But could it have been smaller? Although in 1290 there were strong demand incentives to devote as much land as possible to arable production, common rights, royal forest law, high water tables and a range of other physical and institutional obstacles prevented a good deal of potential tillage from being ploughed. Only later, following reclamation, drainage, enclosure and disafforestation, would this be brought into arable production. A greater reliance upon

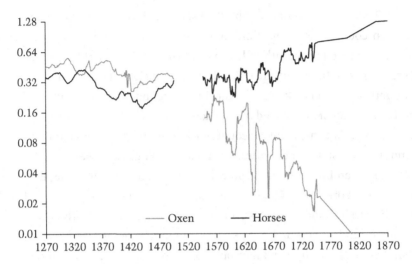

FIGURE 2.01 Numbers of oxen and horses, 1270–1870 (millions, 10-year moving averages, log scale). *Sources and notes:* Derived from the Medieval Accounts Database; the Early Modern Probate Inventories Database; Allen (1994); John (1989); Turner (1998). Further details are given in Chapter 3.

grass-fed oxen for draught power (Figure 2.01) combined with a heavy commercial dependence upon wool production from extensively managed sheep imply the existence of relatively generous supplies of grassland. Lower population densities in much of the north, north-west, and south-west also meant that in these regions there was not yet the need to bring all potential arable land into production. To be realistic, any estimate of the arable acreage in 1290 needs to consider the net effect of these changes in land use between 1290 and the nineteenth-century maximum.

2.4 CHANGING LAND USE, FROM 1290 TO THE MID-NINETEENTH CENTURY

After 1290 major additions to the nation's stock of arable land were made by the drainage and reclamation of many wetland areas, especially the East Anglian fens. Fortunately, these developments have been quantified (Marshall and others, 1978: 255; Grigg, 1989: 29). Harder to estimate are the gains that came from the enclosure and ploughing up of former permanent pasture, from the breaking up of areas previously under forest law, and from the clearance of woodland as coal was substituted for wood as a fuel and timber gave way to brick and iron. For instance, Wrigley (2006: 470) reckons that 'coal, by providing an acceptable substitute for wood and charcoal, endowed the country with the equivalent of many millions of acres of woodland'.

Offsetting these gains, farmland was being lost to quarries, mines, roads, canals, railways, settlement expansion, and the conversion of demesnes and occasionally entire manors into landscape parks. Growing urban demand for meat and dairy produce, especially from middle class consumers in the metropolis, also underpinned the heightened importance of pastoral farming, leading to the lasting conversion of much heavy land from tillage to permanent grass, particularly on the stiff clay soils of the east midlands and south-west midlands. In these regions, strategically well placed between rearing regions to the north and west and the London market to the south and east, physical difficulties and high cultivation costs meant that grassland tended to give better and more reliable financial returns than arable. The widespread phenomenon of village desertion is one legacy of the switch to permanent pasture, a seasonal shift in the timing of early-modern marriages another (Beresford, 1989: 35, 39; Kussmaul, 1990: 79–86, 181–196). For climatic reasons, too, the *potential* arable area was greater in 1300 than in the nineteenth century. Thus, around England's upland margins, the transition after 1300 to the cooler climatic conditions of the Little Ice Age lowered the altitudinal limit of cultivation and meant that land which might once have been used to grow crops was now fit only for permanent pasture (Grove, 2004: 622–30).

2.4.1 The effects of land drainage and reclamation

Work by Marshall and others (1978) has quantified the amount of land brought into use by more effective methods of drainage and Table 2.04, adapted here from Grigg (1989: 29), suggests that nearly 1.39 million acres were thereby brought into use, with the draining of the East Anglian fens accounting for more than half of the total. Most of this

Table 2.04 *The extent of post-medieval wetland reclamation*

Region	Acres (000s)	Acres (000s)
East Anglian fen district		772
Yorkshire and N. Lincolnshire wetlands		180
Vale of Pickering	7	
Beverley and Holderness	10	
Thorne and Hatfield Moors	86	
Ancholme Valley	16	
Lincolnshire Marshes	61	
Somerset Levels		127
Southeastern coastal marshes		119
North Kent marshes	50	
Romney Marsh	57	
Pevensey Levels	12	
Lancashire mosses		89
East Anglian valleys and coast		74
Norfolk river valleys	46	
Essex coast	18	
Suffolk coast	10	
Monmouth moors		20
Other		5
TOTAL		1,386

Source: Grigg (1989: 29).

drained land was being used for arable farming by the mid-nineteenth century, although some of it only since the 1820s (Grigg, 1989: 32). In addition, it has been estimated that some 4.5 million acres were improved by soil underdrainage between 1845 and 1899, with most of this underdrainage taking place in the north and west of England between 1840 and 1870 where it allowed much land to be ploughed for the first time (Phillips, 1989: 242, 217–24).

2.4.2   Conversion from tillage to permanent grass

Quantifying the loss of arable to permanent grass is less straightforward. One guide to the scale and geographical extent of this shift is provided by a simple count of the numbers of deserted medieval villages (DMVs) in each county, taken from the study by Beresford (1989), and reproduced here in the second column of Table 2.05. Combined

Table 2.05 *County distribution and density of deserted medieval villages (DMVs)*

County	Number of DMVs	DMVs per 100,000 acres	DMVs per 100,000 arable acres c.1850
Warwickshire	128	20.6	45.2
Yorkshire, N.R.	171	12.4	39.1
Oxfordshire	103	21.7	38.2
Leicestershire	67	12.6	35.6
Northumberland	165	12.7	35.0
Rutland	13	13.5	31.8
Wiltshire	104	12.2	29.1
Northamptonshire	82	12.8	28.7
Hampshire	156	15.1	26.5
Yorkshire, E.R.	129	17.1	26.2
Lincolnshire	220	12.9	23.9
Buckinghamshire	56	11.8	23.2
Nottinghamshire	67	12.6	22.9
Gloucestershire	67	8.4	22.1
Dorset	42	6.3	21.4
Derbyshire	33	5.1	20.8
Norfolk	148	11.2	17.8
Hertfordshire	44	11.0	16.9
Berkshire	43	8.9	15.4
Yorkshire, W.R.	75	4.1	14.2
Kent	69	6.9	13.7
Huntingdonshire	18	7.6	13.1
Sussex	41	4.4	10.3
Durham	29	4.6	10.1

Table 2.05 (cont.)

County	Number of DMVs	DMVs per 100,000 acres	DMVs per 100,000 arable acres c.1850
Somerset	27	2.6	9.8
Bedfordshire	18	5.9	9.8
Staffordshire	22	3.0	7.7
Herefordshire	11	2.0	5.2
Cambridgeshire	17	3.0	4.2
Suffolk	23	2.4	3.6
Worcestershire	7	1.6	3.5
Westmorland	2	0.4	3.2
Cumberland	8	0.8	3.0
Devon	15	0.9	2.9
Cornwall	8	0.9	2.7
Essex	17	1.7	2.6
Cheshire	4	0.7	2.5
Shropshire	9	1.0	2.4
Surrey	5	1.0	2.3
Middlesex	0	0.0	0.0
Lancashire	0	0.0	0.0
ENGLAND	2,263	7.0	16.3

Source: Beresford (1989: 35, 39).

with the surface area of each county, this yields the density of DMVs per 100,000 acres in the third column of Table 2.05. The density of DMVs per 100,000 acres of arable for the nineteenth-century maximum (column four) is yet more revealing, since this highlights where there was probably less arable in the nineteenth century than there had been before so many villages were deserted following the Black Death (Figure 2.02).

In many parts of England, of course, the existence of DMVs probably reflects little more than the effects of the declining population and associated settlement change, and there may have been little or no enduring loss of land to arable production. Nevertheless, in

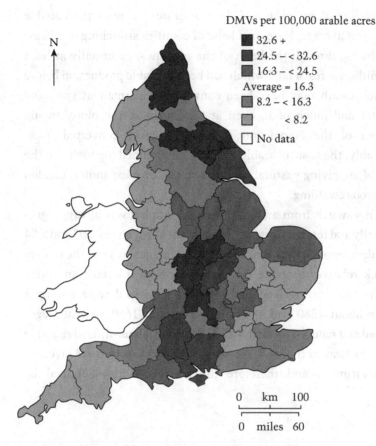

DMVs per 100,000 arable acres

32.6 +
24.5 – < 32.6
16.3 – < 24.5
Average = 16.3
8.2 – < 16.3
< 8.2
No data

N

0   km   100

0   miles   60

FIGURE 2.02 Density of deserted medieval villages (DMVs) per 100,000 acres arable in the mid-nineteenth century. *Source:* Table 2.05.

eighteen counties the density of DMVs is in excess of the national average, with most of them lying along the boundary between the predominantly arable-farming counties of the southeast (where the density of DMVs is mostly below average) and the grassier and more pastoral counties of the northwest and west (where the densities of DMVs are generally lowest of all). In five of these counties (the East Riding of Yorkshire, Rutland, Northamptonshire, Wiltshire and Hampshire) the density of DMVs is at least 50 per cent above average, and in a further five (Northumberland, the North Riding of Yorkshire,

Leicestershire, Warwickshire and Oxfordshire) it is more than double the national average. Here, in a band of counties stretching northeast to southwest through the heart of the midlands, potentially at least half a million acres of land which had been in arable production before the Black Death may have been converted to permanent grassland thereafter and much of it, even at the height of the ploughing-up campaign of the Napoleonic Wars, was never converted back. Presumably, the costs of arable cultivation remained too high and the profits of supplying pastoral products to the ever-expanding London market too rewarding.

This switch from arable to pastoral farming was always a geographically and temporally specific phenomenon. Figures 2.03 and 2.04 set out developments in farm labourers' real wage rates and the ratio of livestock relative to arable prices. These show that cost and price incentives to convert land to permanent grassland were strongest between about 1380 and 1500 and again after 1650, as real wages increased and reduced profitability in the more labour-intensive arable sector. The heavier the land, the greater the unit labour costs involved in cultivating it and therefore the greater savings obtained by

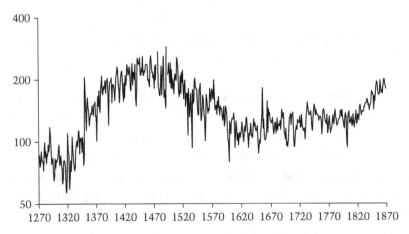

FIGURE 2.03 Indexed daily real wage rate of an unskilled agricultural worker, 1270–1870 (1700 = 100, log scale). *Source*: Clark (2007a).

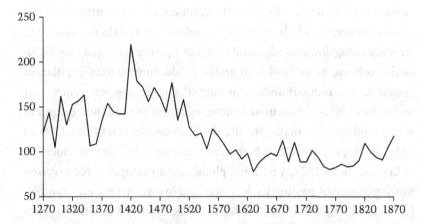

FIGURE 2.04 Ratio of livestock prices to arable prices (decadal averages, 1700 = 100).
Sources and notes: Derived from Clark (2005) with additional data from the Early
Modern Probate Inventories Database. Fuller details are given in Chapters 3 and 5.

switching to some form of pastoral production. In an era of declining
population and tenant scarcity, the excessive drudgery involved in
cultivating such holdings also deterred tenants. Hence the pejorative
talk of villages 'killed by sheep "who eat up men"', although in many
cases partial abandonment had preceded and then precipitated forcible
desertion (Dyer, 1982: 19). This rationalisation of agricultural land use
at a time of high labour costs and slack demand for arable products
subsequently became a specific supply-side specialisation following
comparative advantage in response to the post-medieval expansion of
the London market, thereby ensuring that the associated changes in
land use and farm enterprise remained permanent.

What makes this enduring land use shift so conspicuous is that it
was very much the exception. From the early-sixteenth century until
the mid-seventeenth century farm labourers' real-wage-rates stagnated
while a substantial decline in the price of livestock relative to arable
products favoured the renewed expansion of arable production
(Figures 2.03 and 2.04). Most areas with a comparative advantage in
arable production thus witnessed a significant re-expansion in the

arable area at that time. Later, in the early-eighteenth century, government corn bounties helped bolster cereal output and then, from 1750, strongly rising domestic demand for grain again encouraged those who could to bring more land into arable production. Strong population growth in the industrialising but naturally more pastoral south-west and north-west also stimulated these regions to expand their output of staple food grains. Finally, during the Napoleonic Wars from 1799 to 1815, and especially during Napoleon's attempted economic blockade of England from 1807, a national ploughing-up campaign reconverted much permanent pasture back to arable. This was when, for example, farmers in High Suffolk switched back from livestock to corn production.

During the early modern period the powerful pull of metropolitan market demand encouraged more and more farmers to specialise according to comparative advantage. Kussmaul (1990) sought to identify shifts between arable and pastoral production, and vice versa, at the parish level by examining changes in the seasonal pattern of marriage, for which parish registers provide a wealth of evidence (Table 2.06). Predominantly arable parishes (denoted by A) are identified by a predominance of autumn marriages, following the harvest, while pastoral parishes (denoted by P) are identified by a predominance of spring marriages, following hay-making, calving and lambing. Parishes that displayed neither pattern are identified as proto-industrial (denoted by X). Kussmaul's evidence, summarised in Table 2.06, suggests shifts in both directions during the early modern period between 1561–1640 and 1741–1820 – from pastoral to arable as well as from arable to pastoral – as farming everywhere became more specialised. Again, it would be difficult to argue for a large permanent loss of arable land on the basis of this evidence. With the exception of one parish in Staffordshire, all the parishes that became more arable in their marriage patterns were located south and east of a line from the Wash to the Severn Estuary. Of those that switched in the opposite direction, ten were in the west midlands and southwest (Worcestershire, Herefordshire, Somerset, Dorset, Devon,

Table 2.06 *Parishes shifting between (A) arable and (P) pastoral marriage patterns, between 1561–1640 and 1741–1820*

County	Number of parishes	A to P	P to A	Net % of parishes that switched
From arable to pastoral:				
Durham	3	2	0	67
Lincolnshire	13	4	0	31
Somerset	10	3	0	30
Lancashire	10	2	0	20
Cornwall	5	1	0	20
Herefordshire	6	1	0	17
Devon	15	2	0	13
Dorset	8	1	0	13
Yorkshire, N.R.	8	1	0	13
Nottinghamshire	9	1	0	11
Worcestershire	12	2	1	8
Wiltshire	14	1	0	7
Leicestershire	25	1	0	4
No net change:				
Huntingdonshire	1	0	0	0
Rutland	1	0	0	0
Middlesex	2	0	0	0
Berkshire	3	0	0	0
Derbyshire	3	0	0	0
Cumberland	5	0	0	0
Northumberland	5	0	0	0
Cheshire	7	0	0	0
Yorkshire, E.R.	8	0	0	0
Cambridgeshire	10	0	0	0
Buckinghamshire	17	0	0	0
Shropshire	17	0	0	0
Warwickshire	24	1	1	0
Yorkshire, W.R.	26	0	0	0
Hertfordshire	26	1	1	0
Kent	29	0	0	0
Bedfordshire	31	0	0	0
Northamptonshire	31	0	0	0

Table 2.06 (*cont.*)

County	Number of parishes	A to P	P to A	Net % of parishes that switched
From pastoral to arable:				
Suffolk	29	0	1	3
Gloucestershire	21	0	1	5
Staffordshire	19	0	1	5
Essex	17	1	2	6
Sussex	15	1	2	7
Hampshire	10	0	1	10
Surrey	13	0	2	15
Norfolk	29	0	5	17
Oxfordshire	5	0	1	20
ENGLAND	542	26	19	8

Source: Derived from Kussmaul (1990: 182–94).

Cornwall), and a further ten were scattered from Durham and the North Riding of Yorkshire, through Lincolnshire and Nottinghamshire, to Leicestershire and Wiltshire. This latter group thus complements the pattern of regional specialisation in pastoral production implied by the density distribution of DMVs (Table 2.05 and Figure 2.02). It is also worth noting that at a county level, the proportion of parishes that switched to a pastoral marriage pattern was typically greater than the proportion that adopted an arable regime (Table 2.06).

2.4.3   Other changes of land use

Although firm quantitative evidence is lacking for the other changes of land use, it should be noted that they do not uniformly push in one direction. Factors making for the increase of arable land, including a reduction in the amount of forest and woodland and enclosure of former permanent pasture (both of which benefited permanent grassland as well as arable), were offset by other factors making for a decrease, including the expansion of towns and the transport infrastructure and the conversion of agricultural demesnes into landscape parks. As will be seen from the following reconstruction of the distribution of arable land by county in 1290, the assumption that these effects cancelled out is indeed borne out.

2.5   LAND USE IN 1290

The starting point for the reconstruction of land use in 1290 is the arable acreage in 1871, which, as noted earlier, amounted to 13.9 million acres. Nearly 1.4 million acres of this land came from drainage of former wetlands by methods that were not available in 1290 (Table 2.04) and a further 4 million acres had been underdrained by 1871. On the other hand, there is credible quantitative evidence to suggest that some land used for arable purposes in 1290 had been converted to pasture following the Black Death and had still not been converted back by the nineteenth century (Tables 2.05 and 2.06 and Figure 2.02). Given the concentration of these developments in a narrow band of midland counties, and the subsequent reversal of incentives to switch from arable and pastoral production (Figures 2.03 and 2.04), it is difficult to see how this could have accounted for a permanent net conversion of more than about ½ million acres of arable land to pasture. The maximum arable acreage in 1290 is therefore unlikely to have been more than 12.5 to 13.0 million acres. Whether it was actually as much as this can be tested by deriving a set of county estimates, taking account of the population density in 1290 and the maximum and minimum proportions of arable land use for the nineteenth-century benchmark, and then aggregating the results.

The population density in 1290 matters because of the limited possibilities for trading grain between regions at the time: regions with a higher population density must therefore have had a higher proportion of the county acreage in arable use than those with a lower population density. At this date population densities were highest in a group of eastern counties comprising Norfolk (the most populous county of all), Suffolk, Cambridgeshire, Huntingdonshire and Lincolnshire (Table 2.07). In later centuries, as borne out by a wealth

Table 2.07 *Population density and the share of land use under arable by county in 1290*

Region	County	Population per square mile	% arable	Arable acreage
Eastern England	Norfolk	200	60.0	790,656
	Huntingdonshire	155	62.5	148,000
	Suffolk	147	60.0	574,464
	Cambridgeshire	136	57.5	320,896
	Lincolnshire	134	57.5	981,824
NE midlands	Rutland	146	62.5	60,400
	Northamptonshire	145	62.5	399,200
	Leicestershire	112	47.5	252,928
	Nottinghamshire	102	52.5	279,552
	Derbyshire	83	32.5	210,080
Southeast	Middlesex	331	60.0	113,664
	Bedfordshire	141	57.5	174,432
	Oxfordshire	125	62.5	296,000
	Hertfordshire	123	52.5	209,664
	Kent	118	47.5	475,152
	Buckinghamshire	117	47.5	225,872
	Essex	111	50.0	491,840
	Surrey	95	42.5	206,176
	Berkshire	93	50.0	240,960
	Sussex	85	37.5	350,640
	Hampshire	71	47.5	489,440
SW midlands	Gloucestershire	123	47.5	380,304
	Wiltshire	119	47.5	403,712
	Somerset	105	42.5	443,904
	Dorset	104	42.5	281,248
West midlands	Warwickshire	98	45.0	279,360
	Worcestershire	82	42.5	191,760
	Herefordshire	77	37.5	202,320
	Shropshire	77	37.5	322,560
Northeast	Yorkshire, E.R.	111	57.5	434,240
	Yorkshire, N.R.	70	25.0	344,640

Table 2.07 (*cont.*)

Region	County	Population per square mile	% *arable*	Arable acreage
	Durham	62	25.0	158,880
	Yorkshire, W.R.	52	20.0	363,008
	Northumberland	51	25.0	324,480
Southwest	Devon	60	25.0	418,080
	Cornwall	55	25.0	222,400
Northwest	Staffordshire	58	30.0	222,144
	Cheshire	45	15.0	91,968
	Lancashire	37	15.0	185,184
	Westmorland	37	12.5	63,280
	Cumberland	34	15.0	146,880
ENGLAND		94	39.5	12,772,192

Sources and notes: Population density derived from Campbell (2008: 926); % arable and arable acreage derived as described in the text.

of local historical evidence, most of these counties would add to their arable areas through processes of clearance, reclamation, drainage and the enclosure of common pastures, thereby reinforcing the strong arable bias of their land use. Yet in 1290 as much as 59 per cent of their collective surface area and two-thirds of all their farmland may already have been under the plough (Table 2.08). In the counties of the southeast, the northeast midlands and the southwest midlands, population densities were on average at least 25 per cent lower; hence it is reasonable to suppose that arable constituted a smaller proportion of land use, as it would in many of these counties in the mid-nineteenth century. In fact, in many of the midland counties there may have been a net shrinkage in the arable area between 1290 and the mid-nineteenth century for the reasons discussed above (Tables 2.07 and 2.08).

Williamson (2010), on the basis of systematic parish-by-parish reconstruction of the maximum extent of ploughland from a

Table 2.08 *The regional distributions of population and arable land in 1290*

Region	Total acreage	Estimated total population	Population per square mile	Estimated arable acreage	*Arable as %* *total area*	Arable acres per head
Eastern counties	4,777,600	1,164,457	156	2,810,950	58.8	2.4
NE midlands	2,446,720	428,785	112	1,200,070	49.0	2.8
Southeast	6,757,760	1,155,425	109	3,268,150	48.4	2.8
SW midlands	3,356,800	592,096	113	1,506,550	44.9	2.5
West midlands	2,471,680	321,601	83	994,270	40.2	3.1
Northeast	5,882,240	592,388	64	1,622,420	27.6	2.7
Southwest	2,561,920	232,159	58	639,370	25.0	2.8
Northwest	4,073,600	263,247	41	708,220	17.4	2.7
ENGLAND	32,328,320	4,750,157	94	12,750,000	39.4	2.7

Source: Tables 2.01 and 2.07.

combination of archaeological and historical evidence, has estimated that prior to the Black Death arable may have amounted to as much as 63 per cent of total land use in Northamptonshire. If correct, this implies that almost half of all land in the counties of the northeast midlands (Northamptonshire, Rutland, Leicestershire, Nottinghamshire and Derbyshire) may have been in arable land use. That proportion would shrink to 39 per cent in 1871, following the permanent withdrawal of approximately ¼ million acres from arable cultivation (Table 2.09). In the counties of the south-west midlands (Gloucestershire, Somerset, Wiltshire, and Dorset) the amount of arable land in 1290 may also have been greater (by approximately 200,000 acres) than the amount in 1871 (Table 2.09), since here too there is evidence of village desertion and there were similar incentives to capitalise upon comparative advantage and expand the area devoted to permanent grassland. Conceivably, as much as 45 per cent of land in these counties may have been in arable use before the Black Death. Arable probably accounted for a similar proportion of land use in the south and east, although with much variation from locality to locality on account of the diverse topographical conditions and commercial opportunities prevailing in this large region. Here, however, that proportion rose to 54 per cent in the mid-nineteenth century, since metropolitan growth ensured that these counties became London's bread-basket.

Outside these core regions population densities in 1290 were lower, and in the west midlands, the north-east, south-west, and, especially, the north-west, they were well below the national average and proportionately far lower than they would be in the mid-nineteenth century, by which time the economies of these regions had become far more dynamic. With their low population densities, above average rainfalls, moors, mosses and hill-land, the north-west and south-west can safely be assumed to have had the smallest proportions of arable land in the country. In the southwest this proportion has been set at 25 per cent and in the more mountainous northwest at 17.5 per cent (Tables 2.08 and 2.09). In 1290 mountainous Westmorland must have been the least arable county of all, with

Table 2.09 *Changes in the regional distribution of arable land between 1290 and 1871*

Region	Estimated arable acreage, 1290	Arable as % total area, 1290	Recorded arable acreage, 1871	Arable as % total area, 1871	Net change in arable area, 1290–1871	Net change in % arable, 1290–1871
Eastern counties	2,810,950	58.8	3,056,568	63.0	245,618	4.2
NE midlands	1,200,070	49.0	952,758	39.2	-247,312	-9.8
Northeast	1,622,420	27.6	1,950,640	34.1	328,220	6.5
Northwest	708,220	17.4	1,016,285	24.5	308,065	7.1
Southeast	3,268,150	48.4	3,516,531	51.2	248,381	2.8
Southwest	639,370	25.0	1,031,253	40.6	391,883	15.6
SW midlands	1,506,550	44.9	1,311,922	39.0	-194,628	-5.9
West midlands	994,270	40.2	1,007,413	41.9	13,143	1.7
ENGLAND	12,750,000	39.4	13,843,370	42.8	1,093,370	3.4

Sources: Agricultural Returns for Great Britain for 1871; Table 2.08.

only one-eighth of its land devoted to arable production (Tables 2.03 and 2.07).

Table 2.07 sets out the estimated proportions and amounts of arable land by county, taking account of variations in population density, the location of the drainage schemes identified in Table 2.04, the density of DMVs in Table 2.05, and the effects of urbanisation, which particularly affected Middlesex and Surrey. The net result of these reckonings is an overall arable share in 1290 of 39.5 per cent, amounting to approximately 12.75 million acres (an area equivalent to over half of all farmland). These 12.75 million arable acres differed far more in distribution than quantity from the 13.9 million arable acres for the nineteenth-century benchmark. Proportionately, the arable shrank most in metropolitan Middlesex, where pasture and grazing were in high demand from the capital and the massive horsedrawn traffic that it generated, whereas it grew most in Durham, since cheap grain was needed to feed the growing army of miners who hewed the coal likewise demanded in ever greater quantities by Londoners.

This revised estimate of the arable area in 1290 is very much an upper-bound estimate (Table 2.08). Given prevailing technologies of cultivation, stock management, and drainage, the heavy reliance upon wood for fuel and timber for construction, the underdeveloped economies and sparse populations of large parts of the north and west, and the as yet modest population of London, it is difficult to conceive that more land could have been under arable cultivation at this date, whereas a lower figure is not improbable. These calculations imply that 1.4 million more acres of land were actually in arable production in 1290 than 1801. Overton and Campbell (1996, 1999) and Campbell (2000) have argued against this possibility and proposed that the arable area in 1290 could have been no greater than that in 1801. Moreover, they accepted a more moderate estimate of 10.5 million acres at the later date on the evidence of the 1801 crop return.

In contrast, Clark (2007: 124–5), on an idiosyncratic reading of the early-fourteenth-century *inquisitiones post mortem* and in an attempt to justify a population estimate of almost 6 million in 1315, proposed

that as much as 15.7 million acres may have been in arable production
c.1300: 1.87 million acres more than in 1871. More recently he has
inflated that estimate to 20 million acres (Clark, 2011: 11), taking
reassurance from the fact that this would still be only 62 per cent of
English land area. Yet this is to ignore the very real topographical,
environmental, technological and institutional constraints under
which all pre-modern English agricultural producers had to operate,
farming organically, relying upon animals rather than machines for
farm work, and often hidebound by archaic property rights and local
customs. In fact in 1871, on the evidence of comprehensive and reliable
agricultural statistics, only half a dozen counties had as large a share of
their areas under arable rotations, all of them ranking among the country's premier arable counties: Huntingdonshire, Cambridgeshire,
Norfolk, Suffolk and Hertfordshire plus the East Riding of Yorkshire
(Table 2.03). At the opposite extreme, arable comprised less than 30 per
cent of the respective areas of Somerset, Middlesex and a large block of
northern counties comprising Northumberland, Cumberland,
Westmorland, Lancashire, Cheshire, Derbyshire and the West Riding
of Yorkshire (Table 2.03).

2.6 LAND USE IN 1086 AND 1290

How does the revised figure of 12.75 million arable acres in 1290
compare with the evidence of Domesday Book some two centuries
earlier? Campbell (2000: 386–9) has discussed the difficulties of deriving credible estimates from this most ambiguous of statistical sources.
Lennard (1959) and Maitland (1897) have proposed estimates of 8–10
million arable acres on the basis of the numbers of recorded plough-
lands and plough teams, but these areas are implausibly high for they
are far in excess of the needs and probably also the resources of a
population of 1.7 million people. Cantor's (1982) 11.3 million acres
(derived from land-use shares estimated by Rackham, 1980: 126–7) is
even more implausible (cited by Clark, 2011: 5). Employing a method
of estimation proposed by Seebohm (1883) based upon recorded numbers of land holdings yields a lower and more realistic figure of 5.75–6.0

million arable acres in 1086. If correct, or at least nearer the truth, this implies that the arable area may have slightly more than doubled between 1086 and 1290, when the population grew by a factor of about 2.75. Arable land per head thus declined by approximately 20 to 25 per cent between the two dates, which is consistent with the historical view that by 1290, with an average of less than 2.7 arable acres per head (1 acre of which was probably fallow) (Table 2.08), population was putting considerable pressure upon available agricultural resources (Hatcher and Bailey, 2001: 21–65).

2.7   ARABLE LAND USE, 1270–1871

With benchmark estimates securely established for England in 1290 and the mid-nineteenth century of respectively 12.75 and 13.85 million arable acres (Table 2.10), the final step is the interpolation of corresponding estimates for a range of intermediate dates between 1270 and 1871. For 1801, reliance has to be placed on the crop return which, most writers agree, substantially understated the amount of arable land (Turner, 1981; Grigg, 1989; Holderness, 1989; Prince, 1989). Opting for an upper-bound estimate suggests that at the height of Napoleon's blockade of England, when there were powerful political and price incentives to bring as much land under the plough as possible, approximately 11.35 million acres were under arable cultivation. This was 2½ million acres less than in 1836, by which time parliamentary enclosure, continued substitution of rotational for permanent grass and a raft of new technological improvements had allowed a further extension of arable cultivation. Perhaps more surprisingly, it was 1.4 million acres less than may have been under arable in the early fourteenth century, before permanent grass for commercial pastoral production had become the predominant land use in several former arable-farming regions or temporary grass had become a component of arable rotations.

Substantially more land was nevertheless under arable in 1801 than had been the case a century earlier. Equivalent estimates for 1700 and 1750 have been derived from Chartres (1985) and Holderness

Table 2.10 *The changing availability of arable land per head,
1270–1871*

Years	Total arable (m. acres)	% fallow	Total sown (m. acres)	Arable acres per head	Sown acres per head
1270	12.52	41.0	7.40	2.87	1.70
1290	12.75	35.8	8.19	2.69	1.73
1300	12.72	35.8	8.16	2.69	1.73
1380	9.64	40.4	5.75	3.95	2.36
1420	8.75	40.3	5.21	4.29	2.55
1450	8.44	40.4	5.03	4.42	2.63
1500	8.50	38.1	5.26	3.86	2.39
1600	8.87	24.4	6.72	2.16	1.63
1650	9.63	19.5	7.74	1.81	1.45
1700	9.56	20.0	7.64	1.84	1.47
1750	10.51	15.1	8.92	1.74	1.48
1801	11.35	11.2	10.08	1.27	1.12
1836	13.87	9.4	12.57	0.95	0.86
1871	13.83	3.5	13.35	0.64	0.62

Sources and notes: Total arable: 1290, see text; 1270, 1300, 1380, 1420,
1450, 1500, projected from 1290 using sown acreage data for the manorial
sector and tithe data for the non-manorial sector; 1600, interpolated
between 1500 and 1700 using data on population; 1700, derived from
Chartres (1985: 444), Holderness (1989: 145); 1750, derived from
Holderness (1989: 145), Chartres (1985: 444); 1801, derived from Turner
(1981), Prince (1989: 31), Holderness (1989: 145), Grigg (1989: 39); 1836,
derived from Kain (1986); 1871, derived from Afton and Turner (2000).
Fallow arable and total sown: derived from Medieval Accounts Database,
Early Modern Probate Inventories Database, Holderness (1989), Overton
(1996). Aggregate population estimates from Chapter 1.

(1989), who provided benchmarks linked to 1801. These imply a gain in
the arable area of almost a fifth over the course of the eighteenth
century, as relative prices and dwindling real-wage-rates of farm
labourers encouraged the reconversion of grassland to arable
(Figures 2.03 and 2.04). Private and parliamentary enclosure also

removed some of the institutional barriers which hitherto had kept advance of the plough at bay. Expansion of the arable area made particular progress in the industrialising regions of rapid population growth in the north, midlands and southwest, where demand for potatoes, oats and other cheap food staples was rising strongly (Table 2.09).

Since the population in 1650 was much the same as in 1700, there had probably been little change in the arable area during this marked demographic lull. Relative price shifts which might have encouraged substitution of pasture for arable (Figure 2.04) were countered after 1672 by government corn bounties which provided farmers with a strong financial incentive to maintain the area under tillage and for a time turned England into a net grain exporter (Table 7.06; Thirsk, 1985: 330–4). In 1650, therefore, there may have been approximately 9.6 million acres of arable. Paradoxically, this was at least 3 million acres less than $c.1300$ notwithstanding that the country's population was 0.6 million greater. This underscores the fact that the figure of 12.75 million arable acres $c.1300$ is at the extreme upper end of the range of credible estimates; a figure any higher would be inconsistent with the well-founded post-medieval estimates. It also highlights the scale and durability of the land-use changes that occurred during the century and a half following the Black Death.

Arable estimates for 1270 and 1300, 1380, 1420, 1450 and 1500 have been obtained by projection backwards and forwards from the 1290 benchmark of 12.75 million acres. Manorial case studies and the well-documented trends in sown acreages on seigniorial demesnes indicate that right up to the Great Famine of 1315–22 cultivators were still extending the arable area as and when they could. This was the tail end of a process which had more than doubled the country's arable area since 1086. The amount of land then under the plough would not be eclipsed until the era of 'high farming' prior to repeal of the Corn Laws in 1846. The environmental and demographic setbacks of the second quarter of the fourteenth century then halted and dramatically reversed this process.

As populations shrank and labour costs rose lords began to take marginal land out of cultivation and tenants, faced with greater mobility and choice, began to avoid the challenge of tilling the heaviest and least rewarding soils. During the century of demographic decline following the Black Death the arable area clearly shrank and, when labour costs were at their peak and relative prices most favoured pastoral producers, much of the heaviest and poorest arable was converted to permanent pasture and, in the process, entire villages were reduced in size or abandoned altogether (Tables 2.05 and 2.06 and Figure 2.02). The reducing scale of demesne sown acreages (Campbell, 2012: 124–8) and shrinking volumes of grain tithe receipts (Dodds, 2004; Sapoznik, 2013) leave little doubt of the reality of this trend. By 1450 the arable area had probably shrunk by at least a third to less than 8.5 million acres and it was from this low base that, under the triple stimuli of rising population, cheaper labour and improving relative prices for arable products, it subsequently re-expanded. Nonetheless, that re-expansion was on an altogether more modest scale than the contraction which had preceded it, for in many areas of lowland England the land-use changes of the fifteenth century had become effectively permanent. Interpolation between the arable estimates for 1500 and 1700 using information on population from Wrigley and Schofield (1989) suggests that in 1600 there were still fewer than 9 million arable acres.

Note that although these expansions and contractions of the arable area broadly synchronised with the flow and ebb of population (as reconstructed in Chapter 1), the relationship between these two variables was neither constant nor proportionate (Table 2.10). Where landed resources were in finite supply, in true Malthusian fashion, the potential of populations to grow exceeded the capacity of arable areas to expand. Hence phases of population growth in the thirteenth, sixteenth and later eighteenth and early nineteenth centuries were characterised by shrinking amounts of arable land per head: this was offset by farming the land more intensively, changing the output mix and adapting diets. Conversely, reductions in population, on a grand scale between 1348 and c.1450 and more modestly between the 1650s and 1700s, rarely begot commensurate contractions in arable acreage. At these times, instead of cutting back hard on arable production, farmers typically adopted more extensive methods of production and devoted a larger share of their sown acreages to crops with relatively low food extraction rates as consumers found themselves better able to indulge their dietary preferences. During these episodes the supply per head of arable land therefore improved. The halving of population between 1348 and c.1450 thus resulted in only a one-third reduction in the arable area, as is consistent with documented changes in crop mixes, yields and relative grain prices over the same period (Chapter 3).

One method of varying the intensity of arable cultivation was by varying the proportion of land that was fallowed. Fallowing was a standard method of allowing regeneration of stocks of soil nitrogen by natural processes, cleansing the land of excessive weed growth and augmenting scarce supplies of pasturage and fodder (Overton, 1996: 2). Regular rotational fallowing was typically a formal requirement of the regular commonfield systems which prevailed across a broad swathe of central and southern England and probably achieved their maximum territorial extent at the opening of the fourteenth century. In these systems biennial or triennial fallowing was the norm. Elsewhere, annual fallowing might be more or less frequent, depending upon the requirements of the land and the nature of the prevailing husbandry regime. There were, however, alternatives to fallowing and already by the close of the thirteenth century some cultivators were successfully cropping their land almost continuously and thereby raising the output of their arable land (Campbell, 2000: 269–72, 340–7). Over time, as commonfield regimes became more flexible and better technological alternatives to fallowing became available, a growing number of producers adopted this option.

The changing scale of the fallow acreage can be inferred from what is known about the distribution of different types of field system, the mixes of crops recorded by manorial accounts and probate inventories, actual reconstructions of rotations and the comments of contemporaries. Overton and Campbell (1996, 1999) have made estimates for almost the entire period, as have Holderness (1989) and Overton (1996) for the years 1750–1850. These provide the basis of the estimates given in the third column of Table 2.10. Note the long-term reduction in the amount of fallow from over 40 per cent of the arable in 1270 to just 3.5 per cent in 1871. Provided that soil fertility did not suffer, this will have brought about a significant gain in land productivity. Note, too, that incentives and opportunities to reduce fallows were especially marked when the supply per head of arable was falling. The doubling of population between 1450 and 1600 was accompanied by a halving of the proportion of fallow. Over these years the proportionate gain in the sown area (i.e. the area under arable crops) was consequently significantly greater than the relatively modest expansion of the arable area including fallow. This trend continued and by 1750, with only 15 per cent of the arable fallowed, the sown area finally exceeded that *c*.1300 even though approximately 2.25 million fewer acres were in arable use. By the second quarter of the nineteenth century, following further reform of field systems and property rights and wider adoption of improved agricultural technology, fallows had been reduced to less than 10 per cent of the total and as much land was sown as had been arable some six centuries earlier.

In 1086 the arable area is unlikely to have amounted to more than 6 million acres and maybe almost half of that was fallowed on an annual basis. Thereafter, between 1270 and 1870, the arable area was never less than 8 million or more than 14 million acres, nor the sown area less than 5 million or more than 13.5 million acres. As little as 3.5 per cent of the arable might be bare fallowed or as much as 41 per cent and it was this reserve of up to 5.1 million acres of land that, over the course of time, was brought into more productive use. These were the broad parameters within which English arable production operated. Vital as arable production may have been to national food supplies, at all times, and especially wherever environmental and economic circumstances were ill-suited to tillage, the areas under temporary and permanent grass typically matched or exceeded that under the plough. As the next chapter will show, livestock production was always a large component of English agricultural output and key source of kilocalories, kinetic energy, industrial raw materials and export earnings, and in Wales and Scotland it formed an even greater component.

3   Agricultural production

3.1   INTRODUCTION

This chapter provides annual estimates of output in agriculture, which was the largest sector of the economy during the middle ages, and continued to play an important role throughout the period under consideration. The approach builds on the study of Overton and Campbell (1996), which tracked long-run trends in agricultural output and labour productivity, but was restricted to estimates for a small number of benchmark years. To provide annual estimates, heavy reliance has been made on three datasets assembled for the late-medieval, early modern and modern periods. For the period c.1250 to c.1500, a Medieval Accounts Database has been assembled by Campbell (2000, 2007), drawing upon the archival labours of a number of other historians, including David Farmer, John Langdon and Jan Titow. The information on arable yields and animal stocking densities is taken largely from manorial accounts, but is supplemented by information on the non-manorial sector from tithes. For the period c.1550 to c.1750, an Early Modern Probate Inventories Database has been assembled by Overton, which provides animal stocking densities and indirect estimates of arable yields from the valuation of the assets left by farmers (Overton and others, 2004). From the early eighteenth century, use is made of the Modern Farm Accounts Database assembled by Turner, Beckett and Afton (2001).

The chapter proceeds as follows. Section 3.2 provides a brief introduction to the main data sources for the three periods. Estimates of output for the arable sector are then given in Section 3.3, followed by estimates of livestock-sector output in Section 3.4. The arable and livestock outputs are combined in Section 3.5 to provide estimates of overall agricultural output, while Section 3.6 concludes.

3.2   DATA SOURCES

3.2.1   The late-medieval period, c.1250 to c.1500

The most important data source for the late-medieval period is the Medieval Accounts Database assembled by Campbell (2000; 2007). This relies heavily on manorial accounts, which were drawn up according to a common template by the reeve who managed the demesne under close supervision of the lord's bailiff or steward (Campbell, 2000: 2). These accounts provide detailed information on crops, animals and livestock products and the purchase and maintenance of capital equipment. The number of sampled manorial accounts varies over time, with decadal averages plotted in Figure 3.01, reflecting trends in survival rates and the direct management of demesnes. The fourteenth century is well represented, but the records are less abundant for the

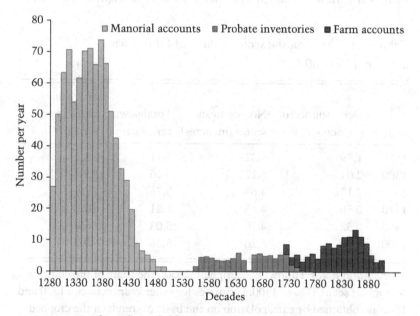

FIGURE 3.01 Numbers of sampled farm enterprises per year, 1250–1900 (decadal averages). *Sources:* Medieval Accounts Database; Early Modern Probate Inventories Database: Modern Farm Accounts Database.

thirteenth and the fifteenth centuries. There is an unavoidable bias within the sample towards large ecclesiastical estates with long runs of data, which provides a challenge to those wishing to generalise from the data. In particular, the geographical coverage is uneven, with a strong, and sometimes exclusive, bias to the south and east of the country. These regional imbalances have therefore been redressed with an appropriate weighting scheme.

Care must also be taken in moving from data on demesnes to inferences about the development of English agriculture as a whole, since the non-seigniorial sector was always larger than the seigniorial sector and the balance between them varied over time. Even at its peak in the early fourteenth century, the seigniorial sector probably accounted for no more than around 25 to 30 per cent of all agricultural land and output (Campbell, 2000: 26). Table 3.01 sets out the seigniorial sector's estimated share of output over time during the late-medieval period. Although evidence on the non-seigniorial sector is

Table 3.01 *The demesne sector's share of total sown acreage, 1250–1500*

Year	Demesne sector (m. acres)	Non-demesne sector (m. acres)	Total sown acreage (m.)	Share of demesne sector (%)
1250	1.79	5.32	7.11	25.2
1300	2.04	6.12	8.16	25.0
1380	1.12	4.63	5.75	19.5
1420	0.56	4.65	5.21	10.8
1450	0.32	4.70	5.03	6.4
1500	0.00	5.26	5.26	0.0

Sources and notes: Following Campbell (2000), the share of the demesne sector was set at 25% in 1300. Estimates for other years between 1270 and 1500 are obtained by extrapolation on the basis of trends in the cropped acreage on demesnes and tithe data in the non-demesne sector (Campbell and others, 1996; Dodds, 2004; Medieval Accounts Database). The demesne sector is assumed to disappear by 1500.

more disparate, data do exist which can be used to verify or qualify trends reconstructed from the manorial accounts. Postan (1962) made use of tax returns to shed light on the relative stocking densities of demesne and peasant holdings, and some of his evidence has been re-examined by Bailey (1989: 115–35). As a result of the pioneering work of Langdon (1982, 1986), much is also known about the relative numbers and types of draught animals on seigniorial and non-seigniorial holdings. More recently, Dodds (2004, 2007) has used tithe records to shed light on annual variations in grain output, and a few tithe series contain wool output. Campbell (2007, 2012: 153–4) shows that there is a close correlation between year-on-year fluctuations in crop yields derived from manorial accounts and annual changes in tithe receipts.

Seigniorial and non-seigniorial producers faced the same environmental conditions and commercial opportunities and employed a common technology. There was also much overlap between their labour-forces. Hence, where peasants led, lords were likely to follow and vice versa (Campbell, 2000: 1). Nevertheless, there were important differences in their respective scales of production, capital resources, consumption priorities, vulnerabilities to risks and hazards and methods of decision-making. Between the mid-thirteenth century and the mid-fourteenth century, factor costs and property rights encouraged lords to manage their demesnes directly and concentrate on arable production. Under the conditions of labour scarcity that followed the Black Death, however, lords found it more difficult to obtain customary labour and increasingly expensive to hire workers. Those lords who continued to farm directly switched away from labour-intensive arable production to mixed husbandry and livestock production, leaving arable production to smaller producers who could rely mainly on family labour and were unburdened by administrative overheads. Once the post-Black Death price inflation had subsided, lords thus found it more profitable to lease out their demesnes, and by the mid-fifteenth century very few remained directly managed and those were mostly home farms provisioning seigniorial households.

3.2.2   The early modern period, c.1550 to c.1750

Probate inventories have been used extensively by historians to provide quantitative information on crops and livestock between the mid-sixteenth and the mid-eighteenth centuries (Overton, 1984; Overton and others, 2004: 13–32). They were made soon after the death of a farmer and record the quantities and values of crops stored on the farm, growing crops, and livestock but exclude fallow, meadow and permanent pasture. From this information, it is possible to derive data directly comparable with those obtained from late-medieval manorial accounts, most straightforwardly crop acreages and livestock numbers, but also grain yields and animal stocking densities (Campbell and Overton 1993). Probate inventories containing this information first become available in the 1550s, but decline in numbers from the early-eighteenth century as church courts ceased to keep the inventories once probate had been granted. The inventories used in this present study cover Norfolk and Suffolk (Overton, 1985), Hertfordshire, Worcestershire, Lincolnshire and Durham (Overton, 2000), and Cornwall and Kent (Overton and others, 2004). The number of sampled inventories is plotted in decadal average form in Figure 3.01, for comparison with the manorial accounts database. As will be seen, the early modern period is currently the less well documented of the two periods.

Crop acreages are directly recorded in inventories (provided the inventory was made at the time of year when crops were growing) but grain yields are not directly recorded since inventories do not give both the crop acreage and the harvested produce from that acreage. Instead, yields can be estimated using the identity $v = py$, where v is the valuation per acre of growing grain recorded in probate inventories, p is the price per bushel after the harvest and y is the yield in bushels per acre (Overton 1979). The yield is thus obtained from the valuation and the price as:

$$y = v/p \qquad\qquad (3.1)$$

However, the calculations are more complex in practice because appraisers subtracted 10 per cent of the gross output taken as a tithe and made allowance for the costs of reaping (r), threshing (t) and carting (c), which affected the value that the appraisers placed on a growing crop. Allen's (1988) valuation equation, accepted by Overton (1990, 1991) and Glennie (1991) thus becomes:

$$v = 0.9 \, (py - ty - c) - r \tag{3.2}$$

Rearranging for comparison with equation (3.1), the yield becomes:

$$y = \frac{v + r + 0.9c}{0.9(p - t)} \tag{3.3}$$

When a growing crop was close to harvest appraisers valued it on the basis of their forecast of the price of grain after the harvest and the yield of the crop. But they could not do this when the crop had not yet developed and so based their valuations of newly sown crops on the costs so far incurred. Allen (1988) filters out these observations by setting a minimum yield of 5 bushels per acre, but excludes genuinely bad harvests. Here, no minimum has been imposed, instead attention has been restricted to valuations in the months of June to August, following Overton (1979: 369).

Although the Early Modern Probate Inventories Database is the best currently available, omission of large parts of northern, midland and southern England means that generalising to the national level from the individual farm observations presents a formidable challenge. Only eight of the country's 43 counties are represented in the database, and five of them – Durham, Lincolnshire, Norfolk, Suffolk, and Hertfordshire – are in eastern England. The midlands are represented solely by Worcestershire and the southern counties by Kent in the east and Cornwall in the extreme southwest. Applying a regional weighting scheme provides some compensation for this extreme imbalance of coverage but is no substitute for the exclusion of so much of the country from the sample. Nor are there continuous runs of data for individual farms, merely one-off observations occasioned by the deaths of farmers. In estimating grain yields and stocking densities, this is dealt with by assuming comparable series in similar agricultural regions, hence introducing a time-series aspect, as suggested by Clark

(2004). Finally, although inventories have survived for a wide range of farm sizes, the very largest and the very smallest farms are under-represented (Overton and Campbell, 1992: 380; Overton and others, 2004: 22–6).

It will be apparent that there remains a statistical Dark Age for grain yields and animal stocking densities between the decline of the manorial sector in the late fifteenth century and the appearance of probate inventories in the mid-sixteenth century. This period is dealt with by using information on prices and income to estimate the demand for agricultural goods, as suggested by Crafts (1976; 1985) and further explored for the modern period by Allen (1994, 2000).

3.2.3   The modern period, c.1700 to c.1870

Paradoxically, the least well-documented period is that nearest the present. To redress this deficiency Turner, Beckett and Afton (2001) collected a sample of farm accounts from the 1720s to the outbreak of World War I in 1914. Although these farm accounts are much less standardised than their late-medieval counterparts, they do provide crucial data on the amount of land in use and crops sown and har-vested, which allows the derivation of grain yields. Perhaps disappoint-ingly, data on numbers of farm animals are not systematically recorded in the accounts and consequently have not been collected, although there are some data on sales of animals. The sample of farm records is also uneven in both temporal and spatial coverage.

Figure 3.01 also sets out the chronological distribution of the sampled farm accounts. The relatively thin coverage for the first half of the eighteenth century can be bolstered by probate inventories. The sample is stronger for the first half of the nineteenth century. The spatial distribution of farm records is more even than for the late-medieval and early modern periods, with the north and west of the country almost as well represented as the south and east (Turner, Beckett and Afton, 2001: 64). Nevertheless, it is still important to apply a regional weighting scheme, as for the earlier periods. There is, of course, a danger that the farmers who kept accounts were a self-selecting minority, more conscientious in their husbandry and commercially astute in their dealings than those who did not bother to do so. It is important therefore to cross-check yields calculated from them against results obtained from probate inventories for the first half of the eighteenth century and official output data from the late nineteenth century.

3.3   ARABLE FARMING IN ENGLAND, 1270–1870

Arable farming output is obtained by multiplying the amount of land sown with each crop by the grain yield for that crop net of deductions for grain used as seed and as fodder for working animals. The key magnitudes are derived from the three main datasets and extrapolated to a national level as described below.

3.3.1   Sown acreage by crop

The starting point for the estimation of arable output is the total area under crop. Having obtained estimates of the overall sown acreage in Chapter 2, the next step is to allocate it between the major crops using information on crop shares calculated from the Medieval Accounts Database for the period before 1500, the Early Modern Probate Inventories Database for the period 1550–1750 and from Holderness (1989) and Overton (1996) for the period 1750–1850. For the late-medieval period, it should be noted that the distribution of crops in the demesne sector is assumed to be broadly representative of all classes of producer, as is borne out by the limited amount of evidence available for the non-seigniorial sector (Dodds, 2007; Sapoznik, 2013).

The regional weighting scheme for the crop shares is shown in Table 3.02, with the regional shares of the sown area in 1290 derived from Table 2.07 as weights for the late-medieval period and the mid-nineteenth century shares derived from Table 2.03 for the early modern and modern periods. Over time the shares of East Anglia, the eastern counties, the southern counties and the southeast remained

Table 3.02 *Regional shares of the total sown area in 1290 and the mid-nineteenth century (%)*

Region	Counties	1290 (%)	c.1850 (%)
East Anglia	Norfolk and Suffolk	10.7	10.7
Eastern counties	Bedfordshire, Cambridgeshire, Essex, Hertfordshire, Huntingdonshire and Lincolnshire	18.2	18.5
Southern counties	Berkshire, Gloucestershire, Hampshire, Herefordshire, Wiltshire and Worcestershire	14.9	14.0
Southwest	Cornwall, Devon, Dorset and Somerset	10.7	7.4
Southeast	Kent, Middlesex, Surrey and Sussex	9.0	8.4
Midlands	Buckinghamshire, Leicestershire, Northamptonshire, Oxfordshire, Rutland and Warwickshire	11.9	9.4
North	Cheshire, Cumberland, Derbyshire, Durham, Lancashire, Northumberland, Nottinghamshire, Shropshire, Staffordshire, Westmorland and Yorkshire	24.6	31.6

Source: Derived from Tables 3.03 and 3.07.

fairly stable, but the north gained somewhat at the expense of the southwest and the midlands. The results for the overall sown acreage by crop are shown in Table 3.03. As already noted in Chapter 2 (Table 2.10), the amount of fallow declined from between a third and a half in the late-medieval period to less than a quarter in the early modern period and eventually just 3.5 per cent in 1871.

Wheat maintained its importance as the principal winter-sown crop throughout the period under examination, but rye and maslin (a mixture of wheat and rye) declined sharply from the early modern period (Overton, 1996: 94–5). Among the spring-sown crops, barley and dredge (a mixture of barley and oats) also remained consistently prominent, whereas oats, until the second half of the eighteenth century, shrank in significance. The greatest changes in cropping mostly

Table 3.03 *Composition of arable land use, 1270–1871 (millions of acres)*

Year	Wheat	Rye/maslin	Barley/dredge	Oats	Pulses	Potatoes	Other crops	Total sown	Fallow arable	Total arable
1270	2.21	0.72	1.23	2.94	0.29	0.00	0.00	7.40	5.13	12.52
1300	2.68	0.60	1.27	3.16	0.45	0.00	0.00	8.16	4.56	12.72
1380	1.83	0.36	1.22	1.87	0.47	0.00	0.00	5.75	3.89	9.64
1420	1.61	0.32	1.17	1.66	0.45	0.00	0.00	5.21	3.53	8.75
1450	1.53	0.31	1.15	1.59	0.44	0.00	0.00	5.03	3.41	8.44
1500	1.58	0.37	1.19	1.56	0.47	0.00	0.10	5.26	3.24	8.50
1600	1.85	0.77	1.44	1.32	0.61	0.00	0.72	6.72	2.16	8.87
1650	2.00	0.39	1.86	1.13	1.02	0.00	1.36	7.74	1.88	9.63
1700	1.99	0.42	1.82	1.15	0.98	0.00	1.30	7.64	1.91	9.56
1750	1.95	0.06	1.50	1.82	0.98	0.08	2.53	8.92	1.59	10.51
1800	2.51	0.06	1.46	1.97	0.83	0.17	2.90	9.91	1.28	11.19
1830	2.12	0.06	1.81	1.27	0.63	0.26	4.46	10.62	1.30	11.91
1871	3.31	0.06	1.96	1.45	0.90	0.39	5.28	13.35	0.48	13.84

Sources: Overton and Campbell (1996: Tables III, V); Campbell and others (1996); Medieval Accounts Database; Early Modern Probate Inventories Database; Holderness (1989); Overton (1996).

occurred after 1700, when a range of new crops – principally potatoes, turnips and clover – began to occupy expanding shares of the arable. Since clover fixes more nitrogen than traditional legumes, its increasing use led to a substantial improvement in soil fertility (Overton, 1996: 110). Turnips enabled fallows to be reduced or eliminated and provided more fodder for the animal stock in winter with the potential for increased recycling of nitrogen through farmyard manure (Overton, 1996: 99–101). Potatoes served some of the same functions but their main advantage was that they provided roughly two-and-a-half times as many calories per acre as did wheat (Overton, 1996:102).

3.3.2 Grain yields

To calculate output from the estimated areas sown with each crop requires information on grain yields per acre, net of seed sown. National average yields per acre, gross of tithe and seed can be obtained from the three main databases, using regression analysis with dummy variables for each farm and for each year, as suggested by Clark (2004). Since the late-medieval evidence relates almost exclusively to demesnes, it is necessary to consider what was happening in the non-seigniorial sector. Although Postan (1966) believed that yields were lower on peasant holdings due to capital deficiencies and a disproportionate dependence upon inferior land, Stone (2006: 21) has recently argued from case-study evidence that yields were around 11 per cent higher in the non-demesne sector, where incentives to maximise output per unit area were stronger for small producers. Sapoznik (2013) has similarly shown that at Oakington in Cambridgeshire petty producers achieved marginally higher unit levels of output than those obtained on the abbot of Crowland's demesne. Yet it does not necessarily follow that this productivity advantage in favour of lesser producers was replicated at a macro scale because demesnes cultivated a much higher proportion of the country's good-quality land. Since the direction of the adjustment is unclear, and would anyway be quite small, it has been assumed here that yields obtained on demesnes are representative of those within agriculture as a whole. For the early modern period several studies have shown that yields are independent of farm size, so there is no reason to adjust the yields derived from inventories (Overton, 1991).

Aggregate trends in grain yields have been obtained from chronologically discontinuous data on individual demesnes and farms using regression analysis. The basic specification for grain yields is as follows:

$$ln(YIELD_{it}) = \alpha + \sum_{i=1}^{I-1} \beta_i LOC_i + \sum_{j=1}^{J-1} \gamma_j REG_j + \sum_{t=1}^{T-1} \delta_t YEAR_t + \varepsilon_{it}$$

(3.4)

where $YIELD_{it}$ is the grain yield on demesne or farm i in year t, α is a constant, LOC_i is a dummy variable for the location of each farm, REG_j is a dummy variable for the region in which each demesne or farm is located, $YEAR_t$ is a dummy variable for the year and ε_{it} is the error term. The dependent variable is entered logarithmically so that the location and regional dummy variables have the same proportional effect on grain yields in all years.

The method produces an estimated national trend in index number form, and the absolute levels of the grain yields are obtained using the regional shares of the sown area in 1290 as weights for the late-medieval period and the mid-nineteenth century shares for the early modern and modern periods. The regional shares in Table 3.04 are specific to each crop and computed by combining the regional shares of the arable acreage from Table 3.02 with the distribution of crops within each region taken from the databases. Table 3.05 shows the estimated values for the regional dummies, together with standard errors and t-values. Yields tended to be high in all crops in East Anglia, the benchmark region, particularly during the early modern and modern periods. This is indicated by the preponderance of negative signs in parts B and C of Table 3.05. Nevertheless, wheat yields were higher in the midlands during the early modern period, as indicated by a statistically significant positive sign. During the late-medieval period, wheat yields were higher in the southern

Table 3.04 *Regional weights for the arable sector by crop, 1290 and 1836/71 (%)*

	Wheat (%)	Rye (%)	Barley (%)	Oats (%)	Pulses (%)
A. 1290					
East Anglia	5.5	22.9	26.1	4.1	22.4
Eastern counties	25.2	4.2	2.3	23.0	8.7
Southern counties	14.9	11.2	20.7	13.7	10.8
Southwest	14.6	4.0	0.6	14.0	3.9
Southeast	5.3	30.7	6.5	11.3	4.6
Midlands	12.6	24.5	12.1	10.0	6.6
North	21.8	2.6	31.7	23.8	43.0
ENGLAND	100.0	100.0	100.0	100.0	100.0
B. 1836/71					
East Anglia	10.8	19.0	15.9	3.4	8.0
Eastern counties	18.9	23.1	17.4	16.3	22.1
Southern counties	15.0	7.9	14.2	12.3	12.2
Southwest	7.0	0.6	8.4	10.3	3.2
Southeast	8.7	5.1	4.9	13.7	8.1
Midlands	9.8	3.9	5.6	15.4	9.1
North	29.8	40.5	33.5	28.6	37.2
ENGLAND	100.0	100.0	100.0	100.0	100.0

Sources and notes: Derived from shares of arable acreage in Table 3.03 and crop distributions within each region from the Medieval Accounts Database, the Early Modern Probate Inventories Database and the Modern Farm Accounts Database.

counties and the southeast, barley yields were higher in the southern counties and the midlands, oats yields were higher in the southeast and pulse yields were higher in the eastern counties and the midlands.

Gross grain are shown in Figure 3.02 for wheat, rye, barley, oats and pulses (beans and peas). From these gross yields it is necessary to subtract grain used as seed (explicitly recorded in the Manorial

Table 3.05 *Values of the regional effects in the arable yield regressions, late medieval, early modern and modern periods*

	Wheat	Rye	Barley	Oats	Pulses
A. Late medieval period					
Constant	2.132 (18.28)	2.542 (2.35)	2.323 (9.51)	2.459 (16.28)	1.103 (1.13)
Eastern counties	−0.007 (−0.13)	OMITTED	OMITTED	−0.494 (−5.94)	0.756 (2.01)
Southern counties	0.382 (8.23)	0.507 (0.79)	0.721 (3.67)	−0.023 (−.032)	OMITTED
Southwest	OMITTED	OMITTED	0.072 (0.25)	OMITTED	OMITTED
Southeast	0.674 (10.17)	−0.253 (−0.37)	−0.622 (−1.71)	0.691 (11.52)	−0.532 (−1.00)
Midlands	0.058 (1.28)	OMITTED	0.46 (2.06)	−0.234 (−3.88)	1.213 (3.25)
North	OMITTED	OMITTED	OMITTED	OMITTED	OMITTED
R^2	0.577	0.604	0.542	0.538	0.428
N	4,955	1,292	4,630	4,999	2,130
B. Early modern period					
Constant	2.833 (6.58)	2.096 (1.18)	2.243 (5.63)	2.934 (4.85)	1.644 (2.45)
Eastern counties	OMITTED	0.013 (0.01)	OMITTED	0.031 (0.13)	OMITTED
Southern counties	OMITTED	OMITTED	OMITTED	OMITTED	OMITTED
Southwest	OMITTED	OMITTED	−0.767 (−2.87)	−0.539 (−2.25)	OMITTED
Southeast	−0.096 (−2.33)	OMITTED	−0.35 (−1.34)	OMITTED	OMITTED
Midlands	0.375 (3.34)	NA	NA	NA	NA
North	OMITTED	NA	OMITTED	OMITTED	0.081 (0.12)
R^2	0.677	0.774	0.524	0.687	0.548
N	799	198	922	445	483

Table 3.05 (cont.)

	Wheat	Rye	Barley	Oats	Pulses
C. Modern period					
Constant	2.78	2.967	3.632	4.105	3.316
	(17.75)	(6.63)	(7.80)	(12.71)	(3.43)
Eastern	−0.022	−0.051	−0.43	−0.34	0.075
counties	(−0.85)	(−0.10)	(−1.02)	(−1.49)	(0.08)
Southern	−0.132	−0.641	−0.199	−0.307	0.334
counties	(−5.02)	(−1.17)	(−0.46)	(−1.73)	(0.36)
Southwest	−0.173	NA	−0.595	−0.206	OMITTED
	(−3.27)		(−1.38)	(−0.43)	
Southeast	−0.235	NA	−0.33	OMITTED	0.179
	(−6.17)		(−0.79)		(0.19)
Midlands	−0.097	OMITTED	OMITTED	−0.429	0.015
	(−0.25)			(−1.09)	(0.01)
North	NA	NA	NA	NA	NA
R^2	0.443	0.837	0.49	0.623	0.578
N	1,300	98	1,196	644	518

Notes: East Anglia is the benchmark region; t-statistics in parentheses; NA indicates that there are no observations available for a particular region; OMITTED indicates that a regional dummy was dropped because of co-linearity.

Accounts Database) to derive the net yields shown in Table 3.06 for all the major crops. For subsequent periods there is ample evidence from farm accounts and contemporary commentators that seeding rates for individual grains were remarkably constant. There are some differences between crops, but the three datasets appear to tell a consistent story, with yields declining from around 1300 to a minimum in the mid-fifteenth century, picking up again from at least the mid-sixteenth century, and growing more rapidly from the early-eighteenth century. The data exhibit a high degree of short run volatility, mainly due to the impact of weather on harvests, which has been smoothed out in Figure 3.02 with 10-year moving averages.

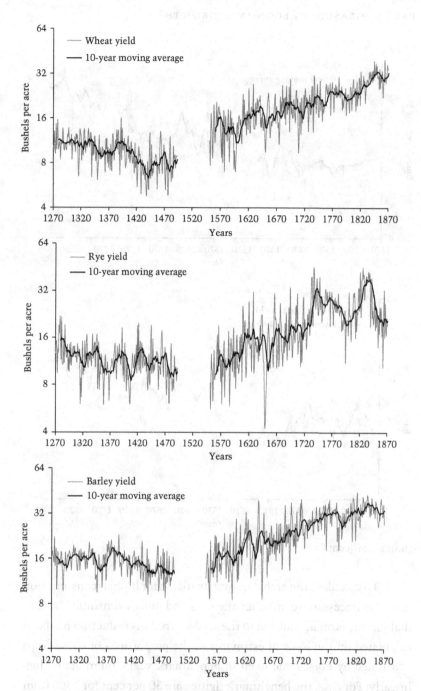

FIGURE 3.02 English weighted national average gross crop yields per acre (bushels, log scale). *Sources:* Derived from the Medieval Accounts Database, the Early Modern Probate Inventories Database and the Modern Farm Accounts Database.

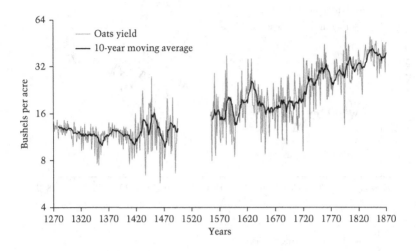

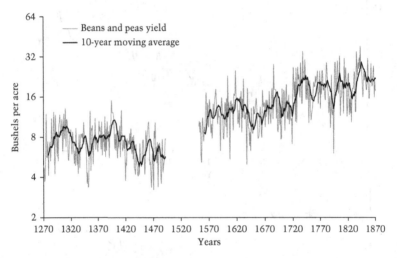

FIGURE 3.02 (cont.)

To calculate the arable output available for human consumption
it is also necessary to subtract the oats and pulses consumed by animals on the farm in addition to the seed sown. This deduction has been
calculated on the basis of estimates of the proportions of these crops
consumed by horses and oxen in benchmark years, interpolated log-
linearly. For oats, the benchmark figures are 30 per cent for 1300 from
Wrigley (2006: 445) and 50 per cent for 1600 and 70 per cent for 1800

Table 3.06 *Weighted national average crop yields per acre, gross of tithes and net of seed, 1270s–1860s (bushels; 10-year averages)*

Decade	Wheat (bus./ac.)	Rye (bus/ac.)	Barley (bus/ac.)	Oats (bus/ac.)	Pulses (bus/ac.)	Potatoes (bus/ac.)
1270s	8.38	12.83	11.70	9.86	2.86	
1300s	7.80	9.19	11.73	8.69	6.36	
1350s	6.32	6.60	8.92	6.74	4.04	
1400s	6.36	5.77	10.74	6.76	4.35	
1450s	5.00	7.88	8.41	8.85	3.67	
1500s	ND	ND	ND	ND	ND	
1550s	9.99	6.35	9.02	10.56	5.74	
1600s	11.06	10.34	12.44	13.17	9.77	
1650s	13.46	9.83	17.87	12.10	9.35	
1700s	14.09	16.04	19.66	10.76	11.56	150.00
1750s	15.54	27.14	26.53	23.28	12.80	150.00
1800s	18.70	21.81	28.58	25.19	18.65	150.00
1850s	26.17	19.74	29.74	33.09	18.54	150.00
1860s	29.43	18.66	29.78	35.05	19.39	150.00

Sources and notes: Gross yield per acre taken from the Medieval Accounts Database, the Early Modern Probate Inventories Database and the Modern Farm Accounts Database. Seed sown per acre from the Medieval and Modern Databases. Pulses for the modern period and all seeds sown for the early modern period are taken from Overton and Campbell (1996), Allen (2005). ND, no data.

from Overton and Campbell (1999: 201). For pulses, the figure of 50 per cent for the pre-1500 period is based on Campbell (2000: 228–9). Allen's (2005) lower figure of 27 per cent for the post-1700 period is taken from the worksheets underlying Clark and others (1995) and the proportion between 1500 and 1700 is interpolated.

3.3.3 Net output from arable farming

The net output of each crop is calculated by multiplying its area by its yield net of seed and fodder for working animals. The results are shown in Table 3.07. During the late-medieval period, output of wheat and

Table 3.07 *Total arable output net of seed and animal consumption, 1270s–1860s (million bushels; 10-year averages)*

Decade	Wheat (m. bus.)	Rye (m. bus.)	Barley (m. bus.)	Oats (m. bus.)	Pulses (m. bus.)	Potatoes (m. bus.)
1270s	18.85	8.94	14.44	20.45	0.44	
1300s	20.88	5.95	14.91	19.12	1.43	
1350s	12.02	2.72	10.91	8.93	0.95	
1400s	10.35	2.02	12.56	7.29	0.98	
1450s	7.69	2.80	9.69	8.58	0.82	
1500s	ND	ND	ND	ND	ND	
1550s	17.08	3.83	11.82	8.14	1.74	ND
1600s	20.70	7.85	18.59	8.44	4.01	ND
1650s	27.01	3.70	33.50	6.14	6.53	ND
1700s	27.94	6.70	35.20	5.70	8.25	1.27
1750s	31.48	1.51	39.67	13.03	9.03	13.56
1800s	46.32	1.36	42.67	14.06	11.07	26.70
1850s	73.69	1.09	58.23	15.93	9.57	44.79
1860s	86.07	0.98	57.00	16.33	11.42	47.72

Sources and notes: Derived from Manorial Accounts Database, Probate Inventories Database and Modern Farm Accounts Database as described in the text. Data reported as decadal averages. ND, no data.

rye, the principal bread grains, declined substantially from a late-thirteenth century peak, with a sharp fall broadly in line with population following the Black Death of the mid-fourteenth century. The output decline was similarly sharp for oats, which fell out of favour as a crop for human consumption. In place of malted oats, malted dredge (a barley/oats mixture) and malted barley became the preferred brewing grains and, since ale consumption per head rose, demand for barley and barley mixtures remained relatively buoyant. The modest decline in the output of pulses reflected a reversion to more land-extensive farming systems.

By the end of the sixteenth century, output of the major grains was back to the peak pre-Black Death level. This was achieved from significantly smaller arable and sown areas (Table 2.10) due to marked improvements in yields (Table 3.06). Controlled comparison of yields calculated from comprehensive datasets of manorial accounts and probate inventories for the single county of Norfolk confirms that the gain in productivity was real (Campbell and Overton, 1993: 66–76). The achievement is the more remarkable given the resistance of yields to significant improvement during the century prior to the Black Death and the fact that most of the more notable technological innovations of the agricultural revolution had yet to take place. Output of wheat continued to increase after 1600, while rye declined, reflecting the growing preference for the more expensive bread grain. The output of barley increased markedly in line with demand for better-quality ale and beer brewed from the best barley malt. Output of pulses also grew rapidly during the early modern period, since their cultivation was instrumental in lengthening rotations and reducing fallows. Later, during the eighteenth century, potatoes became important as a cheap and abundant source of kilocalories. Oats, the cheapest of the grains, was another staple of the poor, especially in the north and west. Everywhere it was vital as a source of fodder for working horses. Net output of oats initially waned as horses displaced oxen as the principal draught animal (see Table 3.14 below) and on-the-farm consumption by working horses rose. Then, during the road and canal transport revolutions of the eighteenth century, as numbers of non-farm horses proliferated, commercial demand for both oats and hay soared and from the mid-eighteenth century output of both rose dramatically. In all these respects changes in demand exercised a profound influence upon the production decisions of farmers (Thompson, 1976).

3.4   LIVESTOCK FARMING IN ENGLAND, 1270–1870

Output of the livestock sector is a function of the numbers of non-working livestock, the proportions of this stock of animals producing milk, meat, tallow, hides, skins and wool on an annual basis, and the respective yields per animal. The magnitudes of each of these components are derived from the three main datasets and extrapolated to a national scale using a system of regional weightings, and, for the late-medieval period, after making allowance for differences in stocking profiles and densities between seigniorial and non-seigniorial producers.

Calculating the output of the livestock sector is more speculative than equivalent calculations for the arable sector, since meat, milk and even wool yields have all attracted less attention from historians than crop yields, despite the wealth of information in manorial accounts. This reflects both an historiographic bias towards grain production and the greater complexity of recorded information on animal products. Until more systematic work is carried out on the available sources the estimates advanced here are necessarily provisional. Their revision depends on more and better information on the numbers of animals, the proportion of those providing outputs in any one year, and the yield of those outputs per animal.

3.4.1 Stocking densities and animal numbers

Contemporary estimates of national numbers of animals are solely available for the modern period. For the late-medieval and early modern periods national totals have to be inferred from farm-specific data on the stocking density of livestock, specifically the numbers of non-working animals per 100 sown acres, taking due account of the influence of farm size. As with the crop yields, regression analysis is employed to generate aggregate trends from the individual observations. The regression equation is as follows:

$$\ln(STOCKDENS_{it}) = \alpha + \sum_{i=1}^{I-1} \beta_i LOC_i + \sum_{j=1}^{J-1} \gamma_j REG_j$$
$$+ \sum_{t=1}^{T-1} \delta_t YEAR_t + \varepsilon_{it} \qquad (3.5)$$

This is essentially the same as equation (3.4), but with the logarithm of the stocking density (STOCKDENS) as the dependent variable rather than the logarithm of the grain yield. The method produces an estimated trend in index number form, and the absolute levels of the stocking densities in benchmark years are obtained as weighted averages of the regional stocking densities, using the regional shares of livestock farming shown in Table 3.08. These regional groupings are different from those in arable farming, reflecting the four main types of livestock farming. Although by 1870 dairying had spread to counties where it had been scarce in 1300, the core activities of many farms, especially in the northwestern counties, had shifted towards the fattening of cattle (Overton, 1986). Table 3.09 shows the estimated values for the regional dummies, together with standard errors and t-values. Strikingly, no particular region stands out as having had higher stocking densities across all livestock or all periods.

Table 3.10 sets out the steps in the derivation of animal numbers for the late-medieval period, starting from detailed data on stocking densities for the demesne sector. Country-wide stocking densities within the demesne sector in Part A are adjusted to national estimates

Table 3.08 *Regional weights for the livestock sector by type of farming, 1300 and 1870*

Type of livestock farming	Counties	%
A. 1300		
Region 1: Mixed enterprises with some dairying on grass/ mixed husbandry	Essex, Herefordshire	7.2
Region 2: Fattening on arable, leys and grass/mainly cattle-based husbandry	Bedfordshire, Cambridgeshire, Huntingdonshire, Lincolnshire, Norfolk, Suffolk, Yorkshire E.R.	27.7
Region 3: Rearing with some fattening/extensive mixed husbandry	Cheshire, Cornwall, Cumberland, Derbyshire, Devon, Dorset, Durham, Gloucestershire, Hampshire, Lancashire, Leicestershire, Northumberland, Nottinghamshire, Shropshire, Somerset, Staffordshire,	42.1

Table 3.08 (cont.)

Type of livestock farming	Counties	%
	Westmorland, Wiltshire, Yorkshire N. R. and Yorkshire W. R.	
Region 4: Primarily dairying/ cattle husbandry	Berkshire, Buckinghamshire, Herefordshire, Kent, Middlesex, Northamptonshire, Oxfordshire, Rutland, Sussex, Surrey, Warwickshire, Worcestershire	23.0
B. 1870		
Region 1: Mixed enterprises with some dairying on grass/mixed husbandry	Berkshire, Buckinghamshire, Hertfordshire, Kent, Northamptonshire, Oxfordshire	14.7
Region 2: Fattening on arable, leys and grass/mainly cattle-based husbandry	Bedfordshire, Cambridgeshire, Essex, Huntingdonshire, Leicestershire, Lincolnshire, Norfolk, Northumberland, Nottinghamshire, Rutland, Suffolk, Sussex, Warwick, Yorkshire E. R.	41.6
Region 3: Rearing with some fattening/extensive mixed husbandry	Cornwall, Cumberland, Devon, Durham, Gloucestershire, Herefordshire, Shropshire, Westmorland, Worcestershire, Yorkshire N. R. and Yorkshire W. R.	25.0
Region 4: Primarily dairying/ cattle husbandry	Cheshire, Derbyshire, Dorset, Hampshire, Lancashire, Middlesex, Somerset, Staffordshire, Surrey, Wiltshire	18.6

Sources and notes: Campbell and Bartley (2006); Orwin and Whetham (1971: 131); Medieval Accounts Database. These weights are based on the arable acreage in each county, derived from Tables 2.03 and 2.07. These shares are interacted with the distribution of stocking densities across animal types within each region to derive animal specific livestock farming weights.

Table 3.09 *Values of the regional effects in the stocking density regressions, late medieval and early modern periods*

	Cattle	Pigs	Sheep	Oxen	Horses
A. Late-medieval period					
Constant	−0.551	−7.204	−2.421	−3.162	−4.425
	(−0.55)	(−3.94)	(−2.60)	(−6.95)	(−22.5)
Region 2	−3.472	OMITTED	OMITTED	1.192	−1.737
	(−4.99)			(1.72)	(−5.22)
Region 3	0.287	2.485	−5.093	1.924	0.091
	(0.59)	(2.74)	(−3.68)	(4.57)	(0.24)
Region 4	−0.715	OMITTED	0.302	1.486	−0.999
	(−1.40)		(0.18)	(3.43)	(−2.76)
R^2	0.682	0.729	0.608	0.743	0.617
N	6.861	2,302	7,984	6,797	6,838
B. Early modern period					
Constant	3.195	2.668	0.980	−10.052	3.134
	(0.75)	(0.48)	(0.13)	(−2.28)	(0.64)
Region 2	OMITTED	OMITTED	OMITTED	OMITTED	−0.059
					(−0.14)
Region 3	OMITTED	OMITTED	5.546	3.358	OMITTED
			(6.45)	(6.36)	
Region 4	NA	NA	NA	NA	NA
R^2	0.269	0.217	0.310	0.438	0.266
N	1,773	1,718	1,718	1,585	1,718

Notes: Definitions of regions listed in Table 3.08; Region 1 is the benchmark region; *t*-statistics in parentheses. Animal numbers are estimated directly for the modern period rather than indirectly from stocking densities, which were not collected systematically in the Modern Farm Accounts Database.

for all classes of producer in Part B on the basis of the share of the demesne sector in total acreage as set out in Table 3.01, combined with four key assumptions. First, because of a negative relationship between farm size and stocking density, drawn from the post-1550 data, the stocking density of cattle was four times higher on

Table 3.10 *Stocking densities, 1270s–1860s*

	Animals per 100 sown acres					
	A. Demesne producers only			B. All producers		
Decade	Cattle (mature + immature)	Sheep	Swine	Cattle (mature + immature)	Sheep	Swine
1270s	8.03	22.90	3.38	18.15	190.61	11.16
1300s	10.25	10.00	3.69	21.29	192.78	12.04
1350s	9.85	28.86	3.04	24.71	256.04	11.15
1400s	8.67	25.64	2.00	22.22	214.77	7.22
1450s	8.01	27.86	2.18	20.67	232.43	8.37
1500s				ND	ND	ND
1550s				20.09	160.49	15.24
1600s				13.71	244.81	13.86
1650s				12.88	157.93	10.63
1700s				9.03	223.95	10.06
1750s				18.42	150.37	13.32
1800s				24.77	204.86	18.03
1850s				26.90	188.52	19.08
1860s				29.19	209.65	18.08

Sources and notes: 1270s–1450s derived from Medieval Accounts Database; 1550s–1750s derived from Probate Inventories Database; 1750s–1860s inferred from Holderness (1989: 147–51); Turner (1998: 159); Mitchell (1988: 708); Perren (1975: 388. ND, no data.

non-demesne lands (Overton and Campbell, 1992: 388–9). However, the scale of this effect has been reduced by following Allen (2005) in assuming that holding farm size constant, the density of cattle was one-third lower on non-demesne lands, due to their high unit capital value. Second, again following Allen (2005), mature cattle have been divided into milk and beef animals in the ratio 53 to 47 per cent. Third, swine, a quintessentially peasant animal, are assumed to have been stocked by non-seigniorial producers at four times the density on demesnes, as is consistent with the observed negative relationship between farm size and swine densities in the post-1550 period (Overton and Campbell,

1992). Fourth, aggregate sheep numbers have been checked for consistency with trends in exports of wool and woollen cloth, inferred levels of domestic demand and the decline in average fleece weights noted by Stephenson (1988: 380). Note that an important constraint on these four key assumptions is the need to obtain consistency between estimated animal numbers in the late-medieval and early modern periods.

In the case of sheep, the trend in demesne-sector numbers has been used to represent that in agriculture as a whole, but the absolute level has been set at 15 million in 1300, in line with the estimate of Wrigley (2006b: 448). This was the number of animals needed to supply the wool export trade as recorded by the customs accounts (Britnell, 2004: 417) plus an allowance for domestic consumption. The latter has been reckoned as annually equivalent to an average of 1.18 square yards of woollen cloth per head, on the assumptions that domestic textile production supplied labourers with 1 square yard, substantial tenants with 2 square yards and landowners with 8 square yards of woollen cloth, weighting the different social classes according to the social tables of Campbell (2008).

The derivation of animal numbers from stocking densities is more straightforward in the early modern period. Table 3.10, gives the regionally weighted stocking densities derived from the probate inventories. Since the demesne sector had disappeared by 1500, these are applied without modification to the national sown acreage to derive the aggregate numbers of livestock set out in Table 3.11. For the ensuing modern period direct estimates of stocking densities are unavailable. Instead, animal numbers for benchmark years after 1750 are taken from contemporary estimates given by John (1989), Mitchell (1988) and Turner (1998). For sheep the conventional estimates of Holderness (1989) are used; however, for cattle and pigs, the Holderness estimates for 1750 and 1800 are too high to align with the early modern estimates derived from the stocking densities. For these animals, the lower estimates of Turner (1998) have been preferred, since they meet up with the early modern data when projected using data on annual sales at Smithfield and the Metropolitan Cattle Market from Mitchell (1988) and Perren (1975).

Table 3.11 *Livestock numbers, 1270s–1860s (millions)*

Decade	Milk cattle (m.)	Beef cattle (m.)	Calves (m.)	Sheep (m.)	Swine (m.)
1270s	0.47	0.42	0.47	14.22	0.83
1300s	0.60	0.54	0.60	15.72	0.98
1350s	0.51	0.46	0.51	15.26	0.67
1400s	0.40	0.36	0.40	11.29	0.38
1450s	0.36	0.32	0.36	11.73	0.42
1500s	ND	ND	ND	ND	ND
1550s	0.41	0.37	0.41	9.55	0.91
1600s	0.32	0.29	0.32	16.75	0.95
1650s	0.35	0.31	0.35	12.29	0.83
1700s	0.24	0.22	0.24	17.36	0.78
1750s	0.57	0.52	0.57	13.58	1.20
1800s	0.84	0.76	0.84	20.21	1.78
1850s	1.12	1.01	1.12	22.88	2.31
1860s	1.23	1.11	1.23	25.75	2.21

Sources and notes: 1270s–1450s derived from Medieval Accounts Database; 1550s–1750s derived from Probate Inventories Database; 1750s–1860s derived from Holderness (1989: 147–51); Turner (1998: 159); Mitchell (1988: 708); Perren (1975: 388). ND, no data.

The animal numbers for the whole period 1270–1870 are plotted in Figure 3.03, using 10-year moving averages to smooth out short-run volatility. Although murrains of sheep and plagues of cattle periodically depressed numbers and short- to medium-term trade-offs clearly existed between different categories of animal, until the second half of the eighteenth century the overall magnitudes of the nation's cattle and pig herds and sheep flock remained broadly stable. The one exception appears to have been a decline in numbers of cattle over the course of the early modern period as farmers disinvested in draught oxen and the herds needed to breed their replacements (see Table 3.14 below). Note that this trend was reversed during the second half of the eighteenth century as demand for milk and beef grew strongly. Earlier, the buoyancy of livestock numbers following the Black Death, at a time when

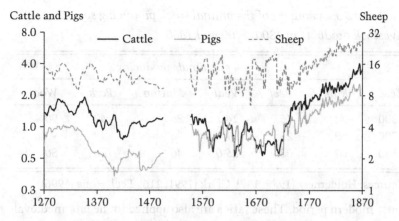

FIGURE 3.03 Numbers of non-working livestock, 1270–1870 (millions, 10-year moving averages, log scale). *Sources:* Derived from the Medieval Accounts Database; Early Modern Probate Inventories Database; Holderness (1989: 147–51); Turner (1998: 159); Mitchell (1988: 708); Perren (1975: 388).

arable output was contracting, meant that the livestock sector had increased its share of agricultural output substantially. That share increased again from the late eighteenth century, this time in conjunction with expanding arable output.

3.4.2 *Proportions of animals producing specific products on an annual basis*

Deriving livestock output from the stock of animals requires two other pieces of information: first, the yields of milk, meat, wool and hides per animal, and second, the proportions of animals that will generate output in a year. For example, cattle kept for beef were not slaughtered until they were at least four years old in the early modern period, so only a quarter of the stock of beef cattle would be producing meat output in a year. Fortunately, there is a broad consensus among historians respecting these proportions. Thus, 90 per cent of cows are reckoned to have been producing milk and 90 per cent of sheep to have yielded wool. For meat, following Holderness (1989: 147), it is assumed that approximately a quarter of the stock of cattle and sheep and around half of all pigs were slaughtered annually in the

Table 3.12 *Percentages of the animal stock producing specific livestock products in 1300, 1700 and 1850*

	% of animals producing					
Year	Milk	Beef	Veal	Mutton	Pork	Wool
1300	90	15	14.1	26	49	90
1700	90	25	21.1	26	49	90
1850	90	33	25.0	40	100	80

Sources: Holderness (1989: 147); Clark (1991: 216); Ecclestone (1996).

early modern period. These ratios are also applied to the late-medieval period for sheep and pigs, in line with slaughter rates documented by Campbell (1995: 164–7). Because few late-medieval herds were kept specifically for beef, slaughter rates for cattle were lower. After 1850 the opposite prevailed, so that slaughter rates increased as animals were finished (i.e. ready to be slaughtered for meat) more rapidly. Similarly, for sheep there was a shift in emphasis from wool to mutton production in the modern period, reflected in a rise in the percentage of animals kept primarily to produce mutton as opposed to wool. Slaughter rates were consistently highest for pigs, as these were the only animals kept exclusively for their meat. Annual reproduction rates were exceptionally high so that butchery rates of almost 100 per cent were possible. The proportions of the stock of animals producing milk, meat and wool in a year are summarised in Table 3.12.

3.4.3 Yields per animal of milk, meat and wool and outputs of hides and hay

The next step in the calculations involves estimating yields of milk, meat and wool per animal, drawn from a number of sources, including Clark (1991), Allen (2005), Stephenson (1988) and Britnell (2004). These data are set out in Table 3.13. For benchmark years in the fourteenth and nineteenth centuries, there is again consensus among researchers concerning the broad orders of magnitude, and the main contribution here concerns the interpolation for intervening years using the ratio of

Table 3.13 *Milk, meat and wool yields per animal,*
1270s–1860s (10-year averages)

Decade	Milk (gals)	Beef (lbs)	Veal (lbs)	Mutton (lbs)	Pork (lbs)	Wool (lbs)
1270s	100.00	168.00	29.00	22.00	64.00	1.63
1300s	100.96	169.26	29.22	22.14	64.11	1.48
1350s	112.27	183.91	31.79	23.81	65.36	1.81
1400s	124.83	199.82	34.59	25.60	66.64	1.49
1450s	138.81	217.11	37.63	27.52	67.94	1.24
1500s	ND	ND	ND	ND	ND	ND
1550s	172.35	257.50	44.74	31.96	70.62	1.64
1600s	200.66	294.44	51.22	36.18	72.00	1.88
1650s	233.63	336.68	58.63	40.97	75.85	2.17
1700s	272.01	384.98	67.12	46.39	86.56	2.51
1750s	316.69	440.22	76.84	52.53	98.78	2.91
1800s	368.72	503.37	87.96	59.49	112.72	3.38
1850s	429.29	575.59	100.69	67.36	128.63	3.92
1860s	443.90	592.82	103.73	69.22	132.42	4.05

Sources and notes: Beef, pork, milk and mutton are obtained from Clark (1991: 216), while veal is taken from Allen (2005: Table 6). Wool yield index from Stephenson (1988: Table 3), with the benchmark of 1.4 lb in 1300 from Britnell (2004: 416). The missing years were interpolated in line with the ratio of product to animal prices. ND, no data.

product prices to animal prices. The basic idea is that an increase in, say, the price of cattle relative to that of beef signifies an increase in the yield of meat per animal (Overton, 1996: 115–16). Price data are taken largely from Clark (2004; 2006), supplemented by Beveridge (1939) and Thorold Rogers (1866–1902). The main result is that although there was some increase in yields during the late-medieval period, the pace of change increased substantially from the mid-sixteenth century.

Additional assumptions are needed to derive output estimates for hay and hides. For hay, the starting point is the number of non-farm horses taken from Wrigley (2006b: 450) for 1300 and from Allen (1994:

102) and Feinstein (1978: 70) for 1700, 1760, 1800 and 1850, with log-linear interpolation for years in between. The number of non-farm horses quadrupled from 50,000 in 1300 to 200,000 by 1750 before quadrupling again to 800,000 by 1850. The assumption of 2.4 tons of hay per horse is taken from Thompson (1983: 60).

For hides, it is necessary to calculate the numbers of working animals as well as the non-working animals given in Table 3.14. For the early modern period, numbers of working animals can be derived directly from stocking densities, which are assumed to apply to the whole agricultural sector. However, for the late-medieval period, the demesne stocking densities have been converted into the numbers of horses and oxen on all lands using Wrigley's (2006b: 449) assumption that the stocking density of working animals on non-seigniorial hold-ings was three-quarters that on demesnes. In making these estimates, allowance has been made for the declining share of demesne acreage. For the modern period, direct estimates of animal numbers are taken from Mitchell (1988), Turner (1998) and Allen (2005), since data on stocking densities are not provided in the Modern Farm Accounts Database. Table 3.14 sets out the numbers of mature working animals in England. Farm horses were already in extensive use in the middle ages (Langdon, 1982, 1986). During the early modern period substitu-tion of horses for oxen as working animals gathered momentum. By the nineteenth century, use of draught oxen had more or less died out and the population of farm horses had quadrupled. The working life of horses and oxen meant that each year approximately an eighth yielded a hide (Clark, 1991: 216). In Table 3.12 the percentages of non-working animals producing hides are the same as those producing meat (with the addition of a figure of 13 per cent for horses and oxen). The yields per animal are taken from Clarkson (1989: 470).

3.4.4   Livestock sector net output

Finally, the information on numbers of livestock, proportions produc-ing milk, meat, wool and hides in a year, and yields of each per animal can be combined to provide the estimates of net output in the

Table 3.14 *Average numbers of working animals in England, 1250–74 to 1850–70 (millions, 25-year averages)*

Years	Mean oxen (m.)	Mean horses (m.)	Mean oxen per horse	Years	Mean oxen (m.)	Mean horses (m.)	Mean oxen per horse
1250–74	0.46	0.33	1.40	1550–74	0.17	0.32	0.57
1275–99	0.47	0.38	1.23	1575–99	0.13	0.34	0.38
1300–24	0.50	0.34	1.48	1600–24	0.12	0.34	0.36
1325–49	0.42	0.41	1.03	1625–49	0.08	0.33	0.24
1350–74	0.47	0.31	1.56	1650–74	0.07	0.39	0.19
1375–99	0.47	0.23	2.01	1675–99	0.06	0.51	0.14
1400–24	0.36	0.25	1.45	1700–24	0.04	0.56	0.08
1425–49	0.30	0.20	1.54	1725–49	0.02	0.63	0.04
1450–74	0.34	0.23	1.47	1750–74	0.02	0.81	0.02
1475–99	0.38	0.30	1.31	1775–99	0.01	0.84	0.02
1500–24	ND	ND	ND	1800–24	0.01	0.94	0.01
1525–49	ND	ND	ND	1825–49	0.01	1.13	0.01
				1850–70	0.00	1.26	0.00

Sources: Derived from the Medieval Accounts Database; the Early Modern Probate Inventories Database; Allen (1994); John (1989); Turner (1998). ND, no data.

Table 3.15 *Total outputs of milk, meat, wool, hides and hay, 1270s–1860s (10-year averages)*

Decade	Milk (m. gals)	Beef (m. lbs)	Veal (m. lbs)	Mutton (m. lbs)	Pork (m. lbs)	Wool (m. lbs)	Hides (m. lbs)	Hay (m. tons)
1270s	42.09	10.57	1.98	81.33	26.13	20.84	6.29	0.12
1300s	54.45	13.72	2.63	90.49	30.82	20.89	7.34	0.11
1350s	51.46	13.52	2.56	94.49	21.33	24.82	7.36	0.12
1400s	45.25	12.39	2.32	75.11	12.38	15.13	6.32	0.10
1450s	44.92	12.83	2.37	83.90	14.06	13.11	6.59	0.09
1500s	ND	ND	ND	ND	ND	ND	ND	ND
1550s	63.94	19.85	3.58	79.32	31.39	14.08	7.54	0.15
1600s	58.56	19.06	3.40	157.49	33.51	28.34	9.90	0.24
1650s	72.52	24.83	4.35	130.85	31.14	23.95	10.51	0.29
1700s	59.10	21.16	3.67	211.92	39.93	39.09	13.12	0.34
1750s	163.19	62.94	10.50	217.12	84.40	34.12	21.73	0.55
1800s	279.75	115.99	18.54	422.49	170.63	56.62	38.50	1.37
1850s	434.05	192.64	28.28	616.27	297.43	71.66	53.08	1.93
1860s	492.79	217.85	31.99	713.12	293.05	83.36	58.34	1.94

Sources and notes: Derived from Manorial Accounts Database, Probate Inventories Database and Modern Farm Accounts Database as described in the text. Data reported as decadal averages. ND, no data.

livestock-farming sector given in Table 3.15. In contrast to the arable sector, where output of all the main products declined with population following the Black Death, output of the main livestock products remained broadly unchanged. Output then grew between the mid-fifteenth and mid-sixteenth centuries until, by the beginning of the seventeenth century, output of all livestock commodities had eclipsed the levels prevailing during the middle ages. Continuing growth raised output to yet more impressive levels by the second half of the eighteenth century. This had little to do with more animals being stocked but reflected considerable gains in livestock yields per animal due to selective breeding, better feeding and greater specialisation in particular livestock enterprises (Overton, 1996: 113–15). The marked dynamism of the livestock sector highlighted by Overton and Campbell (1992, 1996) is thus confirmed.

3.5 TOTAL AGRICULTURAL OUTPUT IN ENGLAND, 1270–1870

Multiplying the volumes of agricultural commodities by their prices yields the total value of net agricultural output. The price data are taken largely from Clark (2004), who synthesises the published data of Beveridge (1939), Thorold Rogers (1866–1902) and the multi-volume *Agrarian history of England and Wales*, as well as integrating new archival material, principally from the unpublished papers of William Beveridge and David Farmer. To these have been added the prices of hides from Thorold Rogers (1866–1902) and of rye from Farmer (1988, 1991), as well as direct evidence from the Early Modern Probate Inventories Database. The price data are used here to calculate the value of agricultural output in both current prices and in constant 1700 prices and will be examined in more detail in Chapter 5.

3.5.1 Agricultural output in constant prices

Figure 3.04 plots arable, livestock and total agricultural output in constant prices on a logarithmic scale, while Table 3.16 summarises the same information in growth-rate form, using 10-year averages to capture long-run trends. Following the Black Death, as the population shrank and, with it, aggregate grain consumption, arable output exhibited a clear downward trend. Livestock output, in contrast, proved more resilient as the surviving population spent part of their increased incomes on greater consumption per head of meat, dairy produce and woollen cloth. Agriculture as a whole thus showed only a modest decline in output.

From the mid-sixteenth century rising demand from a fast-growing population stimulated a sustained re-expansion of agricultural output, with arable output growth initially out-pacing that of the livestock sector. From the mid-seventeenth century, however, as

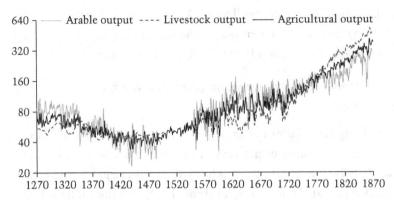

FIGURE 3.04 Total arable, livestock and agricultural output, 1270–1870 (log scale, 1700 = 100). *Sources:* Derived from Medieval Accounts Database; Early Modern Probate Inventories Database; Modern Farm Accounts Database as described in the text.

population pressure eased, livestock output growth accelerated and, significantly, remained ahead of that of the arable sector throughout the eighteenth century notwithstanding the resumption of population growth. What made this possible were the new integrated mixed-farming systems of the agricultural revolution in which fodder cropping with roots, legumes and rotational grass, higher stocking densities and increased on-the-farm recycling of nutrients played a crucial role. Gains in arable productivity, in fact, became contingent upon expansion of the livestock sector. Hence the annual growth rates in excess of 0.5 per cent sustained by both arable and livestock output after c.1750, a combination never before achieved (Table 3.16). Yet even the most advanced organic farming methods were incapable of delivering annual rates of output growth for agriculture as a whole in excess of 1 per cent and for most of the pre-industrial centuries growth rates were substantially lower.

3.5.2   The changing shares of the livestock and arable sectors

Table 3.17 presents the current-price shares of the arable and livestock sectors contributed by individual crop and livestock products. Within

Table 3.16 *Annual real agricultural output growth, 1270s–1860s (constant 1700 prices)*

Decades	Arable sector (%)	Livestock sector (%)	Total agriculture (%)
1270s–1300s	0.12	0.40	0.24
1300s–1340s	-0.19	-0.04	-0.12
1340s–1400s	-0.87	-0.42	-0.66
1400s–1450s	-0.37	0.03	-0.16
1450s–1470s	-0.38	0.00	-0.16
1470s–1550s	0.72	0.18	0.45
1550s–1600s	0.63	0.72	0.69
1600s–1650s	0.34	-0.04	0.21
1650s–1700s	0.24	0.47	0.33
1700s–1750s	0.29	0.90	0.55
1750s–1800s	0.52	1.31	0.93
1800s–1830s	0.98	0.63	0.77
1830s–1860s	0.58	1.08	0.85
1270s–1340s	-0.05	0.14	0.03
1270s–1700s	0.08	0.13	0.11
1270s–1860s	0.21	0.37	0.29
1700s–1860s	0.55	1.02	0.77

Sources and notes: Derived from Medieval Accounts Database; Early Modern Probate Inventories Database; Modern Farm Accounts Database as described in the text. The growth rates are calculated on decadal averages.

the arable sector the most important developments were the decline of inferior grains, as rye fell out of favour as a bread grain and oats as a brewing grain. Within the livestock sector, the importance of sheep in the late-medieval economy is clear from the high shares of wool and mutton. Over time, as the share of wool declined, other types of livestock produce, especially meat and dairy produce, became more important, which implies they were making a modest but growing contribution to diets. Hay also gained in significance as horses

Table 3.17 *Current-price shares of major arable and livestock outputs in English agriculture, 1270s–1860s (10-year averages)*

Decade	Wheat (%)	Rye (%)	Barley (%)	Oats (%)	Pulses (%)	Potatoes (%)	All arable products (%)
A. Arable							
1270s	29.1	3.3	15.0	12.1	0.6		60.1
1300s	25.7	3.2	12.0	8.9	1.3		51.2
1350s	23.7	1.3	15.1	7.4	1.3		48.8
1400s	20.7	1.3	17.1	5.7	1.4		46.3
1450s	17.9	1.9	11.3	6.3	1.0		38.4
1500s	ND	ND	ND	ND	ND	ND	ND
1550s	33.1	3.8	12.2	7.1	2.0		58.1
1600s	31.6	5.7	13.2	4.2	3.4		58.1
1650s	32.8	3.6	20.0	2.8	5.3		64.5
1700s	27.7	4.6	19.4	2.2	5.5	0.4	59.7
1750s	25.6	0.8	16.5	4.7	4.5	5.6	57.8
1800s	25.6	0.5	12.7	2.7	3.8	3.2	48.5
1850s	22.6	0.2	11.3	2.1	2.1	6.5	44.8
1860s	20.3	0.1	9.6	1.8	2.1	6.0	40.0

B. Livestock

	Milk (%)	Beef (%)	Pork (%)	Mutton (%)	Hay (%)	Wool (%)	Hides (%)	All livestock products (%)
1270s	7.8	1.7	4.0	11.1	0.7	14.1	0.6	39.9
1300s	11.7	2.3	5.0	13.4	1.1	14.6	0.7	48.8
1350s	11.9	2.6	4.0	18.0	1.3	12.9	0.6	51.2
1400s	14.2	3.2	3.1	17.6	1.6	13.0	1.1	53.7
1450s	16.8	3.8	4.1	25.2	2.1	8.1	1.4	61.6
1500s	ND	ND	ND	ND	ND	ND	ND	ND
1550s	18.4	2.4	3.6	7.0	3.0	5.6	2.0	41.9
1600s	7.4	1.8	3.1	15.2	3.5	9.5	1.2	41.9
1650s	10.7	2.1	2.1	11.5	4.0	4.2	0.9	35.5
1700s	7.6	1.7	3.4	16.4	4.1	6.1	1.1	40.3
1750s	13.1	3.7	4.8	11.5	5.0	2.9	1.2	42.2
1800s	15.7	4.9	5.4	14.6	7.2	2.8	0.8	51.5
1850s	16.7	5.9	7.4	14.7	6.6	3.2	0.8	55.2
1860s	18.8	6.5	7.6	16.2	6.0	4.2	0.8	60.0

Sources: Derived from Medieval Accounts Database; Early Modern Probate Inventories Database; Modern Farm Accounts Database. ND, no data.

Table 3.18 *Current- and constant-price shares of arable and livestock outputs in English agriculture, 1270s–1860s (%)*

Decade	Current prices		Constant 1700 prices		
	Arable (%)	Livestock (%)	Arable (%)	Livestock (%)	Total agricultural output (1700 = 100)
1270s	60.1	39.9	69.2	30.8	62
1300s	51.2	48.8	66.4	33.6	67
1350s	48.8	51.2	53.3	46.7	51
1400s	46.3	53.7	57.5	42.5	45
1450s	38.4	61.6	53.1	46.9	47
1500s	ND	ND	ND	ND	52
1550s	58.1	41.9	60.5	39.5	56
1600s	58.1	41.9	58.8	41.2	83
1650s	64.5	35.5	64.0	36.0	103
1700s	59.7	40.3	61.5	38.5	112
1750s	57.8	42.2	54.6	45.4	138
1800s	48.5	51.5	45.3	54.7	225
1850s	44.8	55.2	44.2	55.8	341
1860s	40.0	60.0	44.3	55.7	375

Sources and notes: Derived from Medieval Accounts Database; Early Modern Probate Inventories Database; Modern Farm Accounts Database as described in the text. ND, no data.

increased in numbers. These crop and livestock shares, in turn, are used as weights in the construction of the agricultural real output index.

How output is valued makes a difference to the results obtained, as Table 3.18 demonstrates. Measured in constant prices, the livestock sector increased its share of agricultural output during the late-medieval demographic recession, contracted between the 1450s and the 1650s when renewed population growth placed a premium upon grain production, but then expanded again from the mid-seventeenth century when, first, population pressure eased and, then, more advanced

Table 3.19 *Ratio of livestock to arable prices,*
1275–99 to 1700–24 (25-year averages, 1700 = 100)

Years	Mean ratio of livestock to arable prices (1700 = 100)	Years	Mean ratio of livestock to arable prices (1700 = 100)
1275–99	202	1500–24	204
1300–24	224	1525–49	155
1325–49	214	1550–74	130
1350–74	193	1575–99	114
1375–99	207	1600–24	101
1400–24	228	1625–49	90
1425–49	230	1650–74	102
1450–74	242	1675–99	101
1475–99	216	1700–24	104

Source: Derived from Clark (2004).

forms of mixed-farming became widely adopted. When measured in current prices, this ostensibly simple picture is complicated by changes in relative prices. In particular, although the price of livestock products relative to arable products was fairly stable during the late-medieval period, Table 3.19 shows that it trended downwards between the 1480s and 1650s, particularly during the 'Great Inflation' of the sixteenth century. These relative price changes thus amplified the effects of the slower real growth of the livestock sector between the 1450s and the 1650s, so that in current prices, the share of the livestock sector dropped quite substantially during this period. Even so, it never fell below 35 per cent.

No matter how great the demand-side pressure to maximise production of staple bread, brewing and pottage grains, arable output rarely exceeded that of the livestock sector by more than two to one. What impresses most from Table 3.18 is the substantial share of English agricultural output contributed by livestock production, which was never less than 30 per cent, often more than 40 per cent, and in the mid-fifteenth century and again after 1800, over 50 per cent of the total. This testifies to the importance of pastoral land uses – mowable meadow, communal and private pasture, rough grazing – as a proportion of the total but also, as agricultural technology advanced and the arable area expanded to its maximum extent, to the growing contributions of fodder crops and temporary forage in arable rotations to the upkeep of animals. In fact, until the mid-eighteenth century English agriculture supported over four times as many livestock as humans so that it was always necessary to reserve a large share of agricultural resources to meet their needs. It was therefore natural for English agricultural producers to make extensive use of animals for draught power, to the potential benefit of labour productivity in agriculture (an effect further reinforced by the intrinsically higher levels of labour productivity in livestock than arable farming). It was also natural for wool and hides to loom large as medieval exports and for major industries later to develop that processed these livestock raw materials. Finally, producing a mix of crops and animals spread risks and ensured that the population was never exclusively dependent upon grain for its subsistence. Diets may not have been particularly generous if viewed in terms of kilocalories, but, depending upon income, they benefited from incorporation of varying quantities of dairy produce and meat.

3.5.3   Agricultural output during the statistical Dark Age, 1492–1553

It should be noted that there is a gap between 1492 and 1553 as the manorial records come to an end before the probate inventories become available. This gap has been filled at the level of total agricultural output using the demand function approach of Crafts (1985) and Allen (2000). Agricultural consumption per head is assumed to be a function of its own price, the price of non-agricultural goods, and income. Income, own-price and cross-price elasticities are estimated from the data for output (adjusted for net imports), prices and real wages over the periods 1300–1492 and 1553–1700, and used to predict the missing values of output between 1492 and 1553, based upon the known values of prices and real wages for this period.

Crafts (1985) calculated the path of agricultural output in Britain during the industrial revolution with income and price elasticities derived from the experience of later developing countries. The approach was developed further by Allen (2000) using consumer theory. Allen (2000: 13–14) starts with the identity:

$$Q^A = RCN \tag{3.6}$$

where Q^A is real agricultural output, R is the ratio of production to consumption, C is consumption per head and N is population. Real agricultural consumption per head is assumed to be a function of its own price in real terms (P^A/P), the price of non-agricultural goods and services in real terms (P^{NA}/P), and real income (Y). Assuming a log-linear specification:

$$\ln C = \alpha_0 + \alpha_1 \ln(P^A/P) + \alpha_2 \ln(P^{NA}/P) + \beta \ln Y \tag{3.7}$$

where α_1 and α_2 are the own-price and cross-price elasticities of demand, β is the income elasticity of demand and α_0 is a constant. Consumer theory requires that the own-price, cross-price and income elasticities should sum to zero, which sets tight constraints on the plausible values, particularly given the accumulated evidence on elasticities in developing countries (Deaton and Muellbauer, 1980: 15–16, 60–82).

For early modern Europe, Allen (2000: 14) works with an own-price elasticity of –0.6 and a cross-price elasticity of 0.1, which constrains the income elasticity to be 0.5. Allen also assumes that agricultural consumption is equal to agricultural production. The assumption of balanced trade in agricultural goods before 1700 is retained, but the income and price elasticities are estimated from the data for England immediately before and after the statistical Dark Age. It is important that the demand equation should be dynamic, so as to capture the volatility of the agricultural output series. The estimated demand function therefore takes the form:

Table 3.20 *Agricultural demand function, 1300–1700*

	Coefficient	Standard error
A. Dynamic specification (dependent variable: $\ln C_t$)		
Constant	4.05	(1.04)
$\ln C_{t-1}$	0.40	(0.06)
$\ln (P^A/P)_t$	−0.07	(0.10)
$\ln (P^A/P)_{t-1}$	−0.13	(0.13)
$\ln (P^{NA}/P)_t$	0.58	(0.20)
$\ln (P^{NA}/P)_{t-1}$	−0.58	(0.21)
$\ln Y_t$	0.61	(0.12)
$\ln Y_{t-1}$	−0.24	(0.12)
Log likelihood	63.27	
N	342	
DW	2.09	
B. Long-run demand elasticities		
Own-price	−0.34	
Cross-price	0.00	
Income	0.62	

Source: See text. DW, Durbin–Watson statistic.

$$\ln C_t = \gamma_0 + \gamma_1 \ln C_{t-1} + \gamma_2 \ln(P^A/P)_t + \gamma_3 \ln(P^A/P)_{t-1}$$
$$+ \gamma_4 \ln(P^{NA}/P)_t + \gamma_5 \ln(P^{NA}/P)_{t-1} + \gamma_6 \ln Y_t + \gamma_7 \ln Y_{t-1}$$
$$+ \varepsilon_t$$

$$(3.8)$$

where t is a time subscript and ε is an error term. This specification allows the derivation of long-run demand elasticities as follows: the long-run own-price elasticity of demand is given by $(\gamma_2 + \gamma_3)/(1 - \gamma_1)$, the long-run cross-price elasticity of demand by $(\gamma_4 + \gamma_5)/(1 - \gamma_1)$ and the long-run income elasticity of demand by $(\gamma_6 + \gamma_7)/(1 - \gamma_1)$.

Equation (3.8) is estimated by maximum likelihood and the results are shown in Table 3.20. Agricultural output per head is regressed on current and one-period lagged observations of the real agricultural price level, the real non-agricultural price level and the real wage, over the period 1301–1700, with a gap from 1494 to 1550. Because of the one-year lag, there are 342 observations. The agricultural output, the real agricultural price level and the real non-agricultural price level data are all taken from the datasets described in this chapter and Chapter 5, while the real-wage data are from Allen (2001).

The estimated long-run income elasticity of demand is 0.62, which is close to the value of 0.5 assumed by Allen (2000). The price elasticities, however, are somewhat lower than those assumed by him. In particular, the estimated long-run own-price elasticity of –0.34 is substantially lower than Allen's assumed value of –0.6, although the estimated cross-price elasticity of 0 is not very different from Allen's assumed value of 0.1. The constraint that the three elasticities should sum to zero is not strictly met. Nevertheless, the results are encouraging enough to attempt to use the model to estimate the values of agricultural output per head across the gap between 1494 and 1550.

Figure 3.05 plots the estimates of agricultural output per head covering the whole period 1302–1700. The series derived from the late-medieval manorial accounts data and the early modern probate inventories data is labelled 'actual output' and contains a gap between 1492

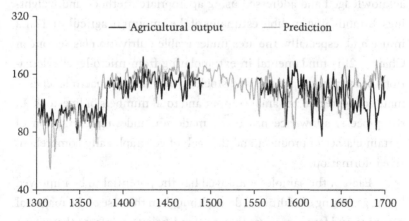

FIGURE 3.05 Actual and predicted agricultural output per head, 1300–1700 (1300 = 100, log scale). *Source:* See text.

and 1553. The series labelled 'predicted output' is derived from the agricultural demand function in Table 3.20. The values of the real agricultural price index, the real non-agricultural price index and the real wage are used to derive the fitted values of agricultural output per head. The predicted series tracks the output series reasonably well during the periods 1300–1492 and 1553–1700. In addition, the predicted series provides estimates for the period 1492–1553, when the data on crop proportions, grain yields, animal stocking densities, slaughter rates and animal yields, necessary for the direct estimation of agricultural output, are unavailable. During these years, data on real agricultural prices, real non-agricultural prices and the real wage remain available, making it possible to estimate agricultural demand across the gap.

3.6 CONCLUSIONS

Generating national estimates of agricultural output over a 600-year period from non-randomly distributed and chronologically discontinuous farm-level data on crops and livestock contained in late-medieval manorial accounts, early modern probate inventories and modern farm accounts is not a task for the faint-hearted. At all stages in the exercise gaps, inconsistencies and biases in the available evidence need to be acknowledged and addressed using appropriate methods and weightings. Establishing credible estimates of the amount of agricultural land in use and, especially, the area under arable cultivation (as set out in Chapter 2) is fundamental in extrapolating from micro-level calculations of average crop yields and stocking densities to macro-level estimates of aggregate net arable output and total numbers of livestock. In the process, allowance has to be made for under-representation of certain classes of producer and the lack of geographically comprehensive information.

Each of the samples employed has the potential to be improved by the gathering of additional data, although in the case of the manorial accounts and farm accounts this is more likely to reinforce than offset existing temporal and spatial biases within the datasets since these are intrinsic to the nature and coverage of the extant sources. The early modern probate inventory dataset is different, insofar as it is altogether more selective in composition and so would benefit from the addition of inventories from under-represented areas. Yet although this would undoubtedly improve the empirical soundness of the results the challenge to generate consistent and valid country-wide results will remain. So, too, will the need to find valid methodological ways of bridging the historical lacuna of the 1490s to 1550s and 'missing' livestock numbers after c.1750. The results presented in this chapter present viable solutions to both these problems.

Although the estimates of land use upon which these output estimates rest are informed by trends in population, the size of the population is not explicitly included in the calculations. The synchronous movement of trends in population and agricultural output

Table 3.21 *Summary trends in agricultural output and productivity, 1270s–1860s (1300s = 100)*

Decade	Population	Arable area	Sown area	Grain yields	Arable share of output	Working horses
A. Arable						
1270s	93	98	91	107	104	106
1300s	100	100	100	100	100	100
1350s	56	78	73	79	80	100
1400s	44	72	67	83	87	74
1450s	41	66	62	75	80	62
1500s	47	ND	ND	ND	ND	ND
1550s	66	68	73	114	91	94
1600s	90	70	82	135	89	85
1650s	113	76	95	159	96	129
1700s	109	75	94	163	93	174
1750s	125	83	109	223	82	235
1800s	192	88	121	253	68	262
1850s	370	103	149	326	67	368
1860s	451	109	164	353	67	374

Table 3.21 (cont.)

	Livestock units	Milk yields	Meat yields	Wool yields	Livestock share of output	Total agricultural output
B. Livestock						
1270s	86	99	99	110	92	93
1300s	100	100	100	100	100	100
1350s	90	111	107	122	139	76
1400s	69	124	115	101	126	67
1450s	65	137	123	84	140	70
1500s	ND	ND	ND	ND	ND	77
1550s	63	171	142	111	118	84
1600s	70	199	159	127	123	124
1650s	65	231	180	147	107	154
1700s	72	269	205	170	115	167
1750s	91	314	235	197	135	206
1800s	127	365	268	228	163	336
1850s	161	425	306	265	166	509
1860s	175	440	315	274	166	560

Sources and notes: See Tables 1.06, 1.08, 3.03, 3.06, 3.10, 3.11, 3.13, 3.14, 3.18. Wrigley and Schofield (1989:353–5). ND, no data.

is therefore one of the most immediately striking features of the results (Table 3.21). Unsurprisingly, farmers expanded or reduced their output, altered its composition, and raised or lowered the intensity of production in response to changes in demand. After the Black Death, when there were fewer mouths to be fed, backs to be clothed and hands to be kept employed, agricultural output contracted; it then re-expanded with the renewal of population growth in the sixteenth century and continued to rise through the seventeenth and eighteenth centuries as numbers climbed ever higher. By 1870 an agricultural output eight times greater than that in the mid-fifteenth century fed and resourced a population which had increased ten-fold. Yet, as these figures imply, successful as were the efforts of English agricultural producers at producing ever more from the land, from the end of the eighteenth century the fast-rising population could not have been adequately fed without drawing upon the agricultural resources of neighbouring Wales, Scotland and Ireland and imports from overseas.

Complicating the relationship between population levels and agricultural output were related changes in relative factor costs and the purchasing power of wages. When real incomes were most under pressure, in the early-fourteenth and mid-seventeenth centuries, arable production was at full stretch and typically accounted for over 60 per cent of total output (Table 3.18). When population pressure eased and real incomes improved, between 1350 and 1450 and again between 1650 and 1700, it was the livestock sector's turn to expand in response to growing demand per head for dairy produce, meat, leather goods and woollen cloth. Since livestock products had a higher value-added component than crops, not least because they required significantly more land per unit of output, these changes in the balance struck between arable and livestock outputs dampened down agriculture's aggregate output responses to the waxing and waning of population. The composition of output might tip from 35 per cent livestock to 35 per cent arable but only exceptionally went further. The mixed-farming character of English agriculture and the trade-offs to be obtained between arable and grass and between crops and livestock were therefore a source of stability, adaptability and strength.

The inherent complementarity between these two activities is especially apparent after 1700 when, in a clear break with the past, the population, arable area, numbers of livestock and the livestock sector's share of total agricultural output all rose together (Table 3.21), as widespread adoption of improved agricultural technology achieved a closer integration between crop and livestock production. In fact, in an age when bread and brewing grains were in greater demand than ever before, as the population finally breached the pre-industrial population ceiling of 5.5 million, livestock production became the most dynamic sector within English agriculture, sustaining general productivity growth through a series of positive-feedback mechanisms. As a result, by 1870, when the arable area was at an unprecedented high, numbers of livestock were at a historic maximum and livestock output accounted for well over half of total production.

Historians have sometimes speculated whether in earlier centuries at times of acute population pressure an inability to reconcile these inherently competitive land uses may have resulted in over-stocking of pastures and/or under-manuring of fields, thereby jeopardising the fragile ecological equilibria upon which the sustainability of production depended (Postan, 1966: 553–9; Outhwaite, 1986). It would be surprising if, at the micro-levels of individual farms and localities, this had not occasionally happened. Nevertheless, at a macro-level and much as Ester Boserup (1965) would have expected, population growth clearly drove up yields of both crops and livestock, while population decline led crop yields at least to fall (Table 3.21). It was in the mid-fifteenth century, when population pressure was weakest and land most abundant, that grain yields sank to their lowest recorded level. Thereafter yields steadily improved as the population grew and the arable area expanded. The impressive gains in agricultural output achieved between 1450 and 1850 arose more from intensifying and rationalising the use of existing resources than by bringing more land into production.

Where medieval cultivators had regularly fallowed the land to restore its fertility, relied upon permanent pasture to support most of their livestock, managed much of their grassland in common, and contented themselves with modest levels of yield, their early modern successors diversified and lengthened their rotations, steadily increased the share of the arable in productive use, enclosed and improved their pastures, expanded cultivation of fodder crops and simultaneously raised the yields of both crops and livestock. Between 1550 and 1700, when the population grew by 65 per cent, the arable area expanded by approximately 10 per cent, the sown area by almost 30 per cent, and net yields of wheat, barley and oats rose by over 40 per cent. Gains in livestock productivity were equally marked: meat yields rose by over 40 per cent and milk and wool yields by more than 50 per cent. Productivity advances between 1700 and 1850 were even more striking. The arable area expanded by 37 per cent, the sown area by almost 60 per cent, grain yields rose by 100 per cent, livestock numbers increased 125 per cent, and meat, milk and wool yields all grew by at least 50 per cent. The upshot was a 200 per cent increase in agricultural output, the greater part of which was brought about by raising the yields of both crops and livestock, and therefore farmland.

Agricultural historians have expended much energy debating whether and which of these episodes of growing population, rising yields and expanding output constituted an 'agricultural revolution', as well as the technological, institutional and economic sources of these productivity gains (Allen, 1992; Overton, 1996: 1–9). This, however, misses the essential point that progress was incremental from the fifteenth to the nineteenth centuries and rarely more than evolutionary in pace, since agricultural output never grew at more than 1 per cent a year until the nineteenth century (Table 3.16). Over several centuries, however, this was sufficient to effect a transformation, as land use was progressively rationalised; rotations lengthened and fallows reduced; cultivation of sown grasses, clover and other legumes blurred the distinction between arable and pasture; grass-fed draught oxen were replaced with fodder-fed working horses; livestock breeds improved; individual farm enterprises became more commercialised and specialised; and adoption of more effective methods of combining crop and livestock production became widespread. At the opening of the fourteenth century advanced organic systems of production were very much the exception, confined to a few environmentally, commercially and institutionally privileged localities (Power and Campbell, 1992). From the mid-eighteenth century they were fast becoming the norm (Wrigley, 2006), as witnessed by the fact that numbers of cropped acres and livestock were rising in parallel, as were yields of grain and of milk, meat and wool (Table 3.21). Little of this would have happened had developments taking place elsewhere within the economy not provided farmers with increasingly powerful incentives to specialise, invest and innovate.

4 Industrial and service-sector production

In 1270 the agricultural sector dominated economic output, dwarfing the industrial and service sectors. By 1870, notwithstanding an eight-fold expansion of agricultural output, this situation had been reversed and industry and services were the fastest-growing and largest sectors. The progress of British industry has been closely scrutinised from 1700 but less so in earlier centuries notwithstanding that the roots of Britain's industrial rise extend back much earlier than the conventional starting date of the industrial revolution in the mid-eighteenth century. The service sector, which already by the mid-nineteenth century had overtaken industry and emerged as the dominant sector within the economy, has received far less attention and awaits systematic investigation from the bottom up. This unevenness of treatment has required adoption of a range of approaches in order to derive valid estimates of industrial and service-sector output and thereby chart these profound changes in the structure of economic activity and volumes of industrial and service-sector output across the 600 years under investigation.

4.2 INDUSTRIAL OUTPUT

From 1700 industry is the one economic sector for which annual data have previously been gathered and analysed on a national scale. Full use has therefore been made of these existing estimates. Pioneering work by Hoffmann (1955) inadvertently overstated the growth rate of industrial output during the industrial revolution as a result of the weighting procedures applied to a dataset which covered only 56 per cent of industrial output. As Harley (1982) and Crafts (1985) separately point out, the problem is that a few industries, most notably cotton and iron, grew more rapidly than the rest of manufacturing, and these atypical industries bulk disproportionately large in Hoffmann's output series. By extrapolating total industrial output from that series he effectively doubled the weights of the most dynamic industries. Harley (1982) and Crafts and others (1989) have overcome this problem by limiting the weights applied to cotton and iron and increasing those applied to other industries, thereby arriving at lower estimates of total industrial output growth. It is these revised British industrial output weights for the period 1700–1870, modified from Hoffmann (1955) in line with Crafts and Harley (1992), that have been employed here but with adjustments to allow for new series available from subsequent scholarship (Table 4.01). The most important of these are King's (2005) series for bar-iron output, Feinstein's (1988: 446) series for building investment, and the British Library's index of new English-language book titles for the output of the printing industry. These improved indices yield securely documented and relatively uncontroversial estimates of trends in British industrial output during the era of most revolutionary growth (Figures 4.01 and 4.05, below).

A number of useful datasets exist before the eighteenth century, especially respecting production of tin, iron, coal and printed books. Further output estimates for textile manufacturing, leather and food processing can be derived from the relevant raw-material inputs supplied from the agricultural sector, net of wool and hide exports, as set out in Chapter 3. Building activity, in turn, has been inferred from trends in population and urbanisation as qualified by independent evidence of major medieval church-building projects. These individual output series, grouped into the three broad sectors of metals and mining, textiles and leather, and other industries, have then been combined to yield a composite output series (Figure 4.01) using the set of weights for England c.1700 summarised in Table 4.01. This does not mean that value-added shares are assumed to have remained constant from 1270 until 1700. For example, since metals and mining grew faster than textiles between 1300 and 1700 (Table 4.03 below), their

Table 4.01 *Industrial output weights, Great Britain 1700–1870 (%)*

1700–1711		
M&M	24.9%	Coal, 11.4; iron, steel and machine building, 11.8; tin, 1.7
Textiles	41.4%	Cotton yarn and cloth, 8.8; silk thread and goods, 11.4; linen yarn and cloth, 21.2
Other	33.6%	Sugar, 0.8; beer, 14.0; malt, 4.4; tobacco products, 2.1; printed matter, 3.6; building, 8.7
1711–1713		
M&M	24.1%	Coal, 10.7; iron, steel and machine building, 11.8; tin, 1.6
Textiles	38.6%	Cotton yarn and cloth, 8.2; silk thread and goods, 10.7; linen yarn and cloth, 19.7
Other	37.3%	Sugar, 0.7; beer, 13.0; malt, 4.1; tobacco products, 2.0; printed matter, 3.6; candles, 5.2; building, 8.7
1713–1722		
M&M	25.9%	Coal, 11.3; iron, steel and machine building, 13.2; tin, 1.4
Textiles	34.5%	Cotton yarn and cloth, 7.3; silk thread and goods, 9.5; linen yarn and cloth, 17.7
Other	39.5%	Sugar, 0.6; beer, 11.7; malt, 3.6; tobacco products, 1.8; paper, 0.8; printed matter, 4.0; soap, 2.6; candles, 4.7; building, 9.7
1722–1727		
M&M	14.9%	Coal, 5.9; iron, steel and machine building, 8.2; tin, 0.8
T&L	55.4%	Cotton yarn and cloth, 4.6; silk thread and goods, 5.9; linen yarn and cloth, 10.8; leather and leather goods, 34.1
Other	29.6%	Sugar, 0.3; beer, 7.1; malt, 2.2; tobacco products, 1.0; paper, 0.5; printed matter, 4.1; soap, 1.6; candles, 2.9; building, 9.9
1727–1739		
M&M	15.3%	Coal, 5.8; copper ore, 0.5; iron, steel and machine building, 8.1; tin, 0.8

T&L	55.0%	Cotton yarn, 4.5; silk thread and goods, 5.8; linen yarn and cloth, 10.7; leather and leather goods, 33.9;
Other	29.7%	Sugar, 0.3; beer, 7.1; malt, 2.2; tobacco products, 1.0; paper, 0.5; printed matter, 4.1; soap, 1.6; candles, 2.9; building, 9.9
1739–1761		
M&M	10.5%	Coal, 4.0; copper ore, 0.4; iron, steel and machine building, 5.6; tin, 0.5
Textiles	64.5%	Cotton yarn and cloth, 2.4; woollen and worsted yarn and cloth, 27.5; silk thread and goods, 4.0; linen yarn and cloth, 7.4; leather and leather goods, 23.2
Other	25.0%	Sugar, 0.3; beer, 5.0; malt, 1.5; tobacco products, 0.8; paper, 0.3; printed matter, 4.1; soap, 1.1; candles, 2.0; building, 9.9
1761–1771		
M&M	11.3%	Coal, 3.9; copper ore, 0.4; iron, steel and machine building, 6.5; tin, 0.5
T&L	64.7%	Cotton yarn and cloth, 6.7; woollen and worsted yarn and cloth, 27.1; silk thread and goods, 3.9; linen yarn and cloth, 7.3; leather and leather goods, 19.7
Other	24.1%	Sugar, 0.3; beer, 4.9; malt, 1.5; tobacco products, 0.8; paper, 0.3; printed matter, 3.4; soap, 1.1; candles, 2.0; building, 9.8
1771–1780		
M&M	11.5%	Coal, 3.8; copper ore, 0.3; iron, steel and machine building, 6.5; copper, 0.4; tin, 0.5
T&L	64.4%	Cotton yarn and cloth, 6.7; woollen and worsted yarn and cloth, 27.0; silk thread and goods, 3.9; linen yarn and cloth, 7.2; leather and leather goods, 19.6
Other	24.0%	Sugar, 0.3; beer, 4.9; malt, 1.5; tobacco products, 0.8; paper, 0.3; printed matter, 3.4; soap, 1.1; candles, 1.9; building, 9.8

Table 4.01 (cont.)

1780–1787		
M&M	11.5%	Coal, 3.8; copper ore, 0.3; iron, steel and machine building, 6.5; copper, 0.4; tin, 0.5
T&L	64.4%	Cotton yarn and cloth, 6.7; woollen and worsted yarn, 12.2; woollen and worsted cloth, 14.8; silk thread and goods, 3.9; linen yarn and cloth, 7.2; leather and leather goods, 19.6
Other	24.0%	Sugar, 0.3; beer, 4.9; malt, 1.5; tobacco products, 0.8; paper, 0.3; printed matter, 3.4; soap, 1.1; candles, 1.9; building, 9.8
1787–1789		
M&M	11.5%	Coal, 3.8; copper ore, 0.3; iron, steel and machine building, 6.5; copper, 0.4; tin, 0.5
T&L	64.6%	Cotton yarn and cloth, 6.7; woollen and worsted yarn, 12.2; woollen and worsted cloth, 14.7; silk thread, 1.3; silk goods, 3.0; linen yarn and cloth, 7.2; leather and leather goods, 19.5
Other	23.9%	Sugar, 0.3; beer, 4.9; malt, 1.5; tobacco products, 0.8; paper, 0.3; printed matter, 3.4; soap, 1.1; candles, 1.9; building, 9.7
1789–1801		
M&M	13.3%	Coal, 3.7; copper ore, 0.3; iron, steel and machine building, 6.5; copper, 0.4; tin, 0.5; shipbuilding, 1.9
T&L	62.8%	Cotton yarn and cloth, 6.7; woollen and worsted yarn, 11.9; woollen and worsted cloth, 14.4; silk thread, 1.2; silk goods, 2.5; linen yarn and cloth, 7.0; leather and leather goods, 19.1
Other	23.8%	Sugar, 0.3; beer, 4.8; malt, 1.4; tobacco products, 0.8; paper, 0.3; printed matter, 3.4; soap, 1.1; candles, 1.9; building, 9.8

1801–1831		
M&M	25.9%	Coal, 8.6; copper ore, 1.0; iron, steel and machine building, 11.5; copper, 0.9; copper products, 0.9; tin, 0.4; shipbuilding, 2.6
T&L	46.4%	Cotton yarn, 5.1; cotton cloth, 10.1; woollen and worsted yarn, 6.9; woollen and worsted cloth, 6.9; silk thread, 0.6; silk goods, 1.4; linen yarn and cloth, 5.3; leather, 1.3; leather goods, 8.8
Other	27.7%	Wheaten flour, 1.4; bread and cakes, 3.0; sugar, 0.5; beer, 0.9; malt, 0.6; spirits, 1.4; tobacco products, 0.6; paper, 1.9; printed matter, 3.9; soap and candles, 2.0; building, 11.5
1831–1870		
M&M	34.0%	Coal, 10.7; copper ore, 0.8; iron, steel and machine building, 12.3; copper, 0.5; copper products, 1.0; lead, 0.3; tin, 0.1; shipbuilding, 1.4; furniture, 2.6; timber products, 4.3
T&L	39.9%	Cotton yarn, 11.4; cotton cloth, 6.4; woollen and worsted yarn, 3.8; woollen and worsted cloth, 4.2; silk thread, 1.0; silk goods, 2.3; linen yarn and cloth, 2.5; leather,1.1; leather goods, 7.1; hemp products, 0.1
Other	26.1%	Wheaten flour, 2.4; bread and cakes, 1.7; confectionary, 0.4; sugar, 0.4; beer, 2.3; malt, 0.4; spirits, 0.6; tobacco products, 0.5; paper, 1.5; printed matter, 3.2; soap & candles, 1.0; vegetable oils, 0.1; building, 11.6

Sources and notes: Derived from Hoffmann (1955: 18–19); Crafts and Harley (1992: 728). M&M, metals and mining; T&L, textiles and leather; Other = all other industries.

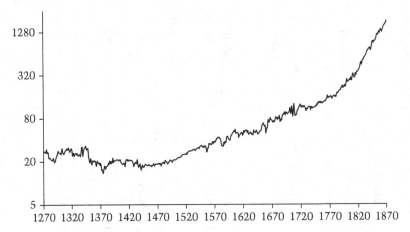

FIGURE 4.01 Industrial output, England 1270–1700 and Great Britain 1700–1870 (1700 = 100, log scale). *Source:* Appendix 5.3.

share of total output must have increased and that of textiles decreased between these two dates. Given data on output indices based on 1700 and the value-added shares in the base year of 1700, following Crafts and Harley (1992: 706–7, 722) implied value-added shares in earlier years can be inferred using the output indices.

Methodologically, industry presents the challenge of dealing with value added and double-counting, when outputs from one activity become inputs to another. Following Crafts and Harley (1992: 706–7, 722), one method of tracking value added over time has been to project back from value-added weights in a specific benchmark year, bearing in mind that infrequent changes in the weights does not necessarily imply the constancy of value-added shares over long periods (this approach has also been used for analysing services). Attempts have also been made where possible to distinguish between variations in the degree of processing, and hence the amount of value added. For example, a distinction is made between pig iron, an intermediate product, and bar iron, a finished product, and between exports of raw wool and those of woollen cloth. For food processing and building, allowances have been made for the output stimulus of urbanisation, while cathedral and abbey building has been estimated separately. Such corrective measures (and there are others) make it unlikely that output will have been overestimated and growth consequently underestimated in these sectors.

4.2.1 Metals and mining

Britain has significant mineral and coal deposits so it is not surprising, despite the pronounced boom-to-bust trajectory of most extractive activities, that metals and mining accounted for a large share of industrial output. Sustaining production was always a challenge and hinged upon constant prospecting for new seams and deposits, adopting technology that facilitated deeper mining and more efficient refinement and smelting of ores, reducing overland transport costs and recruiting a cheap labour-force. The five-fold growth in output of the metals and mining industries between 1300 and 1700 and the fifty-fold growth between 1700 and 1870 were therefore impressive achievements and testify to the progress made on all these fronts (see Table 4.03 below). Although silver, copper and substantial quantities of lead have all been produced at one time or another, output of tin, iron and coal dominated the sector and are relatively well documented. Production of these three activities, which is taken to be diagnostic of the metals and mining sector as a whole, is plotted in Figure 4.02 and summarised in Table 4.02.

Tin produced in Cornwall and Devon was the earliest of these three industries to rise to prominence, largely due to the scarcity of alternative sources of supply within Europe. Annual data on tin output are available with relatively few gaps, from Hatcher (1973: 156–9) for the period before 1550 and from Lewis (1908: 252–9) for the period 1553–1749. Both series have also been reproduced in Mitchell (1988: 303–4). The data are ultimately derived from recorded receipts of coinage dues which, given the government's right of pre-emption, can be taken as a reliable guide to aggregate tin output. Hatcher (1973: 5) certainly believes that the coinage dues provide an accurate picture of the industry's development, notwithstanding that some tin was

Table 4.02 *Output of key industries, England 1270–1700 and Great Britain 1700–1870 (1700 = 100)*

Decade	Tin	Iron	Coal	Textiles	Leather	Foodstuffs	Building	Printed books
1270s	ND	ND	ND	29	47	10	16	ND
1300s	25	ND	ND	20	55	12	17	ND
1350s	14	ND	ND	32	55	5	10	ND
1400s	47	ND	ND	24	47	4	8	ND
1450s	26	ND	ND	24	49	4	9	ND
1500s	43	9	8	23	48	6	11	1
1550s	51	36	27	34	56	10	17	4
1600s	42	124	50	68	74	31	38	12
1650s	19	108	77	57	78	66	72	47
1700	100	100	100	100	100	100	100	100
1750s	186	153	154	170	100	113	142	65
1800s	187	678	456	398	103	136	410	190
1850s	443	7,154	2,366	2,124	139	278	1,368	610
1860s	633	10,329	3,254	2,246	325	332	2,229	617

Sources and notes: See notes to Figures 4.02, 4.03 and 4.04 and Appendix 4.1. ND, no data.

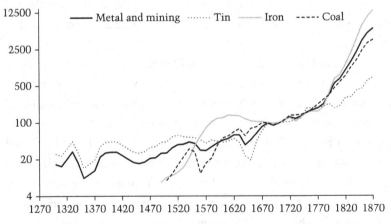

FIGURE 4.02 Output of metals and mining industries, England 1270–1700 and Great Britain 1700–1870 (averages per decade, 1700 = 100, log scale). *Sources and notes:* Tin: Hatcher (1973: 156–9); Hoffmann (1955); Lewis (1908: 252–9); iron: data appendix underlying King (2005), available at www.ehs.org.uk/ehs/Datasets/datasets. asp; Hoffmann (1955); coal: Hatcher (1993); Hoffmann (1955); Pollard (1980); Nef (1932). See Section 4.2.1 for a fuller explanation of the methods.

Table 4.03 *Output of key industrial sectors, England 1270–1700 and Great Britain 1700–1870 (1700 = 100)*

Decade	Metals and mining	Textiles and leather	Other industries	Total industry
1270s	ND	35	11	27
1300s	16	32	12	27
1350s	9	40	6	20
1400s	30	32	5	20
1450s	17	33	5	18
1500s	26	32	7	22
1550s	40	42	11	31
1600s	46	70	31	51
1650s	47	65	65	61
1700	100	100	100	100
1750s	156	151	105	132
1800s	555	298	193	271
1850s	3,638	1,337	566	1,163
1860s	5,052	1,436	802	1,480

Sources and notes: Derived from Table 4.02 using weights from Table 4.01. ND, no data.

smuggled out of the country. Production boomed in the second quarter of the fourteenth century, when the Italian merchant companies were major purchasers of English tin, slumped from the 1340s under the successive impacts of war, trade recession and, following the Black Death, rising labour costs, recovered during the final years of that century but then subsided again as aggregate demand contracted during the great fifteenth-century recession. Output re-expanded as the economy revived during the sixteenth century and then, aided by improved mining technology including introduction of steam pumps, climbed steadily from the late seventeenth century until, by the opening of the nineteenth century it was more than four times the peak level of the early fifteenth century (Figure 4.02 and Table 4.02).

Tin's resistance to corrosion meant it was in demand for a multitude of purposes. Alloyed with copper, it was a key ingredient of bronze, while pewter, which came into increasing use from the six-teenth century, was an alloy of tin, copper and lead. Homer (1991) and Hatcher and Barker (1974) provide data on the number of pewterers in London at roughly decadal intervals between 1310 and 1700, but these reflect the capital's growing importance over these centuries rather than national production of the component metals. Nor, frustratingly, can use be made of Blanchard's (1974, 1978) estimates of national lead production, since they are only available for a small number of bench-mark years. Lead's importance to the building industry, for roofing, fitting window glass and a range of other purposes, does nevertheless mean that it is subsumed into the aggregate estimates of building activity. Silver, in small quantities, was often produced in conjunction with lead, and mostly went straight into the money supply. Northern England had experienced a brief silver rush in the mid-twelfth century but once that passed, production of silver bullion – a royal monopoly – dwindled to trifling proportions (Allen, 2012: 238–52). Tin is therefore the sole non-ferrous metal industry of significance whose output can be tracked with reasonable confidence on an annual basis.

Data for iron production, much of it from low-grade ores, are also quite good, especially from the sixteenth century when fast-expanding military and naval demand for armaments gave the industry a strategic importance. Quantitative research on the late-medieval iron industry has tended to focus on the output of pig iron, an intermediate product, which can be estimated from information on the number of blast furnaces and the average output per furnace (Schubert, 1957; Flinn, 1958; Hammersley, 1973; Hyde, 1977; Riden, 1977). This poses prob-lems for the derivation of annual estimates because of the continuous nature of blast-furnace operation and the need to reline furnaces after each smelting campaign, so that an average annual output of 200 tons over three years may be the product of output of 600 tons in one year followed by two years of zero output. This problem does not affect figures of bar-iron production, since forges did not operate in cam-paigns, so that it is reasonable to assume that output in each forge remained stable across years. King (2005) is thus able to construct an annual series of bar-iron production for the period since 1490 from detailed information on the number of forges and output per forge. His results suggest a period of strong growth in production between about 1540 and 1620, as the indirect process of iron making with a furnace and a forge replaced the traditional direct process in bloomeries (King, 2005: 24). At this stage, of course, the industry was almost exclusively dependent upon charcoal for its fuel, which placed an organic constraint upon the scale and sustainability of production. This partially explains why, according to King's (2005) estimates of bar-iron production, output stagnated from the 1640s until the 1740s. Serious technical obstacles had to be overcome before coke could be substituted for charcoal and this production bottleneck eliminated.

Following Abraham Darby's early-eighteenth-century breakthrough innovation of coke smelting, and a period of further experimentation and refinement, expansion of iron output became rapid and sustained. Riden (1977) and Davies and Pollard (1988) reckon that growth held steady at an impressive 4.5 per cent per year for the better part of a hundred years from the 1740s, while King's figures imply a further acceleration to over 5 per cent between 1785 and 1815 when military demand for iron was at its most insatiable. This period of renewed growth was driven by a number of technological innovations which freed the British iron industry from what Ashton (1948) called 'the tyranny of wood and water' (the latter for power). Blast furnaces relocated to sources of cheap coal where from 1783, following Henry Cort's invention of the puddling furnace, they were joined by the forges which converted pig to bar iron (Hyde, 1977). Meanwhile, substitution of steam engines for water-wheels to drive the bellows relaxed the locational requirement for furnaces to be near fast-flowing water and reinforced the industry's dependence upon access to cheap coal. The industry was now in a position to reap major agglomeration economies which led to Britain's emergence as a net exporter of iron during the final years of the eighteenth century (Deane and Cole, 1967: 225; Hyde, 1977: 45). Iron output grew four-and-a-half-fold during the second half of the eighteenth century and more than tenfold during the first half of the next century (Figure 4.02 and Table 4.02). Underpinned by this seemingly limitless supply, iron came into general use for a whole range of purposes. In particular, its widening use for tools, implements, machines, vehicles, tramways and railways delivered significant efficiency gains to many other economic activities.

Without concurrent expansion of coal output – for forging, smelting and the generation of steam power – these dramatic advances in iron production would not have been possible. Although coal had been mined during the middle ages, the volume of output was insignificant compared with both charcoal production and output levels in later centuries. This situation was transformed in the sixteenth century by surging metropolitan demand for fuel for both domestic and industrial uses, which led to soaring wood and charcoal prices and made it profitable to ship coal mined in Northumberland and Durham from the Tyne to the Thames. Output doubled between 1550 and 1600 and then doubled again over the course of the seventeenth century as, released from its subservience to charcoal and wood, coal-burning London finally overtook Paris to become the largest city north of the Alps (Figure 4.02). The existence of an assured and expanding source of demand from the metropolis sustained investment in the opening up of new mines, extension of tramways and expansion of the coal-carrying fleet.

Output of coal in the 1560s and around 1700 is taken from Hatcher (1993: 68), interpolated using shipments of coal from northeastern ports, also taken from Hatcher (1993: 487–95), updating the earlier work of Nef (1932: 380–1). By 1700 the northeastern coalfield accounted for 50 to 60 per cent of total English production, and 40 to 50 per cent of total British production, so that shipments from the northeastern ports can be taken as representative of the national cycle. There seems to be broad agreement in the literature that, although output could be quite volatile over short periods (as mines became worked out and others opened at new locations), overall the coal industry exhibited strong growth between the early sixteenth century and the end of the seventeenth century (Coleman, 1977: 85; Clay,

1984b: 47). For coal to become the preferred fuel of both domestic consumers and industrial users a host of technical problems nevertheless had to be overcome. To prevent cooked food from becoming tainted and air corrupted, domestic buildings had to be adapted to incorporate improved fireplaces, grates, stoves and chimneys (Hatcher, 1993: 410–18). There was an even greater risk that use of coal as a fuel would spoil industrial products: acceptable solutions were rarely quick to appear and, as in the case of coke smelting of iron, invariably involved much trial and error (Hatcher, 1993: 418–58; Hyde, 1977: 53–75). Progress on all fronts made by the close of the seventeenth century was nonetheless impressive.

From early in the eighteenth century coal became a crucial input for a widening range of other industries as the economy moved from an organic to an inorganic basis (Wrigley, 2004: 29–35). Output grew apace, expanding at a rate of more than 2 per cent from mid-century (Flinn, 1984: 26). More and more energy-intensive industries found ways of substituting the seemingly limitless supplies of stored carbon for wood, although few as a result achieved the spectacular price falls seen in industries such as cotton textiles (Flinn, 1984: 311; Clark and Jacks, 2007: 47). At the same time, technological change facilitated the mining of coal in deeper and less accessible seams. Here, development of the steam engine, used initially for pumping water, constituted the most important technological breakthrough (von Tunzelmann, 1978). Once it was applied to rotary motion, steam power became the first general-purpose technology as its use spread to most other branches of the economy (Crafts, 2004), further boosting demand for coal. Between 1750 and 1850 coal output rose fifteen-fold.

By 1700 outputs of tin, iron and coal were all at an historic high and collectively three to four times greater than the peak levels of the fourteenth century (Figure 4.02 and Tables 4.02 and 4.03). Thereafter, production of the metals and mining sector grew at an accelerating rate, by 0.6 per cent per year between 1700 and 1750, 1.8 per cent from 1750 to 1800 and 2.5 per cent from 1800 to 1850. These industries were at the cutting edge of British industrial expansion and each, but especially iron and coal, gained by tapping into fast-expanding sources of demand. Nevertheless, output of each would have stalled but for constant prospecting for fresh seams of ore, application of ever-greater quantities of labour and capital to the extraction process, and significant technological progress in extraction, refining and transportation.

4.2.2 Textiles and leather

Textiles and leather long ranked among the most important of British industries, since wool and hides were staple products of the country's substantial livestock-farming sector, cloth and leather were in constant and general demand, and surplus labour in many households was available for spinning and weaving. Partly because English wool was considered to be the finest in Europe, cloth was the first native industry to rise to international prominence: exports boomed during the thirteenth century, declined during the international commercial recession that set in from the 1270s, and then revived from the 1340s under the protection afforded by high export duties on raw wool. By the end of the fifteenth century production of a range of wool textiles had grown to become the country's leading export industry, a position which it long retained. Some linen was also produced, although more so in Scotland and Ireland than in England, and cotton manufacture, following mechanisation of the spinning process late in the eighteenth century, enjoyed a meteoric rise (Farnie, 2003). Until the latter became the great success story of the early industrial revolution, the British textile industries remained predominantly wool-based and heavily dependent upon domestic supplies of fibre. This organic dependence limited their capacity to grow.

For the period 1280–1554, annual exports of woollen cloth together with unprocessed wool and wool fells are given by Carus-Wilson and Coleman (1963). It can be presumed that unexported wool was spun and woven into cloth for the domestic market. Total production of raw wool from domestic agriculture is estimated in Chapter 3. Since the scale of manufacturing output was in large measure a function of the supply of wool, production estimates of textile output can therefore be inferred from output estimates of this key agricultural raw material, net of exports. By the end of the fifteenth century wool exports had dwindled to insignificance and the wool-textile industries consumed virtually the entire national clip. Thereafter, output rose with wool production. Output of raw hides and skins, net of exports, similarly determined the output of the leather industries, which included both tanning and curing and an array of trades which ranged from saddlery and harness to boots and shoes. Leather was among the most indispensable raw materials, with the result that leather working was widely represented throughout the rural and urban economies. A few more specialised centres emerged, such as Stratford-on-Avon, where local availability of iron promoted production of wares which combined both materials, such as saddlery and harness. Some of these items entered international trade but for the most part the leather industry never enjoyed the export success achieved by the textile industries.

England's textile industries were at their lowest ebb at the end of the thirteenth century, when rising transaction costs in international trade effectively stifled the once-thriving export trade in cheap, light, undyed cloths produced by mostly urban-based artisans (Munro, 1999). *Circa* 1300 it was consequently raw, unprocessed wool that dominated exports, since this was in high demand from continental textile man-ufacturers who, at this stage, enjoyed a clear competitive advantage over home producers. Insofar as an indigenous cloth industry survived it was largely as a supplier to domestic markets. From an absolute peak during the opening decade of the fourteenth century, wool exports then contracted as sheep murrains depressed output and war-mongering monarchs raised export duties and manipulated the wool trade to suit their own political agenda.

These developments played to the advantage of domestic textile producers and nurtured an incipient industrial recovery (Munro, 2004: 278–9). Some of the former urban centres of production, such as York and Beverley revived, but a number of new rural centres of manufac-ture also emerged, where production was less regulated and labour costs lower. Over the next hundred years England was transformed from Europe's leading supplier of raw wool to a major exporter of woollen cloth. Yet, although the period between the mid-fourteenth and mid-fifteenth centuries was characterised by strong growth of cloth exports, this was offset by a massive contraction in domestic demand as England's population shrank from 4.8 million on the eve of the Black Death to 1.9 million a hundred years later. Rising consumption per head of higher-quality cloths provided inadequate compensation for so great a contraction. Contrary to the impression conveyed by the literature on cloth exports, for which data have long been available, aggregate woollen textile production actually declined over this period (Figure 4.03 and Table 4.02), a trend reinforced by shrinking sheep

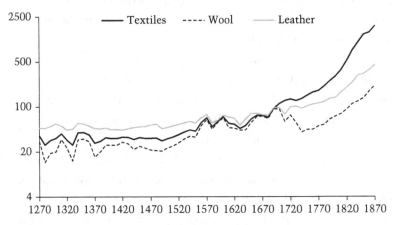

FIGURE 4.03 Output of textiles and leather industries, England 1270–1700 and Great Britain 1700–1870 (averages per decade, 1700 = 100, log scale). *Sources and notes:* Wool: exports of raw wool from Carus-Wilson and Coleman (1963) are subtracted from total wool output estimated in Chapter 3 to obtain the raw wool input which serves as an indicator of the output of the woollen textile industry; leather: output is estimated from the production of raw hides in Chapter 3. After 1700 data are taken from Hoffmann (1955), where the Hoffmann series is extended for silk thread and goods by Mitchell's (1988: 343) series of imports of raw, thrown and waste silk and for linen yarn and cloth by linen imports taken from Schumpeter (1960: 52). Leather is brought back from 1801 with an index of hides and skins charged with duty from Mitchell (1988: 416). See Section 4.2.2 for a fuller explanation of the methods.

numbers and falling fleece weights (Stephenson, 1988; Oldland, 2013; Tables 3.10 and 3.14).

It was not until demand recovered and unit labour costs fell during the sixteenth century that output began to rise once again. Output approximately trebled over the course of that century, as manufacture fastened onto excess labour in both rural and urban households and capitalist clothiers articulated production and marketed the finished product. By the opening of the seventeenth century output was running at more than double its previous late-fourteenth-century peak (Figure 4.03 and Table 4.02). It was during this period of active proto-industrialisation that textile manufacture increasingly gravitated towards regions where cheap land kept the costs of provisions and therefore labour low, well away from major urban markets and the competing labour demands of commercial agriculture. Specialisation in high-quality fulled woollens attracted broadcloth manufacture to locations with surplus water power which could be devoted to mechanised fulling (Carus-Wilson, 1941, 1952; Munro, 2004: 271–3). Hence the rise of substantial textile industries in the southwestern counties, the Stroud valley of the high Cotswolds, the West Riding of Yorkshire, Lancashire and Cumbria. In England's eastern lowlands, where grain milling tended to monopolise the available water-power sites, textile producers were more likely to specialise in light unfulled worsteds, and in the long run it was manufacturers in these locations that tended to have the weakest competitive advantage, especially following the advent of water-powered machine spinning.

The textile industry's national economic importance is beyond dispute. Cloth manufacture made a major contribution to the incomes of many households, bolstered the economies of some of the country's remoter and hillier regions, made a significant contribution to export earnings and pioneered an array of institutional and technological innovations with far-reaching benefits for English industry and commerce. Nevertheless, the industry's dependence upon a mostly home-grown animal fibre severely circumscribed its potential for growth. British farmers responded to the industry's expanding raw-material demands by boosting flock numbers and quadrupling wool yields (Tables 3.11 and 3.14), but these considerable achievements were incapable of liberating wool-textile manufacture from these supply-side constraints. Between the mid-fifteenth and mid-eighteenth centuries textile output grew at an average annual rate of 0.65 per cent. Briefly, during the second half of the sixteenth century, growth was twice as rapid, but it never exceeded a modest 1.5 per cent per year, since, without major raw-material imports, this was the most that domestic wool production could sustain. After 1750 the textile industries bucked this trend (Figure 4.03 and 4.02). Tellingly, the spurt in growth to an unprecedented 1.7 per cent during the second half of the eighteenth century, which more than doubled cloth output within the space of 50 years, came not from traditional woollens but from cotton spun from fibres imported in bulk from tropical and sub-tropical producers.

The English cotton industry had originated to supply the Lancashire linen industry with yarn for the production of fustians, which combined linen warps with cotton wefts (Kerridge, 1985: 124–5). Such was the cheapness of Indian labour that English producers of pure cotton cloth could not hope to compete until protected by imposition of duties on the imported product and adoption of machine spinning and, later, power weaving elevated the productivity of the higher-waged English workers. It was not until the final quarter of the eighteenth century that these twin preconditions were fully met. Output of cotton textiles accelerated dramatically from around 1780, growing at around 10 per cent per year until the end of the eighteenth century and then abating to a moderate 5 per cent during the first half of the nineteenth century (Farnie, 2003). There was, however, a downside to the cotton industry's runaway success, since the cheapness and desirability of the product sent the more traditional wool-textile industries into relative decline. Aggregate textile output consequently grew by the lesser rate of 4.2 per cent between 1800 and 1850.

This turnround in the textile industries' rate of growth reflected a dramatic diversification of raw-material supplies to include imported vegetable fibres combined with a technological and organisational revolution embodied in the emergence of factory-based production. Although the earliest factories were based on water power, swift onset of diminishing returns meant that the steam engine quickly became the main source of motive power once the problem of harnessing it to rotary motion had been solved (Musson, 1976). Agglomeration economies combined with first-mover advantage clinched the pre-eminence of the Lancashire cotton-manufacturing region and confirmed the commercial fortunes of the port of Liverpool, through which the raw cotton was imported and much of the finished cloth exported. With productivity rising rapidly, the price of cotton yarn and cloth fell dramatically in absolute as well as relative terms (Ellison, 1968; Harley, 1998). These productivity and price changes in British cotton textiles led to a major shift of comparative advantage, with Britain first displacing India in export markets and then, from the 1820s, securing a growing share of the Indian domestic market (Broadberry and Gupta, 2009). As mechanised production spread to other textiles, Britain also achieved remarkable export success in woollens and jute, while linen was located mainly in Ireland (Broadberry and others, 2010: 176). These conspicuous achievements have earned the textile industries a leading role in conventional accounts of the British industrial revolution.

In earlier centuries Clarkson (1966: 25) argues that leather was the next most important industry after woollen textiles. It also grew more slowly, a feature it shared with many other branches of manu-facturing: between 1300 and 1700 its output barely doubled (Table 4.02 and Figure 4.03). In part this was because it relied for its principal raw materials on the slaughtering of animals but also due to its lack of technological progress and, in contrast to other industries, limited adoption of mechanical aids (Cherry, 1994: 300). Its omnipresence and wide dispersal meant that it was generally taken for granted by contemporaries and has thus been largely overlooked by historians. In the absence of significant hide imports, its progress to 1700 has been tracked using the production of hides from livestock agriculture, derived from Chapter 3, net of exports as given by Carus-Wilson and

Coleman (1963) for the period 1280–1554. Thereafter, an index of hides and skins charged with duty, from Mitchell (1988: 416), has been used. The industry's unsensational course offers a valuable corrective to the dramatic but atypical achievements of the handful of leading-sector manufactures. Its experience helps to explain why aggregate industrial-output growth rarely exceeded 1.5 per cent a year before 1800 and for most of the pre-industrial centuries was 1.0 per cent or less.

4.2.3 Other industries

In addition to the two industrial sectors of metals and mining and textiles and leather, England before 1700 and Great Britain thereafter supported a diverse group of other industries of varying scales and technological sophistication, many of which were geared towards satisfying consumer demand. Three, in descending order of size, are taken here as representative of this heterogeneous sector as a whole: food processing, building and construction and printed books (Figure 4.04 and Tables 4.02 and 4.03). Output of the food industries is assumed to have grown in line with their specific agricultural inputs, output of the building industry in line with population, but with an allowance for urbanisation, and output of printed books in line with the number of new English-language book titles published in the country. The first two activities were widely suffused throughout the economy, while the last was concentrated in a limited number of urban centres. Collectively, these three industries accounted for a third of all industrial output by 1700, with food processing almost double the combined importance of the other two (Table 4.01).

Although it would in principle be possible to track the output of particular food industries via their specific agricultural inputs, such as barley for the brewing industry, wheat for the flour industry and milk for the dairy industry, there would be no reliable basis for weights at this level of disaggregation. Nor, given the inevitably large gaps in coverage, would this approach yield a comprehensive index of food processing. Instead, output is considered as a function of the

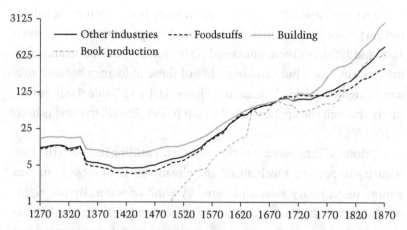

FIGURE 4.04 Output of other industries, England 1270–1700 and Great Britain 1700–1870 (averages per decade, 1700 = 100, log scale). *Sources and notes:* Before 1700 food processing is assumed to grow in line with the agricultural output index from Chapter 3; building: assumed to grow in line with urban population, estimated by multiplying the population estimates from Chapter 1 with the share of the population living in towns from Table 4.01, log-linearly interpolated; books: the number of new titles from the English short-title catalogue. After 1700 all series are taken from Hoffmann (1955) with the following exceptions: beer: prior to 1787 brought back in time using an index of small, strong and table beer charged with duty from Mitchell (1988: 404–5); tobacco products: brought back in time using the value of imported tobacco at official prices from Mitchell (1988: 462–3); paper: paper charged with duty and taken from Mitchell (1988: 43); books: the number of new titles from the *English short-title catalogue*; soap and candles: extended back from 1821 using the series soap charged with duty from Mitchell (1988: 412) and tallow candles charged with duty from Mitchell (1988: 415); building: a constant price series of total buildings and works from Feinstein (1988: 446) with missing data interpolated using a series on timber imports from Mitchell (1988: 462). See Section 4.2.3 for a fuller explanation of the methods.

agricultural output index derived in Chapter 3. Between 1300 and 1450 output of these industries shrank significantly, partly because of the wholesale contraction of population but also due to the greater self-sufficiency of individual households as land became more abundant. By the mid-fifteenth century urbanisation was in abeyance and commercialised production of food and drink was at a low ebb. From this low base substantial growth then ensued at an average annual rate of 1.1 per cent between 1450 and 1750, with a peak rate of 2.3 per cent between 1550 and 1600, as population growth and increasing urbanisation proceeded hand in hand. Progress slowed progressively between 1600 and 1750, but then quickened again as industrialisation and rapid urbanisation took hold and branches of these industries became subject to significant modernisation (Figure 4.04 and Table 4.02), particularly through the application of steam power (Broadberry and others, 2010: 180).

Flour milling pioneered the way. Grain milling had been the first industry to become mechanised and already by 1270 most flour was ground using rotary stones powered by wind or water. By the eighteenth century the greatest of the water-powered mills resembled factories in the scale of their output, capitalisation of their operation and nature of the business methods employed. This remained the prevailing mode of production until large-scale, steam-powered, roller mills introduced at port sites gained market share from the 1830s (Musson, 1978: 234). The scaling up of brewing proceeded concurrently. Large-scale 'common brewers' were already well established by the late eighteenth century (Mathias, 1959) and in England and Wales by 1832 accounted for 54 per cent of total output, with the remainder contributed by small-scale 'private brewers' (such as colleges, hospitals and private gentlemen brewing in country houses for consumption on the estate), publicans brewing beer for sale on their own premises and by licensed victuallers (Gourvish and Wilson, 1994: 69). By 1900, common brewers had expanded their market share to 95 per cent of the total and brewing had become a highly capitalised and predominantly urban activity.

Progress of the building industry proceeded at much the same rate as the food-processing industries until 1700 but thereafter moved ahead and grew faster than industry as a whole at 2.0 to 2.5 per cent per year under the twin stimuli of rapid industrialisation and urbanisation (Figure 4.04 and Table 4.02). This is unsurprising given that construction is assumed to have grown in line with population (as estimated in Chapter 1), but with an allowance for urbanisation, where building activity typically assumed its greatest extent. The urbanisation rate

Table 4.04 *English urban population, 1086–1700*

Year	Urban population (000s)	Total population (000s)	Urbanisation rate (%)
1086	17.8	1,710	1.04
1270	111.2	4,360	2.55
1290	121.4	4,750	2.55
1377	65.0	2,500	2.60
1500	80.0	2,200	3.63
1550	112.0	3,020	3.71
1600	255.0	4,110	6.20
1650	495.0	5,310	9.32
1700	718.0	5,200	13.82

Sources and notes: Urban population: 1086: Russell (1948: 146); 1290: Campbell (2008: 908); 1377: Dyer (2000); 1500–1700: de Vries (1984: 270–8). Total population: Chapter 1. Urbanisation rate: derived by dividing the urban population (those living in towns with at least 10,000 inhabitants) by the total population. For 1270, the urbanisation rate was assumed to be the same as in 1290 and used to derive the urban population.

is derived from a number of sources for benchmark years and log-linearly interpolated. Estimates of the urban population living in towns of at least 10,000 inhabitants are shown in Table 4.04 together with estimates of the total population and the urbanisation rate.

Yet whereas these assumptions may work well for the period after 1520, they fail to do justice to the scale of major late-medieval ecclesiastical construction projects. The pre-1520 estimates therefore make allowance for church building, using data on the number of cathedral and abbey building projects derived from Morris (1979: 179). These prestigious and often lavish building enterprises accounted for an estimated 14 per cent of all construction activity in 1381 and 1,308 out of a total construction workforce of 10,050 at a time when Morris (1979: 179) estimates that a dozen major building programmes were in progress. These figures are based upon the industrial share of the labour-force derived from the 1381 poll tax returns (Chapter 9), a presumed 5.0 per cent share of construction in total industry (interpolated from its 8.8 per cent share in 1700), and an average of 120 workers per project implied by evidence from Westminster Abbey provided by Morris (1979: 216). What is striking is that, even after allowance for these great construction enterprises, the volume of building output c.1300 at the climax of English cathedral-building activity was only a sixth of that in 1700 when more modest secular projects accounted for the bulk of the industry's output. Plainly, it was well within the resources of a relatively poor and underdeveloped economy to undertake conspicuous construction projects of such ambition and scale, especially when the substantial labour input was so cheap.

In contrast, book production was an intrinsically small-scale activity. Until William Caxton set up the first English printing press at Westminster in 1476 all books produced in England were perforce handwritten and therefore slow and expensive to produce. Printing simultaneously increased the supply and reduced the unit costs of printed matter, meeting a demand for books from a relatively literate population. As a result, production of printed books quickly took firm root and displayed impressive growth. Books published before 1500 are known as *incunabula* from the Latin word for cradle and a complete record of these works is provided by the British Library's *Incunabula Short Title Catalogue* (Dittmar, 2011: 1143). After 1500, the numbers of titles published each year have been obtained from the same library's *English Short Title Catalogue* (http://estc.bl.uk/F/?func=fil e&file_name=login-bl-list) (since superseded by a new catalogue, *Explore the British Library*: http://explore.bl.uk/primo_library/lib web/action/search.do?vid=BLVU1). Baten and van Zanden (2008: 220) show that during the fifteenth century, Belgium and Italy had the highest levels of book production per head, but that Holland and England overtook them around 1600. English printed-book production grew at 2.6 per cent a year from 1500 to 1650, making it one of the fastest growing of all early modern industries, slowed to 0.3 per cent between 1650 and 1750 but then recovered to 2.3 per cent from 1750 to 1850 (Figure 4.04 and Table 4.02). These figures would be greater still if account were taken of publication of newspapers, broadsheets and other printed ephemera.

The printing industry's overall scale was modest but its rise illustrates the kind of growth that could be achieved by products targeted at particularly lucrative niche markets. Its growth was, on average, double that of the other industries sector as a whole between 1500 and 1850. From the last quarter of the seventeenth century several other consumer-orientated industries rose to prominence, as witnessed by the changes in consumption discussed in Chapter 7. For example, imports of pottery steadily declined from the mid-seventeenth century as domestic production expanded: numbers of potteries almost doubled between 1680 and 1710 (Weatherill, 1983: 27). Imports of glass also shrank from the closing decades of the seventeenth century, as technical innovation stimulated expansion of the English industry (Thorpe, 1961). Nevertheless, taken as a whole this heterogeneous group of other industries was the slowest-growing manufacturing sector. Many retained a heavy reliance upon hand tools, manual skills and small-scale units of production and hence failed to match the dramatic growth achieved by the textile and especially the metal industries once the industrial revolution got under way. They therefore acted as a counterbalance to these more dynamic industries and slowed overall rates of industrial output growth.

4.2.4 Aggregate industrial production

A combined index of industrial production has been constructed from the individual series for metals and mining, textiles and leather, and other industries (Table 4.03 and Figure 4.05), using the value-added weights set out in Table 4.01. Figure 4.01 plots this master index on a logarithmic scale, while Table 4.05 summarises the same information in growth-rate form over 50-year periods, using 10-year averages to capture long-run trends.

As will be observed, there were substantial fluctuations in aggregate industrial output during the later middle ages. Production drifted down from its modest high-medieval peak during the long era of demographic contraction initiated by the Black Death, with the result that output c.1450 was only two-thirds its pre-plague level (Figure 4.05 and Table 4.05). Since population numbers shrank to a greater extent than industrial output, this implies that output per head grew as higher real incomes enabled households to purchase more manufactured goods. Yet the sheer scale of the contraction in demand, reinforced by the great commercial depression of the mid-fifteenth century (Hatcher, 2002) and a general downturn in foreign trade, meant that this was hardly a period of industrial prosperity.

Rising labour costs did however stimulate a quest for labour-saving technology as exemplified by wider adoption of spinning wheels, broad looms and mechanical fulling and, towards the end of the century, by introduction of the printing press and replacement of bloomeries with blast furnaces (Mokyr, 1990: 44–56). Further, installation of mechanical clocks in many public buildings improved timekeeping and helped promote understanding of cogs and gears and the skills required to construct complex machinery. The same period also witnessed a great deal of industrial relocation as the west country, west midlands and West Riding of Yorkshire all commenced their rise to manufacturing prominence and Britain consolidated its transformation from an exporter of raw wool to one of woollen textiles. A number of positive and formative developments can thus be dated to this period of contraction in industrial output which laid the foundations for England's improved industrial performance during the ensuing period of demographic and economic expansion.

Industrial output finally began to revive during the closing decades of the fifteenth century, when a phase of sustained growth began which returned output to the level of the late thirteenth century by the 1550s and to more than double that level by the 1650s (Figure 4.01 and Table 4.03). Growth was particularly driven by coal and iron, although output of the relatively large wool-textiles industry also played a part and production of printed books is an example of a small consumer industry which grew vigorously (Table 4.02). The buoyancy of these industries meant that the demographic upswing of the sixteenth and early seventeenth centuries was economically more soundly based

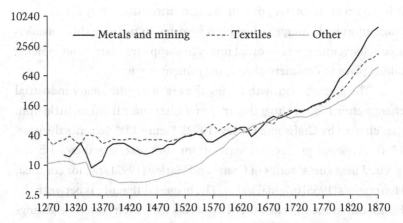

FIGURE 4.05 Industrial output by major sub-sector, England 1270–1700 and Great Britain 1700–1870 (averages per decade, 1700 = 100, log scale). *Sources:* See notes to Figures 4.02, 4.03 and 4.04, and Appendix 4.1.

than the previous upswing of the thirteenth century. In particular, employment in proto-industry helped bolster the incomes of the mounting number of agriculturally marginalised households. The upshot was that per head, England produced twice as much industrial output in 1650 as in 1300 (Table 4.10 below).

The industrial momentum established during the sixteenth and early seventeenth centuries proved unstoppable. From the 1650s population growth effectively ceased but industrial output continued to rise, growing at almost 1.0 per cent per year during the second half of the seventeenth century as the rate of urbanisation increased and the glass and pottery industries underwent unprecedented expansion. Growth then slowed to 0.5 per cent during the first half of the following century (Table 4.05). Output of metals and mining continued to lead growth and, spurred by the introduction of steam pumps, production of tin surged (Tables 4.02 and 4.03). Textile output trebled and coal production doubled between the 1650s and 1750s, whereas the many more traditional craft industries performed less impressively and production of printed books stalled. By the end of this generally expansive era, on the eve of the industrial revolution, industrial output was seven times what it had been at its lowest point in the mid-fifteenth century (Table 4.03). Huge effort and enterprise had been invested in securing this considerable achievement, which owed much to complementary developments taking place in commercial and government services.

The pattern of growth during the era of revolutionary industrial change after 1750 is altogether more familiar since it differs little from that charted by Crafts and Harley (1992). Figure 4.06 presents the post-1700 industrial production series from this text, together with the 'revised best guess' series of Crafts and Harley (1992) and, for contrast, Hoffmann's (1955) original index. The biggest difference is between the Hoffmann index and the other two series with their lesser weightings upon cotton textiles and iron. The new series presented here incorporates King's (2005) data for the iron industry and consequently shows slightly slower growth than the Crafts–Harley index during the early eighteenth century. Thereafter, differences between the two series are relatively minor and the picture presented in Crafts and others (1989) is essentially endorsed.

Table 4.05 presents the annual growth rates of industrial output over the conventional sub-periods calculated using both the raw annual data and 10-year averages, together with the Crafts–Harley estimates for comparison. Industrial output growth doubled after 1760 and doubled again after 1780, when it was running at over 2.0 per cent a year. A further acceleration to over 2.5 per cent occurred after 1800 and from 1830 until 1870 growth approached 3.0 per cent. Metals and mining consistently outpaced all other industries: iron led the way, its output growing by an average of 4.0 per cent a year from 1800 to 1870, with tin, the most ancient of the major metal industries, expanding at less than half that rate (Tables 4.02 and 4.03). The textiles sector performed at close to the national average of 2.5 per cent, as did the building industry, whose outputs were in high demand from expanding cities, factories and transport networks. Most other industries grew more slowly, especially the food-processing industries whose output increased at less than 1.3 per cent, reflecting, of course, the relatively inelastic demand for food.

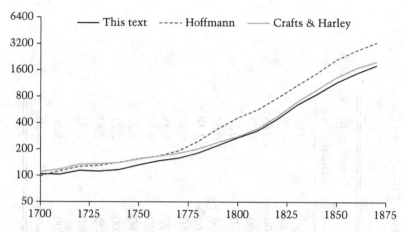

FIGURE 4.06 Alternative estimates of industrial output, Great Britain 1700–1870 (averages per decade, log scale, 1700 = 100). *Sources:* Crafts and Harley (1992); Hoffmann (1955); Appendix 5.3.

None of these growth rates are particularly remarkable by modern standards of industrial growth but in comparison with the preceding five centuries – when the fastest growth was the 2.5 per cent achieved by iron production during the second half of the sixteenth century – they were unprecedented. In fact, as Nef (1934) understood, the Elizabethan age was the precursor of the industrial revolution, insofar as demographic and industrial growth proceeded concurrently, with the latter outpacing the former for much of the time. Adoption of new technology and forms of business organisation helped the metals and mining industries outperform the older-established wool-textile industry, as did new novelty manufactures catering for niche markets such as printed books (Table 4.02). It is also undeniable that both eras far outshone the altogether more modest industrial achievements of the later middle ages, when there was little sign that England would one day become the workshop of the world.

4.3   SERVICE-SECTOR OUTPUT

The service sector has received much less attention from economic historians than agriculture and industry. Consequently, the approach

Table 4.05 Annual growth rates of industrial production, England 1270–1700 and Great Britain 1700–1870 (%)

Period	Crafts–Harley (%)	Present estimates, annual data (%)	Period	Present estimates, decadal data (%)
			1270s–1300s	0.05
			1300s–1340s	0.26
			1340s–1400s	–0.66
			1400s–1450s	–0.27
			1450s–1480s	0.32
			1480s–1553–9	0.61
			1553–9–1600s	1.12
			1600s–1650s	0.35
			1650s–1690s	0.89
1700–1760	0.71	0.49	1700s–1760s	0.58
1760–1780	1.29	1.00	1760s–1780s	1.04
1780–1801	1.96	2.18	1780s–1800s	2.01
1801–1830	2.78	2.59	1800s–1830s	2.87
1830–1870	3.06	3.01	1830s–1860s	2.91
1700–1830	1.39	1.33	1270s–1700	0.30
1700–1870	1.78	1.72	1700–1860s	1.93

Sources: See text; Crafts (1985: 32); Crafts and Harley (1992: 715).

pioneered by Deane and Cole (1967) to estimate service-sector output in eighteenth-century Britain is followed here, albeit with some modifications which have now become standard in historical national accounting. Further, whereas Deane and Cole assumed that commerce grew in line with industry, in this study use has been made of volume indicators of commercial activity in accordance with Feinstein's (1972) work on the United Kingdom from the mid-nineteenth century. The well-documented revenues of central government, quantified by the European State Finance Database, play an important role in quantifying the outputs of certain parts of the service sector, while others have been inferred from trends in population. The work of Crafts (1985) means that estimation is on firmer ground after 1700 than before. As suggested by Deane and Cole, services are broken down into government services, commercial and financial services, and domestic and personal services (including housing). These sub-sectors are then combined into an overall master index of service-sector output (Figure 4.07) using the weights for 1700 and 1841 given in Table 4.06, derived, respectively, from Crafts (1985: 16) and Horrell and others (1994: 547).

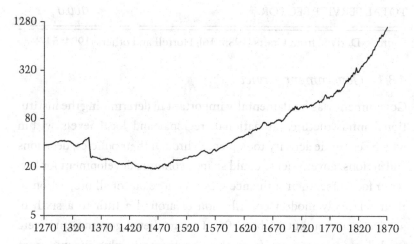

FIGURE 4.07 Service-sector output, England 1270–1700 and Great Britain 1700–1870 (1700 = 100, log scale). *Source:* Appendix 5.3.

Table 4.06 *Service-sector output weights for England in 1700 and Great Britain in 1841*

		Output share%
England, 1700		
Government		16.2
Commerce		37.2
International trade and transport	10.7	
Domestic trade and transport	21.5	
Finance	5.0	37.2
Housing and domestic services		46.6
TOTAL SERVICE SECTOR		100.0
Great Britain, 1841		
Public administration and defence		5.6
Commerce		62.3
Transport	10.3	
Distribution	33.3	
Finance	5.0	
Other commerce	13.7	62.3
Housing		17.6
Domestic services		14.5
TOTAL SERVICE SECTOR		100.0

Sources: Derived from Crafts (1985: 16); Horrell and others (1994: 547).

4.3.1 Government services

Government was fundamentally important in determining the institutional infrastructures at national, regional and local levels within which economic activity took place. Through their policies, decisions and actions, governments could shape economic development for better or for worse; their influence was therefore out of all proportion to their relatively modest contribution of around a fifth to a sixth of service-sector output (Table 4.06). Late-medieval governments were funded out of revenues from the Crown estate plus income from regalian rights and direct and indirect taxes. Over time the balance between these sources of income shifted as the range of tax revenues widened and their relative value rose. Since taxes were in effect granted by parliament, the more financially dependent government became upon taxation the more important became the role of parliament.

Here, it is assumed that the output of government services was proportionate to the combined value of all revenues received. In the case of England and, later, Britain, these are exceptionally well recorded and have been the subject of systematic investigation. In particular, O'Brien and Hunt (1999) have calculated real government revenue for the entire period from 1270 to 1700 and this is available from the European State Finance Database (www.le.ac.uk/hi/bon/ESF DB/frameset.html). For England during the period before 1700, a 10-year moving average of these revenues is used to derive the index of the output of government services. For Britain after 1700, output of government services is assumed to have risen in line with civil government and defence expenditure given by Mitchell (1988: 578–80, 587–8), deflated using the Schumpeter–Gilboy and Rousseaux price indices also from Mitchell (1988: 719–23). Both output series are summarised in Table 4.07 and plotted in Figure 4.08.

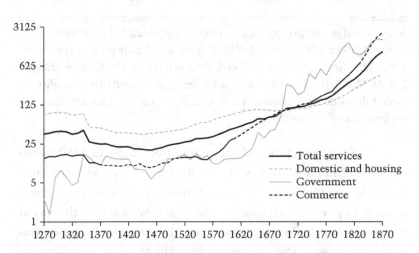

FIGURE 4.08 Service-sector output by major sub-sector, England 1270–1700 and Great Britain 1700–1870 (1700 = 100, log scale). *Source:* See notes to Table 4.07.

Table 4.07 *Output of key service sectors, England 1270–1700 and Great Britain 1700–1870 (1700 = 100)*

| Decade | Government services | Commercial services | | Housing and domestic services | Total services |
		Trade and transport	Finance		
1270s	3	4	73	85	41
1300s	8	6	77	91	46
1350s	14	5	48	51	30
1400s	12	5	36	40	24
1450s	8	5	33	37	21
1500s	14	8	39	43	27
1550s	14	10	28	60	34
1600s	14	25	47	82	49
1650s	40	51	101	103	77
1700	100	100	100	100	100
1750s	363	144	261	120	127
1800s	1,311	319	808	180	244
1850s	1,626	1,473	2,066	353	706
1860s	1,889	2,003	2,402	400	890

Sources and notes: Government services: O'Brien and Hunt (1999); Mitchell (1988: 578–80, 587–8, 719–23); trade and transport: see notes to Table 4.08; finance: Mayhew (2009); Pressnell (1956: 11); Pearson (2004: 374–5); Mitchell (1988: 658, 665); total services: derived using weights from Table 4.06. See Sections 4.3.1, 4.3.2, 4.3.3 and 4.3.4 for a fuller explanation of the methods.

With the exception of the period from 1350 to 1450, when revenues from the Crown estate declined and there was little direct taxation, government revenues and therefore government services displayed a powerful tendency to rise. This was especially the case at times of national emergency and above all whenever the nation was mobilised for war. The campaigns waged by the first three Edwards (r. 1272–1377) in Wales, Scotland, Ireland and France therefore generated a dramatic upsurge in government revenues and concomitant service provision. Between 1270 and 1350 government services grew by almost 2 per cent a year, making this one of the few dynamic sectors within a generally undynamic economy. Government service provision did not breach this early-fourteenth-century peak of activity until the seventeenth century. Change was prompted by the rise of the mercantilist state during the seventeenth century and emergence of Britain as a major colonial, commercial and military power during the eighteenth century. From the accession of James I (VI of Scotland) in 1603 until 1815, when the Napoleonic Wars finally ended, government revenues and services grew at almost 2.5 per cent a year.

Escalating European inter-state conflict played a major part in driving this remarkable growth of British government services, as the state expanded in order to respond to the military exigencies of the day. Advances in military tactics and technology lent momentum to this process, as each new episode of war made ever-greater demands upon resources. This gave government service provision a sharply cyclical character, as it expanded during bouts of warfare and contracted during intervals of peace. The massive and prolonged demands of the French Revolutionary and Napoleonic Wars marked the culmination of these developments when the entire British state was mobilised to sustain a pan-continental war lasting from 1792 to 1815. From 1750 to 1815 government services grew, on average, at over 3 per cent a year. The Allied victory at Waterloo brought a long period of belligerence to a close and ushered in a prolonged peace when government revenues and services subsided and fluctuated around a relatively stable level. From 1815, therefore, government ceased to be a source of growth within the service sector.

4.3.2 Commercial and financial services

4.3.2.1 Trade and transport

By its nature, the country's external trade and transport is more visible than its internal trade and transport. For England before 1700, Carus-Wilson and Coleman (1963) provide export-volume data on an annual basis for wool and cloth from all major English ports between 1280 and 1543, with the national totals conveniently summarised in Mitchell (1988: 358–9). These two commodities accounted for 86.6 per cent of the value of total exports in 1565 and have been aggregated into an index of export volumes using weights of 90 per cent for cloth and 10 per cent for wool, derived from Stone (1949: 37). The series has been extrapolated over the period 1270–1280 using data on domestic wool production, assuming that the export shares of wool and cloth were the same as those in the 1280s. After 1500, data on short-cloth exports through London until 1640 are available from Fisher (1940: 96, 1950: 153). London's over-whelming dominance of that trade is demonstrated for the sixteenth century by Carus-Wilson and Coleman (1963) and for the seventeenth century by Davis (1954: 164–5). Log-linear interpolation has been used to derive values for missing years. After 1640 there is an unfortunate gap in the trade data until new official figures start in 1697. For the period 1570–1700 data are, however, available for the English merchant-shipping tonnage from Davis (1962) and these have been used to interpolate the missing trade values for the years 1640–97 based upon the relationship between the two series during the overlap period 1570–1640. These data also make it possible to capture both the volatility of international commerce and the grow-ing share of that commerce being shipped by English merchants with the encouragement of mercantilist governments (Supple, 1964; Davis, 1973: 46–9).

The share of international trade handled by English merchants and shipped in English-owned ships obviously made a significant difference to the value of this service-sector activity. So, too, did the distances travelled by those exports and the ships that carried them. As long as trade remained largely internal to Europe, the dis-tances goods travelled were not great. That changed in the 1490s with discovery of the Americas and the opening of a direct maritime route round Africa to India, the Far East and China. The distances on these inter-continental routes dwarfed those on intra-European routes and

greatly gained in relative importance over time, with the establishment of international trading companies, foreign trading bases, and,
in the case of the Caribbean and North America, overseas colonies.
For the mid-seventeenth century, Davis (1954: 164–5) provides a
regional breakdown of export destinations and these have been
adjusted to a pre-1500 pattern by eliminating the new trade routes
to Africa, Asia and the Americas. The final pre-1700 index of international trade and transport thereby takes account of the volume of
exports, the growth of English merchant-shipping tonnage and the
distances that goods travelled. Unsurprisingly, the results reveal
little trend growth before the sixteenth century, then a modest step
gain until sustained growth took hold in the second half of the
sixteenth century and continued with little significant loss of
momentum, at an average rate of 1.3 per cent per year, down to the
end of the seventeenth century. By then international trade and
transport had acquired a volume unimaginable in the geographically
circumscribed world of the fourteenth century, when native merchants first began to capture a substantial share of the nation's overseas trade.

Holland, by 1700, was Europe's leading maritime economy and
overseas trade and transport accounted for almost a quarter of Dutch
GDP. The corresponding proportion in England was around a tenth.
Its importance to the country's subsequent economic development
lay less in the income that it generated than in the stimulus it gave to
development of the public and private institutions necessary to sustain commercial growth. States were potentially predatory upon
mercantile profits but in England the ascendancy won by
Parliament over the Crown in the Civil War of 1642–51 and endorsed
by the constitutional revolution of 1688 constrained the ability of the
Crown to act arbitrarily and exploitatively (North and Weingast,
1989; Acemoglu and others, 2005). Instead, with the sanction of
parliament, free enterprise and private property were allowed to
flourish, with the bulk of the profits from trade accruing to those
who had shouldered the risks and invested in it. Post-Civil War

parliaments responded to the influential mercantile lobby and actively championed English commerce, enacting legislation that discriminated in favour of English merchants, shippers and crews and waging war against the commercially dominant Dutch. These protectionist measures may have denied the country the advantages of free trade but they were beneficial in other ways and thereby boosted both domestic and international commerce. Defended by a dominant parliament and secure in legal protection of their assets and property rights, merchant fortunes accumulated, banking houses were established, business activity expanded and capital investment rose. Herein lay the real importance of international trade, for, as O'Brien (1982) has emphasised, its direct contribution to GDP was too small to have had a decisive impact upon the country's economic development. Rather, it helped bring into being the institutional environment within which industry and trade, both internal and external, were able to flourish. This was achieved with the full, and occasionally over zealous, cooperation of the Protestant state. These issues will be discussed further in Chapter 10, in the context of Britain's rise to global economic dominance.

By 1700 Dutch overseas trade exceeded the value of its domestic trade by a ratio of five to two: in England, in contrast, internal trade was the more valuable by a ratio of two to one (Table 4.06). The country was economically more self-sufficient than Holland and its greater size and far more substantial internal market meant that much traded merchandise never left the country. Although the scale of this internal trade is beyond doubt, its measurement is another matter and the clearest indicators of its volume are indirect. Exchange of agricultural and industrial products loomed especially large in domestic trade, as can be inferred from the real output data on agriculture and industry presented in Chapter 3 and Section 4.2 of the current chapter (using the sectoral weights that will be presented in Chapter 5). Changes in the marketed shares of these outputs are captured by the cumulative number of new markets established in the period 1300–1490 taken from Letters (2005) and the growth of the urban share of the population from 1490 to 1700 given in Table 4.04.

The pre-1700 domestic trade and transport series is shown in Table 4.08. From its late-medieval peak in the second quarter of the fourteenth century, the output of domestic trade and transport drifted steadily down until it had reduced to two-thirds of its former level in the third quarter of the fifteenth century. In this period levels of population and agricultural and industrial production were all at their lowest ebb and the stickiness of the urbanisation ratio indicates the absence of commercial dynamism within the economy (Rigby, 2010). Then, in the final decades of the fifteenth century, the tempo of domestic trade and transport quickened, to such an extent that by the 1540s their volume had doubled. Significantly, this upturn began more than half a century before the corresponding upturn in international trade and transport (Table 4.08). From the mid-sixteenth century, however, both were growing together, with domestic trade and transport advancing at the marginally faster rate of 1.7 per cent a year, as it benefited from mutually reinforcing processes of economic specialisation and urban growth and differentiation (Table 4.08). For the next 150 years, international and domestic trade and transport together expanded by an impressive 1.2 per cent a year and by over 1.8 per cent during the second half of the sixteenth century. Moreover, after 1650, when the population ceased to grow, both continued to increase at over 1.3 per cent a year as mercantilist policies pursued by government favoured native merchants and shippers relative to their continental competitors. This onward march of trade and transport is also evidence of increasing dependency upon market exchange.

After 1700, partly due to the dictates of the available data, this bipartite division between international and domestic trade and transport is abandoned. Instead, a distinction is drawn between transport and distribution (Table 4.08). The transport index comprises an unweighted average of shipping tonnage from Mitchell (1988: 534), the length of railways from Mitchell (1988: 541), total investment in

Table 4.08 *Output of trade and transport service sub-sectors, England 1270–1700 and Great Britain 1700–1870 (1700 = 100)*

Decade	Overseas trade and transport	Domestic trade and transport	Transport	Distribution	Other commerce
1270s	8.9	2.4			
1300s	13.1	3.1			
1350s	11.6	2.8			
1400s	12.4	2.7			
1450s	13.0	2.4			
1500s	22.1	3.2			
1550s	20.0	6.3			
1600s	32.5	22.2			
1650s	57.5	48.7			
1700	100.0	100.0	100.0	100.0	100.0
1750s			142.1	145.7	132.3
1800s			237.7	376.3	271.3
1850s			821.7	1,925.4	1,162.7
1860s			1,110.2	2,723.6	1,480.1

Sources and notes: Overseas trade and transport: Mitchell (1988: 358–9); Stone (1949: 37); Fisher (1940: 96; 1950: 153); Davis (1954: 164–5; 1962); domestic trade and transport: agricultural output from Chapter 3 and industrial output from Section 4.2, combined with sectoral weights presented in Chapter 5, and adjusted in line with the share of output marketed, captured by an index of the cumulative number of new markets from Letters (2005) for the period before 1490 and the growth of the urban share of the population after 1490, taken from Table 4.04; transport: Mitchell (1988: 534, 541); Ginarlis and Pollard (1988: 217–19); Bogart (2005: 487); distribution: foreign trade from Mitchell (1988) and industrial production from Section 4.2; other commerce: assumed to grow in line with industrial production from Section 4.2. See Section 4.3.2.1 for a fuller explanation of the methods.

waterways and roads from Ginarlis and Pollard (1988: 217–19) and the number of weekly passenger road services from Bogart (2005: 487). Distribution is a weighted average of the growth of foreign trade from Mitchell (1988) and industry from Section 4.2 of this chapter, with a 60 per cent weight for foreign trade, although varying the weights would make little difference because both series grew at similar rates. All other commerce is assumed to have grown in line with industry, which was Deane and Cole's (1967) assumption for commerce in the eighteenth century. As Table 4.08 shows, distribution consistently grew more rapidly than transport and other commerce and was particularly dynamic during the nineteenth century.

Combining international and domestic trade and transport from before 1700 with transport, distribution and other commerce from after 1700 yields a single trade and transport index spanning the entire period 1270–1870 (Table 4.07 and Figure 4.09). This highlights the broad trends already identified. Growth remained quite strongly positive in the final years of the thirteenth century, at the tail end of the high-medieval commercial revolution. Negative or zero growth then prevailed until the mid-fifteenth century, when aggregate economic activity sank to its

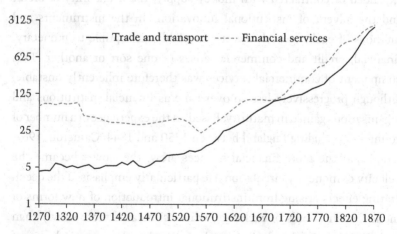

FIGURE 4.09 Output of commercial services, England 1270–1700 and Great Britain 1700–1870 (averages per decade, 1700 = 100, log scale). *Source:* See notes to Table 4.07.

lowest ebb. Then, as economic expansion gathered momentum, trade and transport emerged as one of the most dynamic sectors of the economy, growing at an annual average of 1.2 per cent until the end of the seventeenth century. The first half of the eighteenth century brought a slowdown but the second half a further acceleration. By the first half of the nineteenth century trade and transport were growing at over 3 per cent a year, as improvements to roads, waterways and canals lowered unit transport costs and the ending of European hostilities in 1815 ushered in a great revival of international trade.

4.3.2.2   Financial services

Trade, transport and other commerce had contributed a third of total service-sector output in 1700, rising to over half by 1841 (Table 4.06). Financial services, in contrast, accounted for just 5 per cent at both dates, equivalent to around 1.7 per cent of GDP. This is the share of finance in GDP in 1907, which is the first benchmark year for which current-price sectoral shares are available for Britain with a separate enumeration of finance (Feinstein, 1972: 208). It is likely that this sector's share was even less in the financially less-developed world of the later middle ages. Over the centuries financial sector output expanded or contracted with money supply, the availability of credit and the advent of institutional innovations in the instruments and methods of exchange. Always it was highly susceptible to monetary, financial, credit and commercial crises of one sort or another. This component of commercial services was therefore inherently unstable, although progressively less so over time as financial institutions and organisations gained in maturity. Based on the experience of a number of countries, including England between 1750 and 1844, Cameron (1967) noted that the more financial services grew, the slower became the velocity of monetary circulation. He particularly emphasised the decelerating effects arising from institutional introduction of new forms of money, such as bills of exchange, which circulated more slowly than cash. This implies that declining velocity can be taken as an indicator of the rise of a more sophisticated financial-services sector.

Mayhew (1995b) extended Cameron's analysis of the velocity of circulation back to 1300 and confirmed that velocity underwent a long-run decline during the process of economic development. He also identified a marked but temporary reversal in that relationship during the Tudor debasement of the mid-sixteenth century. Mayhew (2009) provides an update to his earlier study, incorporating revised money-supply data from Allen (2001). The inverse of these revised calculations of the velocity of circulation has been converted into an index of financial service-sector activity using population as a scaling factor. The resultant estimates of financial service activity consequently echo the ebb and flow of population, contracting by 0.56 per cent a year from 1300 until the mid-fifteenth century, then recovering at over 0.3 per cent until thrown dramatically off course by the Tudor debasement of the mid-sixteenth century. Re-establishment of currency stability brought renewed and strengthened financial-services growth at an annual 1.0–1.5 per cent until the mid-seventeenth century, when this phase of financial expansion effectively ceased (Figure 4.09). From this point the financial-services index is based on an unweighted average of the number of country banks from Pressnell (1956: 11) and Pearson's (2004: 374–5) fire-insurance series, interpolated using the drawing accounts of the Bank of England from Mitchell (1988: 658, 665). On the evidence of these series, growth resumed in the eighteenth century and persisted at a steady 2 per cent a year for the next 150 years, as the British financial-services sector emerged as a leading protagonist in the general national and international expansion of trade and commerce. In fact, for much of the eighteenth century, partly due to an element of catch-up and as the fiscal state came into being (North and Weingast, 1989), it appears to have outperformed most other branches of commerce (Figure 4.09 and Table 4.07).

By the nineteenth century the commercial sector as a whole had become firmly established as the most dynamic branch of service-sector activity (Figure 4.08). Whereas individual industries occasionally grew faster, what was notable about the growth of commercial services is that moderate rates of growth had been continuously sustained since the late fifteenth century (Figure 4.09). Since commercial services bore upon all other areas of market-based economic activity, the cumulative effect of such uninterrupted growth over the course of 400 years was to greatly modify the structure and amplify the volume of economic activity.

4.3.3   Housing and domestic services

Housing and domestic services always formed a large part of service-sector output, amounting to almost half in 1700 and a third in 1841 (Table 4.06). Domestic services were labour-intensive tasks, as yet little affected by the advance of technology, whose output was powerfully influenced by the size of the population demanding these services and the availability of labour to supply them. Accordingly, both Deane and Cole (1967) and Crafts (1985) assumed that their output closely tracked population. On the reasonable assumption that productivity improvements were insignificant in this part of the service sector, so that output can be tracked by the labour input, the same procedure has been followed here. This sector also includes the flow of rental services from housing. For the period before 1700, this is also assumed to move in line with population. For the period after 1700, it is inferred from Feinstein's (1988: 389) index of the stock of housing capital at constant prices interpolated using population. Because Feinstein's housing-stock series has a long-run unit elasticity with respect to population, this series moves closely in line with population over the long run as well as the short run.

These assumptions inevitably produce a relatively stable path for output of housing and domestic services, which deviates little from the trend in population (Table 4.07), as is consistent with most assessments of this sector at other times and in other places. Table 4.07 and Figure 4.08 show that, as is to have been expected, both following the Black Death and again during the second half of the seventeenth century, when the population declined the aggregate output of housing and domestic services also contracted. At other times their output displayed modest rates of growth which only exceeded 1 per cent a year during the first half of the nineteenth century when demographic growth rates were at their peak. This was therefore one of the least dynamic components of economic activity and one of the last to benefit from advances in mechanisation and thereby register significant gains in productivity. It was, however, one of the most stable of all sources of employment.

4.3.4 Aggregate service-sector output

Figure 4.07 plots the master index of aggregate service-sector output derived from the component series for commerce, housing and domestic services and government using the weights set out in Table 4.06. Figure 4.08 plots these subsidiary series for England 1270–1700 and Britain 1700–1870. Corresponding service-sector growth rates are presented in Table 4.09, together with the Crafts–Harley estimates for the post-1700 period for comparison. The new growth-rate estimates are very close to the Crafts–Harley data over both the whole period 1700–1830 and the individual sub-periods, whether based on annual data or 10-year averages. The main difference is therefore the fact that the new index is available on an annual basis rather than just the small number of benchmark years provided by Crafts and Harley (1992).

The close correspondence between population and service-sector trends is immediately apparent. Thus, aggregate service-sector output grew with population to 1300, shrank in line with population to 1450, and then re-expanded with population to 1870. This is a function both of the labour-intensive character of most services and the use of population data to infer certain significant service-sector outputs. The only sustained and genuine deviation between the two trends was during the second half of the seventeenth century, when the population contracted slightly but service-sector output, driven forward by the momentum of vigorously expanding trade, transport and government, grew by a steady 0.5 per cent a year.

The service sector's growth resembled that of the population in a further striking respect: it was rarely rapid. Until the second half of the eighteenth century it never exceeded 1 per cent a year, and from 1450

Table 4.09 *Annual growth rates of service-sector output, England 1270–1700 and Great Britain 1700–1870 (%)*

Period	Crafts–Harley (%)	Present estimates, annual data (%)	Period	Present estimates, decadal data (%)
			1270s–1300s	0.39
			1300s–1340s	0.12
			1340s–1400s	-1.15
			1400s–1450s	-0.22
			1450s–1480s	0.30
			1480s–1553–9	0.48
			1553–9–1600s	0.82
			1600s–1650s	0.93
			1650s–1690s	0.56
1700–1760	0.74	0.73	1700s–1760s	0.58
1760–1780	0.77	0.67	1760s–1780s	0.87
1780–1801	1.31	1.41	1780s–1800s	1.89
1801–1830	1.68	1.79	1800s–1830s	1.67
1830–1870	–	2.57	1830s–1860s	2.70
1700–1830	1.05	1.08	1270s–1700	0.22
1700–1870	–	1.43	1700–1860s	1.39

Sources: See text; derived from Crafts (1985: 16–17, 32, 37); Crafts and Harley (1992: 715).

to 1750 averaged 0.6 per cent. It then accelerated to 1.6 per cent from 1750 to 1870 but within that period exceeded 2 per cent only relatively briefly during the first half of the nineteenth century (Figure 4.07). Growth achieved by some component sub-sectors could be more impressive: government services grew at a rate of 2.1 per cent during the first half of the seventeenth century and by 2.6 per cent throughout the eighteenth century, while trade and transport achieved 3.1 per cent growth during the first half of the nineteenth century (Figure 4.09). With the notable exception of government services, however, the fastest growth occurred relatively late. In housing and domestic services, the service sector also contained one of the least dynamic economic sectors of all. The scale and weight of this sector acted as a brake upon growth of the service sector as a whole and ensured that it played a relatively passive role in the story of Britain's lift-off to intensive economic growth. What mattered about the service sector was not the speed of its growth, which was never more than moderate, but the fact that from the late fifteenth century growth occurred more or less continuously. It was an economic tortoise and eventually it drew abreast of and then overtook the industrial hare.

4.4 CONCLUSIONS

The output estimates of industrial and service-sector production presented in this chapter are drawn mainly from the large secondary literature that has developed over more than a century of quantitative investigation by economic historians and, consequently, constitute the best that can be achieved on current knowledge. For Britain after 1700 they broadly affirm the estimates advanced by Crafts and Harley (1992) but do so on an annual basis. For England before 1700 the results are more tentative and highlight where further research is needed. In particular, input–output tables are required for benchmark years earlier than 1700, output series are needed for more industries (lead is an obvious lacuna), and several components of the service sector require far more explicit attention. Until such material is forthcoming reliance has to be placed upon the range of proxy measures presented in this chapter. The results obtained offer provisional chronologies of the two sectors that would eventually grow to dominate the British economy. Substantively, they lend support to the view that the British industrial revolution was long in gestation. The duration of that run-up is brought sharply into focus when, drawing upon the population estimates presented in Chapter 1, the outputs of both sectors and their respective growth rates are expressed per head (Tables 4.10 and 4.11).

Viewed in absolute terms, outputs of the industrial and service sectors achieved their late-medieval peaks at the opening of the fourteenth century and thereafter contracted by respectively a third and a half to their historical minima in the mid-fifteenth century (Table 4.10). Over the same period, however, the population, halved. Service output per head therefore marginally improved and industrial output per head made substantial gains (Table 4.11). This inverts the absolute chronology. For both sectors the lowest points in terms of output per head came around 1300, when many medieval economic historians agree the economy was experiencing considerable difficulties. Temporary high points then occurred in the early years of the fifteenth century, when the problems of income inequality and rural congestion had been much eased by the massive plague-induced reduction in population. In this specific historical context, and much as Bridbury (1962) surmised, the loss of numbers was more of a boon than a misfortune as far as the outputs per head of industry and services were concerned. Indeed, the second half of the fourteenth century stands out as something of a golden age for English industry, with a growth rate per head in excess of 1 per cent, as textile output per head doubled and a tin-mining boom caused mining output per head to quadruple (Table 4.10).

These advances were not maintained and output levels per head of both industry and services tended to sag during the middle years of the fifteenth century, when European commerce likewise sank to a temporal low. It was from this diminished and stagnant state, c.1450, that English industry began its subsequent rise, which in direct contrast to the situation before c.1330 involved the expansion of both

Table 4.10 *Annual growth rates and growth rates per head of the industrial and service sectors, England 1270–1700 and Great Britain 1700–1870 (1700 = 100)*

| | Levels (1700 = 100) | | | | Annual growth (%) | | | | |
| | | | | | Population | Industry | | Services | |
Year	Population	Industry	Services	Period	Absolute	Absolute	Per head	Absolute	Per head
1270	84	27	38	1270–1300	0.27	0.05	-0.22	0.39	0.12
1300	91	27	42	1300–1350	-0.52	-0.59	-0.07	-0.87	-0.35
1350	70	20	27	1350–1400	-1.06	-0.01	1.06	-0.44	0.63
1400	41	20	22	1400–1450	-0.21	-0.27	-0.06	-0.22	-0.02
1450	37	18	20	1450–1500	0.25	0.43	0.18	0.45	0.20
1500	42	22	25	1500–1550	0.65	0.68	0.04	0.48	-0.17
1550	58	31	31	1550–1600	0.62	1.00	0.38	0.74	0.12
1600	79	51	45	1600–1650	0.51	0.35	-0.16	0.90	0.38
1650	102	61	70	1650–1700	-0.04	1.01	1.05	0.71	0.75
1700	100	100	100	1700–1750	0.30	0.56	0.26	0.61	0.31
1750	116	132	135	1750–1800	0.77	1.45	0.68	1.32	0.55
1800	170	271	261	1800–1850	1.34	2.95	1.61	2.15	0.81

Table 4.10 (cont.)

| Year | Levels (1700 = 100) | | | Period | Annual growth (%) | | | | |
| | Population | Industry | Services | | Population | Industry | | Services | |
					Absolute	Absolute	Per head	Absolute	Per head
1850	331	1,163	754	1850–1870	1.54	3.01	1.47	1.96	0.43
1870	416	1,813	1,112						

Sources and notes: Population from Chapter 1; industrial and service-sector output from Sections 4.2 and 4.3, respectively; all total values are 10-year means except 1870.

Table 4.11 *Output per head of key industrial and service sectors, England 1270–1700 and Great Britain 1700–1870 (1300 = 100)*

Decade	Total population	Metals and mining (per head)	Textiles and leather (per head)	'Other' industries (per head)	Total industry (per head)	Trade and transport (per head)	Financial services (per head)	Housing and domestic services (per head)	Government services (per head)	Total services (per head)
1270s	92	ND	118	97	107	77	104	101	33	97
1300s	100	100	100	100	100	100	100	100	100	100
1350s	56	98	220	89	133	159	113	100	309	115
1400s	45	413	221	83	164	200	106	98	325	115
1450s	41	254	250	92	158	223	104	100	241	113
1500s	47	351	209	118	171	305	109	101	347	123
1550s	64	392	201	143	176	267	56	103	254	115
1600s	87	331	248	297	214	488	71	104	188	122
1650s	112	261	178	484	198	773	118	101	428	148
1700s	110	568	281	753	332	1,539	119	100	1,092	215
1750s	128	764	365	677	378	1,908	267	103	3,409	250
1800s	187	1,856	492	854	530	2,893	564	106	8,428	330
1850s	364	6,247	1,134	1,287	1,167	6,851	741	107	5,368	490
1860s	458	6,896	968	1,451	1,181	7,406	685	96	4,955	491

Sources and notes: Population from Chapter 1; industrial and service-sector outputs from Sections 4.2 and 4.3, respectively. ND, no data.

absolute output and output per head. This was a watershed development. Henceforth, gains in absolute output were accompanied and, to
a degree, underpinned by rising industrial output per head. There was
some loss of momentum in gains per head in the early seventeenth
century but this was offset by concurrent advances per head in the
service sector as it, too, embarked upon what proved to be an unstoppable upward course (Table 4.11).

Between 1450 and 1700 English industrial output grew more
than fivefold, while output per head doubled. This was largely the
result of a structural redistribution of labour from agriculture to industry, which will be discussed in Chapter 9, reinforced by adoption of
better technology, improved organisation and, possibly, greater industriousness. Output grew consistently faster than population throughout the sixteenth century, as metals and mining output fluctuated but
nevertheless held up well, textile production prospered, and the
Reformation boosted demand for printed books. This confirms Nef's
(1934) positive verdict on England's industrial performance during the
sixteenth century and the technological foundations then laid for later
industrial growth. That the gains in industrial output per head of the
era of late-medieval population decline were consolidated and maintained during this period of early modern population growth is especially noteworthy and raises intriguing questions as to why the
thirteenth-century economy had been so conspicuously less successful
at marrying the two developments.

Industrial advances were soon followed by corresponding commercial gains, as the trade and transport sector began the process of
expansion that would raise its output per head almost sixfold between
the 1550s and 1700 (Table 4.11). Sparked by the threat of military
invasion, towards the end of Elizabeth I's reign (r. 1558–1603) government services also began to grow apace, a process which once set in
train only ended with the defeat of Napoleon Bonaparte over two
centuries later. These dramatic new developments within the service
sector indicate that the technological achievements of early modern
industrial development rightly emphasised by Nef (1934) need to be

placed within the wider context of the vigorous commercial expansion occurring at the time and the growing power of the state. Within this institutional framework, feedbacks established between industry and commerce impelled England upon a path of Smithian growth, which neither the sharp financial setback arising from the mid-sixteenth century Tudor inflation, nor the return of population and resource problems in the early seventeenth century, nor the stagnation of population growth from the mid-seventeenth century proved capable of derailing.

Continuation of industrial and service-sector output growth after c.1650 in the absence of concurrent population growth was a novel development and, as a result, rates of growth per head turned sharply upwards to levels unmatched since the second half of the fourteenth century when the population had been in marked decline. Between 1650 and 1700 absolute output growth and output growth per head exceeded 0.7 per cent in the service sector and 1.0 per cent in the industrial sector. Trade and transport and government services continued to perform strongly, further highlighting the contribution of these vital sectors to the country's economic development. Meanwhile, most aspects of industrial output registered significant gains per head but none more so than metals and mining, whose output more than doubled (Table 4.11). The close coincidence at this time between commercial and industrial growth is striking and continued during the first half of the eighteenth century, when the rate of growth per head slowed in both sectors.

Within the expanded context of Great Britain rather than just England, growth of absolute output and output per head in the industrial and services sectors continued during the first half of the eighteenth century but at decelerating rates in the face of renewed population growth (Table 4.10). Tempo slowed rather than quickened as the industrial revolution approached. Government services maintained their onward march, especially following the 1688 Glorious Revolution and then union with Scotland in 1707, but expansion of trade and transport saw a marked loss of momentum. The commercial services sector would also have performed relatively poorly but for the spectacularly increased output of financial services following emergence of the fiscal state (North and Weingast, 1989). Within industry, metals and mining and textiles and leather all continued to make headway but other industries did not. In fact, industrial growth rates 1700–50 were less impressive than those of 1550–1600 when population had been rising even faster.

It is possible that processes of Smithian commercial growth were running into diminishing returns as the eighteenth century advanced. Moreover, for all the technological ingenuity of the age, there were limits to the productivity gains that could be achieved, either from further refinements to essentially handicraft methods of production, or from exploitation of deeper, remoter or just poorer-quality seams of tin, lead, iron and coal. The quickening of population growth from mid-century therefore constituted a major challenge to the established economic order. It was not until the final quarter of the eighteenth century that it was overcome by an acceleration of industrial and service-sector growth rates and not until the opening quarter of the nineteenth century that the growth rates per head of the second half of the seventeenth century were significantly bettered (Table 4.10). Yet even then, many lesser branches of the industrial sector and traditional components of the service sector remained little touched by change and, insofar as they grew, did so at essentially pre-industrial rates. During this critical period of industrial revolution it was the metals and mining sector that expanded most rapidly, followed successively by trade and transport, textiles, financial services and 'other' industries. Plainly, as had long been the case, interactions between these industrial and service sub-sectors were mutually reinforcing.

Breakthrough to industrial revolution in the early nineteenth century was the last of a succession of achievements by the industrial and service sectors over the previous five centuries. The first was the dramatic elevation of industrial output per head during the fourteenth century; the second, the consolidation of those gains during the sixteenth century; the third, the fusion of industrial and commercial growth from the late sixteenth century; and the fourth the growing global reach of British trade and industry in the late seventeenth century. Each set the economy on a trajectory that consolidated the gains that had gone before and progressively enhanced the structural importance of these two sectors, thereby raising the likelihood that further positive developments would occur. A fitful but nonetheless real process of economic growth starting from a remarkably early date is implicit in these developments. Its cumulative effect was to make the transformative and self-sustaining growth of the industrial revolution possible.

APPENDIX 4.1
New series in the industrial production index, 1700–1870

The basic data were obtained from Hoffmann (1955), but with the following modifications:

MINING

Coal: Pollard's (1980) decadal estimates, interpolated using the Hoffmann series.

METALS

Iron, steel and machine building: Hoffmann's series is replaced for the period before 1839 using bar-iron output from King (2005): the yearly data can be downloaded from the Economic History Society website at www.ehs.org.uk/ehs/Datasets/datasets.asp.

Shipbuilding: Gross capital formation in ships from Feinstein (1988: 446), interpolated using the Hoffmann series.

TEXTILES

Silk thread and goods: Hoffmann's series is extended back in time using reported imports of raw, thrown and waste silk for 1700–1825 from Mitchell (1988: 343).

Linen yarn and cloth: Hoffmann's series is extended back in time using linen-yarn imports from Schumpeter (1960: 52).

Leather: Hoffmann's series is extended back in time from 1801 to 1722 using an index of hides and skins charged with duty from Mitchell (1988: 416).

FOOD, DRINK AND TOBACCO

Beer: Prior to 1787, Hoffmann's series is extended back in time using an index of small, strong, and table beer charged with duty from Mitchell (1988: 404–5).

Tobacco products: Hoffmann's series is extended back in time to 1700 using an index of the value of imported tobacco at official prices from Mitchell (1988: 462–3).

OTHER MANUFACTURING

Paper: Paper charged with duty is from Mitchell (1988: 413).

Printed matter: An index of new English-language book titles (1700–1800) is from the British Library's *English short-title catalogue* (http://estc.bl.uk/F/?func=file&file_name=login-bl-list) (note: this was replaced in January 2012 by a new catalogue *Explore the British Library*' (http://explore.bl.uk/primo_library/libweb/action/search.do?vid=BLVU1).

Soap and candles: Prior to 1821, separate series for soap and tallow candles charged with duty are available back to 1713 and 1711 from Mitchell (1988: 412, 415).

CONSTRUCTION

Building: The Hoffmann series is replaced with a constant-price series of total buildings and works from Feinstein (1988: 446), available from 1761 but with gaps interpolated using timber imports from Mitchell (1988: 462).

5   GDP and GDP per head

This chapter is concerned with the estimation of real GDP per head. Today, the United Nations, World Bank and several other international organisations publish estimates of GDP per head for most of the world's economies, ranking them in wealth and identifying the most advanced and least developed among them. The difference between the richest and poorest nations is now of the order of two-hundred-fold, whereas until the industrial revolution transformed productivity levels it was rarely more than fivefold. Modern economic growth can be fast and a dozen countries currently have reported growth rates of GDP per head in the range 10–20 per cent; it can also be negative and a dozen others, mostly already poor, have shrinking economies and declining GDP per head. Whereas there are plenty of historical precedents for such negative growth, there are none for such rapid growth, since the highest performing pre-modern economies rarely if ever achieved positive growth rates in excess of 2 or 3 per cent a year and were doing exceptionally well to maintain growth of 0.5 per cent or more for any sustained period of time. In fact, historically it is often presumed that in most countries for long periods there was next to no economic growth at all. This was because economic expansion was always liable to set in train and eventually be outpaced by population growth.

It was the tension between economic and biological reproduction that preoccupied T. R. Malthus, David Ricardo and other classical economists whose pessimistic musings on the potential for unlimited expansion led economics to be dubbed the 'dismal science'. In their day, self-sustaining modern economic growth with its capacity to stay ahead of fast population growth had barely arrived. Its conception was

187

unplanned, gestation long and successful delivery never assured, although ultimately transformative in its consequences. Among European economies, Italy and Flanders showed early promise of achieving a breakthrough but failed to deliver, Holland then overtook both but proved unable to maintain its momentum, and it was left to late-developer Britain to become the first to make the full transition to industrial revolution, closely followed by several of its most immediate European neighbours. Tracing the origins, charting the course and explaining when, how and why Britain became the world's first industrial nation have been key subjects of historical enquiry ever since.

Estimating GDP per head in an age of official statistics is one thing; doing so for historical periods with few if any such data sources is quite another. Nevertheless, it is the task attempted here. Its calculation requires estimates of total population, the subject of Chapter 1, and of real GDP. The basic building blocks of the real GDP series comprise the real value-added output series for the three core economic sectors of agriculture, established from mostly primary historical evidence in Chapter 3, and industry and services, as constructed from largely secondary sources in Chapter 4. Splicing them together into a total real output series entails establishing their changing relative importance over time. For that reason Section 5.2 of this chapter is devoted to the derivation of an appropriate set of sectoral weights based upon current-price data and a detailed input–output table for 1841. The weighted sum of real agricultural, industrial and service-sector output then gives the estimates of real GDP presented in Section 5.3. Whether people were experiencing an actual improvement in their economic situation nevertheless hinges upon whether economic output was expanding, or contracting, at a faster or slower rate than population. Dividing the estimates of real GDP by the estimates of total population presented in Chapter 1 thus gives the estimates of real GDP per head presented in Section 5.4. The result encapsulates all the data, assumptions and estimates set out in Part I of this book and constitutes the best currently available estimate of the performance of the English economy from 1270 to 1700 and the British economy from 1700 to

1870. Section 5.5 then outlines some of the ways in which its credibility will be tested in Part II of this book and highlights a few of the intriguing questions thereby raised about the nature and explanation of economic growth from the thirteenth to the nineteenth centuries.

5.2 SECTORAL SHARES OF GDP

To aggregate the separate real output series for agriculture, industry and services into a single value-added output series for the national economy as a whole requires establishing an appropriate set of sectoral weights which capture the changing structure of the economy. The three components of this task are, first, the real value-added output series of agriculture, industry and services from Chapters 3 and 4; second, nominal or current-price output series for each of those sectors (Section 5.2); and, third, the nominal input–output table for 1841 (see Table 5.01 below) reconstructed by Horrell and others (1994).

5.2.1 Sectoral price indices

Figure 5.01 presents sectoral price indices for agriculture, industry and services. These have been constructed from the array of price series for individual commodities listed in Appendix 5.1, combined using the

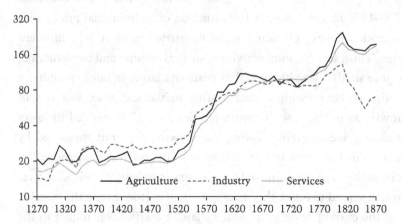

FIGURE 5.01 Sectoral price indices, England 1270–1700 and Great Britain 1700–1870 (averages per decade, 1700 = 100, log scale). *Sources:* see Appendix 5.1.

methods and sub-sector weightings given in Appendix 5.2. With the exception of prices of hides and rye taken, respectively, from Thorold Rogers (1866–1902) and Farmer (1988, 1991), the agricultural price data are those assembled by Clark (2004) and discussed already in Chapter 3.5. Industrial prices are similarly taken from Clark (2006), Beveridge (1939) and Thorold Rogers (1866–1902). There are no corresponding price series for the service sector. Instead, the weighted average of the agricultural and industrial price indices is used as a proxy for the commercial sub-sector before 1700 augmented by some additional price series for finance and transport thereafter. Further, the prices of the labour-intensive domestic and government services are measured, respectively, by Clark's (2006) unskilled and skilled urban wage rates, and the price of housing services is tracked using Clark's (2006) rent series.

Appendix 5.2 outlines the detailed procedures used to construct the three sectoral price indices. Construction of the agricultural price index follows the known current-price shares of arable and livestock commodities summarised in Table 3.17. Derivation of the service-sector price index is also relatively straightforward due to the limited number of price series for this sector: the relevant sub-sector weights for the period 1270–1700 are given in Table A5.2.5 and those for 1700–1870 in Table A5.2.6. Construction of an industrial price index presents a greater challenge since industries grew at very different rates. Thus, fast-growing activities, such as mining and construction, require smaller weights in earlier years and larger in later, in contrast to the slower-growing manufacturing industries. Also, fast output growth, as in the case of cotton textiles after 1700, tended to lower product prices thereby slowing the growth of output measured by value added at current prices. Cotton's success was also gained, in part, at the expense of the older wool-textile industries, whose slower growth served to offset the faster growth of cotton: hence the paradox that the current-price value-added share of textiles was higher in the first half of the eighteenth century than in the nineteenth century. Appendices A5.2.2 and A5.2.3 set out the stages involved in allocating appropriate value-added output shares to individual industries for the periods 1270–1700 and 1700–1870. Tables A5.2.1 and A5.2.3 present the weights allocated to the main industrial sub-sectors, for the six sub-periods 1270–1402, 1402–1582, 1582–1700, 1700–1740, 1740–1770 and 1770–1870, while Tables A5.2.2 and A5.2.4 specify the corresponding output shares of individual industrial commodities.

As will be observed from Figure 5.01, until the nineteenth century all three sectoral price series chart a broadly similar long-run course as a result of changes in the overall price level. This remained essentially trendless throughout the later middle ages, although with considerable volatility from the 1270s to 1370s. Notable short-term deviations included the pronounced inflation that accompanied the agrarian crisis of 1315–22, the sharp deflation that followed outbreak of the Hundred Years War in 1336 and culminated with the credit crunch and financial crisis of 1340–1, and the abrupt inflation that followed the Black Death of 1348–9, when the sudden halving of population effectively doubled coin supply per head. By the final decades of the fourteenth century, however, most of these perturbations had passed and a period of greater price stability prevailed. Prices sagged somewhat during the demographic lull of the mid-fifteenth century, with its accompanying bullion famine and downturn in international commercial activity, but compared to subsequent developments impact of this deflationary episode was slight. In fact, the magnitude of none of these late-medieval price variations bear comparison with those that came later.

Between 1270 and 1870 no change in prices was greater than that set in train by injection of New World silver into the European monetary system after c.1520 (Figure 5.01). In England the price revolution that resulted quadrupled the levels of all three price series between the 1520s and 1620s. A degree of monetary stability was not restored until the second quarter of the seventeenth century (Ramsey, 1971). Stability continued for the next hundred years until, from the mid-eighteenth century, prices began to increase again. The final years of that century brought a steeper price inflation than anything experienced since the mid-sixteenth century, as escalating warfare on land

and sea disrupted commerce and limited British access to continental markets and food and raw-material supplies. Outbreak of war with France in 1792 precipitated an immediate sharp rise in agricultural and service-sector prices and prolongation of that war led them to remain at a much-inflated level until the final defeat of Napoleon in 1815. In 1797 the Bank of England was obliged to suspend convertibility but in 1821 it restored sterling to its pre-war parity with gold. Meanwhile, with the restoration of peace, agricultural and service-sector prices had subsided from their wartime peak but remained above their pre-war level (Figure 5.01). On this occasion, however, they were offset by falling industrial prices delivered by the gathering pace of the industrial revolution. The scale of these variations highlights the need to take account of relative prices and control for changes in the overall price level in all estimates of national income.

5.2.2 Relative prices

It will be plain from Figure 5.01 that the relative levels of the three sectoral price indices varied over time. The relationship between agricultural and industrial prices is particularly revealing. The terms of trade plainly favoured agriculture from the 1270s to 1340s, when industrial output per head was at its lowest ebb (Table 4.10) and demographic pressure upon domestic food resources was at its medieval peak. The return of demographic pressure from the 1590s to 1630s again strongly favoured agricultural over industrial prices, although on this occasion the increasing elasticity of industrial output also had an impact. This was even more the case during the next and most marked shift of the sectoral terms of trade from the 1750s to 1850s, when fast-expanding demand for food boosted agricultural prices while the rapidly increasing output of industry caused the prices of a growing number of manufactured goods to fall. In fact, from the opening of the nineteenth century this fall became general so that by the 1850s the industrial price index was 40 per cent below its peak level of the 1800s. The more elastic the supply of industrial products became, the greater was the divergence between the agricultural and industrial price indices (Figure 5.02).

    The effect of these swings in the relative prices of agricultural and industrial goods was to inflate or deflate their value-added outputs and, consequently, their respective contributions to GDP. High and rising relative prices compensated for the slower growth of agricultural output, just as falling relative prices offset the faster growth of industrial production, especially once the transition to factory production got under way. This largely explains the discrepancies revealed by Tables 5.01 and 5.02 between the value-added sectoral shares of output and those of the labour-force. Figure 5.02 plots the ratio of agricultural to industrial prices and highlights those periods when the most fundamental shifts occurred in the inter-sectoral terms of trade. From the 1270s to 1440s relative prices moved steadily in favour of industrial commodities. After half a century of stability, relative prices then, from the 1500s to 1630s, slowly swung back in favour of agricultural products. Finally, from the 1760s to 1860s and following a further period of stability, prices moved strongly in favour of agricultural products. The upshot of this last shift was that from c.1800 the inter-sectoral terms of trade favoured agriculture more strongly than ever before, as is clearly visible in Figure 5.02. In part this was because

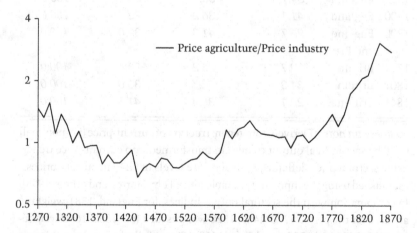

FIGURE 5.02 Inter-sectoral terms of trade between agriculture and industry, England 1270–1700 and Great Britain 1700–1870 (averages per decade, 1700 = 1, log scale). *Sources:* derived from data underlying Figure 5.01.

continuing dependence upon domestic agriculture ensured that food remained dear, but it was also the product of the dramatic falls now taking place in the prices of manufactured goods (Figure 5.01) as mechanised methods of production took hold.

5.2.3 Sectoral output shares

It is a straightforward matter to multiply the sectoral real-output series (Chapters 3 and 4) by the sectoral price indices (Section 5.2.1) in order to obtain indices of sectoral value-added output at current prices. Linking these three current-price output series to the 1841 current-price input–output table for the United Kingdom reconstructed by Horrell and others (1994) but adjusted to a Great Britain basis then gives each sector's current-price output in other years (Table 5.01). This allows

Table 5.01 *Sectoral shares in nominal GDP, England 1270–1700 and Great Britain 1700–1870 (%)*

Year	Territory	Agriculture (%)	Industry (%)	Services (%)	Total (%)
1381	England	45.5	28.8	25.7	100.0
1522	England	39.7	38.7	21.6	100.0
1600	England	41.1	36.2	22.7	100.0
1700	England and Britain	26.7	41.3	32.0	100.0
1759	Britain	29.7	35.2	35.1	100.0
1801	Britain	31.3	32.7	36.0	100.0
1841	Britain	22.1	36.4	41.5	100.0

Sources and notes: Derived from reconstruction of current-price (i.e. nominal) GDP by sector. Real output trends are transformed into current-price trends using sectoral price deflators, with absolute levels of GDP in current prices established using the input–output table for 1841 by Horrell and others (1994). In combination with the sectoral output indices, for England, 1381-weights are used for the period 1270–1450, 1522-weights for 1450–1550, 1600-weights for 1550–1650 and 1700-weights for 1650–1700. Similarly, for Great Britain, 1700-weights are used for the period 1700–40, 1759-weights for 1740–80, 1801-weights for 1780–1820 and 1841-weights for 1820–70.

Table 5.02 *Sectoral shares in the labour-force, England 1381–1700 and Great Britain 1700–1851 (%)*

Year	Territory	Agriculture (%)	Industry (%)	Services (%)	Total (%)
1381	England	57.2	19.2	23.6	100.0
1522	England	58.1	22.7	19.2	100.0
1700	England and Britain	38.9	34.0	27.2	100.0
1759	Britain	36.8	33.9	29.3	100.0
1801	Britain	31.7	36.4	31.9	100.0
1851	Britain	23.5	45.6	30.9	100.0

Source: See Chapter 9.

the derivation of each sector's share of current-price output for the six benchmark years 1381, 1522, 1600, 1700, 1759 and 1801 (Table 5.01). These changes in weights ensure that account is taken of long-run changes in relative prices. Although the weights for each benchmark year are used for calculating real GDP over quite lengthy periods, it should be noted that this does not mean that sectoral shares of output are unchanging between benchmark years. As noted in Chapter 4, differential real growth rates between sectors ensure that sectoral weights are changing implicitly.

With respect to the 1841 sectoral output shares (Table 5.01), note the surprising precociousness of the service sector with already more than 40 per cent of value-added output, compared with industry's 36 per cent and agriculture's still ample 22 per cent. Industry's greater share of employment (Table 5.02) than output at this date reflects the devaluing effect of factory production upon the prices of manufactured goods. For obvious reasons this was a problem which scarcely affected agriculture's share of output. For other years, the results reveal agriculture's progressively contracting and the service sector's progressively expanding shares of value-added output and the intermediate course taken by industry, whose share of output grew to 1700 and then fluctuated around a somewhat reduced level.

Sectoral labour-force shares estimated for most of the same benchmark dates, as described in detail in Chapter 9 and summarised in Table 5.02, offer an interesting counterpoint to these value-added shares. The 1381 and 1522 shares are derived from occupational information contained in the poll tax and muster roll listings for those years, while the 1700, 1759 and 1801 shares are based, respectively, on the social tables of Gregory King [1696], Joseph Massie [1760] and Patrick Colquhoun (1806). The final labour-force shares for 1851 are derived from Shaw-Taylor's (2009a) reworking of the population census material for that year, which is the first to record occupations on a systematic basis.

Note that in both 1381 and 1522 agriculture's share of the labour-force was substantially larger than its value-added share of output in current prices, which was already less than half the total, and that both shares had contracted significantly by 1700, well ahead of the classic period of revolutionary economic change. This accords well with the analyses of writers such as Clark (1951) and Kuznets (1966), who emphasise the low labour productivity of traditional agriculture and regard the release of surplus labour from agriculture as a crucial part of the process of economic development. As a result of its early modern growth spurt, industry was producing more value-added output than agriculture by 1700 and had also emerged as the single largest sector within the economy even though agriculture continued to give more employment. Its greater share of output than employment reflects the gains in productivity arising from technological innovation, better organisation and a fuller division of labour. In due course, however, industry's greater supply elasticity depressed the price of industrial goods relative to commodities with more inelastic supply, so that, once the industrial revolution got under way and markets became flooded with manufactured goods, falling relative prices caused industry's value-added share of output in current prices to shrink. By 1759, as trade, transport, government and administration all expanded as sources of employment, the service sector's output share was already on a par with that of industry and by 1801 it had expanded further to become the largest sector of the economy, with agriculture the

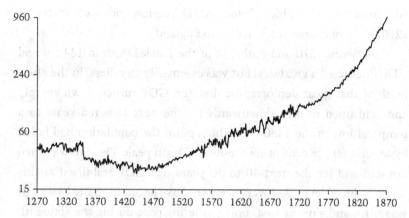

FIGURE 5.03   Real GDP, England 1270–1700 and Great Britain 1700–1870 (log scale, 1700 = 100). *Sources:* Appendix 5.3.

smallest and shrinking fast. Industry nevertheless remained the larger employer of labour and by 1851 45 per cent of the labour-force was engaged in some form of industrial activity.

5.3   REAL AND NOMINAL GDP

The sectoral shares described in Section 5.2.3 provide the weights by which the real value-added outputs of agriculture, industry and services are summed to yield real GDP. The result is plotted on a log scale in Figure 5.03. As explained in Chapter 4, the component output series for industry and services after 1700 relate to the whole of Great Britain, whereas those for agriculture (Chapter 3) apply exclusively to England. The output trend of English agriculture is nevertheless assumed to be representative of the whole of Great Britain after 1700, with the addition of Wales and Scotland merely raising the level of agricultural production whilst leaving the trend and annual fluctuations unchanged. By applying the agricultural index to the GB-adjusted input–output table from Horrell and others (1994), it has therefore been possible to scale up English agricultural output to the whole of Great Britain 1700–1870. It is these enhanced output estimates which are combined with the relevant output series for industry and services to derive the real GDP estimates for Great Britain 1700–1870 depicted in Figure 5.03

and summarised in Table 5.06 (below). The corresponding estimates for 1270–1700, of course, relate solely to England.

Between 1270 and outbreak of the Black Death in 1348–9 real GDP fluctuated a great deal but was essentially trendless. In the aftermath of that great demographic disaster, GDP turned down sharply and continued to drift downwards for the next hundred years to a temporal low in the 1430s, by which point the population had fallen by around 60 per cent of its pre-Black Death peak. Decline was then arrested and for the next 40 to 50 years real GDP stabilised at this much-reduced level. Recovery seems to have begun from the 1480s but was fitful and slow at first, only gathering pace during the sixteenth century and scarcely faltering through the financial turbulence of the Tudor inflation and political and religious turmoil of the Reformation. The momentum of real GDP growth was maintained throughout the seventeenth century irrespective of the cessation of population growth in the 1650s. A literal reading of Figure 5.03 might suggest that there was heightened annual volatility of economic output during this growth phase, and the seventeenth century was certainly very unsettled both climatically and politically (Parker, 2013). Yet this volatility more probably reflects the narrowness of the sample of probate inventories upon which the statistically influential estimates of agricultural output are founded (Chapter 3).

Since Figure 5.03 is plotted on a log scale, the more-or-less straight slope of the real GDP series for practically 200 years indicates that growth took place at much the same rate from the 1480s to 1770s. Table 5.03 shows that annual growth rates were in the range 0.4 to 0.8 per cent. There were individual bad years due to adverse weather, the business cycle and other perturbations, but these setbacks were never more than transitory. After c.1780 the steepening of the slope of the real GDP series indicates a pattern of trend-growth acceleration, as annual growth rates doubled to over 1.5 per cent and then, from the 1830s, increased to well over 2.0 per cent. This is very similar to the pattern identified by Crafts and Harley (1992), whose growth-rate estimates are also presented in Table 5.03 for the conventional

Table 5.03 *Annual growth rates of real GDP, England 1270–1700 and Great Britain 1700–1870 (%)*

Period	Crafts–Harley (%)	Present estimates, annual data (%)	Period	Present estimates, decadal data (%)
			1270s–1300s	0.22
			1300s–1340/8	0.07
			1340/8–1400s	−0.81
			1400s–1450s	−0.18
			1450s–1480s	0.23
			1480s–1553/9	0.56
			1553/9–1600s	0.80
			1600s–1650s	0.41
			1650s–1691/1700	0.74
1700–1760	0.69	0.67	1700s–1760s	0.61
1760–1780	0.64	0.85	1760s–1780s	0.83
1780–1801	1.38	1.46	1780s–1801/10	1.62
1801–1830	1.90	1.64	1801/10–1830s	1.85
1830–1870	–	2.44	1830s–1861/70	2.34
1700–1830	1.06	1.04	1270s–1700	0.21
1700–1870	–	1.37	1700s–1860s	1.32

Sources: See text; Crafts (1985: 45); Crafts and Harley (1992: 715); Appendix 5.3.

periodisation. As Figure 5.03 and Table 5.03 confirm, in no previous period on record had real GDP increased as fast. Growth was slowest in agriculture, faster in services and fastest of all in industry (Table 5.07 below), where adoption of factory-based methods of production was delivering significant gains in productivity and lower prices. These developments were an extension of earlier trends. As is plain from Figure 5.03, rising real GDP had been a feature of the English economy since the end of the fifteenth century and the upturn in growth that set in from the end of the eighteenth century built upon those foundations.

Previous estimates of national income for various benchmark dates in the past by Deane and Cole (1967), Lindert and Williamson (1982), Snooks (1995) and Mayhew (1995a) have all been made in current prices (Table 5.04). To facilitate comparison with these, the figures for real GDP have been reflated with an aggregate price index to give current-price or nominal GDP (Figure 5.04). The aggregate price index has been constructed on the same principles as real GDP: the price indices for the three sectors have been spliced into a single series using the sectoral weights presented in Section 5.3.3. The resultant nominal GDP figures for a series of benchmark years are set out in Table 5.04. They show that Snooks (1995), for instance, appears to have got the level of nominal GDP about right in 1688 but substantially underestimated its level in 1300, thus exaggerating the growth of nominal GDP between 1300 and 1688. Mayhew's (1995a) higher figure for 1300 is closer to, but still lower than, the value suggested here and is estimated for a substantially larger base population of 6.0 million. Lindert and Williamson's (1982) estimate for 1688 also comes close to that proposed here, especially when scaled up to the whole of Great Britain. The degree of consensus respecting the value of England's GDP in 1688 is a tribute to the quality of the dataset assembled for that year by Gregory King.

It is likely that England accounted for 87 per cent of British GDP in 1700, with Wales and Scotland, with their far smaller populations and lower incomes per head, making up the remainder (Scottish incomes were 74 per cent of the British average in 1812, the earliest date for which British income-tax data are available: Lee, 1986: 127, 131). Compared with the estimates advanced here, those of Lindert and Williamson (1982) for 1759 and 1801 are too low, as are the decadal estimates proposed 50 years ago by Deane and Cole (1962) for 1801–61 but not their figure for 1871 (Table 5.04). This suggests that the rate of growth of nominal GDP was significantly faster in the eighteenth century than that implied by Lindert and Williamson (1982) but substantially slower during the first half of the nineteenth century than that proposed by Deane and Cole (1967). After 1851

Table 5.04 *Benchmark estimates of nominal GDP, England 1270–1700 and Great Britain 1700–1870 (£ million current prices)*

12Year	Aggregate price index (1700 = 100)	*Snooks/ †Deane and Cole	°Mayhew/ □Lindert and Williamson	Present estimates, annual data	Present estimates, decadal data
			Nominal GDP (£)		
A. England					
1270	17			£4.44m.	£4.75m.
1300	19	*£4.1m.	°£4.7m.	£5.45m.	£5.25m.
1381	21			£3.98m.	£3.97m.
1500	20			£3.83m.	£4.05m.
1600	65			£23.28m.	£23.61m.
1688	87	*£50.8m.	□£54.4m.	£51.40m.	£52.02m.
1700	100			£65.93m.	£63.51m.
B. Great Britain:					
1700	100		□£75.76m.	£76.01m.	£75.58m.
1759	94		□£75.33m.	£103.46m.	£105.36m.
1801	181	+£232.0m.	□£223.80m.	£329.40m.	£278.73m.
1811	182	+£301.1m.		£381.31m.	£379.39m.
1821	146	+£291.0m.		£349.54m.	£372.35m
1831	130	+£340.0m.		£382.15m.	£394.03m.
1841	129	+£452.3m.		£473.80m.	£479.12m.
1851	99	+£523.3m.		£468.19m.	£541.60m.
1861	120	+£668.0m.		£710.54m.	£737.87m.
1871	134	+£916.6m.		£1,026.13m.	£882.92m.

Sources and Notes: nominal GDP in 1300 and 1688: Snooks (1995: 50); 1300: Mayhew (1995a: 58); 1700–1801: Lindert and Williamson (1982); 1801–71: Deane and Cole (1967). Lindert and Williamson's estimates for England are converted to a Great Britain basis using data on the population share of Scotland and Scottish incomes per head as a percentage of the average for Great Britain from income-tax data in Lee (1986: 127, 131). Aggregate price index and present estimates from Appendix 5.3.

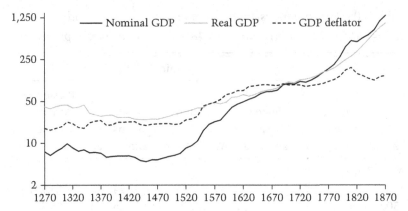

FIGURE 5.04 Real GDP, the GDP deflator and nominal GDP, England 1270–1700 and Great Britain 1700–1870 (averages per decade, 1700 = 100, log scale). *Sources:* Appendix 5.3.

Deane and Cole's (1962) nominal GDP growth estimates are lower than those proposed here. They are, however, broadly consistent with the real GDP growth rates estimated by Crafts (1985) and Crafts and Harley (1992) (Table 5.03).

Figure 5.04 can be used to summarise the division of the increase in nominal GDP between real GDP growth and inflation. For the period 1270–1700, it is clear that most of the increase in nominal GDP was the result of inflation. Whilst real GDP increased by a factor of 2.8, nominal GDP increased by a much greater factor of 17.6, as a result of the price level increasing by a factor of 6.3. Put like this, inflation sounds very high, but compared with the twentieth century, this was relatively mild inflation, at an annual rate of just 0.43 per cent. Furthermore, it is clear that most of the increase in the price level occurred during the 'price revolution' of the sixteenth century, a European-wide and possibly global phenomenon. For the period 1700–1870, most of the increase in nominal GDP was the result of real growth, with only a modest increase in the price level. Although there was a period of substantial inflation during the French Revolutionary and Napoleonic Wars, this was followed by a period of post-war deflation.

5.4   POPULATION, REAL GDP AND GDP PER HEAD

From the mid-fifteenth century the changes in the structure of the economy identified in Section 5.2 of this chapter and the growth of real GDP described in Section 5.3 proceeded more or less continuously and in tandem. The pace of change may rarely if ever have been rapid but it was certainly cumulative so that by 1759, on the eve of the industrial revolution, the economy's structure and scale were conspicuously different from the position in 1381. The share of the labour-force in agriculture had shrunk from 57 per cent to 37 per cent and that in industry had expanded from 19 per cent to 34 per cent (Table 5.01), while value-added output of the industrial and service sectors had risen from 55 per cent to 70 per cent of the total (Table 5.02). Meanwhile, real GDP had grown four-and-a-half-fold whereas the population had increased by less than two-and-a-half-fold, which means that GDP per head must almost have doubled. Plainly the economy had been advancing along an upward growth path long before the industrial revolution got under way. The question, therefore, is not whether the pre-industrial economy grew but when growth began and how continuously and at what pace it proceeded. The answers to these questions lie in the level and rates and direction of change of real GDP per head, as calculated by dividing the estimates of real GDP presented in this chapter by those of population advanced in Chapter 1. This is the result to which the analyses set out in Part I of this book have been leading.

Trends in total population, real GDP and real GDP per head are plotted on a log scale in Figure 5.05. What is remarkable about the GDP per head trend is not the magnitude of its variations, which were narrow, but that from almost the start of the series stability and growth prevailed over decline. Falls in GDP per head did occur but were never as pronounced as the phases of growth, nor as prolonged as the episodes of stability (Table 5.05). With the notable exception of the second half of the thirteenth century and in direct defiance of Malthusian logic, GDP per head tended to hold steady even under conditions of sustained population growth. Such resilience was a considerable achievement,

Table 5.05 *Annual growth rates of real GDP per head, England 1270–1700 and Great Britain, 1700–1870 (%)*

Period	Crafts–Harley (%)	Present estimates, annual data (%)	Period	Present estimates, decadal data (%)
			1270s–1300s	−0.02
			1300s–1340s	0.09
			1340s–1400s	0.54
			1400s–1450s	−0.06
			1450s–1480s	−0.07
			1480s–1553–9	0.00
			1553–9–1600s	0.17
			1600s–1650s	−0.04
			1650s–1690s	0.84
1700–1760	0.34	0.32	1700s–1760s	0.27
1760–1780	0.01	0.22	1760s–1780s	0.10
1780–1801	0.38	0.45	1780s–1800s	0.53
1801–1830	0.47	0.20	1800s–1830s	0.41
1830–1870		1.26	1830s–1860s	1.16
1700–1830	0.32	0.30	1270s–1700	0.17
1700–1870		0.52	1700–1860s	0.48

Sources: See text; derived from Crafts (1985: 16–17, 32, 37); Crafts and Harley (1992: 715); Appendix 5.3.

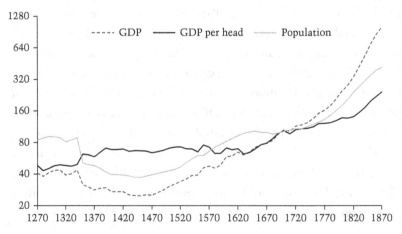

FIGURE 5.05 Real GDP, population and real GDP per head, England 1270–1700 and Great Britain 1700–1870 (averages per decade, log scale, 1700 = 100) *Source:* derived from Appendix 5.3.

Table 5.06 *Population, nominal GDP real GDP and real GDP per head, England 1270–1700 and Great Britain, 1700–1870*

Period	Population (m.)	Nominal GDP (£m.)	Real GDP (£m. constant 1700 prices)	Real GDP per head (£, constant 1700 prices)
A. England				
1270s	4.40	4.75	26.82	6.10
1300s	4.72	5.43	28.65	6.07
1350s	2.65	4.57	20.80	7.85
1400s	2.05	4.03	18.17	8.86
1450s	1.93	3.25	16.36	8.48
1500s	2.23	4.13	20.01	8.97
1550s	3.12	10.66	25.76	8.26
1600s	4.27	26.19	38.52	9.02
1650s	5.35	44.29	47.36	8.85
1700	5.20	65.93	65.93	12.68
B. Great Britain				
1700	6.20	76.01	76.01	12.24
1750s	7.43	98.02	102.90	13.85
1800s	11.17	310.30	188.08	16.84
1850s	21.69	593.72	526.98	24.29
1870	25.84	1,026.13	765.13	29.61

Sources: derived from Appendix 1.5.3.

for, until the industrial revolution was firmly launched on its path, by twenty-first-century standards this was a poor economy, with a GDP per head which remained at late-medieval levels until the final quarter of the seventeenth century (Table 5.06). Nevertheless, its poverty was not absolute and, as will be seen in Chapter 9, even when economic conditions were at their worst in the late thirteenth and early fourteenth centuries English GDP per head was almost double that of the poorest and most underdeveloped economies in the world today. Already there was a significant value-added component to economic output as reflected in the articulated hierarchy of urban centres, existence of an affluent elite possessed of a sophisticated material culture, construction of great cultural monuments, presence of significant numbers of artisans and service workers, and the extensive use made of non-human sources of energy. Over the next five centuries all of these traits became accentuated as GDP per head crept fitfully but ineluctably upwards.

Insofar as an inverse relationship between population and GDP per head ever prevailed, it was during the final stages of the high medieval demographic boom, before proto-industry had absorbed excess labour and when, as a result, numbers were pressing hard on available agricultural resources. Between the 1250s and 1290 England's population increased by an estimated 12 per cent, whereas a tentative reconstruction of GDP per head back to 1253 suggests the latter shrank by 14 per cent. At the same time, real wage rates of farm labourers also deteriorated (Clark, 2007a: 131–2). This is the clearest example of a negative Malthusian scenario during the entire period under review, with the 1280s the single worst decade on record (Figure 5.06). To blame was the devastating sheep-scab epizootic of 1279–80, which simultaneously depressed flock sizes, fleece weights, wool prices, wool-textile production and revenues from international trade and

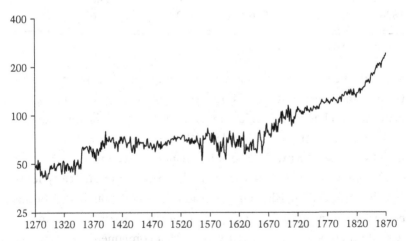

FIGURE 5.06 Real GDP per head, England 1270–1700 and Great Britain 1700–1870 (log scale, 1700 = 100). *Sources:* derived from Appendix 5.3.

commerce. The substantial negative economic ramifications of this disease outbreak nevertheless soon passed and, although scab did not disappear, it never recurred with such ferocity.

By the 1290s, notwithstanding a run of poor harvests, outbreak of war on three fronts, and a major international credit crisis, agricultural output and the economy were in recovery and for the next fifty years GDP per head fluctuated at a low level, below that of the 1250s but above that of the 1280s. Further negative shocks during this environmentally, politically and commercially most unstable of half-centuries set it plunging again, most notably during the harvest crisis of 1316–18 and international credit crunch of 1339–40, but GDP per head invariably returned to its pre-crisis level. Even the outbreak of the Hundred Years War in 1336 had an economic silver lining, insofar as it boosted expansion of government services, enabled English merchants to enlarge their share of overseas trade, and revenue-raising customs duties on wool exports helped revive the flagging native cloth industry (Section 4.2.2 above; Lloyd, 1977: 144–92; Bolton, 1980: 200–1; Ormrod, 1990: 181–3, 188–94). These positive developments partially offset the proliferation of under-resourced and underemployed households in both town and countryside whose low productivity and lack of purchasing power constituted a growing dead weight upon the economy thwarting any prospect of economic growth (Campbell, 2005). Yet, seemingly against all the odds, GDP per head exhibited no tendency to decline and from the 1290s to 1340s remained essentially trendless.

This status quo was abruptly and dramatically transformed by outbreak of the Black Death which in 1348–9, within the space of 18 months, reduced the population by 46 per cent. Had fourteenth-century England, like Spain and many other parts of Europe, been underpopulated such a massive haemorrhaging of numbers might have constituted a serious economic setback (Álvarez-Nogal and Prados de la Escosura, 2013). Instead, the opposite applied and the huge death toll resolved an intractable economic problem. Relieved of its heavy burden of poverty, the economy registered an immediate gain in GDP per head of 30 per cent. Further 'isostatic uplift' followed over

Table 5.07 *Annual growth rates of population, agricultural output, industrial output, service-sector output, real GDP and real GDP per head, England 1270–1700 and Great Britain, 1700–1870*

Period	Annual growth rate (%)					
	Population	Agriculture	Industry	Services	Real GDP	Real GDP per head
A. England						
1270s–1300s	0.27	0.24	0.05	0.39	−0.02	−0.29
1300s–1350s	−0.52	−0.52	−0.59	−0.87	−0.64	−0.12
1350s–1400s	−1.06	−0.43	−0.01	−0.44	−0.30	0.76
1400s–1450s	−0.21	−0.10	−0.27	−0.22	−0.06	0.15
1450s–1500s	0.25	0.35	0.43	0.45	0.40	0.15
1500s–1550s	0.65	0.31	0.68	0.48	0.51	−0.14
1550s–1600s	0.62	0.69	1.00	0.74	0.81	0.19
1600s–1650s	0.51	0.21	0.35	0.90	0.41	−0.10
1650s–1700	−0.04	0.20	1.01	0.71	0.78	0.82
1270s–1700	0.04	0.10	0.31	0.23	0.22	0.18
B. Great Britain						
1700–1750s	0.30	0.63	0.56	0.61	0.49	0.19
1750s–1800s	0.77	0.93	1.45	1.32	1.21	0.44
1800s–1850s	1.34	0.78	2.95	2.15	2.08	0.74
1850s–1870	1.54	0.99	3.01	1.96	0.12	0.58
1700–1870	0.84	0.79	1.72	1.43	1.31	0.48

Source: Derived from Appendix 5.3.

the next thirty years as sequel outbreaks of plague thwarted any demographic recovery. The annual rate of GDP per head growth during this quite exceptional half-century averaged 0.76 per cent and would not be bettered until the second half of the seventeenth century (Table 5.07). By the early fifteenth century, when this growth phase ended, GDP per head had been elevated to 50 per cent above its pre-Black Death level.

Until this point the loss of numbers had clearly been a boon: the proportion of families living at a bare-bones level of subsistence diminished, holding sizes expanded, real wage rates rose, household incomes improved and spending power per head increased to the benefit of bakers and brewers, tanners and weavers, and the array of artisans, clerks and other service providers who plied their crafts, wares and skills throughout the countryside and its many small towns. As observed in Chapter 4, for industry this was something of a golden age and no other sector of the economy fared as well (Table 5.07). Beyond the 1420s, however, further gains in GDP per head were not forthcoming, notwithstanding that conditions of resource abundance continued to apply and, if anything, became more pronounced as the population drifted down to its temporal minimum of less than 2 million in the mid-fifteenth century. In fact, in the middle decades of the century GDP per head slipped back slightly, as population, bullion supplies, markets and international commerce all shrank. Such circumstances were not propitious for growth, hence GDP per head at the close of the fifteenth century was little different from what it had been at the middle and beginning of the century. The urbanisation ratio also appears to have stayed stubbornly at the same level (Rigby, 2010). Real wage rates alone kept rising (Clark, 2006; Allen, no date; Munro, no date), but for all the implied improvement in living standards the economy's performance remained flat.

Towards the end of the fifteenth century the population began to increase once again and it is from this point that real GDP commenced its sustained long-term rise (Figure 5.05 and Table 5.06). For the next 150 years population and GDP were growing together and since they grew at much the same rate there was little erosion of the GDP per head gains bestowed during the late-fourteenth-century era of demographic contraction. It is tempting to treat the absence of any substantial improvement in GDP per head during this long period as evidence that little was changing. That, however, is to overlook the significant amount of economic restructuring that was taking place as labour moved out of agriculture and into industry (Section 5.2). From 1450 to 1600 industrial output grew consistently faster than both agricultural output and the population (Table 5.07). Moreover, to return to an issue raised in Chapter 1, contrary to the Malthusian model there was no significant decline in GDP per head as the population rose. Certainly, GDP per head suffered when subsistence pressures were at their most acute, in the 1550s, 1590s and 1640s and especially during the Civil War of 1642–51 (Figure 5.06), but, as in the early fourteenth century, none of these downturns persisted much beyond the specific circumstances responsible for them. Again, GDP per head proved resilient.

By the 1620s numbers were as great as they had been in the 1340s but GDP per head was 40 per cent higher. Thirty years later, as the population attained its seventeenth-century peak of 5.3 million, GDP per head was actually nudging upwards. This capacity to retain, and in small measure improve upon, the GDP per head gains of the post-Black Death period despite substantial population growth testifies to the qualitative improvements made to the country's economy and its institutional infrastructure over the intervening 300 years. It was a rare achievement at the time. Holland was even more successful at marrying economic and demographic growth in contrast to the once-leading economy of Italy where, from the sixteenth century, each increment of population brought about a corresponding reduction in GDP per head (van Zanden and van Leeuwen, 2012; Malanima, 2011). Holland's economy was smaller, more open and commercially far more entrepreneurial than was England's, and was the runaway economic success story of the sixteenth and early seventeenth centuries. England's progress was more measured. It was founded upon the expansion of industry (building upon the advances made by its late-medieval wool-textile industry, the re-expansion of tin mining, and, from the end of the sixteenth century, the rise of iron smelting and coal mining), the fusion of industrial with commercial growth, and a greatly enhanced role for the state. It contributed to the divergence that was opening between a small group of dynamic economies around the southern North Sea – Brabant, Holland and England – and the once leading but increasingly stagnant economies of southern Europe (Allen, 2001; van Zanden, 2009). This issue will be explored in more depth in Chapter 10.

England's take-off to rising GDP per head took place a century and a half after Holland's, during the politically turbulent and climatically challenging second half of the seventeenth century. As Figure 5.06 shows, between the end of the Civil Wars and the Glorious Revolution of 1688 the trend in GDP per head turned irreversibly upwards for the first time since the post-Black Death era (North and Weingast, 1989). By the early 1680s GDP per head was double the level of the early fourteenth century and such was the vigour of growth that by the 1690s it was on a par with the GDP per head of Italy at the height of its commercial revolution and Holland during the most buoyant phase of its Golden Age. That GDP per head was able to move ahead so strongly was in part because the population had stopped growing and even shrank a little (Table 5.07). This episode therefore fails to meet one of Kuznets's (1966) criteria for modern economic growth, namely that rising population and GDP per head should take place concurrently. Rather, it exemplifies the kind of growth envisaged by Adam Smith, based upon the positive-feedback mechanisms set in motion by commercial expansion and market growth. That there was no significant reduction in population size was therefore material to the economy's continued expansion, since any greater contraction would have had a detrimental effect upon market size. By earlier English standards, the annual growth rate achieved of over 0.8 per cent was unprecedented and even by later standards, when growth was being driven by heavy investment in improved technology, it was remarkable (Table 5.07). It illustrates what could be achieved by what Wrigley (2000, 2006b) has termed an advanced organic economy increasingly engaged in international commerce and with a demographic reproduction rate in part restrained by adoption of an array of preventive checks. These measures included restriction of nuptiality, significant rural to urban migration (thereby relocating population from lower- to higher-mortality locations) and net emigration.

Significantly, the rate of GDP per head growth slackened in the eighteenth century as the rate of GDP growth slowed (Table 5.04) and the population began again to increase (Figure 5.06 and Tables 5.06 and

5.07). As the pace of population growth quickened from mid-century GDP per head growth slowed further (Table 5.05). The immediate prelude to the initial water-powered phase of the industrial revolution was therefore an unmistakable slowing of the rate of economic growth as the lead of GDP growth over population growth narrowed. While production remained organised along traditional lines and mostly employed established technology any more favourable outcome was unlikely. There were, after all, limits to what could be achieved by Smithian growth alone. Fortunately, this loss of economic momentum proved temporary and from the 1780s annual GDP per head growth improved to over 0.5 per cent as the transition to the machine age began.

Growth of GDP per head during the opening phase of the industrial revolution was real but unimpressive and it was not until the 1830s that it comfortably exceeded 1.0 per cent per year (Table 5.05). Paradoxically, the economy performed better during the Napoleonic Wars, despite the inflationary impact of that event upon the price level (Figure 5.01), than it did during the peace that followed (Table 5.05). Looking at growth of GDP per head on its own, it may be tempting to see the period 1780–1830 as unexceptional and certainly a good deal less dynamic than portrayed by Deane and Cole (1962) with their estimates of faster growth (Table 5.03). Yet consideration of population trends underscores the significance of the developments that were under way, since for the first time the Kuznets condition of simultaneous growth of both GDP per head and population was being met (Table 5.07). Slow and uneven though it was, this was undeniably modern economic growth, and it persisted irrespective of the acceleration of population growth to 1.0 per cent and then 1.5 per cent a year, faster than at any other time in Britain either before or since.

The dire economic warnings contained in Malthus's [1798] *First essay on population* were published when population growth was approaching its historical peak. Yet with hindsight it is clear that growth of real GDP was still maintaining its long-established lead. Contrary to The *First essay*'s most pessimistic predictions, diminishing returns did not set in. Far from lagging, economic growth rose to the demographic challenge; GDP per head growth remained strongly positive and from the 1830s increased further to over 1.0 per cent. An expanding share of value-added output was now being contributed by the fast-growing industrial and service sectors and a shrinking proportion by the slow-growing agricultural sector (Table 5.02). The transformation from a majority agrarian to a majority non-agrarian economy was at last complete and by 1851, for the first time, town-dwellers outnumbered those living in the countryside. By 1870 British GDP per head was almost five times the English level at the end of the thirteenth century when output per head had been at its lowest, four times the English level on the morrow of the Black Death, and double the British level on the eve of the industrial revolution (Table 5.06).

Between 1270 and 1700 annual growth of GDP per head had averaged 0.18 per cent, although much of this was concentrated into the two great growth surges of the second half of the fourteenth and second half of the seventeenth centuries (Table 5.07). Then, from 1700 to 1870, British GDP per head growth increased to an annual rate of 0.48 per cent, with the fastest growth occurring after 1780 and especially after 1830 when the population was also rising fast (Table 5.05). Modern economic growth may have commenced with the industrial revolution but economic growth per se did not. Bit by bit, for centuries before, the economy had been inching forward, rarely slipping back for very long. The first substantial GDP per head gains were registered during the far-reaching readjustment of factor inputs that followed the Black Death. Thereafter, GDP per head changed little but the structure of the economy a great deal (Tables 5.01, 5.02 and 5.06). This endowed it with the resilience to hold onto these GDP per head gains throughout the period of demographic recovery from 1500 to 1650. During the latter part of this phase the economy became commercially a great deal more mature with the result that further substantial gains then accrued during the demographic lull of the second half of the seventeenth century. These, too, were consolidated over the course of the eighteenth century as the wider British economy further developed its ability to cope with population growth. By the close of that century the economy was successfully delivering sustained gains in *average* living standards to a rapidly increasing population. This late breakthrough represents the first example of a successful transition to modern economic growth. Five hundred years after this process began, the economy was finally growing at well over 1.0 per cent a year and rising living standards had become the norm rather than the exception.

5.5   CONCLUSIONS

Estimation of GDP per head for contemporary economies is an intrinsically inexact process: for historical economies, with their less complete and more problematic datasets, precision is even more elusive. That is why here the data, methods and assumptions involved at each step in the estimation process have been made explicit. Improvement is certainly possible with more and better production series for a wider cross-section of activities, but that is a task for the future. Although further systematic work in the archives is likely to repay dividends, certain statistical lacunae are bound to endure due to the paucity or absence of relevant historical information. Bridging the documentary discontinuity between the late-medieval and early modern periods will always present a challenge and obtaining direct evidence of many aspects of service-sector activity before 1700 may never be possible. Methodological resourcefulness will always be required if these gaps and discontinuities are to be overcome. Fortunately, the national accounting approach offers a number of well-established ways of developing proxy measures of activities not directly recorded. Without resort to such measures the current estimates could not have been made.

With so many assumptions, qualifications and uncertainties, can historical national income estimates ever be convincing? Ultimately, their credibility hinges upon whether or not they can be falsified. That is why every effort has been made to ensure that those advanced here are free from internal contradictions and inconsistencies, especially where the outputs of one sector or sub-sector comprise the inputs of another. In addition, Part II of this book, 'Analysing economic growth', subjects these estimates to a number of tests. One of the most obvious is a comparison with the independent chronology of the returns to labour offered by real wage rates, especially the well-known wage-rate indices of building and agricultural labourers (Allen, no date; Munro, no date; Clark, 2006). Real wage rates are often treated as surrogate measures of living standards and GDP per head, although, as Angeles (2008) has highlighted, they were also influenced by changes in the factor returns to land and capital as also by the market supply of labour per head (in terms of hours worked per day and days worked per year). Nevertheless, there ought to be some correspondence between real wage rates and real GDP per head; hence any significant divergences between them, such as occurred in the fifteenth and again in the late eighteenth centuries, need to be explicable. Reconciling the somewhat contrasting chronologies of these two measures of economic wellbeing is the subject of Chapter 6.

Two further cross-checks considered in Chapters 7 and 8 are whether agriculture and net imports together delivered enough food to feed the population and whether total estimated national income, when disaggregated, was sufficient to meet the income requirements of all socio-economic groups. In the case of food, Livi-Bacci (1991) reckons that an average daily intake per head of 2,000 processed kilocalories was the minimum required to maintain a population at the nutritional standard required for economic and biological reproduction. To test whether this requirement could be met requires converting the physical outputs of crops and livestock products into their kilocalorie equivalents and then estimating their respective food-extraction rates after allowance for losses from food processing and waste. Allowance also needs to be made for any net gains or losses from foreign trade. Generally, the less that crops were processed, the fewer the potential kilocalories that were lost, so much depended upon the form in which foodstuffs were consumed. Here, it is customary to draw a distinction between a 'bare-bones basket' of the cheapest and most basic of staple consumables with relatively high kilocalorie extraction rates, such as pottage, potatoes and milk, which nonetheless needed to be affordable to the poorest households, and a higher-quality and more generous 'respectability basket' of consumables with lower extraction rates – white bread, ale and meat – which pandered more to dietary and other consumer preferences (Allen, 2009a: 35–8). The budgetary boundary between these two baskets of consumables constitutes the poverty line. A key issue is therefore what proportion of households was below the poverty line and what, if any, difference rising GDP per head made to that proportion. Obviously, it was these households that were most vulnerable to harvest shortfalls, hikes in food prices and collapses in employment. Socio-economic tables reconstructed for a series of benchmark years track the proportion of households falling into this category and the emergence of new social groups able to afford the superior 'respectability basket' of consumables. At the same time they demonstrate that the aggregated incomes of all socio-economic groups match the national income estimates presented in Section 5.4.

Material rewards were always in substantial part a function of labour productivity, which was intrinsically higher in some tasks than others. This issue is the subject of Chapter 9. Agriculture potentially had quite high labour productivity due to its extensive employment of animal power. If it was well supplied with working animals, English mixed farming did not need a large labour-force other than during the harvest season. This natural productivity advantage could be seriously compromised if morcellation and involution entrapped excessive numbers on the land and encouraged substitution of the spade for the plough. A key to maintaining and improving labour productivity in agriculture therefore lay in the displacement of surplus labour into other activities. Expansion of part-time and full-time industrial employment from the fifteenth century served this purpose, although many industrial activities were initially even more dependent than agriculture upon human labour. Proto-industrialisation was therefore likely to be self-defeating unless labour productivity could be improved via a greater division of labour and adoption of improved technology.

The food-processing industries led the way in harnessing inanimate power to grind grain. Water power was then applied to the fulling of cloth and, from the end of the fifteenth century, to the smelting and forging of iron. Mechanisation of many other manufacturing processes was, however, long delayed which is why so much ingenuity was expended on improving the efficiency of essentially manual tasks with spinning wheels and jennies and flying shuttles. Eventually, the steam engine became the universal motor that powered the industrial revolution and elevated labour productivity to previously unimaginable levels. Steam pumps were helping to drain mines and raise tin and coal output from the close of the seventeenth century thereby boosting the profits and incomes of those who owned and operated the mines. Throughout these developments the service sector became the last bastion of unmechanised labour-intensive methods. The service sector's expansion therefore partially offset some of the dramatic labour productivity gains that were being made in industry and the slower but nonetheless steady advances accruing to agriculture. This helps to explain why growth of GDP per head remained so slow for so long. Identifying these productivity shifts helps to resolve the when, where and why of economic growth and link it to an earlier historiography which focused upon these technological issues.

A final test of the credibility of these estimates of GDP per head for England 1270–1700 and Great Britain 1700–1870 is whether they make sense when compared with those now available for a number of other pre-industrial economies in both Europe and Asia. This helps establish whether they are of the right relative order of magnitude and clarifies when Britain overtook other economies. As Chapter 10 demonstrates, in Western Europe the key comparisons are with Italy, the leading economy of the twelfth and thirteenth centuries and still far ahead of all but the Flemish economy in the early Renaissance, and with Holland, which grew faster and became richer than any other European economy during the sixteenth and early seventeenth centuries. In the mid-fifteenth century Italian GDP per head was approximately double that of England whereas Holland's was still more or less on a par.

Subsequently, England performed less well than Holland, although both, along with Brabant and probably Flanders, fared better than Italy and Spain, whose economic fortunes waned. This relocation of economic dynamism from the Mediterranean to a small group of countries around the southern shores of the North Sea has become known as the Little Divergence. The bigger question is whether by the sixteenth century or even earlier this group of fast-developing North Sea economies was already ahead of their counterparts in East Asia, especially China's Lower Yangzi province and Japan, or whether that profound shift in the world's economic centre of gravity occurred much later. Estimates of GDP per head provide an ideal tool for evaluating such macro comparative issues while the coherence or otherwise of the patterns they reveal provides a pragmatic test of whether the estimates themselves ring true. In all these respects the figures of GDP per head presented in this chapter constitute a beginning rather than an end.

APPENDIX 5.1

Price-data sources

A5.1.1 COMMODITIES USED IN THE AGRICULTURAL PRICE INDEX, 1270–1870

Arable prices: Wheat, rye, barley, oats, peas, beans, potatoes, hops, straw, mustard seed, saffron: all from Clark (2004), with additional information on rye from Farmer (1988, 1991).

Livestock and hay product prices: Hay, cheese, butter, milk, beef, mutton, pork, bacon, tallow, wool, eggs: all from Clark (2004); hides: from Thorold Rogers (1866–1902).

A5.1.2 COMMODITIES USED IN THE INDUSTRIAL PRICE INDEX, 1270–1700

Textiles: Linen cloth, woollen cloth, work gloves, stockings: all from Clark (2006); shirting: from Thorold Rogers (1866–1902, 4: 583–8).

Metals: Iron manufactures, nails, pewter: all from Clark (2006); horse-shoes, lead (rolled, pig): from Thorold Rogers (1866–1902, 1: 554–9; 4: 482–7).

Other manufactures: Candles, charcoal, firewood, lamp oil, parchment, soap: all from Clark (2006); hurdles, ligatures, paper: from Thorold Rogers (1866–1902, 1: 554–9, 561–6; 4, 605–6).

Construction: Bricks, wages of building labourers: from Clark (2006); laths, plain tiles, crest tiles, slates, lime, planks, boards: all from Thorold Rogers (1866–1902, 1: 515–20; 4: 404–9, 468–72; 5: 538–44).

Mining: Coal: from Clark (2006).

Foodstuff: Wheat, flour, beer: all from Clark (2006).

A5.1.3 COMMODITIES USED IN THE INDUSTRIAL PRICE INDEX, 1700–1870

Textiles: Cotton, cotton cloth, wool, woollen cloth, silk thread, linen cloth: all from Clark (2006); leather (the average of Naval Stores leather, backs and hose): from Beveridge (1939).

Metals: Iron manufactures, pewter: from Clark (2006).

Other manufacturing: wood, paper-foolscap, books, soap, candles, lamp oil, coal gas: all from Clark (2006).

Construction: Bricks, wages of building labourers: from Clark (2006); paving, roof, and plain tiles (the average of Winchester, Eton, Westminster, Sandwich, Greenwich, Office of Works and Naval Stores but omitting ridge and paving tiles from the Naval Stores because these were outliers compared to the other series), laths (the average of Greenwich and Office of Works), lime (the average of Winchester, Eton, Westminster, Sandwich, Greenwich, Office of Works and Naval Stores), masons' sand and gravel, and sand (the average of Westminster, Office of Works and Naval Stores), cement and tarras (the average of cement, mortar, and tarras from Greenwich and Westminster), lead (the average of lead, milled sheet, sheet and cast, pipe from Westminster, Greenwich, Office of Works and Naval Stores): all from Beveridge (1939).

Mining: Coal: from Clark (2006).

Foodstuff: Wheaten flour, bread, bacon, treacle, sugar, beer, spirits, tobacco: all from Clark (2006); malt (the average of Winchester, Eton, Westminster, Greenwich and Navy Victualling in London, Portsmouth and Plymouth): from Beveridge (1939).

A5.1.4 COMMODITIES USED IN THE SERVICE-SECTOR PRICE INDEX, 1270–1700

Housing: Rent: from Clark (2006).

Domestic service: Wages of building labourers: from Clark (2006).

Government: Wages of craftsmen: from Clark (2006).

Commerce (distribution): Weighted average of agriculture and industry prices.

A5.1.5 COMMODITIES USED IN THE SERVICE-SECTOR PRICE INDEX, 1700–1870

Housing: rent: from Clark (2006).

Domestic service: Wages of building labourers: from Clark (2006).

Government: Wages of craftsmen: from Clark (2006).

Distribution: Weighted average of agriculture and industry prices.

Finance: Fire insurance: from Pearson (2004: 374–80).

Transport: Unweighted average of shipping: from Harley (1988: 873–5); goods road transport (interpolated decadal figures, 1700–1830), passenger road transport (interpolated decadal figures, 1750–1830): from Bogart (2005: 505–6).

APPENDIX 5.2

Price-index weighting schemes

A5.2.1 WEIGHTS FOR THE AGRICULTURAL PRICE INDEX

The current price shares of the arable and livestock products are given in Table 3.18.

Table A5.2.1 *Sub-sector weights for the industrial price index,*
1270–1700 (%)

Commodity	1270–1402 (%)	1402–1582 (%)	1582–1700 (%)
Foodstuff	27.6	27.0	21.3
Textiles	51.0	51.9	41.4
Metal manufactures	18.8	11.9	13.5
Other manufactures		0.5	3.6
Construction	2.6	4.2	8.8
Mining		4.5	11.4
Total industry	100.0	100.0	100.0

Sources: Derived from Hoffmann (1955); Crafts and Harley (1992).

A5.2.2 WEIGHTING SCHEME FOR THE INDUSTRIAL PRICE
INDEX, 1270–1700

The first step is to trace back the shares of the major sub-sectors from
1700, using the volume indicators from Chapter 4. The resulting
weights are presented in Table A5.2.1.

The next step is to allocate the weights of the available commodities within each sub-sector (where no information is available on their
relative importance, sub-sector weights are allocated equally). These
commodity weights are given in Table A5.2.2.

A5.2.3 WEIGHTING SCHEME FOR THE INDUSTRIAL PRICE
INDEX, 1700–1870

Again, a two-level weighting scheme is adopted. The major sub-sector
weights for the period 1700–1870 are derived by projecting back from
1870 using the volume indicators from Chapter 5. The resulting
weights are presented in Table A5.2.3.

In the second level, the weights of the available commodities
within each sub-sector are allocated in accordance with the weights of
Crafts and Harley (1992) (Table A5.2.4).

Table A5.2.2 *Weights of commodities in the industrial price index, 1270–1700 (%)*

Commodity	1270–1402 (%)	1402–1582 (%)	1582–1700 (%)
A. Textiles			
Woollen cloth	33.3	33.3	60.2
Work gloves	33.3		
Linen cloth	33.3	33.3	16.2
Shirting		33.3	
Stocking			23.6
Total textiles	100.0	100.0	100.0
B. Metal manufactures			
Iron manufactures	30.6	45.9	45.9
Nails	30.6	45.9	45.9
Pewter	8.2	2.7	4.1
Horseshoes	30.6		
Lead pig		2.7	4.1
Lead rolled		2.7	
Total metal manufactures	100.0	100.0	100.0
C. Other manufactures			
Candles wax	3.8	2.5	2.5
Candles tallow	3.8	2.5	2.5
Firewood	11.0	16.5	16.5
Oil lamp	0.5	0.5	0.5
Parchment	9.4	49.5	49.5
Paper		9.4	9.4
Hurdles	11.0		
Ligatures	49.5		
Soap		2.5	2.5
Charcoal	11.0	16.5	16.5
Total other manufactures	100.0	100.0	100.0
D. Construction			
Bricks	21.0	21.0	21.0
Laths	13.0	13.0	4.3
Plain tiles	16.0	1.5	
Crest tiles		1.5	

Table A5.2.2 (cont.)

Commodity	1270–1402 (%)	1402–1582 (%)	1582–1700 (%)
Lime		3.0	16.0
Slates		10.0	
Board			4.3
Plank			4.3
Labourers' wages	50.0	50.0	50.0
Total construction	100.0	100.0	100.0
E. Foodstuffs			
Wheat	100.0	100.0	
Flour			57.6
Beer			42.4
Total foodstuffs	100.0	100.0	100.0

Sources and notes: Derived from Hoffmann (1955); Crafts and Harley (1992). Coal has a weight of 100 per cent in the mining sub-sector.

Table A5.2.3 *Sub-sector weights for the industrial price index, 1700–1870 (%)*

Commodity	1700–1740 (%)	1740–1770 (%)	1770–1870 (%)
Metal manufactures	9.0	7.4	15.6
Mining	5.9	4.1	12.4
Textiles	55.5	64.6	39.4
Foodstuffs	10.6	7.5	8.7
Construction	9.9	9.7	11.4
Other manufactures	9.1	6.7	12.5
Total industry	100.0	100.0	100.0

Sources: Derived from Crafts and Harley (1992).

A5.2.4 WEIGHTS FOR THE SERVICE-SECTOR PRICE INDEX

Weights for the service-sector price index are provided for England 1270–1700 in Table A5.2.5, and for Great Britain 1700–1870 in Table A5.2.6. They are derived by projecting back from the 1700

Table A5.2.4 *Weights of commodities in the industrial price index,*
1700–1870 (%)

Commodity	1700–1740 (%)	1740–1770 (%)	1770–1870 (%)
A. Textiles			
Cotton yarn			36.0
Cotton cloth		14.9	20.1
Woollen and worsted yarn	25.5	25.5	12.1
Woollen and worsted cloth	34.7	34.7	13.1
Silk threads	23.6	8.7	10.5
Linens	16.2	16.2	8.3
Total textiles	100.0	100.0	100.0
B. Metal manufactures			
Iron and steel	91.8	88.6	87.2
Copper	6.8	9.5	
Lead/tin/copper	1.4	1.9	12.8
Total metal manufactures	100.0	100.0	100.0
C. Other manufactures			
Candles wax	3.8	2.5	2.5
Candles tallow	3.8	2.5	2.5
Firewood	11.0	16.5	16.5
Ligatures	49.5		
Soap		2.5	2.5
Charcoal	11.0	16.5	16.5
Total other manufactures	100.0	100.0	100.0
D. Construction			
Bricks	21.0	21.0	21.0
Timber	12.0	12.0	12.0
Tiles	3.0	3.0	3.0
Lime	3.0	3.0	3.0
Sand	3.0	3.0	3.0
Cement and tarras	3.0	3.0	3.0
Lead	5.0	5.0	5.0
Labourers wages	50.0	50.0	50.0
Total construction	100.0	100.0	100.0

Table A5.2.4 (cont.)

Commodity	1700–1740 (%)	1740–1770 (%)	1770–1870 (%)
E. Foodstuffs			
Wheaten flour	46.1	41.1	40.9
Bread			
Confectionery			2.1
Sugar	4.4	4.0	2.1
Beer	26.5	23.7	23.5
Malt	4.6	4.1	4.1
Spirits	6.9	6.2	6.1
Tobacco products		10.7	11.0
Meat	11.5	10.3	10.2
Total foodstuffs	100.0	100.0	100.0

Sources and notes: Derived from Hoffmann (1955); Crafts and Harley (1992). Coal has a weight of 100 per cent in the mining sub-sector.

Table A5.2.5 *Weights for the service-sector price index, 1270–1700 (%)*

Commodity	1270–1402 (%)	1402–1582 (%)	1582–1700 (%)
Housing	32.4	41.5	32.8
Domestic services	13.9	17.8	14.1
Government	19.5	8.7	15.9
Commerce	34.2	32.1	37.3
Total services	100.0	100.0	100.0

Source: Derived from Crafts (1985).

Table A5.2.6 *Weights for the service-sector price index, 1700–1870 (%)*

Commodity	1700–1725 (%)	1725–1870 (%)
Housing	21.6	20.4
Domestic	17.8	16.8
Government	6.9	6.5
Distribution	41.0	38.6
Finance		5.8
Transport	12.7	11.9
Total services	100.0	100.0

Sources: Derived from Crafts (1985); Horrell and others (1994: 547).

and 1841 benchmarks, respectively, using the volume indicators from Chapter 4.

APPENDIX 5.3

Indexed sectoral real output, real GDP, population and real GDP per head, England 1270–1700 and Great Britain 1700–1870 (1700 = 100)

The data series are provided in index number form for England 1270–1700 and then Great Britain 1700–1870. Indexing both series on their respective values in 1700 allows continuous rates of change to be tracked across these 600 years. All sectoral and GDP output values have been estimated in constant prices. Those for the outputs of agriculture, industry and services are provided solely in index number form. Those for GDP, population and GDP per head can be converted into absolute values using the following real values for England and Great Britain in 1700.

Territory	GDP (£m.)	Population (m.)	GDP per head (£)
England 1700	65.93	5.20	12.68
Great Britain 1700	76.01	6.21	12.24

Year	Agriculture	Industry	Services	GDP	Population	GDP per head
1270	64.6	28.2	37.0	40.6	84.0	48.3
1271	63.9	27.4	37.4	40.2	84.1	47.7
1272	69.0	27.7	37.5	41.7	84.3	49.4
1273	61.4	26.9	37.6	39.3	84.4	46.6
1274	60.5	27.0	37.7	39.2	84.5	46.3
1275	76.9	29.8	37.9	44.8	84.7	52.9
1276	62.3	26.5	37.7	39.4	84.8	46.4
1277	71.1	27.3	37.7	42.1	84.9	49.5
1278	77.6	26.8	38.0	43.6	85.1	51.3
1279	56.9	22.5	37.9	36.2	85.2	42.5
1280	59.3	22.3	38.1	36.8	85.8	42.9
1281	67.1	22.8	38.4	39.1	86.3	45.3
1282	64.0	22.1	38.3	38.0	86.9	43.7
1283	57.8	21.5	38.5	36.1	87.4	41.3
1284	62.9	21.2	38.9	37.4	88.0	42.5
1285	65.2	20.8	39.1	37.9	88.6	42.8
1286	62.6	21.0	39.3	37.4	89.1	41.9
1287	73.0	22.6	39.8	40.9	89.7	45.6
1288	69.8	21.5	40.2	39.7	90.3	44.0
1289	61.2	19.7	40.4	36.7	90.9	40.3
1290	61.7	20.2	41.1	37.2	91.4	40.7
1291	60.7	20.8	41.2	37.3	91.4	40.8
1292	64.6	22.7	41.3	39.3	91.4	43.0
1293	65.4	24.3	41.3	40.2	91.3	44.0
1294	63.8	24.7	41.0	39.9	91.3	43.7
1295	70.0	27.0	41.4	42.7	91.2	46.8
1296	73.9	28.3	41.7	44.4	91.2	48.7
1297	68.7	26.8	42.2	42.5	91.1	46.6
1298	77.4	26.5	42.5	44.7	91.1	49.1

(*cont.*)

Year	Agriculture	Industry	Services	GDP	Population	GDP per head
1299	71.2	26.6	42.2	43.0	91.0	47.3
1300	70.0	26.5	42.5	42.7	91.0	47.0
1301	73.0	25.4	42.6	43.0	90.9	47.3
1302	72.1	28.5	42.1	44.2	90.9	48.6
1303	74.9	30.7	42.4	46.0	90.8	50.6
1304	64.8	26.9	42.4	41.6	90.8	45.8
1305	69.9	26.3	42.8	42.7	90.7	47.1
1306	67.5	25.4	42.2	41.5	90.7	45.8
1307	72.5	26.9	42.2	43.5	90.6	48.0
1308	72.8	28.0	41.9	44.0	90.6	48.6
1309	75.3	28.9	41.8	45.1	90.5	49.8
1310	72.2	29.4	41.9	44.5	90.5	49.2
1311	76.0	30.5	42.0	46.1	90.4	50.9
1312	73.1	29.4	42.1	44.8	90.4	49.6
1313	75.7	29.9	41.9	45.6	90.3	50.5
1314	73.1	31.5	41.5	45.7	90.3	50.6
1315	58.8	29.3	41.9	41.0	90.2	45.5
1316	54.2	27.5	40.9	38.7	89.1	43.5
1317	60.1	28.2	40.7	40.5	87.9	46.1
1318	73.7	30.0	40.1	44.7	86.8	51.5
1319	74.3	30.5	39.3	44.9	85.7	52.4
1320	71.3	29.1	39.3	43.4	84.5	51.3
1321	55.0	24.3	38.5	36.7	83.5	44.0
1322	60.0	26.1	37.7	38.6	82.4	46.9
1323	64.8	26.5	37.7	40.1	81.3	49.3
1324	56.4	24.0	36.9	36.5	80.2	45.5
1325	66.6	25.1	36.4	39.5	79.2	49.9
1326	68.2	25.9	36.3	40.2	79.7	50.5
1327	65.3	26.2	36.8	39.8	80.3	49.6
1328	56.7	25.4	36.9	37.2	80.8	46.0
1329	62.9	26.2	37.5	39.4	81.4	48.3
1330	61.7	25.1	37.6	38.6	82.0	47.1
1331	57.1	24.2	37.8	37.0	82.5	44.8
1332	63.9	24.8	38.1	39.2	83.1	47.1

(cont.)

Year	Agriculture	Industry	Services	GDP	Population	GDP per head
1333	68.3	25.3	38.3	40.6	83.6	48.5
1334	64.7	24.8	38.7	39.5	84.2	46.9
1335	60.5	23.8	39.1	38.1	84.8	44.9
1336	63.3	26.6	39.0	40.1	85.4	47.0
1337	71.8	31.6	39.2	44.7	86.0	52.0
1338	74.1	32.1	40.3	45.9	86.5	53.0
1339	55.1	24.3	41.8	37.7	87.1	43.2
1340	68.1	27.0	42.3	42.5	87.7	48.4
1341	64.5	30.0	43.0	43.2	88.3	48.9
1342	70.1	31.4	43.7	45.5	88.9	51.1
1343	66.3	31.4	43.7	44.5	89.5	49.6
1344	75.3	33.2	44.2	47.8	90.2	53.0
1345	67.6	30.6	44.7	44.8	90.8	49.3
1346	61.6	29.4	45.3	42.8	91.4	46.8
1347	67.3	30.0	46.0	44.7	92.0	48.6
1348	71.0	30.7	46.4	46.1	92.7	49.8
1349	49.9	24.0	38.8	35.3	75.5	46.8
1350	51.5	21.7	32.2	32.8	61.5	53.3
1351	53.9	19.5	27.0	30.8	50.1	61.6
1352	56.7	20.6	26.4	31.9	50.0	63.8
1353	54.3	22.2	26.1	32.0	49.9	64.0
1354	52.9	19.3	27.3	30.6	49.9	61.3
1355	58.6	18.2	27.0	31.5	49.8	63.2
1356	52.7	20.6	26.7	31.0	49.7	62.3
1357	54.9	20.4	26.8	31.5	49.6	63.5
1358	56.4	20.0	26.6	31.6	49.6	63.8
1359	56.5	20.7	26.4	31.9	49.5	64.5
1360	55.6	20.5	26.6	31.7	49.4	64.1
1361	51.9	20.3	26.2	30.5	49.3	61.9
1362	52.0	18.3	26.5	29.7	49.3	60.2
1363	50.7	17.4	26.0	28.8	49.2	58.5
1364	57.8	20.5	25.5	31.9	49.1	65.0
1365	53.0	19.9	25.6	30.4	49.0	62.1
1366	57.9	19.2	25.5	31.3	48.9	64.0

(cont.)

Year	Agriculture	Industry	Services	GDP	Population	GDP per head
1367	50.9	18.9	25.5	29.3	48.9	60.0
1368	49.6	19.3	24.9	29.1	48.8	59.6
1369	44.8	17.9	24.8	27.1	48.7	55.7
1370	55.5	19.1	24.4	30.3	48.6	62.4
1371	53.7	17.8	24.6	29.3	48.6	60.4
1372	47.4	15.2	24.5	26.5	48.5	54.6
1373	54.9	15.6	24.7	28.6	48.4	59.1
1374	47.8	14.5	24.8	26.3	48.3	54.4
1375	44.8	13.9	25.2	25.3	48.3	52.4
1376	56.5	15.8	24.9	29.2	48.2	60.6
1377	57.1	17.4	24.6	30.0	48.1	62.4
1378	54.9	16.9	25.5	29.5	47.7	61.7
1379	47.2	15.9	25.0	26.8	47.4	56.7
1380	48.4	17.1	25.3	27.8	47.0	59.3
1381	50.0	17.2	25.4	28.4	46.6	60.8
1382	52.7	17.5	25.2	29.1	46.2	62.9
1383	46.7	17.9	24.8	27.6	45.9	60.2
1384	57.0	19.2	25.2	31.0	45.5	68.1
1385	47.5	18.3	24.9	28.0	45.2	62.1
1386	55.7	20.5	24.7	31.1	44.8	69.5
1387	56.6	19.9	24.8	31.1	44.4	70.0
1388	48.7	18.9	24.6	28.6	44.1	64.8
1389	50.0	20.2	24.2	29.4	43.7	67.1
1390	44.1	19.0	24.3	27.3	43.4	63.0
1391	54.6	20.3	23.5	30.4	43.1	70.7
1392	64.6	22.5	23.5	34.1	42.7	79.7
1393	46.5	19.6	23.5	28.0	42.4	66.1
1394	54.9	20.6	23.4	30.6	42.0	72.8
1395	49.3	20.6	23.3	29.1	41.7	69.8
1396	49.3	20.7	23.2	29.2	41.4	70.5
1397	46.5	20.9	22.7	28.4	41.0	69.1
1398	53.0	21.3	22.5	30.2	40.7	74.2
1399	47.8	21.3	22.4	28.9	40.4	71.4
1400	44.7	21.4	21.9	27.9	40.1	69.6

(*cont.*)

Year	Agriculture	Industry	Services	GDP	Population	GDP per head
1401	43.9	21.1	21.7	27.5	40.0	68.7
1402	47.0	20.6	22.2	28.2	40.0	70.6
1403	48.4	21.1	21.7	28.7	40.0	71.8
1404	49.5	21.4	21.8	29.1	39.9	73.0
1405	50.6	21.0	21.6	29.2	39.9	73.2
1406	44.6	19.5	21.9	27.0	39.8	67.9
1407	45.1	19.4	21.8	27.1	39.8	68.0
1408	38.6	18.6	21.9	25.0	39.8	62.9
1409	42.1	18.3	22.1	25.9	39.7	65.1
1410	47.9	18.7	21.9	27.5	39.7	69.2
1411	44.9	19.1	21.8	26.9	39.6	67.8
1412	42.9	18.9	21.7	26.2	39.6	66.3
1413	36.2	17.2	22.0	23.8	39.5	60.1
1414	43.4	20.2	21.9	27.0	39.5	68.3
1415	43.1	21.4	22.2	27.6	39.5	70.0
1416	40.3	21.0	22.0	26.6	39.4	67.5
1417	48.8	21.4	22.2	29.1	39.4	73.8
1418	44.9	20.3	22.2	27.6	39.3	70.1
1419	48.9	21.2	22.3	29.0	39.3	73.8
1420	46.4	21.0	22.3	28.3	39.3	72.1
1421	39.8	20.6	22.3	26.4	39.2	67.3
1422	42.5	20.9	22.4	27.3	39.2	69.6
1423	47.2	21.1	23.0	28.7	39.1	73.4
1424	49.4	20.6	22.6	29.0	39.1	74.1
1425	45.5	20.7	22.4	27.9	39.1	71.5
1426	44.3	19.8	22.0	27.1	39.0	69.4
1427	43.5	18.9	21.7	26.4	39.0	67.6
1428	40.7	17.1	21.4	24.7	38.9	63.5
1429	41.7	18.5	21.1	25.6	38.9	65.7
1430	44.0	19.0	20.7	26.3	38.9	67.7
1431	43.3	19.7	20.7	26.4	38.7	68.2
1432	43.8	18.7	20.6	26.1	38.6	67.4
1433	45.8	19.4	20.4	26.8	38.5	69.6
1434	48.3	21.4	20.2	28.4	38.4	73.9

(cont.)

Year	Agriculture	Industry	Services	GDP	Population	GDP per head
1435	41.3	18.4	20.4	25.2	38.3	65.8
1436	37.9	16.9	19.9	23.5	38.2	61.4
1437	33.9	16.9	20.1	22.5	38.1	59.1
1438	35.7	18.1	20.3	23.6	38.0	62.1
1439	39.3	18.5	20.1	24.6	37.8	65.0
1440	43.3	16.3	20.7	24.8	37.7	65.8
1441	34.3	15.4	20.2	21.9	37.6	58.3
1442	34.6	16.9	20.1	22.7	37.5	60.5
1443	50.7	18.0	20.4	27.4	37.4	73.3
1444	52.5	16.9	20.3	27.4	37.3	73.4
1445	38.5	16.7	20.0	23.6	37.2	63.4
1446	43.7	16.9	20.2	25.1	37.1	67.6
1447	44.8	17.8	19.8	25.6	37.0	69.4
1448	46.5	18.4	20.2	26.5	36.9	71.8
1449	39.4	18.1	19.3	24.3	36.8	66.0
1450	42.0	17.9	19.8	25.0	36.6	68.2
1451	43.3	17.6	19.7	25.1	36.8	68.3
1452	42.2	17.7	19.6	24.9	36.9	67.4
1453	43.0	17.8	19.7	25.1	37.0	68.0
1454	42.7	18.3	19.3	25.2	37.1	68.0
1455	43.3	17.6	19.5	25.1	37.2	67.4
1456	43.9	17.8	19.9	25.4	37.3	68.1
1457	36.2	17.7	19.2	23.3	37.4	62.3
1458	41.6	17.7	19.6	24.7	37.5	65.9
1459	41.8	17.0	19.4	24.4	37.6	64.8
1460	41.4	17.6	19.0	24.4	37.7	64.8
1461	41.8	17.6	19.2	24.6	37.8	65.0
1462	49.9	18.3	19.2	27.0	38.0	71.0
1463	50.7	18.7	19.0	27.3	38.1	71.8
1464	43.4	17.5	19.4	25.0	38.2	65.5
1465	40.8	17.7	18.9	24.3	38.3	63.5
1466	38.3	18.5	19.2	24.2	38.4	63.0
1467	41.2	18.5	19.4	25.0	38.5	64.9
1468	45.6	18.6	19.4	26.1	38.6	67.6

(cont.)

Year	Agriculture	Industry	Services	GDP	Population	GDP per head
1469	44.6	18.4	19.7	25.8	38.7	66.7
1470	41.8	18.5	19.5	25.2	38.9	64.7
1471	37.6	18.6	19.3	24.1	39.0	61.8
1472	39.6	19.0	19.8	24.9	39.1	63.8
1473	40.3	18.4	19.8	24.8	39.2	63.3
1474	43.9	18.9	20.5	26.2	39.3	66.6
1475	41.9	18.5	20.4	25.4	39.4	64.5
1476	36.6	17.4	20.7	23.6	39.5	59.8
1477	38.7	18.6	20.8	24.8	39.7	62.5
1478	40.3	19.2	20.9	25.5	39.8	64.2
1479	45.9	19.0	21.7	27.0	39.9	67.8
1480	48.2	19.7	21.5	27.9	40.0	69.6
1481	44.1	19.2	21.7	26.7	40.1	66.5
1482	40.3	18.7	21.9	25.6	40.2	63.5
1483	42.2	20.8	21.1	26.8	40.4	66.5
1484	42.0	20.2	21.5	26.6	40.5	65.8
1485	37.7	19.8	21.0	25.2	40.6	62.1
1486	48.6	19.8	21.2	28.0	40.7	68.8
1487	42.2	18.6	20.7	25.6	40.8	62.8
1488	43.3	18.8	21.4	26.2	41.0	64.0
1489	44.4	19.2	22.1	26.8	41.1	65.4
1490	43.4	19.9	22.4	27.1	41.2	65.7
1491	43.9	20.3	22.3	27.3	41.3	66.1
1492	43.3	21.0	22.7	27.7	41.4	66.9
1493	42.3	20.6	23.0	27.3	41.6	65.7
1494	46.9	20.7	23.4	28.6	41.7	68.7
1495	46.7	20.1	23.0	28.1	41.8	67.3
1496	44.0	19.6	23.2	27.3	41.9	65.1
1497	47.9	20.6	24.5	29.1	42.0	69.3
1498	48.3	20.9	24.8	29.5	42.2	69.9
1499	48.8	21.2	24.4	29.6	42.3	70.1
1500	47.2	21.1	24.5	29.2	42.4	68.8
1501	43.0	21.2	24.5	28.2	42.5	66.2
1502	47.0	21.2	24.6	29.2	42.7	68.5

(cont.)

Year	Agriculture	Industry	Services	GDP	Population	GDP per head
1503	51.8	21.5	24.4	30.5	42.8	71.2
1504	51.3	21.9	24.5	30.6	42.9	71.3
1505	51.7	22.3	24.6	30.9	43.0	71.9
1506	51.7	22.6	24.5	31.1	43.2	72.0
1507	49.3	22.6	24.6	30.5	43.3	70.5
1508	51.3	22.7	24.3	31.0	43.4	71.3
1509	56.8	22.8	24.5	32.4	43.5	74.5
1510	51.7	23.0	24.6	31.3	43.7	71.7
1511	53.7	23.3	24.6	31.9	43.8	72.9
1512	47.0	23.8	24.7	30.5	43.9	69.5
1513	50.4	24.6	25.0	31.9	44.1	72.4
1514	49.2	24.8	25.4	31.8	44.2	72.0
1515	51.9	25.1	25.5	32.7	44.3	73.8
1516	50.6	25.1	25.8	32.4	44.4	73.0
1517	50.6	25.2	26.0	32.5	44.6	73.0
1518	51.0	25.3	26.0	32.7	44.7	73.2
1519	50.0	25.3	26.1	32.4	44.8	72.3
1520	48.5	25.1	26.1	32.0	45.0	71.1
1521	48.9	26.4	26.0	32.7	45.1	72.6
1522	53.6	25.4	25.9	33.3	45.2	73.7
1523	53.2	26.7	26.9	34.2	45.7	74.9
1524	54.2	27.5	27.2	34.9	46.2	75.6
1525	53.3	27.9	27.3	34.9	46.6	74.9
1526	55.0	27.9	27.3	35.4	47.1	75.1
1527	45.6	27.9	27.3	33.0	47.6	69.4
1528	47.8	27.9	27.2	33.5	48.1	69.8
1529	49.9	28.3	27.2	34.3	48.6	70.6
1530	52.2	28.4	27.3	34.9	49.0	71.2
1531	47.9	28.5	27.5	33.9	49.5	68.5
1532	52.1	29.0	27.8	35.3	50.1	70.6
1533	51.6	29.2	28.0	35.4	50.6	69.9
1534	58.2	29.8	27.6	37.2	51.1	72.8
1535	49.6	29.2	27.7	34.8	51.6	67.5
1536	50.6	28.4	27.8	34.6	52.1	66.4

(cont.)

Year	Agriculture	Industry	Services	GDP	Population	GDP per head
1537	60.5	29.1	28.1	37.5	52.7	71.3
1538	51.8	29.7	28.2	35.7	53.2	67.2
1539	61.9	30.5	28.7	38.8	53.7	72.2
1540	57.3	30.5	29.0	37.7	54.3	69.5
1541	51.6	31.0	29.3	36.6	54.5	67.2
1542	57.2	31.1	30.1	38.3	55.2	69.4
1543	54.1	30.2	30.2	37.1	55.5	66.9
1544	58.7	32.2	30.9	39.4	56.1	70.3
1545	52.5	32.5	31.2	38.2	56.0	68.1
1546	53.2	33.0	31.5	38.7	56.0	69.1
1547	64.4	33.6	31.7	41.8	56.0	74.6
1548	60.4	32.8	31.9	40.4	56.8	71.2
1549	56.7	31.7	32.0	39.0	57.4	68.0
1550	54.6	32.5	32.3	39.0	58.1	67.0
1551	54.3	31.2	32.2	38.4	59.0	65.0
1552	49.0	31.7	31.6	36.8	59.4	61.9
1553	69.0	33.2	31.3	43.2	59.9	72.2
1554	57.9	32.3	31.2	39.6	60.4	65.5
1555	59.1	31.4	31.0	39.4	60.8	64.8
1556	41.5	27.2	30.7	32.5	61.8	52.5
1557	51.6	27.7	30.2	35.5	61.7	57.5
1558	80.1	30.7	30.0	45.1	60.3	74.7
1559	67.0	31.0	30.0	41.3	58.4	70.7
1560	60.3	35.5	30.1	41.2	58.0	71.1
1561	64.4	34.6	30.2	42.1	58.4	72.1
1562	64.3	34.7	30.4	42.2	59.1	71.4
1563	77.0	35.3	30.8	46.3	59.7	77.6
1564	72.5	34.4	31.3	44.7	59.9	74.7
1565	73.1	34.5	32.0	45.2	60.6	74.5
1566	87.6	37.5	32.8	50.9	61.1	83.4
1567	78.3	37.1	33.1	48.1	61.7	77.9
1568	81.6	35.4	33.6	48.5	62.6	77.5
1569	77.7	38.1	33.5	48.4	63.0	76.8
1570	66.2	38.1	32.3	44.7	63.4	70.4

(*cont.*)

Year	Agriculture	Industry	Services	GDP	Population	GDP per head
1571	68.4	37.2	31.8	44.9	63.7	70.4
1572	62.0	38.6	32.2	43.7	64.3	67.9
1573	79.5	41.4	32.9	50.2	64.7	77.6
1574	60.4	41.3	33.1	44.6	65.1	68.5
1575	76.0	42.7	33.8	50.0	65.7	76.0
1576	81.1	43.5	34.2	51.9	66.4	78.2
1577	56.6	42.7	34.3	44.4	67.2	66.1
1578	77.7	43.3	34.9	51.0	67.9	75.2
1579	78.7	41.4	35.1	50.6	68.5	73.8
1580	70.7	41.2	35.4	48.2	69.3	69.6
1581	70.4	38.0	35.5	46.9	69.9	67.1
1582	61.1	33.4	35.7	42.3	70.7	59.8
1583	80.9	33.3	36.3	48.2	71.6	67.3
1584	76.8	33.0	36.6	46.9	72.5	64.7
1585	58.6	32.4	36.6	41.4	73.1	56.6
1586	49.4	36.8	37.1	40.6	73.9	55.0
1587	67.3	34.9	37.5	45.2	74.3	60.9
1588	81.6	37.8	37.8	50.7	74.0	68.5
1589	63.2	36.2	38.0	44.7	74.8	59.8
1590	70.9	37.6	38.8	47.8	75.7	63.1
1591	63.7	43.4	39.2	48.2	75.8	63.6
1592	74.7	44.6	39.8	52.1	75.9	68.6
1593	85.1	44.4	40.0	55.1	75.9	72.7
1594	55.1	41.6	40.0	45.2	76.6	59.0
1595	58.0	40.5	40.5	45.7	77.5	58.9
1596	51.6	39.9	40.8	43.6	78.1	55.9
1597	45.7	39.4	40.6	41.6	78.0	53.4
1598	65.6	43.5	41.0	49.3	77.5	63.6
1599	85.7	46.4	41.9	56.7	78.2	72.5
1600	76.0	47.2	42.3	54.3	79.2	68.5
1601	72.6	49.2	42.9	54.3	80.1	67.7
1602	79.8	50.5	43.8	57.2	80.6	71.0
1603	89.6	51.7	44.3	60.7	81.0	75.0
1604	99.6	53.8	44.9	64.7	81.2	79.7

(cont.)

Year	Agriculture	Industry	Services	GDP	Population	GDP per head
1605	80.4	51.9	45.1	58.4	82.2	71.0
1606	85.0	55.9	45.9	61.6	83.0	74.2
1607	76.9	49.3	45.9	56.5	83.9	67.3
1608	67.6	49.5	46.1	53.9	84.6	63.7
1609	95.6	50.2	47.2	62.7	85.4	73.5
1610	108.5	50.2	47.5	66.6	85.6	77.8
1611	91.9	49.3	47.5	61.4	86.2	71.2
1612	92.2	43.1	47.2	58.8	86.6	67.9
1613	80.7	46.2	47.7	56.8	87.0	65.4
1614	73.4	46.4	47.9	54.8	87.0	63.0
1615	86.3	48.8	48.2	59.7	87.6	68.1
1616	76.4	48.6	47.5	56.5	87.9	64.3
1617	93.5	50.2	48.3	62.4	88.0	70.9
1618	93.0	50.3	48.8	62.5	88.6	70.5
1619	82.7	45.9	48.5	57.5	89.4	64.3
1620	110.7	49.0	49.6	67.4	90.2	74.7
1621	104.9	53.7	50.3	67.8	91.3	74.3
1622	81.2	50.6	50.3	59.6	92.9	64.1
1623	75.7	53.7	51.0	59.4	93.5	63.5
1624	101.3	53.6	51.6	67.1	93.0	72.2
1625	101.5	54.5	52.0	67.6	92.8	72.9
1626	93.2	52.7	51.4	64.3	91.6	70.1
1627	97.7	50.4	52.0	64.8	92.3	70.2
1628	121.9	54.2	55.0	74.4	94.2	78.9
1629	67.8	47.8	53.8	55.5	95.7	58.0
1630	65.4	47.9	53.6	54.8	95.5	57.4
1631	68.1	48.5	53.4	55.8	94.8	58.8
1632	88.4	51.1	55.5	63.4	96.0	66.1
1633	76.5	50.8	55.8	59.9	98.4	60.8
1634	84.7	47.7	57.0	61.3	99.6	61.6
1635	89.9	49.0	58.2	63.8	100.1	63.7
1636	82.8	46.8	57.6	60.6	98.0	61.9
1637	78.7	47.3	58.4	59.8	100.0	59.8
1638	87.4	54.4	58.8	65.4	99.4	65.8

(*cont.*)

Year	Agriculture	Industry	Services	GDP	Population	GDP per head
1639	95.5	51.4	59.0	66.6	100.2	66.5
1640	102.1	50.7	59.4	68.4	100.3	68.2
1641	75.8	50.1	58.0	60.0	98.7	60.8
1642	91.4	52.9	59.7	66.2	99.9	66.3
1643	104.0	54.0	61.3	70.9	101.4	69.9
1644	109.1	51.0	60.9	71.0	100.4	70.7
1645	82.6	47.9	60.5	61.8	101.0	61.2
1646	83.0	48.3	60.8	62.2	100.7	61.8
1647	81.1	50.3	62.0	62.8	102.3	61.4
1648	82.6	50.8	62.4	63.6	102.2	62.2
1649	74.4	52.7	64.3	62.5	102.3	61.1
1650	63.6	53.2	65.6	59.9	102.2	58.6
1651	71.5	54.5	67.7	63.2	102.2	61.9
1652	92.8	60.4	70.6	72.3	103.8	69.7
1653	114.8	64.8	72.7	80.7	103.7	77.8
1654	107.9	66.2	71.1	78.9	102.3	77.2
1655	118.9	68.8	72.9	83.5	103.9	80.3
1656	104.9	63.3	71.9	77.2	103.8	74.4
1657	92.4	61.2	71.1	72.7	103.8	70.0
1658	82.1	63.6	70.1	70.6	102.4	69.0
1659	64.3	49.7	67.2	59.2	101.4	58.4
1660	78.3	53.7	67.2	64.6	101.0	64.0
1661	76.6	58.6	67.7	66.3	101.6	65.3
1662	82.9	58.2	66.9	67.6	100.2	67.5
1663	95.6	76.2	68.8	79.0	99.5	79.4
1664	88.2	71.1	68.4	74.8	100.9	74.1
1665	97.1	70.3	69.2	77.1	99.8	77.3
1666	121.4	76.8	71.8	87.1	100.6	86.5
1667	116.6	81.4	71.0	87.5	98.3	89.0
1668	91.4	76.8	70.9	78.8	100.2	78.7
1669	100.5	75.0	71.8	80.8	100.1	80.7
1670	91.5	75.1	71.6	78.4	100.0	78.4
1671	88.0	70.4	71.4	75.4	99.3	75.9
1672	82.2	71.5	72.2	74.6	98.9	75.4

(*cont.*)

Year	Agriculture	Industry	Services	GDP	Population	GDP per head
1673	83.8	73.9	73.9	76.5	99.5	76.9
1674	75.3	70.7	74.3	73.1	99.8	73.2
1675	75.9	74.2	75.2	75.0	99.8	75.1
1676	111.4	82.7	77.2	88.6	99.8	88.8
1677	88.7	82.3	76.7	82.2	99.9	82.3
1678	100.5	81.7	77.9	85.5	100.3	85.3
1679	87.1	76.4	77.4	79.6	100.0	79.6
1680	111.5	82.2	79.1	89.0	99.4	89.5
1681	85.1	78.4	77.5	79.9	98.3	81.2
1682	91.7	82.6	76.9	83.2	95.5	87.1
1683	108.9	86.6	77.9	89.7	95.3	94.2
1684	81.6	71.4	74.4	75.1	95.2	78.9
1685	98.0	77.5	76.1	82.5	96.5	85.6
1686	80.7	74.6	75.8	76.6	96.9	79.0
1687	105.6	76.0	77.1	84.3	95.8	87.9
1688	105.7	88.6	78.7	90.0	95.2	94.6
1689	96.9	88.0	80.2	87.9	97.1	90.5
1690	109.3	92.7	82.4	93.8	97.0	96.7
1691	114.9	91.4	84.3	95.4	98.0	97.3
1692	129.7	97.7	88.2	103.2	98.1	105.2
1693	87.6	88.5	87.0	87.8	98.6	89.1
1694	132.3	95.9	91.7	104.3	98.3	106.0
1695	112.6	96.8	92.9	99.8	98.3	101.4
1696	101.4	92.9	94.1	95.5	98.5	97.0
1697	100.5	91.2	94.9	94.9	99.1	95.7
1698	101.6	95.5	97.1	97.6	99.6	98.0
1699	87.5	95.4	98.0	94.1	99.9	94.2
1700	100.0	100.0	100.0	100.0	100.0	100.0
1701	111.1	111.9	103.5	109.0	100.6	108.3
1702	117.7	101.1	103.0	106.2	101.3	104.8
1703	104.7	92.6	103.6	99.4	102.2	97.2
1704	131.2	117.0	109.1	118.3	102.7	115.2
1705	127.0	105.9	108.2	112.3	102.9	109.1
1706	98.7	85.4	104.6	95.1	103.3	92.1

(cont.)

Year	Agriculture	Industry	Services	GDP	Population	GDP per head
1707	115.2	98.3	110.8	106.8	103.7	103.0
1708	91.2	127.2	115.0	113.7	104.0	109.3
1709	77.5	102.6	110.7	98.5	104.3	94.5
1710	72.2	86.8	107.6	89.6	104.6	85.7
1711	93.2	88.5	113.2	97.6	104.4	93.5
1712	100.3	88.5	106.9	97.5	104.2	93.6
1713	77.2	94.2	105.8	93.4	104.4	89.4
1714	95.8	103.4	107.5	102.7	104.8	98.0
1715	84.4	104.2	107.1	99.8	104.9	95.1
1716	85.4	109.9	110.6	103.6	105.6	98.1
1717	95.9	117.1	110.7	109.4	106.3	103.0
1718	115.8	117.5	113.0	115.6	107.0	108.1
1719	95.7	124.9	113.9	113.6	107.7	105.4
1720	132.4	119.7	112.5	120.8	107.4	112.5
1721	128.7	112.8	109.9	116.1	107.2	108.3
1722	118.3	118.7	114.8	117.3	107.3	109.3
1723	109.7	118.4	113.5	114.5	107.7	106.3
1724	114.3	112.9	113.2	113.4	108.1	104.9
1725	117.2	117.0	114.8	116.3	108.5	107.2
1726	100.4	119.3	114.6	112.7	109.5	103.0
1727	104.7	114.1	115.6	112.1	110.1	101.8
1728	121.7	110.8	116.4	115.5	109.0	105.9
1729	117.7	101.1	112.2	109.1	107.3	101.7
1730	113.6	108.6	113.6	111.6	106.0	105.3
1731	110.5	106.4	113.6	109.8	105.9	103.7
1732	131.3	110.5	113.8	117.1	106.4	110.1
1733	130.5	115.9	115.5	119.7	106.9	111.9
1734	125.6	115.7	118.6	119.2	108.1	110.4
1735	115.5	115.0	118.9	116.4	109.0	106.8
1736	146.2	115.6	119.6	125.1	109.9	113.8
1737	142.6	104.4	116.2	118.4	110.6	107.1
1738	130.8	115.5	118.7	120.6	111.1	108.6
1739	130.6	113.2	119.2	119.8	111.8	107.2
1740	128.3	109.9	119.1	117.8	112.4	104.8

(cont.)

Year	Agriculture	Industry	Services	GDP	Population	GDP per head
1741	131.6	113.8	122.2	121.2	112.7	107.6
1742	141.8	112.4	123.7	124.0	111.5	111.2
1743	128.1	113.1	125.4	121.1	111.5	108.6
1744	117.8	114.7	126.9	119.4	112.2	106.4
1745	121.7	116.1	127.4	121.1	113.4	106.8
1746	129.0	119.8	128.5	125.0	114.1	109.5
1747	149.5	117.6	131.3	130.6	114.6	114.0
1748	128.0	126.8	134.1	129.2	114.9	112.5
1749	129.0	123.5	134.7	128.5	115.6	111.1
1750	128.0	134.3	128.8	130.3	116.4	112.0
1751	124.0	129.5	129.2	127.5	117.1	108.9
1752	137.6	134.4	131.2	133.8	117.8	113.6
1753	140.2	135.3	131.6	135.0	118.7	113.8
1754	136.3	129.4	130.3	131.2	119.5	109.8
1755	136.5	136.2	134.2	135.2	120.3	112.4
1756	133.5	128.6	138.4	132.9	121.3	109.6
1757	156.4	132.0	138.5	140.6	121.8	115.4
1758	162.9	129.8	141.6	142.5	122.1	116.8
1759	157.4	133.4	148.6	144.8	122.5	118.2
1760	164.7	134.0	154.3	149.0	123.2	120.9
1761	172.4	138.8	160.3	154.9	124.0	124.9
1762	161.7	137.2	157.9	150.6	124.5	120.9
1763	163.4	137.7	154.5	150.1	124.2	120.8
1764	161.3	147.1	145.5	150.0	124.8	120.2
1765	153.5	148.0	147.3	148.8	125.8	118.3
1766	132.9	166.0	149.4	150.8	126.3	119.4
1767	159.2	153.3	145.7	151.8	126.6	119.9
1768	165.8	151.9	145.9	153.2	127.0	120.7
1769	181.9	158.1	151.5	161.9	127.8	126.7
1770	164.7	157.2	153.3	157.5	128.7	122.4
1771	175.4	157.4	153.2	160.4	129.5	123.9
1772	150.7	163.4	154.3	156.3	130.4	119.9
1773	175.8	155.0	151.7	159.1	131.4	121.1
1774	169.2	148.6	153.7	155.6	132.4	117.5

(cont.)

Year	Agriculture	Industry	Services	GDP	Population	GDP per head
1775	173.6	157.2	155.2	160.5	133.7	120.0
1776	179.9	159.1	163.2	165.7	135.0	122.8
1777	187.0	162.7	167.6	170.5	136.3	125.1
1778	180.0	165.0	167.2	169.3	137.7	123.0
1779	184.2	157.6	170.7	168.9	139.0	121.5
1780	197.2	163.5	176.2	176.6	139.7	126.4
1781	216.9	157.5	176.8	181.6	141.2	128.6
1782	193.1	170.3	183.8	179.8	142.3	126.4
1783	188.1	181.3	176.0	178.9	142.6	125.5
1784	192.2	177.5	177.3	179.6	143.9	124.8
1785	176.8	182.9	184.2	178.3	145.2	122.8
1786	188.5	188.9	176.3	181.5	146.8	123.6
1787	168.9	196.1	180.4	178.4	148.5	120.2
1788	166.8	195.3	182.0	178.0	150.0	118.7
1789	171.1	199.2	185.9	182.0	152.0	119.7
1790	195.5	211.5	191.1	195.8	153.8	127.4
1791	194.3	209.8	196.4	196.7	155.7	126.3
1792	197.5	227.4	200.6	204.6	157.5	129.9
1793	198.7	213.7	202.0	201.3	159.1	126.5
1794	170.1	212.1	212.8	194.7	160.5	121.3
1795	213.3	220.4	224.6	215.9	162.3	133.0
1796	212.4	231.7	226.7	219.8	164.0	134.0
1797	206.5	218.9	239.5	218.2	166.1	131.3
1798	211.5	224.2	236.0	220.3	168.0	131.1
1799	204.1	245.9	240.8	226.1	170.0	133.0
1800	201.9	280.4	244.1	237.1	171.1	138.6
1801	236.6	257.2	236.7	239.2	172.2	138.9
1802	223.8	256.7	258.1	241.9	173.6	139.3
1803	211.1	265.4	247.8	236.8	175.6	134.8
1804	202.7	269.2	252.1	236.6	178.1	132.9
1805	228.3	277.9	260.9	250.9	180.7	138.8
1806	222.9	270.3	270.3	249.9	183.4	136.3
1807	239.9	293.8	280.3	266.3	185.9	143.2
1808	234.7	267.7	272.3	253.8	188.3	134.8

(*cont.*)

Year	Agriculture	Industry	Services	GDP	Population	GDP per head
1809	238.8	274.4	285.7	261.8	190.8	137.2
1810	231.5	319.6	301.8	278.6	193.2	144.2
1811	210.5	334.5	300.6	275.7	195.7	140.8
1812	209.7	306.5	293.1	264.3	198.7	133.0
1813	253.5	297.7	299.8	278.7	201.9	138.0
1814	222.0	293.7	316.7	272.5	205.1	132.9
1815	235.7	338.5	348.5	301.6	208.5	144.7
1816	224.5	317.1	332.3	285.8	212.0	134.8
1817	242.9	340.4	306.7	290.6	215.4	134.9
1818	223.1	357.5	310.2	290.3	218.7	132.7
1819	216.4	351.7	308.0	285.5	221.8	128.7
1820	261.5	365.1	319.3	308.7	225.2	137.1
1821	258.6	377.5	328.0	314.0	228.9	137.1
1822	251.9	391.3	341.4	320.1	232.8	137.5
1823	255.0	417.0	347.3	329.6	236.6	139.3
1824	262.9	453.4	364.3	347.7	240.1	144.8
1825	263.3	481.5	367.3	355.6	243.5	146.0
1826	241.5	442.9	362.1	336.5	246.7	136.4
1827	263.6	488.7	380.2	362.5	249.9	145.1
1828	235.3	517.7	392.3	363.6	253.4	143.5
1829	245.5	515.2	392.1	366.7	256.9	142.7
1830	253.8	553.8	403.2	383.2	260.3	147.2
1831	258.8	562.0	405.4	387.8	263.8	147.0
1832	279.8	574.8	408.8	399.8	266.9	149.8
1833	261.0	600.4	418.9	402.9	269.9	149.3
1834	266.4	617.5	428.4	412.7	273.4	150.9
1835	308.2	661.2	442.2	443.7	277.1	160.1
1836	293.7	697.4	471.6	458.5	280.8	163.3
1837	303.7	696.1	452.8	454.3	284.1	159.9
1838	305.3	735.0	473.5	472.2	287.4	164.3
1839	290.0	739.1	477.6	469.2	291.5	161.0
1840	313.4	769.1	496.3	492.3	295.4	166.6
1841	289.7	759.0	500.3	482.8	299.0	161.5
1842	315.6	704.0	496.5	478.1	302.7	157.9

(cont.)

Year	Agriculture	Industry	Services	GDP	Population	GDP per head
1843	315.8	757.7	524.8	501.9	306.5	163.8
1844	346.0	852.1	552.7	546.1	310.2	176.0
1845	326.1	941.5	581.9	571.1	314.0	181.9
1846	319.1	943.9	586.8	571.1	317.7	179.7
1847	339.2	888.2	583.9	564.4	321.5	175.6
1848	319.2	955.1	622.7	588.1	325.2	180.8
1849	337.2	948.9	647.6	603.2	329.0	183.4
1850	309.7	957.4	654.3	597.8	332.7	179.7
1851	323.2	1,004.4	682.0	624.7	336.5	185.7
1852	344.8	1,062.4	698.0	652.5	340.2	191.8
1853	297.5	1,170.3	735.9	675.2	344.0	196.3
1854	370.0	1,191.0	738.7	707.9	347.7	203.6
1855	339.1	1,156.1	747.6	691.9	351.4	196.9
1856	341.1	1,233.9	816.3	738.2	355.2	207.9
1857	322.5	1,296.4	819.0	746.9	358.9	208.1
1858	344.3	1,224.3	807.2	733.5	362.6	202.3
1859	319.3	1,330.6	845.2	764.2	366.3	208.6
1860	281.6	1,393.5	884.0	780.4	370.0	210.9
1861	308.8	1,344.2	882.9	778.5	373.7	208.3
1862	300.2	1,271.7	854.9	747.3	378.2	197.6
1863	409.4	1,351.7	889.1	819.8	382.8	214.2
1864	408.5	1,419.2	912.1	844.3	387.4	217.9
1865	361.3	1,519.3	954.5	867.1	392.1	221.1
1866	354.7	1,583.8	998.0	897.0	396.9	226.0
1867	359.0	1,583.8	1,010.0	903.4	401.6	224.9
1868	386.5	1,667.0	1,053.1	950.0	406.5	233.7
1869	398.1	1,667.1	1,070.2	961.2	411.4	233.6
1870	383.7	1,813.2	1,112.4	1,006.6	416.4	241.7

PART II
Analysing economic growth

6 Real wage rates and GDP per head

6.1 INTRODUCTION

Part I of this book has presented a predominantly positive picture of long-run economic growth and development in Britain from the Black Death of 1348–9 until 1870. Between the early fourteenth century and 1700 GDP per head approximately doubled and it doubled again between 1700 and 1870. Before 1780 progress was fitful, with the greatest gains concentrated into the twin periods of demographic decline in the second halves of the fourteenth and seventeenth centuries, but, crucially, there was little erosion of these gains during the sequel episodes of population growth in the sixteenth and eighteenth centuries. In fact, well before the industrial revolution got under way population and GDP per head were rising together. Malthus [1798], however, in his *Essay on the principle of population*, was convinced that the relationship between population growth and output per head was otherwise, since, sooner or later, diminishing returns to labour were bound to accrue. This is possibly exemplified by the inverse correlation between population and GDP per head that appears to have prevailed during the second half of the thirteenth century. It is without parallel over the next five centuries: later phases of population growth certainly brought their quota of socio-economic difficulties but, for the most part, declining GDP per head was not one of them.

Britain's post-Black Death fitful but nonetheless progressively incremental improvement in output per head is at variance with the picture often painted of Malthusian stagnation – or, *l'histoire immobile*, as Emmanuel Le Roy Ladurie (1974) dubbed it – across much of Europe before the mid-nineteenth century. Especially influential in shaping this view have been long-run series of building workers' real wage rates, which have been widely used as proxies for material living standards and, thus, GDP per head. Across the continent these show that late-medieval real wage rates were not significantly bettered until at least the final decades of the nineteenth century (Allen, 2001), leading to the supposition that there had been little improvement in output per head in the interim. The pioneering work in Britain was undertaken by Phelps Brown and Hopkins (1955, 1956; corrected and revised by Munro, no date), who memorably showed that the purchasing power of a building labourer's daily wage rate was greater in the mid-fifteenth century than at any subsequent point until the 1880s. Further, their series suggested that until well into the nineteenth century, trends in real wage rates and population were inversely related, much as Malthus might have supposed. Thus, the zero demographic growth of the 1440s–80s and 1730s–40s coincided with real-wage-rate peaks and the real-wage-rate minima of 1295, 1316, 1597, 1631 and 1801 all mark years when population had been growing rapidly and subsistence pressures were especially acute (Campbell, 2009). In true Malthusian fashion, each successive wave of population growth, in the thirteenth, sixteenth, early seventeenth and eighteenth centuries appears to have culminated in a serious subsistence crisis when living standards were squeezed hard, excess deaths mounted and fertility, for a time, was curbed.

This pessimistic view of English economic development right up to the industrial revolution has recently been endorsed by Clark (2004, 2005, 2007a), who refines the Phelps Brown and Hopkins building workers' wage-rate series, adds a wage-rate series for agricultural labourers and constructs a new aggregate price index. In addition, he provides new time-series for land rents and capital income and combines those with real wage rates to reconstruct GDP per head from the income side (Clark, 2010a). Unsurprisingly, because this new GDP per head series is dominated by the real wage rate, it essentially endorses the chronology identified by Phelps Brown and Hopkins over 60 years ago. Thus, Clark infers that early-nineteenth-century Britain was no wealthier per head than mid-fifteenth century England, with much of the so-called economic 'progress' during the intervening years merely absorbed in maintaining an enlarged population at pre-existing standards of living. De facto, any economic growth over this long period was transitory, negligible or non-existent.

It would, however, be unwise to rely too exclusively on the real-wage-rate evidence. As Hatcher (2011) has recently pointed out, Phelps Brown and Hopkins (1956: 296) specifically warned against interpreting their series as a measure of living standards since, on the income side, it takes no account of how many days' work labourers were getting and what other resources they had, and, on the outlay side, lacks information on important costs and is heavily reliant upon wholesale rather than retail prices. Moreover, a condition for the reconstruction of a long wage-rate series is that workers are engaged on tasks little affected by the refinements of skill and advances in technology that are integral to long-run economic progress. Nor are the wage-rate data themselves unproblematic, with the highest rates recorded during the very period when their documentary base is thinnest and possibly skewed towards the higher rates paid to casual workers on short-term contracts (Hatcher, 2011). Any exaggeration of wage levels during the fifteenth-century 'golden age' of wage earning will naturally reinforce the impression that there was scant scope for improvement thereafter.

Wage rates paid to adult males performing specific tasks should not be equated with earnings, let alone household incomes. After all, throughout pre-industrial Europe it was the household, comprising men, women, children and sometimes servants, that was the primary unit of economic production and consumption. Households had the capacity to vary their contribution to the workforce according to their wants and needs and the availability of paid employment and its alternatives. They might offset falling real wage rates by working more days, trade drudgery for leisure and work less when wage rates rose, or embrace consumerism and work longer in order to acquire more goods in what de Vries (1994) has described as an 'industrious revolution'. The most straightforward way to reconcile the real-wage-rate evidence with the output-based GDP per head estimates is therefore to assume that the number of days worked per worker did not remain constant over time.

Plainly, these conspicuous discrepancies between the chronologies of real wage rates and those of GDP per head, and between income-based and output-based estimates of GDP per head, warrant closer examination. Accordingly, Section 6.2 compares the output-based and income-based measures of GDP per head and shows how the long-run stagnation in the income-based measure of GDP per head is driven largely by the daily real-wage-rate series. Section 6.3 then demonstrates how the long-run stagnation of daily real wage rates can be reconciled with the trend growth of GDP per head measured from the output side by an increase in the number of days worked per worker during the early modern period, although a subsidiary issue of the representativeness of the nominal wage series is also considered. Section 6.4 examines the implications of the trend growth of GDP per head for those more pessimistic verdicts on British economic development which emphasise the negative effects of population growth. Section 6.5 concludes, drawing attention to the fit between rising urbanisation rates and GDP per head after c.1500.

6.2   INCOME-BASED AND OUTPUT-BASED MEASURES OF GDP PER HEAD

Lindert and Williamson (1982), Snooks (1995) and Mayhew (1995a) have all offered income-based estimates of current-price GDP for individual benchmark years, constructed for the most part by summing the incomes of all socio-economic groups, landed and landless, rural and urban, rich and poor (Table 5.04). Clark (2010a) approaches the task differently and constructs decadal estimates of GDP over a seven-century period by summing factor incomes from labour, land and capital. Labour income is obtained by multiplying average wages of male employees by the number of male and female workers (in male equivalents), assuming a constant share of the population participating in the labour-force and a constant number of days worked per year. Rental income is the average rent per acre multiplied by the farmed acreage, which is also assumed to have been constant over time. Capital income is derived from estimated average annual rates of return (interest rates) multiplied by the stock of capital. The resulting nominal GDP is deflated by an aggregate price index to obtain real GDP, which is then divided by population to yield GDP per head. By contrast, the real GDP per head series presented in this study (Chapter 5) has been built up from the output side, as far as possible on an annual basis, using volume indicators. Nominal income is obtained in this approach by reflating the real outputs for each sector using sector-specific price indices, as described in Section 5.2.1. To facilitate comparison with Clark's income-based GDP series these annual results are here averaged on a decadal basis.

Figure 6.01 sets out the very different trajectories for GDP per head suggested by the two approaches. Note that the output-based series starts lower and ends higher than the income-based series. Each

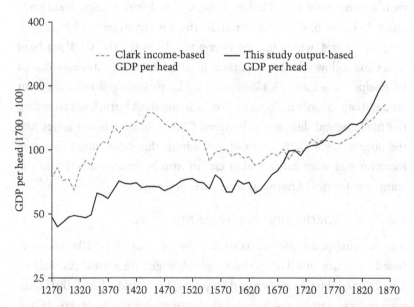

FIGURE 6.01 Alternative estimates of real GDP per head, England 1270–1700 and Great Britain 1700–1870 (decadal averages, 1700 = 100, log scale). *Sources*: Clark (2010a); Appendix 5.3.

is characterised by decline during the thirteenth century to respective low points in the 1280s and 1310s. Thereafter, both exhibit substantial growth during the fourteenth century across the Black Death, although the increase is greater in amplitude and longer in duration in the case of the income-based series, which does not peak until a full generation after the output-based series has ceased to rise. Moreover, whereas the latter then holds steady until the 1640s, apart from minor dips in the 1580s–90s and 1630s, the income-based series declines fairly continuously from the 1450s to a low-point in the 1630s–40s, by which time most of the post-Black Death gains have been eliminated. From the 1650s both series begin to move in tandem again, with the output-based series rising more steeply than the income-based series. In fact, the latter grows more slowly throughout the eighteenth and nineteenth centuries than either the output-based series or the well-regarded series constructed by Crafts and Harley (1992).

Clark's (2010a) income-based real GDP per head series works primarily in nominal terms before being deflated with an aggregate price index. In Figure 6.02, it is clear that its trend is driven largely by the real-wage-rate series, which has the largest weight in the real GDP per head series and follows the broad pattern of daily real wage rates established by Phelps Brown and Hopkins (1956). The inclusion of incomes from land and capital only makes a difference in the short term. Understanding the fundamental differences between Clark's income-based series and the output-based GDP per head series from this study must therefore focus on real wage rates, which can in turn be broken down into the component series of nominal wage rates and prices.

6.2.1   Alternative nominal-wage-rate series

The starting-point for the construction of Clark's (2010a) income-based estimate of GDP is the nominal-wage-rate series. As well as Clark (2005), Phelps Brown and Hopkins (1955) and Allen (2001) offer money-wage-rate series. Because the focus of this study is on real GDP and the extent of inflation over the period 1270–1870, it is convenient to plot these three variant money-wage-rate series deflated by the same

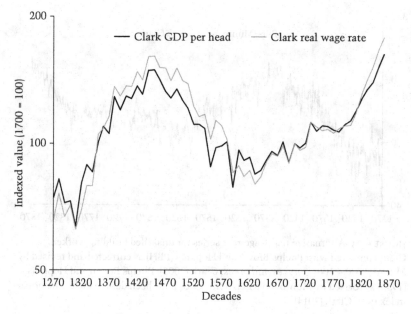

FIGURE 6.02 Clark's real factor incomes, 1200–1870 (1700 = 100, log scale). *Source*: Clark (2010a).

aggregate price index in Figures 6.03 and 6.04. This means that the alternative real-wage-rate series can differ only because of the money-wage-rate series, and makes it easier to assess the contribution of choices about the latter to differences in the former. The price deflator used for this purpose has been taken from Clark (2010a), since Clark's (2005) nominal-wage-rate series is the benchmark in this exercise. Figure 6.03 compares the Clark (2005) and Phelps Brown and Hopkins (1955) money-wage-rate series for building labourers, both deflated by the Clark (2010a) price index. The differences are minimal, suggesting that Clark's real wage rate and hence his real GDP-per-head series, despite all its refinements, ends up merely reproducing the findings of Phelps Brown and Hopkins. A very similar picture emerges if the same exercise is done for building craftsmen.

Figure 6.04 compares the Clark (2005) money-wage-rate series for building labourers with Allen's (2001) equivalent series for London,

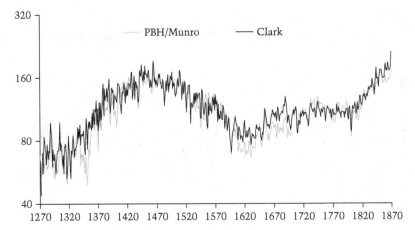

FIGURE 6.03 Alternative real-wage-rate series for unskilled building workers: Clark compared with Phelps Brown and Hopkins (PBH) as corrected and revised by Munro (1700 = 100). *Sources and notes*: Clark (2005); Phelps Brown and Hopkins (1955) as revised by Munro (no date). Both series have been deflated with the price index from Clark (2014).

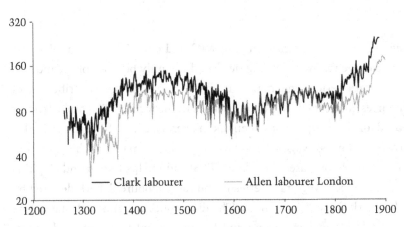

FIGURE 6.04 The alternative real-wage-rate series for unskilled building workers of Clark and Allen, 1250–1900 (1700 = 100, log scale). *Sources and notes*: Clark (2005); Allen (2001). Both series have been deflated with the price index from Clark (2010a).

again with both series deflated by the Clark (2010a) price index. In contrast to the almost complete agreement evident in Figure 6.03 between the Clark (2005) and Phelps Brown and Hopkins (1955) wage-rate series, Figure 6.04 does reveal some significant differences between the Clark (2005) and Allen (2001) wage-rate series. Nevertheless, the broad patterns are not dissimilar. Indeed, as will be shown later, if the two series are based on the mean of 1270–1870 = 100 rather than 1700 = 100, their paths appear close together for a much greater proportion of the period (see Figure 6.07 below). This suggests that the choice of the particular nominal-wage-rate index is not crucial for determining the long-run stagnation of real GDP per head constructed from the income side.

6.2.2   *Alternative aggregate price indices*

If alternative nominal-wage-rate series make little difference to the trend of Clark's (2010a) real GDP-per-head series, does the same apply to the choice of the aggregate price index used to deflate nominal incomes? Figure 6.05 plots the GDP deflator from Clark (2010a) together with the aggregate price index from this study. Before 1700 the two aggregate price indices move closely together over both the short and the long runs; after 1700, however, the Clark (2010a) index rises more during the French Revolutionary and Napoleonic Wars and falls less thereafter. Since most of the individual price series used in construction of the aggregate price index in this study are taken from Clark (2006), these divergences are largely caused by alternative weighting schemes. Here, the most important difference is the greater weight given to industrial prices in this study, particularly as the relative price of industrial goods declined during the industrial-revolution period. By focusing on the price of agricultural goods, based largely on budget studies for working-class families, Clark (2010a) understates the gain in real incomes that arose from the greater affordability of industrial goods.

Figure 6.06 plots Clark's real GDP-per-head series deflated using the aggregate price index from this study as well as the Clark (2010a)

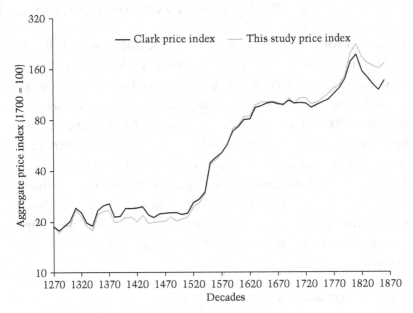

FIGURE 6.05 Alternative aggregate price indices, 1270–1870 (1700 = 100). *Sources*: Clark (2010a); Appendix 5.1.

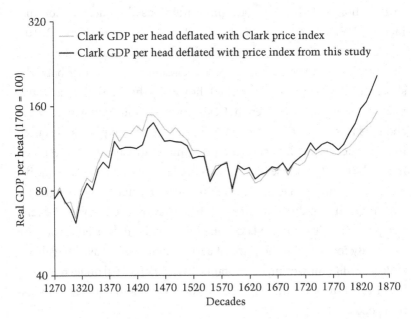

FIGURE 6.06 The effect of alternative price deflators upon Clark's estimate of real GDP per head, 1200–1870 (1700 = 100). *Sources and notes*: Clark's (2010) nominal GDP per head series has been deflated with price indices from (i) Clark (2010a) and (ii) Appendix 5.1.

price index. It is clear that this makes a substantial difference to the path of GDP per head after 1700, raising the annual growth rate from 0.31 per cent to 0.48 per cent. This is sufficient to explain all the difference between the income-based and output-based GDP-per-head series for the period 1700–1870. Note, however, that whereas use of the aggregate price index from this study raises the real growth rate of Clark's (2010a) series, use of the Clark aggregate price index has no equivalent effect on the real growth rate of the output-based series, which is derived from volume indicators. Rather, use of the Clark aggregate price index with the real GDP-per-head series from this study would lower the growth of nominal GDP. In the case of the pre-1700 period, it makes little difference to the path of real GDP per head which aggregate price index is used, since the two indices follow much more similar paths between 1270 and 1700.

6.3   RECONCILING INCOME-BASED AND OUTPUT-BASED MEASURES OF GDP PER HEAD

The previous section has established that the trend in Clark's income-based GDP per head series is driven by his real-wage-rate series. Since the former is not available on an annual basis, the focus here is on the latter, which is plotted together with the output-based GDP per head series in Figure 6.07. As noted in Section 6.2.1, although Allen's (2001) real-wage-rate series is sometimes seen as presenting a different view of the long-run evolution of living standards from that of Clark (2005) (Figure 6.04), if all three indices are plotted together with the mean of 1270–1870 set equal to 100, it is clear that both real-wage-rate series diverge significantly from the output-based GDP-per-head series. Long phases of congruence between real wage rates and GDP per head between, first, 1270 and c.1350 and then c.1580 and c.1750, are separated by two extended periods of divergence. In the first, real wage rates increased more rapidly than GDP per head between the 1350s and 1450s and then declined from the 1450s to 1640s while GDP per head remained essentially stable. The peak real wage rates of the mid-fifteenth century were not seen again until the late nineteenth century

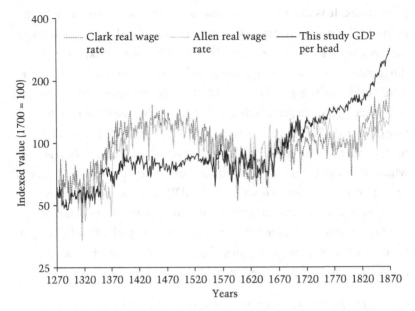

FIGURE 6.07 Daily real wage rates of unskilled building workers and GDP per head, 1270–1870 (log scale, mean of 1270–1870 = 100). *Sources*: Clark (2005); Allen (2001); Appendix 5.3.

and hence play an important role in creating the impression of no long-run progress in living standards. In the second, as the industrial revolution took off during the second half of the eighteenth century, it was real wage rates that stagnated while GDP per head continued to grow steadily.

Neither of these divergences between real wage rates and GDP-per head was exclusive to Britain. GDP-per-head estimates are now available for Spain from the 1280s, the centre and north of Italy from the 1310s and Holland from the 1350s, together with real-wage-rate series for building labourers (although the Amsterdam wage series does not start until the 1410s) (Álvarez-Nogal and Prados de la Escosura, 2013; Malanima, 2011; van Zanden and van Leeuwen, 2012). In Figure 6.08 GDP per head and real wage rates are indexed against their respective means for the period 1400–1849 and real wage rates then divided by GDP per head. The two English divergences

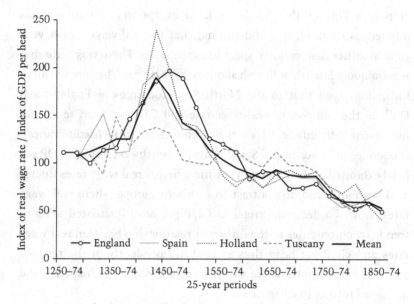

FIGURE 6.08 England, Spain, Holland and Tuscany: index of real wage rates of building labourers divided by index of GDP per head, 1250/74 to 1850/74 (25-year averages, real wage rates and GDP per head are indexed on their respective means 1400–1849). *Sources*: England: this text; Spain: Álvarez-Nogal and Prados de la Escosura, 2013; Holland: van Zanden and van Leeuwen, 2012; Tuscany: Malanima, 2011.

already identified show up clearly, with wage rates rising relative to GDP per head in the fifteenth century and the inverse after *c*.1750. So, too, do equivalent divergences in Spain and Holland (albeit with the fifteenth-century peak in favour of real wage rates occurring a quarter of a century earlier). Tuscany alone is different, with a lesser inflation of real wage rates after the Black Death and quicker return to their mean relationship with GDP per head. Thereafter, however, the ratio between these two variables falls broadly into line with those in England, Spain and Holland and shares with them the marked negative divergence between real wage rates and GDP per head after *c*.1750.

 Synchronous swings in the ratio between wage rates and GDP per head in four independently constructed time-series suggest that they are neither a figment of the evidence nor a product of the methodologies employed. Further, they imply, with the exception of certain obvious differences of amplitude and timing, that these divergences have a general rather than country-specific explanation. There was little that was uniquely English or British about either of them. They are the more intriguing given that in the North Sea economies of England and Holland the component real-wage-rate and GDP-per-head series followed markedly different trajectories from those of the Mediterranean economies of Tuscany and Spain. Thus, in northwest Europe GDP per head exhibited a rising trend over time whereas real wage rates fluctuated without trend, in contrast to southern Europe where real wage rates showed a declining trend as GDP per head fluctuated without trend. Synchronicities in the divergent relationship between real wage rates and GDP per head thus existed independently of the reversal in the economic fortunes of the two regions noted in Chapter 5 and discussed further in Chapter 7.

6.3.1 Explaining divergences between real wage rates and GDP per head

Angeles (2008) provides a general framework for reconciling real wage rates and GDP per head with reference to the divergence that emerged from the mid-eighteenth century. He starts with the definition of labour's share of income (α) as the product of the daily wage rate (w) and the number of days worked (L) divided by nominal GDP which is the product of real GDP (Y) and the price of GDP (p^Y). The wage bill is thus equal to labour's share of nominal GDP:

$$wL = \alpha\, p^Y\, Y \tag{6.1}$$

Now divide both sides by the consumer price index (p^C) and by population (N) to yield:

$$\left(\frac{w}{p^C}\right)\left(\frac{L}{N}\right) = \alpha\left(\frac{p^Y}{p^C}\right)\left(\frac{Y}{N}\right) \tag{6.2}$$

which can be rearranged to bring the labour-supply term to the right-hand side and invert the relative-price term:

$$\left(\frac{w}{p^C}\right) = \frac{(\alpha)\left(\frac{Y}{N}\right)}{\left(\frac{L}{N}\right)\left(\frac{p^C}{p^Y}\right)} \tag{6.3}$$

This yields an equation for relating changes in real wage rates (w/p^C) over time to changes in GDP per head (Y/N), labour's share of income (α), labour supply (L/N) and the price of consumption goods relative to the GDP deflator (p^C/p^Y):

$$\frac{\left(\frac{w}{p^C}\right)_1}{\left(\frac{w}{p^C}\right)_0} = \frac{\left(\frac{Y}{N}\right)_1}{\left(\frac{Y}{N}\right)_0} \frac{(\alpha_1)}{(\alpha_0)} \left[\frac{\left(\frac{L}{N}\right)_1}{\left(\frac{L}{N}\right)_0}\right]^{-1} \left[\frac{\left(\frac{p^C}{p^Y}\right)_1}{\left(\frac{p^C}{p^Y}\right)_0}\right]^{-1} \tag{6.4}$$

Angeles (2008: 157) demonstrates that it is possible to explain the slower growth of real wage rates compared with GDP per head from the mid-eighteenth century largely by increases in the numbers of hours worked per day and days worked per person, although part of the divergence was also due to a declining share of labour income in GDP, with relative price changes playing no significant role. In effect, more people were participating in the labour-force and, for a variety of mutually reinforcing reasons, working longer and harder. They were doing so partly to make ends meet but also to avail themselves of the widening array of consumer goods. Unfortunately, Angeles (2008) was unable to comment on the pre-1700 period, for which he lacked data on GDP per head.

Table 6.01 conducts a similar exercise for the longer period, using Clark's (2006, 2010a) data on real wage rates, consumer prices and labour's share of income, together with the GDP per head series from this study. Equation (6.4) is used to derive a simulated path for labour supply. Since relative prices and labour's share of income changed only modestly, consistency requires a large increase in days worked per year, particularly during the period between the 1450s and 1650s when daily real wages fell dramatically but GDP per head held steady. Mid-fifteenth-century labourers had enjoyed an exceptionally favourable work/leisure balance; their seventeenth-century counterparts did not and had to substitute work for leisure in order to satisfy the needs and wants which their fifteenth-century predecessors had

Table 6.01 *Explaining the divergence between GDP per head and real wage rates, 1300s–1860s (1700 = 100)*

Variable	Percentage change over the period						
	1300s–1340s	1340s–1450s	1450s–1650s	1650s–1750s	1750s–1800s	1800s–1860s
Real wage (w/p^C)	+5.5	+75.0	-50.4	+15.2	-3.6	+59.7
GDP per head (Y/N)	+2.8	+30.6	+4.2	+48.3	+19.6	+46.5
Labour's share (α)	-5.1	+15.3	-8.5	-1.7	-0.2	+12.1
Relative prices (p^C/p^Y)	+4.4	-6.4	+8.0	-0.7	+9.2	+1.6
Simulated labour supply (L/N)	-11.5	-8.0	+78.0	+27.4	+13.4	+1.2

Sources and notes: Real wage: Clark (2006); GDP per head: derived from Appendix 5.3; labour's share: Clark (2010a); relative prices: Clark (2006) and Appendix 5.1. The growth rates are calculated on decadal averages.

been able to take for granted. This broadly fits the timing of the industrious revolution, hypothesised by de Vries (1994) to have occurred after the Reformation, but raises the question whether the scale of the increase in days worked is too large to be credible. To answer this it is necessary to turn to independent estimates of labour supply per head.

6.3.2 Variations in labour supply per head

Table 6.02 sets out the currently available data on days worked per year. The evidence is strongest for the industrial-revolution period, where Voth (1998, 2001) uses court records from London and the north of England to infer the decline of the pre-industrial practice of not working on Mondays (known colloquially as St Monday) (Reid, 1976). Clark and van der Werf (1998) infer days worked by comparing wages paid to workers hired on annual contracts and those on daily rates in various parts of England for a period stretching from the second half of the sixteenth century to the late nineteenth century. Their figures are broadly consistent with those of Voth for the nineteenth century, although Voth's figures suggest a more sudden increase after 1760. Clark and van der Werf's data also overlap with a set of figures covering the fifteenth and sixteenth centuries calculated by Allen and Weisdorf (2011: 721) from a study by Blanchard (1978) of workers who combined farming with lead mining in the Mendips. The total number of days worked is derived as the sum of days worked in agriculture (135) plus the share of the remaining 130 workdays spent in mining. Again there is broad consistency between the two sources in the overlapping years in the second half of the sixteenth century. Especially interesting is the finding of the low number of days worked in the fifteenth and early sixteenth centuries, which would be consistent with the notion of an early modern industrious revolution.

Although he did not use the term, the idea of an early modern industrious revolution can be traced back to Max Weber's (1930) controversial work on the protestant ethic. Hayami (1967) subsequently coined the term industrious revolution in the context of early modern Japan. It was then applied to post-Reformation Europe by de Vries (1994),

Table 6.02 *Estimates of the annual days worked per person,*
1433–1870

Period	Blanchard/Allen and Weisdorf	Clark and van der Werf	Voth
1433	165		
1536	180		
1560–1599		257	
1578	260		
1584	210		
1598	259		
1600–1649		266	
1650–1699		276	
1685		312	
1700–1732		286	
1733–1736		295	
1760			258
1771		280	
1800			333
1830			336
1867–1869		293–311	
1870		318	

Sources and notes: 1433–1598: Allen and Weisdorf (2011: 721), derived
from Blanchard (1978: 24) as the number of days worked in agriculture
(135) plus the share of the remaining 130 workdays spent in mining.
1560–1599 to 1870: Clark and van der Werf (1998: 838). 1760–1830:
Voth (2001: 1078).

with whose work the term is now most widely associated. Although
there are a number of components in his concept of the industrious
revolution, the basic idea is that people worked harder to obtain new
goods made available through long-distance trade and industrial innovation. At the same time, reform of the religious calendar reduced the
number of holidays. This interpretation seems to fit the British case
well, with commercial expansion from the sixteenth century dramatically increasing availability of sugar and tobacco from the New World

and tea, coffee, sugar, spices, silk, cotton and porcelain from Asia (Davis, 1973: 26–40; Clay, 1984, 121–41, 154–63; de Vries, 2008: 181–5). This was paralleled by increased domestic output of furniture, cutlery, cooking utensils, clocks, cloth, pewter, pottery, ironware and printed books (Figure 4.04) as British industry innovated and expanded (Nef, 1934; Weatherill, 1988; Overton and others, 2004). Since 1450 industrial output had been growing faster than population (Table 4.09). By 1522 industry's share of the labour-force was 23 per cent and had expanded to 34 per cent by 1700 (Table 5.02), when its share of value-added output was 41 per cent (Table 5.01). Here were the expanding labour-market opportunities that enabled more people to work more days per year and the increasingly affordable wave of consumer goods that provided them with the incentive to do so.

6.3.3 The representativeness of the wage-rate data

A rather different way of reconciling the real-wage-rate and GDP-per-head evidence is offered by Hatcher (2011), who argues that the pattern of real wage rates charted by Phelps Brown and Hopkins (1956), Clark (2005, 2007a) and others is unrepresentative of labour incomes more generally. Hatcher demonstrates that the impressive daily real wage rates of the mid-fifteenth century could not have been earned throughout the year by most workers. Although the wage rates in Figures 6.03 and 6.04 are for unskilled urban building labourers, Clark (2007a) claims a similar pattern for agricultural labourers. Yet, as Hatcher (2011) shows, the agricultural wage index is based largely upon rates paid to casual labourers, which were much higher than those earned by agricultural workers on long contracts (*famuli*) and rarely available for more than short periods during the peak season. Further, he shows that if employers had paid labourers at these rates throughout the year they would have been left worse off than their workers, while large landowners doing likewise would have been bankrupted. Since this inversion of income distribution clearly did not occur during the fifteenth century, Hatcher concludes that Clark's agricultural wage-rates are 'unreal'. Blanchard's (1978) evidence on the small number of days worked by lead miners in the Mendips at the beginning of the sixteenth century would also be consistent with Hatcher's analysis.

Although with the current state of research, it is not possible to rule out Hatcher's (2011) argument, the fact that similar trends can be seen in other European real-wage-rate series (Figure 6.08) suggests that it would be unwise to rely too heavily on a case that depends on circumstances specific to England. Accepting the daily wage-rate series at face value, the evidence seems to point towards a progressive withdrawal of labour from the labour-force between c.1350 and c.1450 and re-engagement thereafter. As suggested by de Vries (1994), that re-engagement was reinforced from the mid-sixteenth century by a widespread industrious revolution, of which England, Holland and Flanders were by no means the only exemplars. While the European dimensions of these developments await further investigation, it is already clear that the relationships between wage rates, earnings and household incomes were less consistent and more complex than is usually appreciated. Patently, for good reasons, labour supply per head was anything but constant over time. To take the real-wage-rate series currently in use as representative of annual living standards without further corroboration, as emphasised by the authors of the first such series (Phelps Brown and Hopkins, 1956: 296), is therefore imprudent. Supplementing them with output-based estimates of GDP per head offers a more complete picture of long-run growth and highlights significant shifts in the economic priorities and strategies of households and their attitudes to work and leisure.

6.4 BREAKING OUT OF THE MALTHUSIAN INTERPRETATION OF PRE-INDUSTRIAL ECONOMIC DEVELOPMENT

6.4.1 The Malthusian framework

Malthusian theory has long exercised a powerful influence upon interpretations of economic development during Britain's pre-industrial past (Hatcher and Bailey, 2001: 21–65; Clark, 2007b). Its central tenet is that population growth is bound to exceed the growth of food supply so that, in the long run, living standards eventually regress to the minimum necessary to maintain subsistence. This hangs upon two key assumptions. First, that population responds positively to real incomes, so that, if the real wage rate rises, fertility will increase and mortality decline until the consequent increased supply of labour exerts downward pressure on wage rates, thereby reducing opportunities for marriage and family formation and leading to worsening nutrition, hygiene, sanitation and public health and, hence, heightened mortality (the positive check). Second, with land in fixed supply, wage rates respond negatively to population because of the inescapability of diminishing returns to labour. In the first, 1798, edition of his *Essay on the principle of population*, Malthus famously claimed that while populations grow biologically in geometric progression, output can only increase in arithmetic progression, until the widening disparity between population and output precipitates such severe crises of subsistence and public health that the two are brought back into line. This, in turn, creates the preconditions for onset of a new cycle of growth, crisis and contraction. Each cycle is mirrored in the chronology of real wages rates, which decline as the population grows, sink to their nadir when major positive checks strike, and then recover as the population contracts.

These principles are illustrated diagrammatically in Figure 6.09, derived from Weir (1998). The left-hand diagram shows the relationship

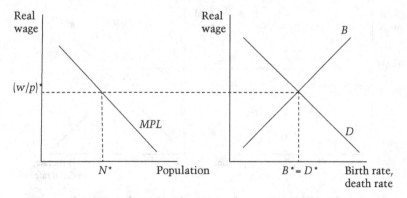

FIGURE 6.09 The Malthusian framework. *Source*: Derived from Weir (1998). For explanation, see text.

between the real wage rate and the level of population, characterised as the downward sloping marginal product of labour schedule (MPL), reflecting the diminishing returns to labour. In this simple framework, assuming unchanging labour supply per person, the real wage rate is equated to real income per head. The right-hand diagram shows the relationship between the real wage rate and the flows of births (B) and deaths (D). As the real wage rate declines, the death rate increases (termed the positive check) and the birth rate decreases (termed the preventive check). Where the birth and death schedules intersect, the birth rate is equal to the death rate. This yields the equilibrium of the system, with births equal to deaths ($B^* = D^*$), a stable population (N^*) and an equilibrium real wage $(w/p)^*$.

Malthusian theory predicts that any increase in the real wage rate will in due course engender a corresponding increase in population. This in turn exerts downward pressure on the real wage rate and causes it to return to the equilibrium level, which is normally interpreted as bare-bones subsistence income. Due to the iron law of wages the economy therefore remains ensnared in a 'Malthusian trap'. Consider in Figure 6.10 what happens if there is a positive shock to the marginal product of labour (MPL) schedule through, say, technological progress in agriculture. At the initial population level, N^*, the real wage rate increases from $(w/p)^*$ to $(w/p)'$ and workers experience a

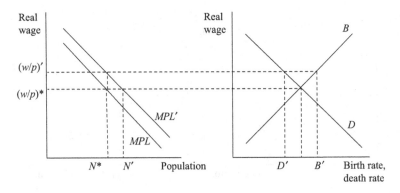

FIGURE 6.10 The Malthusian trap. *Source:* Derived from Weir (1998). For explanation, see text.

higher standard of living. Next consider what happens to the flows of births and deaths in the right-hand diagram: with a higher real wage rate, the preventive and positive checks are weaker so that fertility increases and mortality declines. With births (B') now exceeding deaths (D'), the population must be increasing. In the left-hand diagram, as the population increases, the real wage rate falls, and this process continues until the real wage rate reduces back to $(w/p)^*$, at which point the population has reached its new equilibrium level (N') at the subsistence real wage.

One way to stop this return to the subsistence real wage is through what Malthus called 'moral restraint', whereby marriage is delayed, more women never marry and conceptions outside marriage are discouraged. As illustrated in Figure 6.11, this shifts the whole relationship between the real wage rate and fertility; moving the fertility schedule from B^* to B', raising the equilibrium real wage rate from $(w/p)^*$ to $(w/p)'$, and lowering the equilibrium population from N^* to N'. Such behaviour, of course, curbs population growth, cushions it against potential positive shocks and ensures that living standards of a greater proportion of households remain above bare-bones subsistence (Mokyr and Voth, 2010: 15). Malthus introduced moral restraint as a theoretical possibility in the revised [1803] second edition of his

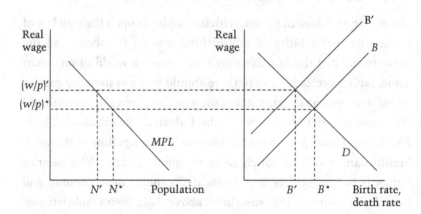

FIGURE 6.11 Fertility control. *Source*: Derived from Weir (1998). For explanation, see text.

Essay on the principles of population but did not think it likely to be of any practical significance.

Except perhaps in the thirteenth century (Postan, 1972), the evidence for pre-industrial England presented above is clearly not consistent with the 'strong' version of the Malthusian model as articulated in the first edition of the *Principles of population*. First, the fact that the European marriage pattern is known to have been in place from at least the end of the middle ages suggests that moral restraint was important in practice as well as in theory (Hajnal, 1965; Smith, 1979; Wrigley and Schofield, 1989: 422–24; Wrigley and others, 1997: 128–39). Second, although population numbers had matched the level of the 1340s by the 1620s, the enlarged value-added contributions of the industrial and service sectors ensured that incomes per head remained two-thirds higher and from the 1650s were creeping steadily upwards. Third, as will be demonstrated in Chapter 8, the proportion of people at the bottom of the income distribution, living at or close to bare-bones subsistence, progressively shrank over time and was never again as great as in the early fourteenth century (Table 8.07). Slowly but surely the proportion of households living above the poverty line was expanding.

6.4.2   The Smithian alternative

The strong Malthusian model, with its emphasis upon the iron law of wages, the inevitability of diminishing returns to labour and the inescapability of the positive check, envisages a world of recurrent demographic cycles in which 'there should be no systematic gain in living standards on average across societies between earliest man and the world of 1800 on the eve of the Industrial Revolution' (Clark, 2007b: 40). These gloomy predictions are less compelling in the weak Malthusian model, in which there is moral restraint, the balance struck between fertility and mortality is more indeterminate and household incomes are sustained above bare-bones subsistence. Relaxing the assumption of diminishing returns to labour opens further possibilities.

For Adam Smith [1776], significant productivity gains could be generated through greater division of labour, contingent upon growth of the market. His stress upon the gains to be obtained from exchange is the most important alternative to the Malthusian framework for understanding pre-industrial economic development (Persson, 2010: 21–41). Under conditions of Smithian growth, higher population densities expand the size of the market, increase the potential for greater division of labour and lead, via a series of positive-feedback mechanisms, to establishment of a gradually ascending spiral of progress. Maintaining population levels thus becomes material to sustaining economic prosperity, as was most conspicuously the case in Italy during its twelfth- and thirteenth-century commercial revolution and Holland during its sixteenth- and early-seventeenth-century Golden Age (Campbell, 2014).

Boserup (1965, 1981) also hypothesises a positive relationship between population density and real income levels. In its simplest form this effect is manifest in the processes of land-use substitution and steady reduction in the share of fallow in the cultivated acreage noted in Chapters 2 and 3 (Boserup, 1965). But this positive relationship is also apparent in the influence of the expanding London market upon land-use specialisation and the organisation of agricultural production within the surrounding metropolitan region. This was already apparent in the late-medieval period, long before the industrial revolution, with Campbell and others (1993) identifying a hierarchy of concentric zones around London. These were characterised by different types and intensities of agricultural production according to levels of economic rent, as predicted by the theoretical model of von Thünen [1826] (Hall, 1966) but qualified by the confounding role of topography, soil fertility, access to cheap water transport and an array of rural institutions. They argue that insofar as the provisioning of London at that date was subject to constraints, these arose less from the capacity of the city's hinterland to raise output and generate surpluses than from the, as yet, limited demand incentives provided by a city of 60–80,000 inhabitants to specialise, innovate, intensify and invest (Campbell,

1997). From the sixteenth century, in contrast, London's rapid growth to a quarter of a million by 1610 and over half a million by 1700 transformed it into an engine of growth (Wrigley, 1967, 1985).

Boserup's (1981) second positive effect operates through investment in infrastructure in the metropolitan centre, which is dependent upon population density, thus creating increasing rather than diminishing returns. This is most evident in the service sector. In transport, London was early the focus of the national road network and by the fourteenth century had become the most important port in Britain, handling the vast majority of international trade (Davis, 1954: 164–5; Campbell, 2008: 914–15). In finance, the City of London overtook Antwerp and eventually Amsterdam and during the eighteenth century grew to become the most important financial centre in northwest Europe and eventually in the world (Neal, 1990). From modest beginnings it also became the single greatest source of investment capital in the country. Over the course of the sixteenth, seventeenth and eighteenth centuries, the city's growth as a centre of concentrated demand and conspicuous consumption stimulated development of capitalist agriculture within its ever-widening hinterland and boosted production of a host of industrial manufactures at many remoter locations, with Londoners providing much of the capital that was invested in such ventures (Fisher, 1948; Langton and Hoppe, 1983; Boulton, 2000). James I (r. 1603–25) may have railed at London's gargantuan appetite for goods and commodities supplied from all corners of the realm, but in so doing failed to recognise the efficiency gains that stemmed from such extensive reorganisation and restructuring of production to meet the demands emanating from the city. Here, after all, was Smithian growth.

None of this is to deny that negative relationships could and did exist between the level of population and incomes per head. Indeed, Persson (2010: 60) has suggested that most of the key elements of pre-industrial economic development are best captured by combining the Smithian framework with elements of the weak Malthusian model. Thus it seems likely that Smithian multiplier effects were weakening in England before the Black Death due to the stiffness of foreign competition and rising transaction costs in international trade, so that urban growth stagnated and industrial employment shrank (Munro, 1999). This resulted in an unhealthy overdependence upon agriculture and much under- and unemployment on the land, to the detriment of labour productivity, wage rates, household incomes and aggregate demand. It is hardly surprising therefore that during the first half of the fourteenth century real wage rates and GDP per head both plumbed some of the lowest levels on record, especially during the succession of acute harvest failures and devastating livestock panzootics that punctuated the period (Figure 6.07; Campbell, 2010). Malthusian positive and preventive checks are both in evidence at this time, as famines precipitated significant excess mortality, poverty undermined the reproductive capacity of the poorest households (Razi, 1980: 71–93) and scarcity drove many couples to postpone marriage (Campbell, 2008: 292–5; Kelly and Ó Gráda, 2012). While this combination of demographic, economic and commercial circumstances prevailed there was little prospect of reversing the process by kickstarting Smithian growth. Shrinking international markets and the dead weight of a swollen and impoverished underclass were against it.

This adverse situation was transformed by the massive excess mortality inflicted by the Black Death and its sequel plague outbreaks, which almost at a stroke redressed the imbalance between population and resources, relieved society of the heavy burden of poverty, reflated demand per head and initiated an immediate increase in incomes per head (Figures 5.05 and 6.04). It was a pattern England shared with a number of other Western European countries, where the sudden labour scarcity precipitated a steep rise in real wage rates and sparked a rash of legislation intended to curb wage demands and restrict the mobility of workers (Allen, 2001; Cohn, 2007). Yet although output per head and incomes both rose, the sheer scale of the population losses meant that overall demand contracted and this set limits to the amount of Smithian growth that could be achieved, especially in an international context where transaction costs remained high. This problem was all the greater in those countries and regions which had not been burdened with excess numbers on the eve of the Black Death. Spain is probably representative of wide areas of late-medieval Europe (Kitsikopoulos, 2012: 336–9). It had remained a thinly peopled frontier economy during the re-conquest period with a vibrant but fragile urban sector. Here, therefore, loss of numbers undermined commercial networks, rendered existing levels of specialisation unsustainable, and depressed levels of income per head (Álvarez-Nogal and Prados de la Escosura, 2013). This profound loss of economic momentum postponed the onset of demographic recovery.

In England, too, in defiance of Malthusian theory, demographic recovery was long delayed in part because recurrent disease outbreaks kept mortality levels high. Yet the absence of population pressure and the favourable resource balance did not lead to rising prosperity due to the circumscribed scale of overall demand,. In fact, rising real wage rates imply that the working day and year were shortening as labourers opted for more leisure and less drudgery rather than more goods, which is why there was no corresponding rise in GDP per head or the urbanisation ratio. Towards the end of the fifteenth century, however, this situation changed. As the population recovered after 1480, although real wage rates began to trend down, GDP per head held steady and the urbanisation ratio began slowly to rise.

By substituting work for leisure and engaging more actively in the expanding industrial sector, sixteenth-century households maintained their incomes at the sacrifice of real wage rates. Over the course of the next 150 years, therefore, the level of GDP per head held remarkably firm in the face of strongly rising population. Any Malthusian tendency towards declining output per head was thwarted by a strengthened work ethic and lengthened working year in combination with structural economic change. Then, in 1597, enactment of a national poor law codified the welfare entitlements of the poorest and most vulnerable individuals during hard times. From early in the seventeenth century, a growing body of circumstantial evidence suggests that the living standards of many, if not all, social groups were improving.

Alongside the growth of publicly funded welfare provision (Slack, 1990), this includes the virtual elimination of famines (Campbell and Ó Gráda, 2011), greater diversity of diets (Feinstein, 1995; Woolgar and others, 2006), availability of new and cheap consumer goods (Spufford, 1984; Weatherill, 1988; Hersh and Voth, 2009), increasing wealth of testators (Overton. 2006), rising literacy levels (Schofield, 1973; Cressy, 1980; Houstan, 1982), diversification of occupations (Goose and Evans, 2000), transformation of the urban built environment (de Vries, 1984; Clark, 2000) and the rebuilding of the rural environment (Platt, 1994; Overton and others, 2004: 122–5).

This was a society developing the economic, social and institutional means of coping with demographic pressure while building a more productive and dynamic economy. The clearest measure of its success is that by the 1650s, when the population reached its seventeenth-century peak, GDP per head was double the level of the impoverished 1280s and set to rise higher (Figure 5.05 and Table 5.06). The vigorous GDP per head growth which then took place between 1650 and 1700 occurred against a backdrop of sagging population numbers, but when demographic growth resumed from 1700, the upward trend in GDP per head continued albeit at a slower pace (Table 5.07). In one of history's great ironies, the British economy finally broke free from Malthusian constraints half a century before Malthus's birth. By the time he published the first edition of his *Essay on the principle of population*, population growth was increasing fast but output was increasing faster (Table 5.07). As noted in Chapter 5, the combined demographic and GDP-per-head growth achieved during the industrial revolution represents the culmination of a process that began at least as far back as the late-medieval period. In a striking inversion of the situation in the fifteenth century, however, from c.1750 these gains in GDP per head were unmatched by commensurate gains in real wage rates. Another industrious revolution was in progress as the new work discipline of workshops, factories and offices took hold and the working day and year lengthened again. Meanwhile, as the capitalisation of production proceeded apace, the returns to labour as a factor of production declined. Hence the paradoxical situation, apparent in Holland, Spain and Italy as well as Britain (Figure 6.08) and diagnosed by Angeles (2008), that real wage rates were deteriorating relative to GDP per head.

6.5   CONCLUSIONS

Real wage rates emerge from this analysis as by no means the neutral measure of living standards for which they have so often been used. As Angeles (2008) identified, temporal changes in income distribution, labour supply per head and relative factor prices all had their impact. Real wage rates were likely to rise whenever labour rose in price relative to land and capital and household members substituted leisure for work and thus reduced the amount of labour per head supplied to the market, as appears to have been the case during the 100 years or so that followed the Black Death. When the opposite conditions prevailed and labour became cheaper as a factor of production, workers had to labour longer and harder to maintain household incomes. Consequently, real wage rates declined still further, as they did from $c.1500$ to $c.1650$ and again from $c.1750$. The end result was that by the early nineteenth century the majority of adult male labourers were working a six-day week with only a few days of holiday per year (Table 6.02). The desire to maintain accustomed subsistence standards was one reason for working harder; post-Reformation reductions in the number of religious holidays another; imposition of stricter work disciplines in workshop, factory and office a third; and a desire to acquire the means to purchase new consumer goods a fourth. This increase per head in the amount of time devoted to remunerated work has become known as the industrious revolution and it helps to explain why, from the end of the fifteenth century in England, real wage rates improved less than GDP per head.

Phelps-Brown and Hopkins (1956: 296) were therefore wise to mistrust real wage rates as an impartial index of living standards, as was Maddison (2003: 252–3) to doubt their capacity to serve as a proxy measure of economic growth. As has been demonstrated in Section 6.2 above, income-based estimates of GDP per head (e.g. Clark, 2010a) in which the wage-rate data loom large, suffer from many of the same

limitations and are no substitute for independently constructed estimates of GDP per head based upon output, such as those presented in
this study. The latter are powerfully endorsed by the evidence for
parallel divergences between real wage rates and GDP per head found
in Spain, Holland and Italy notwithstanding their otherwise very different economic fortunes and circumstances (Figure 6.08). Plainly, the
trends towards, first, dearer labour and less work per head from c.1350
to c.1450 and, then, the opposite from c.1500 to 1650 and, again, from
c.1750, were not unique to England or Britain.

Once the intrinsic limitations of the real-wage-rate data are
recognised, one of the key evidential planks of the Malthusian interpretation of long-term economic development is removed and the
apparent contradiction between the long-run stagnation of daily real
wage rates and the trend growth of GDP per head measured from the
output side disappears. Instead, worsening real wage rates become a
symptom of the profound structural economic changes taking place as
the industrial and service sectors grew in significance and a culture of
thrift and hard work took hold. De Vries's (1994) concept of an industrious revolution is certainly consistent with what is known about
the progressive growth of English industrial employment and output
after c.1450 and especially from c.1550, when it may have been leant
momentum by the religious reforms of the Reformation. By embracing
these expanding industrial-employment opportunities and working
harder the increasing numbers of urban and artisanal households maintained their incomes and improved their consumption of material
goods in an era of rising population, growing resource scarcity and
falling real wage rates. The consequent gains in value-added output
per head prevented GDP per head from declining in the way that it had
done during the second half of the thirteenth century or returning to
the same reduced level of the first half of the fourteenth century. This
was a singular achievement and went hand in hand with a socio-
demographic regime which curbed female fertility and promoted geographical mobility of surplus labour, thereby keeping population growth
rates within bounds. These developments in household employment,

household structures and demographic behaviour are a key part of the story of how England escaped from Malthusian constraints and embarked upon a course of Smithian growth.

Urbanisation ratios provide further corroboration of the picture of market-based economic growth conveyed by the GDP per head estimates. For Kuznets (1966: 271), urbanisation represents 'an increasing division of labour within the country, growing specialisation, and the shift of many activities from non-market-oriented pursuit within the family or the village to specialised market-oriented business firms'. Other things being equal, therefore, 'a rising level of real income per head and a rising proportion of urban dwellers are likely to be linked phenomena in a pre-industrial economy' (Wrigley, 1985: 683). Tellingly, and in direct contrast to the static situation in the fifteenth century, the percentage resident in towns of at least 5,000 inhabitants increased progressively from just 5 per cent c.1500 to 8 per cent by 1600, 17 per cent by 1700 and 21 per cent by 1750 (Wrigley, 1985: 688). Over the same period, London's population grew almost exponentially from around 50,000 to 675,000, as the state and the economy both became more centralised and the city's role in international trade and commerce was enhanced. The capital's impressive growth was both a symptom and a cause of the far-reaching economic and demographic changes then underway, since its expansion was contingent upon sustained supplies of migrants, provisions, fuel and manufactures (Wrigley, 1967). Producers across an ever-widening hinterland responded to its concentrated demand by specialising according to comparative advantage (Fisher, 1935). Again, such positive developments sit ill with the notion that the English economy was in a state of Malthusian stagnation during this dynamic transitional period and chime far better with Goldstone's (2002: 353–9) characterisation of it as an era of 'efflorescence', when expanding populations, widening and deepening markets and Smithian gains from trade and specialisation generated modest rates of economic growth (Persson, 2010).

7 Consumption

7.1 INTRODUCTION

Chapter 6 has argued that workers responded to changes in real wage rates by adapting how hard they worked so as to maintain their earnings. Household incomes therefore tracked GDP per head rather than real wage rates and progressively improved over time, doubling between the early fourteenth and late seventeenth centuries and doubling again over the course of the industrial revolution. Higher incomes translated into changing patterns of consumption and the forms these consumption choices took are the subjects of this chapter. Section 7.2 reconstructs the kilocalorie value and composition of diets based on the agricultural-output estimates presented in Chapter 3, augmented by information on imported foodstuffs. Given that populations require an average daily food intake per head of 2,000 kilocalories (Livi-Bacci, 1991: 27) to provide sufficient nourishment for both economic and biological reproduction, these calculations also provide a useful cross-check on the consistency of the agricultural-output and population estimates. Section 7.3 then considers non-food consumption drawing upon early modern evidence of material culture as revealed by probate inventories. Again, these trends need to be consistent with those of industrial output reconstructed in Chapter 4.

Price, habit, fashion and status all shaped the budgetary decisions taken by households. Demand for food was inelastic up to the point where basic subsistence needs had been met, but as incomes rose there were clear trade-offs to be obtained between increasing consumption of cheap sources of kilocalories such as pottage, potatoes and salted herrings on the one hand, or indulging in more expensive refined bread, quality ale and beer, dairy produce and meat, plus the imported luxuries of wine, sugar, tea, cocoa and tobacco, on the other. In effect, higher incomes allowed more households to trade up to a respectability basket of foodstuffs providing a more varied and processed diet but not necessarily more kilocalories. The changing relative prices of arable, livestock and luxury products influenced these consumption decisions, while the relative cheapness or dearness of food determined how much disposable income could be devoted to the increasingly varied and tempting array of non-food consumer goods (Figure 5.02). According to de Vries (1994), these were the items that people were prepared to work longer and harder to acquire, as the luxuries of one generation became the essentials of the next. The household goods thereby accumulated show up increasingly in the probate inventories which become available in great numbers from the mid-sixteenth century. These document increased consumption of a wide variety of goods both traditional and new, prosaic and exotic, British-made and imported from abroad (Weatherill, 1988; Overton and others, 2004: 87–120).

7.2 FOOD CONSUMPTION

The products of Britain's mixed-farming systems yielded kilocalories at very different rates, at different costs and in forms of varying desirability. Potatoes yielded kilocalories at a higher rate per unit area and required less processing than any other food. Hence, as demand for food rose steeply from the mid-eighteenth century, they were increasingly adopted as a staple foodstuff of the poor (Table 3.07), displacing the pottages of legumes and oatmeal upon which those living at a bare-bones level of subsistence had previously relied. Meat represented the opposite extreme: its production required far more land and capital, yielded kilocalories at a substantially lower rate per unit area, and had a much lower food extraction rate. Nevertheless, meat was very attractive to consumers because it provided kilocalories in a concentrated form and the expense of the better cuts of meat gave it social kudos. Few, however, could afford to consume it on a regular basis and in quantity with the result that British diets long remained overwhelmingly grain based. Refined wheaten bread and ale and beer brewed from the best barley malt were the preferred staples of those living above the poverty line, with legumes, vegetables, dairy produce, fish and modest quantities of meat (of which bacon was the cheapest) adding variety and nutritional balance. The simplest way to assess the adequacy of these diets and their changing volume and composition is to convert each of their component elements into its kilocalorie equivalents following the method of Overton and Campbell (1996).

7.2.1   The kilocalorie supply of foodstuffs

Estimating the kilocalorie food value of agricultural output involves three basic stages. First, as set out in Table 7.01, outputs of arable products measured in volume (Table 3.07) and of livestock products measured in either weight or fluid capacity (Table 3.15) need to be converted to their kilocalorie equivalents using the official conversion ratios established by McCance and Widdowson (1960), as interpreted and modified by Campbell and others (1993) (Table 7.01). Second, post-harvest losses from storage and waste need to be deducted, at a flat rate for all grains of 10 per cent (Table 7.02). Third, allowance has to be made for further losses incurred in the conversion of these raw kilocalories into consumable kilocalories via processes of milling, stewing, baking and brewing, as well as in the conversion of milk into butter and cheese (Tables 7.02, 7.04 and 7.06). Note that brewing entailed particularly heavy losses of raw kilocalories of approximately 70 per cent, which is why curtailing the scale of brewing activity became a standard official response to serious harvest shortfalls. In all cases, the more that crops and livestock products were processed, the lower their food extraction rates.

Switching grain from bread to ale and beer production, as in the case of barley, was particularly likely to depress extraction rates. Here, in line with Campbell and Overton (1996: 295), the proportion of barley that was brewed is assumed to have jumped from 50 per cent before the Black Death to 80 per cent thereafter, reducing to 65 per cent by c.1600 before re-expanding to 80 per cent by 1800 and then rising to effectively 100 per cent by 1870 (Table 7.03). On the whole, the greater the prevailing level of food security the greater the proportion of grain

Table 7.01 *Kilocalories per unit of agricultural output*

Output	Unit	Kilocalories per unit
Wheat	Bushel	86,667
Rye	Bushel	83,810
Barley	Bushel	71,429
Oats	Bushel	63,889
Beans	Bushel	24,000
Potatoes	Pound (lb)	368
Milk	Gallon	3,185
Butter	Pound (lb)	2,270
Cheese	Pound (lb)	1,032
Beef	Pound (lb)	1,035
Mutton	Pound (lb)	1,039
Pork	Pound (lb)	1,003

Sources and notes: Campbell and others (1993: 41), based upon McCance and Widdowson (1960: 117). Potatoes are taken from McCance and Widdowson (1960: 149).

Table 7.02 *Kilocalorie losses through grain storage and food processing*

Process	Percentage loss
Grain storage	10%
Milling and baking wheat into bread	20%
Milling and baking rye into bread	20%
Milling and baking barley into bread	22%
Milling and baking oats into bread	44%
Malting and brewing barley into ale/beer	70%
Converting fresh milk to butter	36%
Converting fresh milk to cheese	71%

Sources and notes: Overton and Campbell (1996: Table XIII). Butter and cheese estimated from Table 7.01 assuming that 1 gallon of fresh milk made 0.9 lbs of butter or cheese.

Table 7.03 *Proportions of barley brewed and quantities of oats fed to non-farm horses, 1270s–1860s*

Decade	Proportion of barley that was brewed (%)	Number of non-farm horses (000s)	Annual oats consumption per horse (bushels)	Total oats consumption by non-farm horses (m. bushels)
1270s	50	40	17.63	0.63
1300s	50	50	17.69	0.89
1310s	50	50	17.84	0.88
1380s	80	30	18.91	0.65
1420s	80	30	19.55	0.54
1450s	70	20	20.04	0.43
1600s	65	50	22.75	1.20
1650s	65	90	24.43	2.11
1700s	70	130	26.23	3.40
1750s	75	210	28.16	6.02
1800s	80	570	30.04	17.09
1830s	80	710	30.04	21.40
1840s	90	770	30.04	23.07
1850s	95	800	30.04	24.12
1860s	100	810	30.04	24.33

Sources and notes: Brewing proportions derived from Overton and Campbell (1996: Table XIII): the proportion of barley brewed was lowest before the Black Death, rose in the aftermath of that disaster, but then is assumed to have decreased from the 1450s to 1600s before rising again from the 1650s. Non-farm horses for benchmark years are taken from Wrigley (2006b: 450) for 1300, and from Allen (1994: 102) for 1750, 1800 and 1850, based on Feinstein (1978: 70). Horse numbers for other years are obtained by log-linear interpolation. The figure of 30.04 bushels per horse in 1800 is derived from the consumption per farm horse in Chapter 3, adjusted upwards by 17.5 per cent to reflect the fact that on farms, 35 per cent of horses were immature and consumed only 50 per cent of the oats of a mature horse. The consumption per horse was lower in earlier years, in line with the lower assumed share of oats consumed by farm horses and oxen, 30 per cent in 1300 from Wrigley (2006b: 445), compared with 50 per cent in 1600 and 70 per cent in 1800 from Overton and Campbell (1999: 201).

that could be devoted to brewing and, consequently, the lower the overall food extraction rate. When population pressure upon available food resources was particularly acute extraction rates might be pushed as high as 55 per cent, whereas in times of relative abundance rates as low as 43 per cent were manageable and indicate that substantial proportions of grain were being consumed in highly refined and processed forms (see Table 7.06 below).

Feeding grain to livestock was an especially extravagant use of available kilocalories. This was particularly the case with oats and estimates of total national oats production given in Table 3.07 are net of livestock consumption on the farm. To estimate the quantity of oats kilocalories remaining for human consumption, oats consumed by non-farm horses must also be subtracted, as set out in Table 7.03. Given the expanding trade and transport sector's heavy reliance upon horsepower, catering for the rising population of non-farm horses became a growing burden upon English agriculture. Their numbers quadrupled between 1300 and 1700 and by 1850 had quadrupled again to 800,000 (Feinstein, 1978: 70; Allen, 1994: 102; Wrigley, 2006b: 450). Meanwhile, selective breeding increased their strength and demand for their labour grew so that annual consumption of oats per horse increased from 17.63 bushels in 1300 to 27.98 bushels in 1750 and 30.04 bushels by 1800 and 1850 (Table 7.03). The latter figure is broadly consistent with Vancouver's (1808) estimate that in Devon during winter horses ate 0.125 bushels a day. By that date over half a million non-farm horses were consuming 2.14 million quarters of oats, an increase of almost twenty-fold on their consumption in 1300.

One further step involves the allocation of total milk production from Table 3.15 between fresh milk, butter and cheese as shown in Table 7.04. Only a tenth of the total was consumed as fresh milk during the late-medieval period, but this rose to over a quarter by 1700 and more than a third by 1870. Milk processed into butter also became more important over time. The high share of cheese in dairy output during the late-medieval period was due to the fact that butter spoiled quickly and hence was not a practical way of preserving the nutrients in milk

Table 7.04 *Dairy consumption patterns and kilocalorie extraction rates, 1270s–1860s*

Decade	Total milk output (m. gallons)	Fresh milk (m. gallons)	Cheese (m. lbs)	Butter (m. lbs)	Estimated kilocalorie extraction rate (%)
1270s	42.09	4.21	24.62	11.36	48
1300s	54.45	5.44	31.85	14.70	48
1310s	47.93	4.79	28.04	12.94	48
1380s	38.77	3.88	22.68	10.47	48
1420s	32.78	3.28	19.17	8.85	48
1450s	44.92	4.49	26.28	12.13	48
1600s	58.56	9.77	29.24	16.86	53
1650s	72.52	15.26	33.69	21.49	57
1700s	59.10	15.42	25.69	17.99	62
1750s	163.19	41.27	71.28	50.39	61
1800s	279.75	54.57	126.14	97.45	59
1830s	309.99	89.55	123.92	91.51	63
1840s	341.67	112.62	131.17	95.41	65
1850s	434.05	153.20	163.13	117.71	67
1860s	492.79	173.94	185.21	133.64	67

Sources and notes: The division of total milk production between fresh milk, cheese and butter for the medieval period was derived from Biddick (1989); for the modern period, Holderness (1989: 169–70) provides estimates for 1750, 1800 and 1850; other years are obtained using log-linear interpolation.

(Dyer, 1988). From the early eighteenth century this changed as a result of improvements in hygiene and the introduction of the barrel churn, mounted on a wooden stand so that it could revolve, and fitted with handles to turn it (Fussell, 1963: 217). The significance of these shifts is that 36 per cent of the kilocalories present in fresh milk were lost when converted to butter and 71 per cent when converted to cheese (Table 7.02). The net effect of these consumption changes was therefore to raise food extraction rates of dairy produce from less than 50 per cent in 1300 to 60 per cent by 1700 and 67 per cent in 1870 (Table 7.04).

Although the main outputs of domestic agriculture's arable and livestock sectors contributed the majority of kilocalories consumed, it is also necessary to consider net imports of food. During the first half of the eighteenth century a prospering agricultural sector began to export grain, so that by 1750 roughly 8 per cent of the grain crop was exported. Thereafter, as population grew faster than domestic output (Table 5.07), the trend was reversed and Britain became a net importer of grain (Mitchell, 1988: 221–5, 233). By 1800 grain imports were already making a critical difference and their dietary contribution grew further during the nineteenth century, especially following repeal of the Corn Laws in 1846, so that by 1870 almost half the kilocalorie needs of the country were supplied from overseas (Overton, 1996: 88–9) (see Table 7.06 below). In contrast, the contribution of imported livestock products to English diets was altogether more modest. Substantial meat imports only really began in the late nineteenth century, as transport costs declined and refrigeration facilitated long-distance shipments from the New World.

Much earlier, of course, a range of high-status exotic commodities had spearheaded the food-import trade. Wine was already firmly established as a significant import trade in the middle ages (James and Veale, 1971) and in due course a range of other foreign-produced foodstuffs – tobacco, sugar, tea, coffee and spirits – found a ready demand in England. The broad trends in annual consumption per head of these items from the 1670s can be seen in Table 7.05, taken from de Vries (2008). Tobacco rapidly established itself as a national addiction from early in the seventeenth century; subsequently, sugar and then tea were increasingly consumed by all who could afford them, especially following establishment of British-owned overseas plantations. Consumption of spirits also rose substantially, particularly during the first half of the eighteenth century when Hogarth satirised the effects of gin upon the poorer classes of London. Coffee drinking, in contrast, did not catch on beyond a narrow cosmopolitan elite. Contrary to the situation in continental Europe, it was tea that established itself as the nation's preferred beverage (de Vries, 2008: 183).

Table 7.05 *Annual consumption per head of imported exotic foodstuffs, 1670s-1840s*

Decade	Sugar (kg)	Tea (kg)	Coffee (kg)	Tobacco (kg)	Spirits (litres)
1670s	c.1.0			0.42	
1680s					0.35
1690s					
1700s	2.6		0.05	1.05	
1710s					1.5
1720s	5.0	0.28			1.9
1730s					
1740s					c.6.0
1750s	7.5	0.50	0.05	0.88	
1760s					
1770s	10.5				
1780s	7.7	0.61	0.03		
1790s				0.51	
1800s	9.3	0.79	0.03		
1810s				0.44	
1820s					
1830s	9.2	0.86		0.44	3.5
1840s	9.6	0.84	0.23		

Source: De Vries (2008: 181–5): There is a break in the series for sugar, which refers to England until the 1770s, but to Great Britain from the 1780s.

Yet although these commodities gratified many needs and in several cases established themselves as dietary essentials, their collective contribution to the country's kilocalorie supply was slight.

More significant were the kilocalories obtained from other sources of food: these included vegetables, fruit, berries, nuts, poultry, game, and freshwater and salt-water fish (both fresh and preserved). Often it was these that made the difference between scarcity and sufficiency. Budget studies from Prest (1954) suggest that fish and poultry were contributing around 200 kilocalories per head per day at the close of the nineteenth century, which is broadly in line with recent estimates for the late-medieval period. Extrapolating from the evidence of well-documented religious households, Slavin (2008, 2009, 2010) reckons that before the Black Death poultry may have provided around 90 kilocalories per head per day, ranging from 150 kilocalories in elite and urban households to maybe half that amount in peasant households. He estimates that the equivalent average figure for fish was around 165 kilocalories per head per day, with members of higher-status households again consuming at a higher rate than those of lower status. If horticultural crops and wild food sources provided just another 45 kilocalories per head a day, this would mean that a collective total of around 300 kilocalories was obtained from all three subsidiary food sources before the Black Death, which then shrank to around 200 kilocalories as meat and other preferred foodstuffs were partially substituted for them. For the want of equivalent detailed studies of later periods, this level of supply is assumed to have held more or less steady for the remainder of the period under investigation.

7.2.2   Trends in kilocalorie consumption per head

Combining the estimated daily supply per head of kilocalories from arable output, livestock output, net imports of arable and livestock products, and minor food sources (including fruit and vegetables, poultry and fish) gives the results summarised in Table 7.06. Note that over most of the period under review the level of kilocalorie consumption remained within ±10 per cent of the 2,000 kilocalories per head per day deemed by Livi-Bacci (1991: 27) to have been the minimum necessary to provide an adequate diet. Only during the late fourteenth and fifteenth centuries when land was abundant and during the late nineteenth-century when food imports were growing rapidly was the supply of kilocalories significantly above this threshold, so that the population was both generously fed and well buffered against adversity. At all other times national food supplies closely matched the subsistence needs of the population. In fact, on several occasions, most conspicuously in the 1310s, 1650s and 1830s, this minimum requirement was clearly under pressure (Table 7.06). Coping strategies

Table 7.06 *Composition of daily kilocalorie consumption per head in England, 1270s–1860s*

		Arable kilocalories from grains and legumes				Livestock kilocalories		Other kilocalories	
Decades	Population (millions)	Net of seed	Net of seed, losses and fodder	*% food extraction rate*	From net imports	From meat and dairy produce	From meat imports	From vegetables, poultry and fish	Total kilocalories daily per head
1270s	4.40	3,628	1,786	*49*	0	117	0	300	2,203
1300s	4.72	3,017	1,625	*54*	0	131	0	300	2,056
1310s	4.63	2,938	1,576	*54*	0	122	0	300	1,998
1380s	2.36	4,170	2,076	*50*	0	191	0	200	2,467
1420s	2.03	3,662	1,716	*47*	0	230	0	200	2,145
1450s	1.93	3,594	1,712	*48*	0	264	0	200	2,176
1600s	4.27	3,226	1,698	*53*	0	206	0	200	2,103
1650s	5.35	3,026	1,576	*52*	0	169	0	200	1,945
1700s	5.26	3,451	1,777	*52*	0	210	0	200	2,187
1750s	6.07	4,051	1,734	*43*	−75	319	0	200	2,178
1800s	9.06	3,337	1,436	*43*	154	385	0	200	2,176
1830s	13.83	2,825	1,300	*46*	139	311	0	200	1,949
1840s	15.58	2,908	1,359	*47*	293	308	6	200	2,166
1850s	17.47	2,382	1,073	*45*	500	328	10	200	2,112
1860s	20.07	2,233	1,035	*46*	886	320	22	200	2,462

Sources and notes: Derived from the agricultural output data in Chapter 3, using the assumptions set out in Tables 7.01 to 7.05.

under these circumstances included switching crops from animal to human consumption and diverting grain from brewing to baking, thereby boosting extraction rates. Such substitutions endowed the nation's food supply with considerable elasticity.

That food supplies were less than adequate in the 1310s is hardly surprising, for the population was close to its medieval peak and this was the decade of the Great European Famine and the disastrous back-to-back harvest shortfalls of 1315 and 1316 and sequel livestock pan-zootics of sheep murrain and cattle plague (Campbell, 2011). All the available evidence suggests that the economy was under considerable pressure at this time, making it hard to see how a population much above the average of 4.72 million over the decade 1300–09 could have been sustained, given realistic estimates of cropped areas (Chapter 2) and crop yields (Chapter 3). A second period of pressure can be seen as the population regained and then exceeded its medieval peak during the first half of the seventeenth century when poor harvests again placed living standards under pressure (Hindle, 2008), but the situation eased with the cessation of population growth from the 1650s and as rising agricultural productivity (Figure 3.02 and Table 3.06) brought a return to sufficiency. A third and final period of pressure then emerged during the early nineteenth century, before repeal of the Corn Laws, steam shipping and railroads allowed imports from America to grow sufficiently to meet the demands of the rapidly rising and increasingly urban population (Table 7.06).

Although the country's food supplies were periodically stretched, this does not necessarily mean that they were not improving. The first big nutritional advance came after the Black Death, when daily kilocalorie consumption per head increased substantially. Grain continued to contribute 80 per cent of all kilocalories consumed but a reduction in food extraction rates implies that less of it was being consumed as pottage and more processed into bread and especially ale. This is consistent with changes in crop mix as output of rye declined relative to wheat and of oats relative to barley (Table 3.07). Consumption of livestock products also rose from a mere 6 per cent of kilocalories in the early fourteenth century to maybe 12 per cent in the mid-fifteenth century (Table 7.06). Diets at this time had more calories, were of superior quality, better balanced and contained more processed and refined foodstuffs than those of the early fourteenth century.

The sixteenth and early seventeenth centuries brought some erosion of these high standards, but without a complete return to the straitened diets of before the Black Death. Although the ascendancy of wheat and barley was maintained (Table 3.07), the daily kilocalorie allowance per head shrank and grain extraction rates rose as the share of grain processed into bread expanded at the expense of that brewed into ale and beer. Also, fewer livestock products were consumed (Table 7.06). Demographic pressure on available food stocks eased from the 1650s and by the end of the seventeenth century dietary standards were clearly qualitatively better and more varied than they had been at the opening of the fourteenth century. Nonetheless, the net gain was substantially smaller than the doubling of GDP per head which had occurred over the same period (Table 5.06). In part this was because, as will be discussed in Section 7.2.3 below, households were trading dietary improvements for increased consumption of non-food goods whose relative price was falling (Figure 5.02).

After 1700 the continuing rise of GDP per head (Table 5.06) meant that households could increasingly enjoy both better diets and greater non-food consumption. From this time grain was never again as overwhelmingly prominent in diets as it had been and lower extraction rates indicate that the forms in which grain was consumed were more highly processed (Table 7.06). At the same time, encouraged by lower relative prices (Figure 2.04), livestock products were making a modestly increased contribution to diets, as more meat was consumed and more milk consumed directly or turned into butter rather than being processed into cheese. Extraction rates of dairy produce consequently rose (Table 7.04). Potatoes and other root crops also expanded as important supplementary sources of kilocalories, especially for those on the lowest incomes, and the Columbian Exchange further widened the range of foodstuffs on offer.

As in earlier periods, these minor food sources, including fish, added colour, flavour, variety and nutritional balance to diets.

The magnitude of these eighteenth-century developments should not be overstated but they do point to a modest but nonetheless significant improvement in the diversity of diets and the ability of an expanding proportion of households to indulge their dietary preferences for wheaten bread, beer brewed from barley malt, milk and butter, and meat. This range of items was only affordable to the growing proportion of households living above the poverty line. To anticipate the results presented in Chapter 8, approximately 63 per cent of the population were able to afford the respectability basket of consumables in 1290, rising to 76 per cent in 1688, 86 per cent in 1759 and then 80 per cent in 1801/3 (Table 8.07). All poorer households had to settle for diets that were mostly limited to inferior grains and crops which required only limited processing or, in the case of potatoes, none at all. Such households consumed few of their kilocalories from the livestock sector, whose lavish requirements of land and working capital made them the most costly to produce. In fact, the scale of the livestock sector would probably have been unjustified but for the fact that livestock were also vital suppliers of draught power, manure and a range of essential raw materials.

7.2.3 Alternative estimates of kilocalorie consumption per head

For the period since 1600 several alternative estimates of daily kilocalorie consumption are available. Compared with the results obtained from this study (Table 7.07C summarising Table 7.06), those produced by Floud and others (2011) for the years 1700–1850 (Table 7.07A) using the estimates of Holderness (1989: 147–70) envisage a larger contribution from livestock products (24–37 per cent) and ascribe a smaller dietary role to grain (50–65 per cent). Their estimated total daily allowance per head of 2,100–2,500 kilocalories is marginally more generous than the 2,200 ± 70 reckoned here and differs further in registering a marked improvement during the second half of the eighteenth century, which is

Table 7.07 *Alternative estimates of daily kilocalorie consumption per head, 1600–1850*

Years	Grain	Fruit and vegetables	Fish etc.	Meat	Dairy products	Other	Total
A. Floud, Fogel, Harris and Hong							
1700	1,461	167	24	*538		39	2,229
1750	1,246	189	24	*786		83	2,327
1800	1,382	247	24	*708		113	2,472
1850	1,396	338	24	*599		147	2,504
B. Muldrew							
1600	1,968			514	580		3,062
1700	2,682			423	474		3,579
1770	3,985			579	483		5,047
1800	3,189			428	360		3,977
C. This study							
1600s	1,698	+200		*206			2,103
1650s	1,576	+200		*169			1,945
1700s	1,777	+200		*210			2,187
1750s	1,659	+200		*319			2,178
1800s	1,590	+200		*385			2,176
1850s	1,573	+200		*338			2,112

Sources and notes: Floud and others (2011: 167); Muldrew (2011: 156). The published version of Floud and others (2011) shows a lower figure for 1750, due to a spreadsheet error: we are grateful to Bernard Harris for providing the corrected data. * = Meat and dairy products; + = Fruit, vegetables and fish, etc.

delayed until after 1860 in Table 7.06. So substantial an increase in kilocalorie consumption between 1750 and 1800 would be unexpected given the inability of domestic agricultural output to match the accelerating growth of population occurring at that time (Table 5.07). Furthermore, data on the heights of male military recruits aged 20–23 in Table 7.08 do not indicate an increase in net nutritional status during the second half of the eighteenth century. The height estimates of Floud and others (1990) indicate a net gain of only 1.5 centimetres between cohorts born in the 1760s and 1800s, followed by a marked deterioration

Table 7.08 *Average heights of English military recruits aged 20–23, by birth cohort (centimetres)*

Birth decade	Floud, Wachter and Gregory: height (cm)	Komlos: height (cm)
1760s	167.4	171.1
1780s	168.0	164.6
1800s	168.9	164.6
1820s	170.7	167.2
1830s	170.7	165.6
1850s	165.3	164.7

Sources and notes: Voth (2004: 271), derived from Floud and others (1990); Komlos (1993, 1998).

after 1830. In contrast, the later estimates of Komlos (1993, 1998) suggest a net loss of 6.5 centimetres between the 1760s and 1780s/1800s and no improvement throughout the first half of the nineteenth century. In the light of this demographic, agricultural and anthropometric evidence, the dietary estimates of Floud and others (2011) look overly optimistic. Nevertheless, they do at least appear to be of the right general order of magnitude.

Muldrew (2011), in contrast, paints an altogether more optimistic picture of living standards in England during the seventeenth and eighteenth centuries, with daily kilocalorie consumption per head already above 3,000 in 1600 and rising to over 5,000 by 1770 before reducing to a generous 4,000 by 1800 (Table 7.07B). These high estimates appear to arise from a combination of optimistic assumptions respecting both arable and livestock production in England (Kelly and Ó Gráda, 2013). Thus, Muldrew's agricultural estimates differ from those presented in Chapter 3 in assuming, first, a higher acreage for most crops, but particularly for oats and for wheat in later years; second, higher yields for most crops, but particularly for oats; third, lower consumption of oats by horses; fourth, higher extraction rates, particularly for barley, where losses through brewing are set at 27 per cent rather than 70 per cent; and, fifth, substantially higher livestock yields. In the light of the evidence of land use and agricultural output discussed in Chapters 2 and 3 and the kilocalorie extraction rates summarised in Table 7.02, it is therefore difficult to regard Muldrew's estimates of daily kilocalories per head as anything other than a gross overestimation.

Contrary to the favourable assessment of Floud and others (2011) and even more optimistic verdict of Muldrew (2011), Clark and others (1995) argue that food consumption per head in Britain showed little improvement between 1770 and 1850. To them this constituted a paradox, or 'British food puzzle', for incomes per head were rising over the same period. In fact, as the results presented in this chapter indicate, the British food puzzle extends over a much longer period of time. Part of its explanation lies in the trade-off between the quantity of kilocalories and the quality and diversity of diets, with populations displaying a preference for the latter over the former, raising when they could their consumption of refined wheaten bread, quality ale and beer, fresh dairy produce, meat and imported luxuries. What changed over time was not so much the quantity of kilocalories that were consumed but their composition. The other component of the explanation is the rising relative price of food, which became particularly important after 1700 as the price of manufactured goods declined sharply (Figures 5.01 and 5.02). This means that the growth of consumption per head should be easier to detect in the non-food sector.

7.3 NON-FOOD CONSUMPTION

Household decisions about whether or not to spend more on food were influenced by the opportunity cost of what else they might do with the money. When the relative price of food declined, as it did between 1270 and 1450, it made economic sense to consume more food, hence the diets of the fifteenth century were more refined and abundant and workers were reluctant to labour longer and harder in order to acquire non-food consumables. Conversely, when food became relatively dearer, as it did from c.1510 to c.1630 and especially from c.1720 to 1850, spending more on an improved diet gave poor value relative to the alternatives. During these periods, once basic food needs had been satisfied, spending more on the increasingly tempting and affordable array of consumer wares on offer proved irresistible. It was therefore the industrial and service sectors which were the principal beneficiaries of the rise in household spending power after 1650, as witnessed by the fact that the industrial sector's shares of output and employment were expanding over time (Tables 5.01 and 5.02). Whereas spending on sports and entertainments has left little trace, greater consumption of durable manufactured items is evident in probate inventories. In England these inventories come on stream in the mid-sixteenth century and are available in large numbers until the mid-eighteenth century (Arkell, 2000: 72). They provide the best currently available evidence of trends in non-food consumption during this critical 200-year period.

7.3.1 Wealth per testator

The valuations of household effects provided by inventories leave little doubt that households were gaining in material wealth over these years. Data assembled by Overton (2006) on the total values of inventoried goods for the five sample counties of Lincolnshire, Hertfordshire, Kent, Worcestershire and Cornwall (Appendix 7.1) provide a guide to what was happening to personal wealth in England between 1550 and 1750. It is unlikely that inventories were made for the poorest 40 per cent of the population, so the figures have been adjusted to include these missing individuals whose goods are assumed to have been worth no more than £1. This assumption does not affect the median which provides the best indicator of average wealth since the distribution is highly skewed. It is plotted in Figure 7.01 alongside GDP per head and the real wage rate. Note the tendency for all three series to sag in the 1580s and 1590s, which for a combination of reasons were among the most difficult years of the sixteenth century, and the depressed real wage rates and testator wealth of the 1600s to 1630s. In fact, the 1630s stand out as an economically adverse decade on all three counts. Thereafter, however, median wealth bounced back and over the next ten decades grew

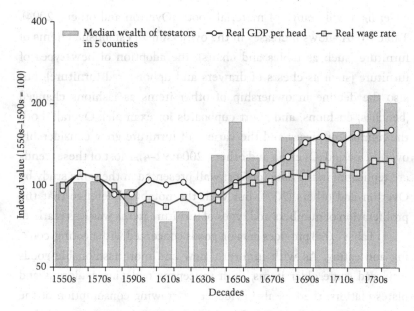

FIGURE 7.01 Real GDP per head, real wage rates and the median wealth of testators in five counties, 1550s–1740s (decadal averages indexed on 1550s–1590s, log scale). *Sources and notes:* Real GDP per head from Section 5.4; real wage rates = Allen (2001) and Clark (2007a) combined; median wealth of testators at constant prices adjusted for the poor in the five counties of Cornwall, Hertfordshire, Kent, Lincolnshire and Worcestershire, from Overton (2006).

two-and-a-half-fold (as did mean wealth shown in Appendix 7.1) from £8.57 to £22.35 in constant prices, at an average annual growth rate of 0.88 per cent per year. This was roughly 50 per cent higher than the concurrent growth of real income per head which, in turn, was 20 per cent greater than the growth rate of real wage rates. The inventory evidence thus leaves little doubt that economic growth from the 1640s was delivering steadily improving material living standards to at least the better-off members of society.

7.3.2 Household goods

Use of probate inventories to study household goods is well established (Weatherill, 1988). Here increasing consumption is exemplified through a case study of Kent spanning the years 1600–1749 and covering a wide range of material goods (Overton and others, 2004). Table 7.09A shows increases in the ownership of established items of furniture (such as tables and chairs); the adoption of new types of furniture (such as chests of drawers and upholstered furniture); but also the decline in ownership of other items as fashions changed (benches, cushions, and court cupboards for example). Overall, both the number of pieces and the variety of furniture grew considerably over the period (Overton and others, 2004: 92–4). Most of these trends are replicated in the data for Cornwall presented in the same study by Overton and others (2004) but with the notable difference that the proliferation of numbers and types of furniture items was less marked.

Table 7.09B provides data on goods concerned with heating, cooking and eating. As with furniture, new and more fashionable goods displaced some older items, with saucepans replacing cauldrons and plates platters; there is also evidence of growing consumption of the products of newly developing home industries such as pottery and glass (Overton and others, 2004: 100–08). Although Kent was generously supplied with woodland, the county's increasing reliance upon coal for domestic purposes reflects the convenience with which it could be supplied, along with London, by sea from the northeast. The same did not apply to Cornwall (Overton and others, 2004: 98), which in all other respects followed much the same trends. Tables 7.09C and 7.09D document the changing ownership of linen, clocks, mirrors, pictures, window curtains, books and weapons. Most Kent households were already well furnished with linen at the beginning of the seventeenth century, so increased consumption is reflected in the rising numbers of sheets, towels, tablecloths and napkins inventoried. In Cornwall, by contrast, only the larger households indulged in this trend. Particularly significant is the ownership of new English-produced consumer goods, including clocks, mirrors, pictures and window curtains. Ownership of printed books reflects a slightly earlier fashion trend: Clark (1976: 99) notes a sharp increase in ownership between the 1560s and 1630s for Canterbury and in Kent likewise their ownership peaked during the 1630s. Overall, acquisition of these material consumer goods increased

Table 7.09 Ownership of selected consumer goods recorded in Kent probate inventories, 1600–1749

	1600–1629	1630–1659	1660–1689	1690–1719	1720–1749
A. Furniture and furnishings					
Chests of drawers (%)	0	2	19	39	59
Press cupboards (%)	15	21	30	33	34
Chairs (median no.)	3	4	6	10	13
Tables (median no.)	2	2	3	3	5
Upholstered furniture (%)	16	32	69	79	74
Feather beds (%)	44	48	55	62	51
Court cupboards (%)	12	20	26	12	2
Benches (%)	76	75	73	65	47
Carpets (%)	18	20	26	10	3
Cushions (%)	37	40	38	15	9
All furniture (median no. items)	12	13	20	23	24
Variety of furniture (median no. types)	7	9	11	12	12
B. Heating, cooking and eating					
Coal (%)	4	8	13	17	27
Saucepans (%)	0	0	2	11	33
Glass bottles (%)	1	1	4	24	30
Knives and forks (%)	0	0	1	5	13
Plates (median no.)	2	2	3	13	19
Cauldrons (%)	22	11	4	0	0
Platters (%)	85	74	53	50	33

Table 7.09 (cont.)

	1600–1629	1630–1659	1660–1689	1690–1719	1720–1749
C. Linen					
Linen (median no.)	28	28	41	51	50
Sheets (median no.)	14	14	16	20	20
Towels (median no.)	5	6	8	12	12
Tablecloths (median no.)	4	3	6	6	8
Napkins (median no.)	12	12	18	18	18
D. Miscellaneous goods					
Clocks (%)	1	1	18	41	54
Mirrors (%)	3	10	18	36	52
Pictures (%)	2	6	5	6	25
Window curtains (%)	6	8	11	16	22
Books (%)	19	31	25	25	20
Weapons (%)	38	35	23	17	21

Source: Overton and others (2004: 91, 99, 109, 111).

Table 7.10 *Ownership of certain items by quartiles of pooled material wealth in Kent and Cornwall probate inventories, 1600–1749 (percentages)*

Item	Kent (%)			Cornwall (%)		
	1600–49	1650–99	1700–49	1600–49	1650–99	1700–49
Upholstered furniture						
1st quartile	0.0	3.6	50.0	0.6	0.4	0.5
2nd quartile	1.4	37.1	42.9	0.0	2.7	3.6
3rd quartile	21.7	59.6	66.7	0.9	9.5	10.5
4th quartile	61.7	92.3	84.2	4.7	23.9	17.9
Plates						
1st quartile	1.7	12.9	28.6	1.0	7.9	54.0
2nd quartile	2.7	18.6	57.4	2.1	20.5	71.4
3rd quartile	18.1	34.8	82.8	5.5	33.6	85.9
4th quartile	40.5	66.4	84.0	7.3	49.1	89.4
Mirrors:						
1st quartile	1.8	4.1	22.2	0.4	1.5	1.5
2nd quartile	1.4	8.8	18.3	0.7	3.2	4.7
3rd quartile	3.8	16.0	41.7	1.6	6.6	8.9
4th quartile	11.2	31.0	53.1	2.2	10.4	9.4
Hot drinks:						
1st quartile	0.0	0.0	5.6	0.0	0.0	0.0
2nd quartile	0.0	0.0	8.5	0.0	0.0	2.7
3rd quartile	0.0	0.3	11.4	0.0	0.0	3.3
4th quartile	0.0	0.6	16.8	0.0	0.0	5.1

Source and notes: Overton and others (2004: 144). Pooled material wealth = the total value of inventoried goods excluding real estate and debts owed by the deceased (Overton and others, 2004: 138. 1st quartile, poorest testators; 4th quartile, wealthiest testators.

in pace from the mid-seventeenth century, and continued to grow during the first decade of the eighteenth century.

Although there were strong social and spatial dimensions to this rising tide of consumerism, the overall increase in consumption was strongly related to wealth. Table 7.10 tracks the ownership of four groups of new consumer goods – upholstered furniture, plates, mirrors, hot drinks – by quartiles of the distribution of pooled material wealth for Cornwall and Kent. Although there is an inevitable relationship between wealth and the ownership of goods, since wealth is calculated by summing the value of goods, some clear patterns are evident. First, ownership levels of these items in both counties was positively correlated with wealth, including items with relatively low values such as utensils for hot drinks. Second, in virtually every case ownership levels within each quartile tended to increase over time in both counties. Third, acquisition of most of these items tended to catch on earlier, and rise to high levels sooner in Home Counties Kent than remote and provincial Cornwall (Overton and others, 2004: 137–47).

Inventoried individuals of all degrees of wealth were acquiring more consumer goods between 1600 and 1749 and doing so with increased vigour from $c.1650$, in line with steadily rising levels of recorded wealth and GDP per head (Figure 7.01). Whereas contemporary improvements in diets were modest, the domestic contexts within which food was prepared and consumed changed a great deal. By the mid-eighteenth century, in contrast to the early seventeenth century, meals in better-off households were increasingly cooked using saucepans on a coal range, eaten with knives and forks off ceramic rather than pewter plates or trenchers, by diners seated on chairs rather than benches, at tables dressed with linen tablecloths, in rooms furnished with a degree of style and comfort. Social differences were marked but the trend towards higher levels of consumption per head is unmistakable and new fashions, such as those for hot drinks such as tea and coca, spread fast (Table 7.10).

7.4   CONCLUSIONS

This chapter has shown that rising consumption per head was concomitant with rising GDP per head, so that by the eve of the industrial revolution the majority of households were significantly better fed, clothed and housed than their predecessors before the Black Death. Throughout this halting and slow process consumption choices were made between more abundant or better-quality diets and between foodstuffs and material goods. Relative prices were a powerful influence upon such choices. Cheaper livestock prices from the seventeenth century (Figure 2.04) encouraged people to consume more meat and dairy produce (Tables 7.04 and 7.06), while, at the same time, cheaper manufactured goods meant devoting surplus income to the acquisition of luxuries and consumables (Tables 7.09 and 7.10) gave better value than spending more on food and drink. Given the strong budgetary constraints that bound most households, strong consumer preferences for dietary quality rather than quantity and for more goods rather than more kilocalories together explain the 'British food puzzle' (Clark and others, 1995), whereby food consumption per head appeared to stagnate during the industrial revolution notwithstanding that GDP per head and household incomes both rose (Kelly and Ó Gráda, 2013). In fact, the 'British food puzzle' far pre-dated the industrial revolution.

What is most striking is how modest were the changes in British diets between 1270 and 1870 (Table 7.06) relative to the magnitude of developments taking place in real wage rates and GDP per head (Figure 6.07). Daily food intake per head mostly fluctuated around the 2,000 kilocalories that were the minimum necessary for demographic reproduction and only rose to a more generous 2,500 kilocalories during the underpopulated late fourteenth and fifteenth centuries and, five centuries later, when from the mid-nineteenth century cheap imports finally transformed the nation's food supplies. Until these imports released the country from dependence upon domestic food sources, grain processed into pottage, bread, ale and beer typically contributed at least three-quarters of all kilocalories consumed, whereas livestock products – milk, butter, cheese and meat – contributed no more than 15 per cent, and all other food sources – fruit, vegetables, poultry, game, fish, and exotic imports – the remainder. Any changes in diets were effectively rung within these tight constraints, mainly by modifying the grain and livestock components of the diet. Thus, more livestock produce was consumed in the fifteenth century, less in the sixteenth and early seventeenth centuries, and more again in the eighteenth and early nineteenth centuries. Meanwhile, foodstuffs became more refined and highly processed, as pottages and gruels were replaced with bread and ale with beer. As demand became more discriminating, agricultural producers replaced rye with wheat, oats with barley, and sheep with cattle, and expanded specialist production of dairy produce and meat. Finally, imported spices, sugar, wine, tea, cocoa, coffee and tobacco added colour, flavour, variety and prestige to meals.

By dint of these mostly undramatic dietary changes English people in the mid-eighteenth century may have eaten little more than those living in the early fourteenth century but, on the whole, they ate better. Their foods were more highly processed, livestock produce featured more prominently, and exotic commodities were more widely enjoyed. Moreover, proportionately fewer households were obliged to settle for a cheap, coarse and monotonous diet at a very basic level of subsistence. New crops, improved breeds of livestock and generally more advanced farming methods coupled with more efficient markets meant that food supplies were more assured and, thanks to the Poor Law, the food entitlements of the poorest and most vulnerable were better protected. Individually, there was little that was remarkable about any of these advances but collectively they constituted real nutritional progress, especially given that from c.1700 food prices were rising faster than those of most other commodities (Figure 5.02).

As, with population growth, foodstuffs became relatively more expensive and, with expanding output, industrial goods became cheaper, households favoured expenditure on non-food items. Rising consumption per head is evident in the probate inventory data assembled and analysed by Overton and others (2004), which leaves little doubt that from the mid-seventeenth century the material wealth of those leaving inventories was more than keeping abreast of GDP per head (Figure 7.01). It is reflected in more and better furnishings, cooking and eating implements, linen and such fashionable new items as clocks and mirrors (Table 7.09), which began as luxuries but rapidly became essentials. This chimes with the marked expansion in industrial output documented in Chapter 4, which took place over the same period and to a substantial degree was directed towards satisfying domestic demand. The ramifications of these developments went further, for Allen and Weisdorf (2011) have proposed that it was urban and artisanal households that were in the vanguard of this early modern consumer revolution, willing to stint themselves of food and work longer and harder in order to follow fashion, ape their betters and acquire some of the new material goods and luxuries of the age. The more these households multiplied the more entrenched became this bias in consumer spending towards non-food items.

APPENDIX 7.1

Probate inventory valuation totals for Cornwall, Hertfordshire, Kent, Lincolnshire and Worcestershire at constant prices adjusted for the poor, 1550s–1740s

Decade	Mean (£)	Median (£)	Standard deviation (£)	Skewness	Coefficient of variation	Gini coefficient
1550s	34.17	11.31	63.69	1.08	1.86	0.65
1560s	35.29	11.41	72.44	0.99	2.05	0.69
1570s	40.75	11.44	82.60	1.06	2.03	0.70
1580s	40.21	10.59	79.80	1.11	1.98	0.71
1590s	47.44	10.69	95.47	1.15	2.01	0.73
1600s	40.30	9.54	79.51	1.16	1.97	0.74
1610s	41.21	8.15	94.11	1.05	2.28	0.76
1620s	47.01	8.87	112.71	1.02	2.40	0.77
1630s	48.09	8.57	109.32	1.08	2.27	0.76
1640s	63.39	14.28	160.62	0.92	2.53	0.76
1650s	57.90	19.02	95.08	1.23	1.64	0.70
1660s	67.03	14.02	144.83	1.10	2.16	0.76
1670s	83.00	15.23	221.44	0.92	2.67	0.78
1680s	87.33	16.67	235.63	0.90	2.70	0.78

(*cont.*)

Decade	Mean (£)	Median (£)	Standard deviation (£)	Skewness	Coefficient of variation	Gini coefficient
1690s	90.38	16.72	174.87	1.26	1.93	0.75
1700s	89.50	16.54	180.41	1.21	2.02	0.76
1710s	109.42	17.45	233.44	1.18	2.13	0.76
1720s	110.78	18.63	227.02	1.22	2.05	0.76
1730s	125.43	23.94	306.32	0.99	2.44	0.75
1740s	123.72	22.35	240.47	1.26	1.94	0.75

Source: Overton (2006).

8 The social distribution of income

8.1 INTRODUCTION

Income distribution in England between 1270 and 1870, as elsewhere in Western Europe, was profoundly unequal due to entrenched inequalities in access to the land, capital, education and political power upon which personal wealth depended. Gender, rank and servility and their differential legal rights were determined at birth. Privilege, patronage and position ensured that rent-seeking was rife, while warfare created opportunities for ransom and plunder to the enrichment of those in command and impoverishment of the vanquished. Everywhere, as a result, there were rich men in their castles and poor men at their gates. Moreover, as van Zanden (1995) and Milanovic and others (2007) have demonstrated, the effect of economic growth was to magnify rather than mitigate these inequalities and widen the income gap between those at the top and bottom of the social pyramid.

The rich became richer as average wealth grew because the more wealth there was the greater the opportunities for those with power and privilege to enrich themselves at the expense of the weak and disadvantaged majority. In Holland one legacy of the prosperity achieved during the Dutch Golden Age was a greatly increased inequality of incomes, which was more marked in towns than rural villages and greatest of all in major cities (van Zanden, 1995). In England, similarly, Milanovic and others (2007) claim that inequality rose with average incomes between 1688 and 1801/03, thereby confirming Kuznets' (1955) observation that income inequality typically increased during the early stages of economic growth and only declined relatively late in the modernisation process. Prior to 1870, therefore, increasing inequality can be treated, like urbanisation, as a characteristic and unavoidable manifestation of economic growth.

Income inequality is typically measured using Gini coefficients, expressed as a percentage with the higher the coefficient the greater the inequality. Van Zanden (1995) estimates that between 1561 and 1732, when Dutch GDP per head improved by 10 per cent, Gini coefficients for rural and urban Holland increased, respectively, from 35 to 38 per cent and from 53 to 59 per cent. Milanovic and others (2007) reckon that Gini coefficients of pre-industrial economies were typically in the range 25–65 per cent and invariably lower than the maximum theoretically attainable because of the ineffectiveness of elites at expropriating to themselves all wealth surplus to subsistence. Using Gregory King's social table they estimate that England in 1688 had a maximum potential Gini coefficient of 72 per cent but an actual Gini coefficient of only 45 per cent: in other words, 37.5 per cent of the wealth that might have been expropriated was retained by those who produced it. By 1801/03, on the evidence of Colquhoun's social table, the potential had risen to 80 per cent and actual to 51.5 per cent; on which figures inequality would appear to have been rising both absolutely and relatively but by less than it might otherwise have done.

Significantly, Milanovic and others (2007) obtain a Gini coefficient of approximately 37 per cent for England in 1290, based upon Campbell's (2008) reconstructed social table for that year. Despite the country's highly polarised feudal distribution of power, land and wealth and the supposed immiserising effects of serfdom, the country was too poor to sustain a greater degree of inequality. These English results suggest that income inequality grew substantially over the five centuries from 1290 to 1801/03 in tandem with the threefold rise in GDP per head. Hoffman and others (2002) claim that after 1600 the same was true of Europe.

Nevertheless, the fact that the well-off were becoming wealthier does not necessarily mean that the poor were becoming poorer or that more households were being oppressed into poverty. It did not require a big hike in incomes for those scraping a frugal existence at a bare-bones standard of subsistence to be able to afford a more diverse and desirable basket of consumables that maintained them in a degree of comfort, security and respectability. In fact, it is reasonable to suppose that economic growth and rising mean incomes enabled more households to lift themselves above a poverty line defined by the ability to afford such a 'respectability basket' of food, clothing and housing (Allen, 2009a). No doubt it was the aspiration to enjoy such a lifestyle that encouraged many workers to labour longer and harder, thereby boosting mass demand for the manufactured goods and imported exotic commodities available in increasing supply from the seventeenth century. Certainly, persistence of a massive underclass of impoverished households leading a hand-to-mouth existence at a bare-bones standard of subsistence, as in the late thirteenth and early fourteenth centuries, is more likely to have hampered than encouraged a process of economic growth. If, as Chapter 6 has indicated, employment in England's expanding industries and services was growing and people were successfully maintaining and even improving their earnings and household incomes by working longer and harder, then the incidence of abject poverty should at least have diminished.

This chapter explores these issues by defining in Section 8.2 the economic poverty line for the seven benchmark years 1290, 1381, 1522, 1620, 1688, 1759 and 1801/03 and then in Section 8.3 estimating from social tables the proportions of households – and, later, families – living above and below that line. Following Allen (2009a), the poverty line is taken to be the minimum income required to enable a family of two adults and two children to afford a 'respectability basket' of preferred consumption goods: bread, quality ale or beer, eggs and cheese, with moderate quantities of meat, textiles and fuel and an allocation for housing rent. The substantially cheaper 'bare-bones basket' contains a narrower range of items, with greater reliance upon coarser and less processed food staples, but nonetheless providing sufficient kilocalories and protein to support a working adult. Since women and children require fewer kilocalories than a working adult man, a two-parent and two-child family is assumed to have required the cost of three bare-bones baskets to survive at what Rowntree (1901) called merely physical efficiency.

If the fruits of economic growth became more widely spread through society, then the proportion of households able to afford the respectability consumption basket should have risen with time and the numbers living below the poverty line reduced. This is assessed in Section 8.2 by measuring the estimated annual earnings of a wage-earner (derived from information on daily money wage rates on the assumption of constant annual days worked) against the reconstructed costs of the bare-bones and respectability baskets. Alternatively, relaxing the assumption of constant days worked, Section 8.3 assesses the costs of the two baskets against estimates of family income derived from social tables. This dual exercise lends support to the view that economic growth between 1350 and 1800 helped bring about a significant reduction in poverty principally by reducing the proportion of households with incomes that placed them below the poverty line.

8.2 THE DIVIDING LINE BETWEEN SUFFICIENCY AND WANT

Table 8.01 sets out the estimated cost to a family of four, with an aggregate consumption need equivalent to that of three adults, of the bare-bones and respectability baskets of consumables, plus the reconstructed earnings of agricultural and building labourers and building craftsmen assuming a constant working year of 200 days, together with the ratios of earnings to the costs of these two consumption baskets. The quantities and prices of the items in these baskets are detailed in Appendices 8.1 to 8.7. The quantities per person per year are taken from Allen (2009a: 36–7), with the exception of the amount of bread in the respectability basket which has been lowered by almost a fifth from Allen's 234 kilograms to 190 kilograms. This is because his higher bread allowance would have resulted in an overall consumption of kilocalories well above that capable of being supplied by the amount of grain grown in Britain given the agricultural output and kilocalorie estimates presented in Chapters 3 and 7. The bread consumed in quantity by those able to afford the respectability basket is replaced in the bare-bones basket by oats, the cheapest grain, which was

Table 8.01 *Wages and the cost of the bare-bones and respectability subsistence baskets, 1290–1801/03*

	1290	1381	1522	1620	1688	1759	1801/03
Annual costs, 3 adult equivalents (£)							
Bare-bones basket	1.13	1.25	1.38	4.76	5.69	5.70	10.15
Respectability basket	3.02	3.43	4.08	13.77	16.82	17.19	32.13
Daily wage (pence)							
Farm labourer	1.59	3.30	4.14	10.00	12.00	12.00	18.30
Building labourer	1.75	3.00	4.00	8.00	12.00	16.00	24.00
Building craftsman	3.00	5.00	6.00	12.00	18.60	24.00	37.20
Annual wage working 200 days (£)							
Farm labourer	1.33	2.75	3.45	8.33	10.00	10.00	15.25
Building labourer	1.46	2.50	3.33	6.67	10.00	13.33	20.00
Building craftsman	2.50	4.17	5.00	10.00	15.50	20.00	31.00
Ratios							
Building labourer's wage / bare-bones basket	1.29	2.00	2.41	1.40	1.76	2.34	1.97
Building craftsman's wage / respectability basket	0.83	1.22	1.23	0.73	0.92	1.16	0.96
Skilled wage / unskilled wage	1.71	1.67	1.50	1.50	1.55	1.50	1.55
Respectability basket / bare-bones basket	2.67	2.74	2.96	2.89	2.96	3.02	3.17
Mean income / bare-bones basket	2.40	4.02	4.59	4.17	5.53	7.26	7.79
Mean income / respectability basket	0.90	1.46	1.55	1.44	1.87	2.41	2.46

Sources and notes: Daily wages from Allen (2001); family subsistence and respectability baskets derived from Appendices 8.1 to 8.7 on the basis of 3 adult-equivalent baskets. 240 pence = £1.

typically either mixed with beans or peas and stewed into pottage or lightly ground and cooked into oatcakes. The respectability diet also contains considerably more meat and dairy produce, along with items such as eggs and beer which do not appear in the bare-bones diet. Those living at this superior income level are also assumed to have spent more on cloth and other household items such as soap, lighting and heating. To avoid unrepresentative years, the prices used to cost the two baskets are 10-year averages.

In 1290, when an unskilled agricultural labourer earned around 1½ pence a day, a farmhand would need to have worked for 150–160 days in order to afford the respectability basket of ale, bread, beans and peas, meat, eggs, butter, cheese, soap, cloth, candles, lamp oil, fuel and rent (estimated at an additional 5 per cent, in line with household budgets for later periods: Allen, 2009a: 38), all costed at current prices. For a single man that was a realistic possibility, especially if he was employed on an annual contract, but his wages would have fallen far short of the income needed to support a wife and two children, which would have remained the case irrespective of whether his wife was earning. Even to provide a family of four with the coarser and narrower bare-bones subsistence basket of oatmeal pottage augmented by limited quantities of beans and peas, frugal helpings of meat and butter and Spartan quantities of soap, cloth, candles, lamp oil, fuel and rent, would have required 170–180 days' waged employment. At this stage in England's economic development attempting to maintain a family on wages alone was therefore precarious, especially given the seasonally and annually varying demand for farm labour. Hence the importance of supplementing waged work with additional income or food sources from smallholding, common rights, fishing, mining or craft working. Contributions made by women and children to the household budget were also important and often made the difference between poverty and a modicum of comfort.

Most rural families needed some land of their own, or rights of access to common resources, as a hedge against the difficulty of securing sufficient regular paid work (Britnell, 2001: 10–14; Campbell, 2005:

60–74). Without these extra sources of support servanthood and landless labouring were viable solely for those who remained single. Only
skilled workers paid a premium wage of 3 pence or more a day and able
to secure employment for at least 242 days could have earned the
60s. 5d. which, by 1290, was the annual cost of providing a family of
four with a respectability basket of consumables. Even these workers,
therefore, had little prospect of enjoying a lavish lifestyle.

It was households that provided skilled and unskilled workers
with economic security and constituted the basic units of production
and consumption. Those without household support typically lapsed
into vagrancy and destitution. Harvest failure, trade recession, war and
the biological lottery of disease could swell vagrant numbers to
socially and politically alarming proportions. This was the case during
the economically straitened final decade of the sixteenth century
when, in 1597, the government introduced a national system of poor
relief, subsequently enshrined in the Elizabethan Poor Law of 1601.
The origins of this formalised system of poor relief lay in earlier developments at the local level, reaching back to the late-medieval period
(Dyer, 2012) as well as the early Tudor period (Slack, 1988; Hindle,
2004; McIntosh, 2012). Implemented at parish level, funded out of
obligatory means-tested contributions levied upon rate payers and
policed by the Justices of the Peace, it provided the deserving poor
with a vital safety net when in years of extreme scarcity the cost of
even a bare-bones standard of subsistence became more than they
could afford.

As will be observed from Table 8.01, the lowest earners were
hardest hit in the late thirteenth century since in all subsequent benchmark years the earnings of unskilled workers afforded a greater margin
over the cost of the bare-bones subsistence basket. For building labourers, the greatest gain in purchasing power came a generation after the
crisis of the Black Death in the mid-fourteenth century. By 1381 one
building labourer working for at least 200 days could have purchased
two bare-bones subsistence baskets. That ratio increased further until
1522 before falling back during the sixteenth century to a second low

point in the early seventeenth century. By 1688 the ratio had recovered significantly and by 1759 it was back to the elevated level of 250 years earlier. Although it then fell back somewhat, the ratio remained substantially higher at the beginning of the nineteenth century than it had been at the close of the thirteenth century. Note that the purchasing power of a building craftsman's earnings relative to the cost of the more expensive respectability basket followed a similar trend but did not improve to the same extent. One reason is that the skill differential, as measured by the ratio of the skilled to the unskilled wage (Table 8.01) narrowed over time, dropping substantially between 1290 and 1522 and then remaining at this lower level. For another, the relative prices of the goods in the respectability basket grew more rapidly than those in the bare-bones basket, as is manifest in the widening ratio of the cost of the respectability basket to that of the bare-bones basket.

The net effect of these changing ratios is likely to have been a reduction in the incidence of poverty amongst the labouring classes. Although the respectability basket became progressively costlier, the bare-bones basket became more affordable so that more households could afford more than the barest subsistence minimum. This also gave them a greater buffer against hard times. These calculations would, however, be upset if, as seems probable (Chapter 6), the number of days worked per year did not remain constant. For skilled artisans in particular there were strong incentives to labour more industriously (de Vries, 1994; Voth, 1998; Allen and Weisdorf, 2011). Accordingly, it will be useful in the next section to examine the changes in the costs of the subsistence and respectability baskets in relation to estimates of family income embodied in social tables for five of these seven benchmark years.

8.3   SOCIAL TABLES AND THE PROPORTIONS OF HOUSEHOLDS LIVING IN POVERTY

Milanovic and others (2007) drew upon social tables to analyse income inequality in fourteen pre-industrial societies ranging in time from the

Roman Empire to British-India in 1947. This study makes use of five: two for England in 1290 and 1381 derived from Campbell (2008) and three others from the long eighteenth century compiled by contemporary political economists – Gregory King [1696], Joseph Massie [1759] and Patrick Colquhoun [1801/03] – but reworked by Lindert and Williamson (1982). Each combines information on the numbers of families, their occupations and incomes, within an accounting framework that ensures consistency with the population totals established in Chapter 1 and the nominal GDP totals established in Chapter 5. The social table reconstructed for 1290 is also constrained to conform with the estimate of total arable land advanced in Chapter 2. Since these five social tables are consistent with the other key parameters presented in this study, they provide specific opportunities when the proportions living above and below the poverty line, as defined in Table 8.01, can be established.

The Domesday Survey of 1086 provides the earliest opportunity to examine England's socio-economic structure at a time when the country's population numbered only 1.7 million (Chapter 1) and its nominal GDP amounted to maybe £0.39 million (Walker, 2008). Although this was an economy with considerable agricultural resources still in reserve, the country's limited commercial development meant it was far from rich. William I (r. 1066–87) and the country's new Norman elite may have been possessed of fabulous wealth, but, as in all relatively underdeveloped and overwhelmingly agrarian economies with limited specialisation and trade, the incomes per head of most people were close to subsistence level (Walker, 2008). Significant extra-economic rental transfers of resources from those who worked the land to those who de facto owned it maintained and perpetuated this polarity. Whereas tenants-in-chief and their under-tenants comprised 2.5 per cent, and townsmen 8.8 per cent, of the population, everyone else was rural based and often legally bound to the land: unfree tenants (villeins, bordars, cottars and coscets) made up a massive 65.5 per cent of the population, slaves and other minority groups a further 8.7 per cent, and free and semi-free tenants the final

14.5 per cent (calculated from Darby, 1977: 89, 337). The most lowly of these groups with the smallest holdings and often quite onerous rental burdens – the bordars, cottars, coscets and slaves – accounted for 35 per cent of the population and no doubt mostly lived below the poverty line. In a society thus constituted it is unsurprising that townspeople were so few in number since scope for the emergence of and retention of wealth by middling groups of merchants, traders, craftsmen and administrators remained limited.

There is no later counterpart to Domesday but a remarkable constellation of detailed sources at the end of the thirteenth century has enabled reconstruction of a social table for England in 1290, including information on the average incomes of social groups. Much of the relevant evidence was assembled by Dyer (1989) and then systematised by Mayhew (1995a) to produce a social table and estimate of national income reckoned on the basis of a population of 6.0 million. Additional data on seigniorial and clerical incomes was then gathered by Campbell (2005), who produced a fresh social table for a population of 4.0 million; Table 8.02 now offers a further revision of that estimate constrained to conform to an estimated population of 4.75 million (Chapter 1), arable area of 12.75 million acres (Chapter 2) and national income at current prices of £4.30 million (Chapter 5). At this date the cost of the most basic of bare-bones baskets for a family of two adults and two children would have been £1.13, rising to £3.02 for the respectability basket (Table 8.01). As will be observed from Table 8.02, the bare-bones basket was within the budget of more or less everyone, except perhaps those reduced to beggary and without family, land or employment, whose premature deaths and malnourished remains are beginning to be revealed by archaeology (Connell and others, 2012). The respectability basket, on the other hand, was affordable to probably at most 60 per cent of households, containing approximately two-thirds of the population. The larger share of population than households reflects the fact that those who could afford the respectability basket were very likely to have had larger completed family sizes and certainly lived in larger households than those living below the poverty

Table 8.02 *A revised social table for England in 1290*

Socio-economic group	Number of households	Assumed mean household size	Total population	Assumed mean acres per rural household	Total acres (000s)	Total income (£, 000s)	Mean income per household (£)
Minor clergy, lawyers, professionals, merchants, tradesmen, builders, craftsmen, urban labourers	130,000	5.50	715,000	0	0	722	5.55
Landowners (spiritual lords, aristocracy, gentry, clergy)	21,000	8.50	178,500	120	2,520	588	28.00
Substantial tenants	12,500	7.00	87,500	50	625	150	12.00
Yardlanders	180,000	5.50	990,000	30	5,400	1,125	6.25
Smallholders	300,000	4.00	1,200,000	12	3,600	938	3.13
Cottagers and agricultural labourers	240,000	3.50	840,000	2	480	360	1.50
Rural craftsmen, non-agricultural labourers, paupers, vagrants	160,000	3.50	560,000	0.75	120	288	1.80

Table 8.02 (cont.)

Socio-economic group	Number of households	Assumed mean household size	Total population	Assumed mean acres per rural household	Total acres (000s)	Total income (£, 000s)	Mean income per household (£)
Miners, men-at-arms, sailors, fishermen	50,000	3.50	175,000	0	0	130	2.60
TOTAL	1,093,500	4.34	4,746,000	13.95	12,745	4,300	3.93

Sources and notes: Based from Campbell (2008: 940) but recalculated for a total population of 4.75 million, total arable area of 12.75 million acres and total current-price GDP of £4.30 million. The dotted line represents the poverty line of £3.02, below which incomes are insufficient for a family comprising one adult male, one adult female and two children to afford the respectability basket.

line (Razi, 1980: 83–8). Notwithstanding two centuries of vigorous commercial development and urban growth, the substantial proportion of the population living below the poverty line in 1290 was little different from that in 1086.

As historians have long recognised and these figures demonstrate, one consequence of the population's increase by a factor of 2.6 during the twelfth and thirteenth centuries was a dramatic expansion in the proportion of families living close to the subsistence minimum (Postan, 1966: 563–5). Moreover, when, in 1293–4 and, more seriously, in 1315–16, back-to-back harvest failures turned their narrow surpluses into deficiencies, that proportion was likely to double. At the close of the thirteenth century those leading this precarious existence included households of most petty smallholders and cottagers provided with just a garden, an acre or two of land and/or common rights, many rural and urban artisans, most miners, fishermen and sailors, and all agricultural, non-agricultural and urban labourers, plus, of course, paupers and vagrants. None of these groups possessed enough landed resources to be self-sufficient and, in one way or another, all depended in part for their survival upon the market. Yet in times of scarcity market forces squeezed them hard, depriving them of employment and earnings, inflating food prices to unaffordable levels and generally disentitling them of licit means of providing for their most basic subsistence needs. According to both Munro's (no date) reworking of the Phelps-Brown and Hopkins real-wage-rate series and Clark's (2007a) farm-wage-rate index, famine in 1316 squeezed the living standards of wage-earners harder than in any other year on record. In that grim year the Gaol Delivery Rolls report a massive resort to property crime in the desperate effort to bridge the shortfall between incomes and subsistence needs (Hanawalt, 1979; Campbell, 2010).

There can be no question that these land-deficient groups constituted a far larger component of English society in 1290 than in 1086. Moreover, in a striking inversion of status and income, many of them were free, for it was free tenants whose numbers had multiplied most rapidly and whose holdings had succumbed to the most extreme

morcellation during the intervening two centuries. In fact, the proliferation of petty free holdings by a combination of piecemeal reclamation, subdivision and sub-letting, aided and abetted by the unrestrained
working of an active land market, is one of the most striking features of
the age (Campbell, 2005: 45–70; Bekar and Reed, 2013). Customary
holdings were not immune to these processes but lords were in a
stronger position to regulate and restrain them (Kanzaka, 2002). The
free, as a result, were the new poor, whereas villein yardlanders now
ranked among the better off with average incomes double those needed
to purchase a respectability basket of consumables (Table 8.02).

Within the space of a generation, between 1348 and 1375, the
massive mortality triggered by the Black Death and its sequel outbreaks provided a drastic but enduring solution to the congestion
that had developed on the land. By 1377 the population had reduced
from a pre-plague peak of 4.8 million to 2.5 million, real wage rates had
risen by 45 per cent, and GDP per head had received a 25 per cent boost.
As is plain from Table 8.01, provided that workers continued to labour
for at least 200 days a year, a building craftsman's earnings were now
more than sufficient to purchase the respectability consumption basket and those of agricultural and building labourers were double the
cost of the bare-bones basket. Undoubtedly, living standards of those
who survived the plagues had improved. Table 8.03 offers a provisional
social table of England in 1381, the year when frustrated rising expect-
ations and grievances against the poll taxes and Statute of Labourers
sparked the Peasants' Revolt. The country's income distribution in
that eventful year has been reconstructed by projecting forward from
the 1290 social table in conformity with estimated reductions in population and national income (Chapters 1 and 5). Note that the social
table has been reduced from eight to four income groups. Note, too,
that the number of households estimated to have been living below the
poverty line has contracted from 450,000 to 134,000, halving propor-
tionally from 41 per cent to 22 per cent of the total. Given the smaller
size of poor households, by 1381 the proportion of individuals living
below the poverty line must have been less than 20 per cent and might

Table 8.03 *A provisional social table for England in 1381*

Socio-economic group:	Number of families	Total income (£)	Income per family (£)
Landowners (spiritual lords, aristocracy, gentry, clergy)	18,815	553,772	29.4
Substantial tenants	100,598	1,558,850	15.5
Yardlanders, smallholders, minor clergy, lawyers, professionals, merchants, tradesmen, builders, craftsmen, urban labourers, miners, men-at-arms, sailors, fishermen	351,587	1,475,379	4.2
Cottagers, labourers, rural craftsmen, paupers, vagrants	134,000	401,999	3.0
TOTAL	605,000	3,990,000	6.6

Sources and notes: the dotted line represents the poverty line of £3.43, below which incomes are insufficient for a family to afford the respectability basket. The table is constructed by forward projection from that for 1290 (Table 8.02). Total numbers of families are adjusted downwards from 1290 in line with population (Chapter 1). The proportional breakdown of family numbers across the four social classes is derived from the proportions of taxpayers contributing at four different rates to the 1381 poll tax, on the assumption that these differences in payments reflected differences in income (Goldberg, 1990: 195). Average family income in each social group is obtained by forward projection of 1290 to 1381 using data on nominal GDP per head from Chapter 5 for the highest three social classes and the unskilled building wage from Allen (2001) for the lowest social class. The average income per family in the lowest class is determined by the unskilled wage, that of the three high social classes by the requirement that the summed income of all four social groups should add up to a nominal GDP of £3.99 m. for 1381.

conceivably have been as low as 15 per cent. Poverty had most certainly not gone away but it was massively reduced.

The next available social table is the well-known and much-used profile assembled by Gregory King [1696] for England in 1688, the year of the Glorious Revolution. During the interim much had happened to the country's economy, society and political institutions. By 1688 the population was double that of 1381 and GDP per head had risen by a further 40 per cent: agriculture had shrunk in relative importance, while services had expanded and industry had become the largest sector of the economy in terms of output and was rapidly catching agriculture as the premier employer of labour (Tables 5.01 and 5.02). Those deriving their livelihoods from commerce, manufacturing, construction and the armed forces are consequently more strongly represented in Gregory King's social table than those for 1381 or 1290. As Table 8.01 shows, the incomes of those earning their livings by labouring for 200 days a year had improved less and remained unequal to the price of a respectability basket of consumables. Due to increases in relative prices, the latter also remained slightly out of budgetary reach of building craftsmen working the same number of days.

The income profile presented in Table 8.04 is a revision of Lindert and Williamson's (1982) reworking of Gregory King's [1696] data, with figures scaled down to conform to this study's slightly lower estimate of nominal GDP. Only the incomes of labouring people and out-servants remain unchanged since any downward adjustment would have made it difficult to reconcile them with the wage-rate data, especially given the evidence presented in Chapter 6 that many must now have been working considerably more than the 200 days a year assumed in Table 8.01. For the higher social classes, a number of Gregory King's categories have been combined, since the interest of this study lies more in the distinctions at the lower end of the income distribution. In 1688 approximately three-quarters of families would have been able to afford the respectability basket of consumables, even though the relative prices of several of its core components were rising. The cheaper and coarser contents of the bare-bones basket meant that it was less affected in this way. It remained the subsistence staple of cottagers and paupers and may also have been affordable to vagrants as individuals, who now potentially qualified for poor relief from their home parishes.

Table 8.04 *A social table for England in 1688*

Socio-economic group	Number of families	Total income (£)	Income per family (£)
High titles and professions	62,586	12,802,127	205
Commerce	128,025	10,507,431	82
Agriculture, excluding labourers	227,440	11,054,906	49
Industry and building	256,866	9,237,285	36
Military and maritime	94,000	2,054,478	22
Labouring people and out-servants	284,997	4,844,949	17
Cottagers and paupers	313,183	1,963,512	6
Vagrants	23,489	45,312	2
TOTAL	1,390,586	52,510,000	38

Sources and notes: Derived from King [1696]; the dotted line represents the poverty line of £16.82, below which incomes are insufficient for a family to afford the respectability basket.

Although almost a quarter of families had incomes that kept them below the poverty line, Allen (2009a: 50) estimates that only 18.3 per cent of individuals were in this position, mainly because those on low incomes had smaller than average completed family sizes and a number had no families. By 1688 the wider range of available employment opportunities in combination with an effective system of poor relief meant that economic survival without family support was becoming more viable. Poverty in late-seventeenth-century England remained substantial but those able to obtain employment and willing to work longer and harder were less exposed to its worst rigours than their predecessors before the Black Death. Not only did their modest incomes go that little bit further in terms of the items contained in the bare-bones and respectability baskets, but they also had a parish poor-law system to fall back on should their circumstances deteriorate too much. Poverty, in short, had become more manageable and the Overseers of the Poor were now in a position to dictate the terms upon which it was relieved.

Table 8.05 *A social table for Great Britain in 1759*

Socio-economic group	Number of families	Total income (£)	Income per family (£)
High titles and professions	75,070	20,324,232	271
Commerce	200,500	16,915,288	84
Industry and building	366,252	14,140,114	39
Agriculture (excluding labourers and husbandmen)	244,848	17,518,619	72
Military and maritime (excluding common soldiers)	68,000	2,269,860	33
Labouring people	240,000	5,070,964	21
Husbandmen	134,160	2,591,697	19
Common soldiers	18,000	304,258	17
Cottagers and paupers	178,892	1,511,925	8
Vagrants	13,418	51,842	4
TOTAL	1,539,140	80,698,799	52

Sources and notes: Derived from Massie [1760]; the dotted line represents the poverty line of £17.19, below which incomes are insufficient for a family to afford the respectability basket.

It is generally acknowledged that Joseph Massie's [1760] social table for 1759 is not as reliable as Gregory King's for 1688 (Lindert and Williamson, 1982: 394–5). Massie's table was constructed to prove a particular political point and King had access to more and better data. For all its shortcomings it is nevertheless of great value in depicting Great Britain on the eve of the industrial revolution. Massie's figures have been reworked by Lindert and Williamson (1982) and are further revised in Table 8.05 to yield a substantially higher total national income at current prices of £80.70 million, in line with the estimates presented in Chapter 5. Accordingly, the incomes of most groups have been scaled up by 13.3 per cent, except when the result would be at variance with the evidence of wage rates and potential wage earnings. The estimates strongly suggest that the numbers of families living below the poverty line had continued to shrink and may now have comprised as little as 14 per cent of the total and possibly only one in eight of all individuals.

Out of a total of 1.54 million families in 1759, 210,300 were unable to afford the respectability basket. Cottagers, paupers and vagrants still dominated this lowest income group. Even so, cottagers and paupers with average incomes of £8 were comfortably able to afford the bare-bones subsistence basket of £5.70 (Table 8.01) and vagrants alone were close to the subsistence level for an individual of £1.90. At £17.19, the cost of a full respectability basket of goods was also just beyond the budget of common soldiers, with average annual incomes of £17.00. The bulk of the 567,000 families who earned their livings from commerce, manufacturing and construction were nevertheless well able to afford the material comforts of a respectable lifestyle. Never before had the proportion of families on middling incomes (those more than able to afford the respectability basket but less affluent than the aristocracy and professional classes) been as great. These were families with significant disposable income and it was their demand for manufactured goods, services and imported luxuries which had been so conspicuously absent in 1290 when the economy had lost whatever forward momentum it might once have possessed.

The final social table captures Great Britain in 1801/03 on the cusp of profound socio-economic change, at the height of the Napoleonic Wars and at the point when union between Ireland and Great Britain came into effect. It is based on data assembled by Scottish statistician, philanthropist and businessman Patrick Colquhoun in his *Treatise on indigence* (1806). Colquhoun was able to draw upon a wealth of official and unofficial quantitative information, including the first national census of 1801, whose compilation stemmed from the constitutional reforms that followed the Glorious Revolution (Maddison, 2007: 252–84). Since Colquhoun was preoccupied with the links between poverty, indigence and crime the numbers and condition of the poor are particular strengths of his *Treatise*.

Malthus's *Essay on the principle of population* [1798] had stoked contemporary debate about the conditions, costs, benefits and consequences of relieving the poor. Also, and as if on cue, serious back-to-back harvest failures in 1799 and 1800 had once more highlighted the continuing vulnerability of those on low incomes to scarcity and high prices and the consequent resort of many to crime. Meanwhile, engrossing and enclosure were dispossessing many commoners and smallholders from the land at the very time that competition from the new factories was extinguishing opportunities for employment in traditional domestic industries (Shaw-Taylor and others, 2010). Unsurprisingly, adaptation to these profound structural and organisational changes brought short-term hardship to many. Economic progress may have been gathering pace but those with the least education, skill and resources had yet to experience its benefits.

Table 8.06 draws upon Colquhoun's (1806) study as reworked by Lindert and Williamson (1982). Since Lindert and Williamson greatly underestimate Britain's national income, most incomes have been scaled up by 42.5 per cent to conform to the considerably higher nominal GDP presented in Chapter 5. The scale of this adjustment largely reflects the use of 10-year average nominal data in this study during a period of rapid wartime inflation, although it should be noted that these higher nominal values are also used to construct the poverty lines. Note that the average incomes of labouring people, at £45, are well above the poverty line of £32.13 as defined by the cost of purchasing a respectability basket of consumables. Incomes of members of the armed forces are also well above that line and over 1 million families who obtained their livelihoods from farming, commerce, manufacturing and construction could all, on average, afford the respectability basket several times over. Four out of five families therefore received incomes that were mostly more than sufficient to keep them well above the poverty line. Cottagers, paupers and vagrants remained below the line and their incomes would have purchased less than half the respectability basket.

Table 8.06 *A social table for Great Britain in 1801/03*

Socio-economic group:	Number of families	Total income (£)	Income per family (£)
High titles and professions	102,043	65,763,253	644
Commerce	205,800	57,485,115	279
Industry and building	541,026	74,885,817	138
Agriculture (excluding labourers)	320,000	55,715,417	174
Military and maritime	244,348	15,222,931	62
Labouring people	340,000	15,453,697	45
Cottagers and paupers	260,179	3,814,732	15
Vagrants	175,218	2,569,038	15
TOTAL	2,188,614	290,910,000	133

Sources and notes: Derived from Colquhoun (1806); the dotted line represents the poverty line of £32.13, below which incomes are insufficient for a family to afford the respectability basket.

Between 1759 and 1801/03 the number of families living in such straitened circumstances had doubled from 210,000 to 435,000, which represents a proportionate increase from 14 per cent to 20 per cent. Neither figure is surprising, given the speeds with which the population was then growing and the economy changing, but the upsurge in poverty was nonetheless dramatic enough to alarm contemporaries and prompt political economists to reflect upon its individual and systemic causes and the measures that might be adopted to alleviate and reduce it. Continued economic growth was part of the solution, reduced rates of population growth another, and educational and welfare reforms intended to improve the skills and employability of the unskilled and shore up the incomes of the deserving poor, a third. State funding of schools for poor children began in England in 1833 and in 1834 the New Poor Law instituted workhouses. From the mid-nineteenth century, reductions in the cost of living also had a big impact. In particular, increased food imports helped bring down the relative cost of the dietary component of both the bare-bones and subsistence baskets of consumables.

8.4 CONCLUSIONS

Inequality and poverty were inescapable features of all pre-modern societies but measuring them is at best an imprecise science. Conventionally, income inequality is quantified using Gini coefficients, with the expectation articulated by Kuznets (1955) that until modernisation was far advanced inequality was likely to rise with mean incomes. Economic growth obviously did a great deal to boost the incomes of privileged elites, merchants and financiers, industrial entrepreneurs and all those with scarce and highly valued skills. It did little to alter the incomes of the remainder, who laboured with little skill and less education in an over-supplied labour market and led a hand-to-mouth existence at living standards close to the lowest compatible with physical subsistence. For their incomes to improve the returns to labour as a factor of production had to rise, the cost of living fall, and access to training, education, skills and opportunity become more universal: welfare measures intended to protect the subsistence needs of the poorest and most vulnerable members of society also made a difference.

How much rising wealth percolated down to those at the base of the social pyramid is obviously captured to some extent by trends in the purchasing power of wages, although as Chapter 6 has demonstrated the relationship between wage rates and actual incomes is less straightforward than often assumed due to variations in the hours per day and days per year that labourers were prepared to work. An alternative approach, pioneered by Allen (2009a) and applied in this chapter, is to reconstruct the social distribution of incomes, define the minimum income required to afford a 'respectability' basket of consumables, and then measure the proportions of households, families and individuals whose annual incomes placed them below that budgetary poverty line. The results are summarised in Table 8.07, together with

Table 8.07 *Measures of wealth, poverty and inequality, England 1290, 1381 and 1688, and Great Britain 1759 and 1801/03*

Date:	GDP per head (1290 = 100)	Ratio of wage to consumption basket		% living below the poverty line		Gini coefficient (%)
		Unskilled to bare-bones	Skilled to respectability	Families	Individuals	
1290	100	1.29	0.83	41.2	33.2	33
1381	144	2.00	1.22	22.1		37
1688	212	1.76	0.92	24.2	18.3	49
1759	276	2.34	1.16	13.7		45
1801/03	319	1.97	0.96	19.9		48

Source: Derived from Tables 8.01 to 8.06; the bare-bones and respectability consumption baskets are defined and priced in Appendices 8.1 to 8.7; the figure for individuals in 1688 is from Allen (2009a: 50). Results for 1290, 1381 1688 are for England and for 1759 and 1801/03 for Great Britain.

corresponding estimates of the purchasing power of wages and Gini coefficients calculated on the income distributions set out in Tables 8.02 to 8.06.

On all the available indicators England was poorer and the incidence of household, family and personal poverty greater in 1290 than at any of the four subsequent benchmark dates examined. The cost of a respectability basket of consumables was beyond the budget of two out of five households, including skilled craftsmen receiving wages for 200 days' work a year. The poverty of these low-income households meant that they had lower reproduction rates than those of the better off, with the result that fewer individuals than households were poor (as was also the case in 1688). Nevertheless, roughly a third of the population was subsisting on some version of the bare-bones consumption basket, with little margin to cushion themselves against poor harvests, scarce employment and high food prices. It is therefore hardly surprising that the dismal harvests of 1293–4 caused genuine hardship (Schofield, 1997). Yet although the richest 2 per cent of the population enjoyed average incomes nineteen times greater than those of the poorest 22 per cent, the fact that the average income was less than the price of the respectability consumption basket limited the amount of surplus extraction that even the most rapacious feudal landlords could expropriate (Brenner, 1976). Poverty in effect constrained income inequality (Milanovic and others, 2007), as reflected by the low Gini coefficient of 33 per cent.

By 1381 the situation had been transformed by the massive plague-induced collapse in population. In the aftermath of the Black Death GDP per head, the purchasing power of unskilled and skilled wages and income inequality all increased (Table 8.07) and windfall gains in living standards lifted greatly increased proportions of both households and individuals above the poverty line. Poverty still affected two out of nine households but it was less grinding than in 1290 since the incomes of even these poorest households now bought more. It seems likely that over the next hundred years poverty decreased further until rising population and falling wage rates again squeezed incomes during the sixteenth and early seventeenth centuries. As Chapter 6 has shown, individuals and households responded to these renewed pressures by working longer and harder, with the result that although poverty grew it never became as crushing or burdensome to the economy as it had been in the late thirteenth century. A lengthened working year, expanding industrial employment and establishment in 1597 of a parish-based national Poor Law all helped take the strain.

At the end of the seventeenth century, when GDP per head was more than double that of 1290, about a quarter of families and two out of eleven individuals were unable to afford the respectability basket of consumables. This was clearly an economy on the move and the overall gain in wealth brought a significant increase in income inequality, for the fruits of economic progress were unequally shared. Over the next 70 years wealth per head advanced further and the rewards of economic growth became diffused more widely, so that by 1759, on the eve of the industrial revolution, the purchasing power of wages had improved, income inequality eased somewhat and the proportion of families living below the poverty line reduced to perhaps just 14 per cent.

Thereafter, poverty evidently rebounded as population growth accelerated and industrialisation, with all its disruptive socio-economic side effects, advanced apace. By 1801/03 the proportion of families unable to afford the respectability basket was back to one fifth (Table 8.07). Floud and others (2011: 91) arrive at the same proportions for 1688 and 1801/03 from the social tables of both King and Colquhoun but are sceptical of the reduction in poverty implied by Massie's social table for 1759. Instead, they prefer to interpolate geometrically between 1688 and 1801/03 to arrive at a figure of 21.4 per cent living in poverty in 1759. Yet a fall in poverty to 1759 and rise thereafter is entirely consistent with the improvement in the purchasing power of wages from 1688 to 1759 and deterioration from 1759 to 1801/03 (Table 8.07). It is also consistent with what Allen (2009b) calls 'Engels' pause', namely, that during the early stages of industrialisation gains in wages lagged behind advances in output per worker for the reasons explained by Angeles (2008). The fact that employers seem to have been profiting more than their employees probably accounts for the higher Gini coefficient in 1801/03 than 1759, although the rise in income inequality is less marked than that estimated by Milanovic and others (2007).

For all the understandable concern of informed contemporaries at the conspicuous proliferation of poor households and individuals seeking parish relief at the turn of the eighteenth and nineteenth centuries, the proportion of families thus entrapped was half that of five centuries earlier when the economy was substantially poorer and less dynamic, with little beyond private charity to relieve those who had fallen upon hard times. Between 1290 and 1801 the effect of economic growth was to reduce the incidence of poverty at the price of raising income inequality. From 1597 a national Poor Law did much to dampen down the surges in vagrancy which had followed serious harvest failures and trade recessions, often bringing disease outbreaks in their train. Employment growth, especially in manufacturing, also helped bolster household incomes. In 1801 poverty remained an intractable problem, and when concentrated into the expanding industrial cities brought additional problems of crime and public health, but was no longer on such an overwhelming scale that it stifled demand for consumer goods and inhibited economic growth. By the nineteenth century poverty had become a burden that could be carried and institutions were in place that protected the poorest in society from the worst of its consequences. These achievements had not been won overnight but sprang from developments first set in train in the aftermath of the Black Death and then consolidated during the sixteenth and seventeenth centuries when, paradoxically, the social distribution of income was becoming ever more polarised.

APPENDIX 8.1

Contents, prices and costs of the bare-bones and respectability consumption baskets in 1290

Commodity	Quantity per person per year	Price (d. per unit)	Expenditure (d.)	Expenditure share (%)	Kilocalories per day	Grams of protein per day
A. Bare-bones basket						
Oats	155 kg	0.23	35.7	41.4	1,657	72
Beans/peas	20 kg	0.42	8.4	9.8	187	14
Meat	5 kg	0.79	3.9	4.5	34	3
Butter	3 kg	2.27	6.8	7.9	60	0
Soap	1.3 kg	4.59	6.0	6.9		
Linen	3 m	3.75	11.3	13.1		
Candles	1.3 kg	2.92	3.8	4.4		
Lamp oil	1.3 lt	2.64	3.4	4.0		
Fuel	2.0 M BTU	3.43	6.9	8.0		
TOTAL			86.1	100.0	1,938	89
Rent (5%)			4.3			
TOTAL including rent			90.4			
B. Respectability basket						
Bread	190 kg	0.47	88.7	38.6	1,276	64
Beans/peas	40 kg	0.42	16.8	7.3	370	28
Meat	26 kg	0.79	20.5	8.9	178	14
Butter	5.2 kg	2.27	11.8	5.1	104	0
Cheese	5.2 kg	1.09	5.7	2.4	54	3
Eggs	52 each	0.06	3.1	1.4	11	1
Beer	182 lt	0.12	20.9	9.1	212	2
Soap	2.6 kg	4.59	11.9	5.2		
Linen	5 m	3.75	18.8	8.2		
Candles	2.6 kg	2.92	7.6	3.3		
Lamp oil	2.6 lt	2.64	6.9	3.0		
Fuel	5.0 M BTU	3.43	17.2	7.5		
TOTAL			229.8	100.0	2,205	112
Rent (5%)			11.5			
TOTAL including rent			241.3			

Sources: Expenditure derived using quantities from Allen (2009a: 36–7) and prices from Allen (2001); prices are averages of the years 1286–95.

APPENDIX 8.2

Contents, prices and costs of the bare-bones and respectability consumption baskets in 1381

Commodity	Quantity per person per year	Price (d. per unit)	Expenditure (d.)	Expenditure share (%)
A. Bare-bones basket				
Oats	155 kg	0.22	34.1	35.9
Beans/peas	20 kg	0.44	8.8	9.3
Meat	5 kg	0.84	4.2	4.4
Butter	3 kg	2.42	7.3	7.6
Soap	1.3 kg	6.68	8.7	9.1
Linen	3 m	4.64	13.9	14.6
Candles	1.3 kg	4.25	5.5	5.8
Lamp oil	1.3 lt	3.35	4.4	4.6
Fuel	2.0 M BTU	4.16	8.3	8.7
TOTAL			95.2	100.0
Rent (5%)			4.8	
TOTAL including rent			100.0	
B. Respectability basket				
Bread	190 kg	0.53	99.9	38.2
Beans/peas	40 kg	0.44	17.6	6.7
Meat	26 kg	0.84	21.8	8.4
Butter	5.2 kg	2.42	12.6	4.8
Cheese	5.2 kg	1.17	6.1	2.3
Eggs	52 each	0.08	4.4	1.7
Beer	182 lt	0.10	18.0	6.9
Soap	2.6 kg	6.68	23.2	6.6
Linen	5 m	4.64	25.4	8.9
Candles	2.6 kg	4.25	11.1	4.2
Lamp oil	2.6 lt	3.35	8.7	3.3
Fuel	5.0 M BTU	4.16	20.8	8.0
TOTAL			261.5	100.0
Rent (5%)			13.1	
TOTAL including rent			274.6	

Sources: Expenditure derived using quantities from Allen (2009a: 36–7) and prices from Allen (2001); prices are averages of the years 1377–86.

APPENDIX 8.3

Contents, prices and costs of the bare-bones and respectability consumption baskets in 1522

Commodity	Quantity per person per year	Price (d. per unit)	Expenditure (d.)	Expenditure share (%)
A. Bare-bones basket				
Oats	155 kg	0.28	43.4	41.3
Beans/peas	20 kg	0.71	14.2	13.5
Meat	5 kg	1.10	5.5	5.2
Butter	3 kg	2.68	8.0	7.7
Soap	1.3 kg	5.14	6.7	6.4
Linen	3 m	5.09	15.3	14.5
Candles	1.3 kg	2.65	3.5	3.3
Lamp oil	1.3 lt	3.38	4.4	4.2
Fuel	2.0 M BTU	2.07	4.1	3.9
TOTAL			105.0	100.0
Rent (5%)			5.3	
TOTAL including rent			110.3	
B. Respectability basket				
Bread	190 kg	0.71	135.1	43.5
Beans/peas	40 kg	0.71	28.4	9.1
Meat	26 kg	1.10	28.5	9.2
Butter	5.2 kg	2.68	13.9	4.5
Cheese	5.2 kg	1.60	8.3	2.7
Eggs	52 each	0.14	7.3	2.4
Beer	182 lt	0.13	24.2	7.8
Soap	2.6 kg	5.14	13.4	4.3
Linen	5 m	5.09	25.4	8.2
Candles	2.6 kg	2.65	6.9	2.2
Lamp oil	2.6 lt	3.38	8.8	2.8
Fuel	5.0 M BTU	2.07	10.3	3.3
TOTAL			310.6	100.0
Rent (5%)			15.5	
TOTAL including rent			326.1	

Sources: Expenditure derived using quantities from Allen (2009a: 36–7) and prices from Allen (2001); prices are averages of the years 1518–27.

APPENDIX 8.4

Contents, prices and costs of the bare-bones and respectability consumption baskets in 1620

Commodity	Quantity per person per year	Price (d. per unit)	Expenditure (d.)	Expenditure share (%)
A. Bare-bones basket				
Oats	155 kg	1.36	210.8	58.1
Beans/peas	20 kg	0.88	17.6	4.9
Meat	5 kg	4.99	25.0	6.9
Butter	3 kg	11.42	34.3	9.4
Soap	1.3 kg	10.32	13.4	3.7
Linen	3 m	7.93	23.8	6.6
Candles	1.3 kg	9.89	12.9	3.5
Lamp oil	1.3 lt	9.05	11.8	3.2
Fuel	2.0 M BTU	6.70	13.4	3.7
TOTAL			362.8	100.0
Rent (5%)			18.1	
TOTAL including rent			380.9	
B. Respectability basket				
Bread	190 kg	2.72	516.6	49.3
Beans/peas	40 kg	0.88	35.3	3.4
Meat	26 kg	4.99	129.7	12.4
Butter	5.2 kg	11.42	59.4	5.7
Cheese	5.2 kg	5.72	29.7	2.8
Eggs	52 each	0.66	34.3	3.3
Beer	182 lt	0.52	94.6	9.0
Soap	2.6 kg	10.32	26.8	2.6
Linen	5 m	7.93	39.7	3.8
Candles	2.6 kg	9.89	25.7	2.5
Lamp oil	2.6 lt	9.05	23.5	2.2
Fuel	5.0 M BTU	6.70	33.5	3.2
TOTAL			1,048.9	100.0
Rent (5%)			52.4	
TOTAL including rent			1,101.3	

Sources: Expenditure derived using quantities from Allen (2009a: 36–7) and prices from Allen (2001); prices are averages of the years 1615–24.

APPENDIX 8.5

Contents, prices and costs of the bare-bones and respectability consumption baskets in 1688

Commodity	Quantity per person per year	Price (d. per unit)	Expenditure (d.)	Expenditure share (%)
A. Bare-bones basket				
Oats	155 kg	1.48	229.5	52.9
Beans/peas	20 kg	2.78	55.7	12.8
Meat	5 kg	6.42	32.1	7.4
Butter	3 kg	11.86	35.6	8.2
Soap	1.3 kg	9.92	12.9	3.0
Linen	3 m	10.50	31.5	7.3
Candles	1.3 kg	10.47	13.6	3.1
Lamp oil	1.3 lt	9.23	12.0	2.8
Fuel	2.0 M BTU	5.48	11.0	2.5
TOTAL			433.6	100.0
Rent (5%)			21.7	
TOTAL including rent			455.3	
B. Respectability basket				
Bread	190 kg	3.06	582.2	45.4
Beans/peas	40 kg	2.78	111.4	8.7
Meat	26 kg	6.42	167.0	13.0
Butter	5.2 kg	11.86	61.7	4.8
Cheese	5.2 kg	7.79	40.5	3.2
Eggs	52 each	0.70	36.4	2.8
Beer	182 lt	0.67	121.5	9.5
Soap	2.6 kg	9.92	25.8	2.0
Linen	5 m	10.50	52.5	4.1
Candles	2.6 kg	10.47	27.2	2.1
Lamp oil	2.6 lt	11.10	28.8	2.3
Fuel	5.0 M BTU	5.48	27.4	2.1
TOTAL			1,281.8	100.0
Rent (5%)			64.1	
TOTAL including rent			1,345.9	

Sources: Expenditure derived using quantities from Allen (2009a: 36–7) and prices from Allen (2001); prices are averages of the years 1683–92.

APPENDIX 8.6

Contents, prices and costs of the bare-bones and respectability consumption baskets in 1759

Commodity	Quantity per person per year	Price (d. per unit)	Expenditure (d.)	*Expenditure share (%)*
A. Bare-bones basket				
Oats	155 kg	1.36	210.8	*48.5*
Beans/peas	20 kg	2.29	45.8	*10.5*
Meat	5 kg	7.32	36.6	*8.4*
Butter	3 kg	15.82	47.5	*10.9*
Soap	1.3 kg	16.09	20.9	*4.8*
Linen	3 m	10.50	31.5	*7.3*
Candles	1.3 kg	15.06	19.6	*4.5*
Lamp oil	1.3 lt	8.21	10.7	*2.5*
Fuel	2.0 M BTU	5.59	11.2	*2.6*
TOTAL			434.5	*100.0*
Rent (5%)			21.7	
TOTAL including rent			456.2	
B. Respectability basket				
Bread	190 kg	2.91	552.9	*42.2*
Beans/peas	40 kg	2.29	91.6	*7.0*
Meat	26 kg	7.32	190.3	*14.5*
Butter	5.2 kg	15.82	82.3	*6.3*
Cheese	5.2 kg	3.86	20.1	*1.5*
Eggs	52 each	0.75	39.0	*3.0*
Beer	182 lt	0.83	151.1	*11.5*
Soap	2.6 kg	16.09	41.8	*3.2*
Linen	5 m	10.50	52.5	*4.0*
Candles	2.6 kg	15.06	39.2	*3.0*
Lamp oil	2.6 lt	8.21	21.3	*1.7*
Fuel	5.0 M BTU	5.59	27.9	*2.1*
TOTAL			1,310.0	*100.0*
Rent (5%)			65.5	
TOTAL including rent			1,375.5	

Sources: Expenditure derived using quantities from Allen (2009a: 36–7) and prices from Allen (2001); prices are averages of the years 1755–64.

APPENDIX 8.7

Contents, prices and costs of the bare-bones and respectability consumption baskets in 1801/03

Commodity	Quantity per person per year	Price (d. per unit)	Expenditure (d.)	Expenditure share (%)
A. Bare-bones basket				
Oats	155 kg	2.83	438.6	56.7
Beans/peas	20 kg	1.87	37.4	4.8
Meat	5 kg	17.64	88.2	11.4
Butter	3 kg	26.01	78.0	10.1
Soap	1.3 kg	23.15	30.1	3.9
Linen	3 m	14.70	44.1	5.7
Candles	1.3 kg	23.15	30.1	3.9
Lamp oil	1.3 lt	8.62	11.2	1.5
Fuel	2.0 M BTU	7.83	15.7	2.0
TOTAL			773.4	100.0
Rent (5%)			38.7	
TOTAL including rent			812.1	
B. Respectability basket				
Bread	190 kg	6.15	1168.5	47.7
Beans/peas	40 kg	1.87	74.8	3.1
Meat	26 kg	17.64	458.6	18.7
Butter	5.2 kg	26.01	135.3	5.5
Cheese	5.2 kg	7.83	40.7	1.7
Eggs	52 each	1.39	72.3	2.9
Beer	182 lt	1.33	242.1	9.9
Soap	2.6 kg	23.15	60.2	2.5
Linen	5 m	14.70	73.5	3.0
Candles	2.6 kg	23.15	60.2	2.5
Lamp oil	2.6 lt	8.62	22.4	0.9
Fuel	5.0 M BTU	7.83	39.1	1.6
TOTAL			2,447.7	100.0
Rent (5%)			122.4	
TOTAL including rent			2,570.1	

Sources: Expenditure derived using quantities from Allen (2009a: 36–7) and prices from Allen (2001); prices are averages of the years 1798–1807.

9   Labour productivity

England's aggregate output per head doubled between the 1290s and the 1690s, trebled by the 1800s and had quadrupled by the 1850s: self-evidently, the productivity of labour was rising across this long period. Whether it was rising equally across all three sectors is another matter. Deane and Cole's (1967) once influential account of British economic development since 1688 was premised on an eighteenth-century agricultural revolution releasing labour to industry at the very time that mechanisation and the division of labour were raising the productivity of labour in manufacturing. British-made goods thereby became unbeatable in world markets so that industry became the most dynamic employment sector within a fast-growing economy. Yet evidence of agricultural innovation a century earlier (Kerridge, 1967) suggested that agricultural output and probably labour productivity were rising from the seventeenth century, so that the share of the labour-force in agriculture was already much reduced before the industrial revolution got under way. Initially controversial, this view has since gained considerable legitimacy (Allen, 1992, 1999; Overton, 1996, 80–2, 121–30). Indeed, it would be difficult to account for an English urbanisation ratio which rose from 5.25 per cent in the 1520s to 17.0 per cent by 1700 and then 27.5 per cent in 1801 (Wrigley, 1985: 688) if there were no concurrent improvements in agricultural labour productivity.

The post-1700 output estimates of Crafts (1985) and Crafts and Harley (1992) accepted the revisions of the agricultural historians and, in turn, proposed that industrial growth was slower during the eighteenth century than estimated by Deane and Cole, notwithstanding the continued transfer of labour out of agriculture and into industry.

On this scenario eighteenth-century agriculture was more successful at shedding labour than industry was at expanding output: hence the paradox that, at the very time that Britain was becoming the workshop rather than the granary of the world (Crafts, 1989), productivity growth in agriculture apparently exceeded that in industry.

Clark and others (2012; Clark, 2013) repudiate all these views with their premise of economic growth and claim instead that there was no significant change in the share of the population employed in farming, fishing and forestry between 1379–81 and 1652–60, which they estimate respectively at 56–9 and 59 per cent (although the latter figure relates to males only and would reduce to approximately 50 per cent if female occupations were taken into account). In fact, Clark (2010a) asserts that there was little substantial reduction in the farm share of employment until after $c.1817$. Relying upon a provisional sample-based estimate by Shaw-Taylor and Wrigley (2008) for adult males employed in the primary sector, he reckons the proportion of the population employed in farming, fishing, forestry and coal mining to have been 42 per cent and equivalent, after agricultural imports have been taken into account, to an *effective* share of 52 per cent. Following full analysis of this occupational dataset, however, Shaw-Taylor (2009a) revised the male primary-sector share down to 38 per cent and, by eliminating those employed in forestry, fishing and mining, obtained a male farm share of 35 per cent for $c.1817$. Adjusting for females then gives the final agricultural employment share of 31 per cent used here (see Tables 9.07 and 9.08 below) but overlooked by Clark (2010a, 2013). Consequently, the latter's claim that the second quarter of the nineteenth century witnessed the greatest fall in the farm share of employment and corresponding surge in agricultural labour productivity does not withstand scrutiny.

Clark's estimates have been cleverly constructed to support his explicitly Malthusian view that England was little richer $c.1800$ than it had been in the 1650s, 1560s or 1380s and therefore that little real economic growth had occurred in the interim. The post-1700 revised GDP-per-head growth rates estimated by Crafts and Harley (1992) and post-1350 growth rates advanced by this study (Table 5.05) suggest otherwise. So, too, do the doubling of urbanisation ratios between the 1520s and 1650s and their doubling again by the 1800s (Wrigley, 1985: 688), none of which would have been possible if labour productivity in agriculture and agriculture's share of the labour-force had remained unchanging. The results now emerging from Shaw-Taylor (2009a) and others' (2010) painstaking researches into the occupations recorded in parish registers, benchmarked against the secure profiles of the country's occupational structure provided by the 1851 and 1861 censuses, lend further credence to this view. They find that only 43 per cent of males were employed in agriculture by 1710 and, further, that this share reduced from approximately 44 per cent in 1755 to 35 per cent in 1813–20, before shrinking to 24 per cent in 1861. Since proportionately fewer women than men were employed in agriculture, including females reduces these shares to 31 per cent in 1813–20 and 21 per cent in 1861. These securely grounded figures supersede the preliminary estimates for males only by Shaw-Taylor and Wrigley (2008) and used by Clark (2010b, 2013), who misrepresents them by applying them to the entire population and failing to discount the primary-sector workers not employed in agriculture but included in them.

Thanks to the new occupational data systematically assembled and analysed by Shaw-Taylor (2009a) and others (2010) the issue as to whether labour-productivity growth in agriculture preceded, accompanied or followed that in industry and services is becoming much clearer. This chapter sheds further light on the matter by reconstructing the output shares (Section 9.2) and labour-force shares (Section 9.3) of the three principal sectors of agriculture, industry and services for the six benchmark years 1381, 1522, 1700, 1759, 1801 and 1851. In so doing particular attention is paid to the differing sectoral participation rates of male and female workers and the effects of relative prices upon value-added output. In Section 9.4 estimates of output per worker in each sector are then derived for these same benchmark years and corresponding annual growth rates in labour productivity calculated. The nineteenth-century estimates are anchored against those of

Shaw-Taylor (2009a) and Shaw-Taylor and others (2010) and the lat-ter's estimates for the long eighteenth century are used to cross-check those obtained in this study from the social tables of Gregory King [1696], Joseph Massie [1760] and Patrick Colquhoun [1806]. Likewise, those of Clark (2013) for 1379–81 provide an independent cross-check on those derived from the 1381 poll tax returns.

It will be demonstrated that the results obtained from these social tables are consistent with the view that the critical structural shift of labour away from agriculture to industry occurred during the early modern period of vigorous industrial, commercial and urban growth. In fact, so much progress had been made by 1759, and espe-cially during the economically dynamic second half of the seventeenth century, that the shift of labour from agriculture to industry during the industrial revolution was smaller than that proposed by Crafts and Harley. This reinstates industry as the sector with the fastest labour productivity growth during the classic industrial revolution period. Although there was substantial agricultural labour productivity growth between 1759 and 1851, it was at a slower pace than in industry and it also slowed over time, thus reversing the most counter-intuitive conclusion of Crafts and Harley (1992) and reconciling their esti-mates with traditional views of a technologically dynamic industrial revolution.

9.2 SECTORAL OUTPUT SHARES

The estimates of sectoral output in nominal value added used in Section 9.4 for the estimation of sectoral labour productivity are those derived from Chapters 3 and 4, assembled in Section 5.2 and presented in Table 5.01. Indices of real output constructed by sector have been transformed into current price terms using sectoral price deflators (Section 5.2.1), with absolute levels of GDP in current prices for each sector and for the total economy established using the input–output table for 1841 from Horrell and others (1994) adjusted to a Great Britain basis, with a further adjustment to an England-only basis at 1700. The results are set out in Part A of Table 9.01. Corresponding labour-force

Table 9.01 *Sectoral shares in GDP and the labour-force, and output per worker in each sector relative to the economy as a whole, England 1381–1700 and Great Britain 1700–1851*

Sector	1381	1522	1700	1759	1801	1851
A. Output shares (%)						
Agriculture	45.5	39.7	26.7	29.7	31.3	18.7
Industry	28.8	38.7	41.3	35.2	32.7	32.1
Services	25.7	21.6	32.0	35.1	36.0	49.2
GDP	100.0	100.0	100.0	100.0	100.0	100.0
B. Labour-force shares (%)						
Agriculture	57.2	55.6	38.9	36.8	31.7	23.5
Industry	19.2	23.5	34.0	33.9	36.4	45.6
Services	23.6	20.9	27.2	29.3	31.9	30.9
GDP	100.0	100.0	100.0	100.0	100.0	100.0
C. Output per worker						
Agriculture	79.5	71.4	68.7	80.8	98.9	79.6
Industry	150.1	164.5	121.5	103.8	89.7	70.3
Services	109.1	103.8	117.9	119.9	112.9	159.3
GDP	100.0	100.0	100.0	100.0	100.0	100.0

Sources and notes: Part A: Table 5.01. Part B: Tables 9.02 to 9.07. Part C: derived by dividing Part A by Part B.

shares from Section 9.3 are given in Part B and derived estimates of output per worker for each sector relative to the economy as a whole in Part C.

In 1700 agriculture's share of current value added was lower than that assumed by Crafts (1985: 16), who worked with a figure of 37 per cent, rather than the 26.7 per cent reported here. By the beginning of the nineteenth century, however, as noted by Crafts (1985: 61), agriculture no longer had an income per worker significantly below the economy-wide average (Table 9.01C). The explanation seems to lie with the marked gain in the price of agricultural goods relative to the price of industrial goods which occurred during the long eighteenth century (Figure 5.02). This offset the effects of agriculture's below-average real output growth, so that agriculture's output share in current prices changed comparatively little. In contrast, incomes in industry and services were both higher than the economy-wide average before 1700 (Table 9.07C). Thereafter, whereas industrial incomes were regressing to the mean, service-sector incomes were increasingly rising above the economy-wide average as commercial services grew in importance relative to domestic service.

9.3 SECTORAL LABOUR-FORCE SHARES

The shares of the labour-force engaged in the three main sectors of agriculture, industry and services have been constructed for England from the occupational information contained in the 1381 poll tax returns, the 1522 muster rolls and King's social table for 1688. Following Deane and Cole (1962) and Crafts (1985), the 1688 shares are assumed to apply to Great Britain in 1700. For Great Britain in other years, the social tables of Massie and Colquhoun for 1759 and 1801, and the census for 1851 are used. In each case, occupations have been classified according to Wrigley's (2006a) Primary–Secondary–Tertiary (PST) scheme, but with mining included in the industrial sector, following Shaw-Taylor (2009a). One obvious difficulty with allocating workers to specific occupations before the nineteenth century is the fact that many individuals combined more than one occupation. Both Saito (2010) and Shaw-Taylor (2009b) have investigated the issue of by-employment for the early modern period and each concluded that a statistical assumption of complete occupational specialisation is unlikely to misrepresent too seriously the actual allocation of workers across the three main sectors. Clark (2013: 9–10) agrees. The reason for this is that where by-employment data do exist, they suggest that flows between sectors occurred in both directions, with only a relatively small net effect. Unfortunately, for the late-medieval period no systematic investigations of by-employment have been made. Pending fuller quantitative research into this issue, the same basic assumption, that any net effects of inter-sectoral flows in secondary occupations were small, has therefore been made for both the early modern and late-medieval periods in the estimates that follow.

9.3.1 Late-medieval labour-force shares

The poll tax returns of 1381, made accessible recently in Fenwick (1998, 2001, 2005), provide the earliest securely documented basis for estimating the occupational structure of England. Information is available for 30,292 individuals (approximately 2 per cent of all adults), resident in 892 vills, covering 95 hundreds in 22 counties stretching across England from Kent in the southeast to Lancashire in the northwest and from Dorset in the southwest to Yorkshire in the northeast. A particular strength of the poll tax returns is that information is given on female as well as male occupations, which are treated separately in Table 9.02.

The first step in the derivation of national labour-force estimates from this partial evidence involves allocating male and female workers with known occupations across agriculture, industry and services. The 15.0 per cent of male workers and 16.4 per cent of female workers with the non-sector specific designation 'labourer' present a particular problem, common to all the pre-census benchmark data. They have been assigned to agriculture and non-agriculture in proportion to the identified workers in these sectors, but with all non-agricultural labourers allocated to industry. The results are not particularly sensitive to this procedure, since for example, if labourers were allocated in proportion to the shares of identified workers in all sectors, there would be no change to the share of agriculture but an improbable 4.4 per cent of the labour-force would be redistributed from industry to services. Finally, because the sample is biased towards urban and semi-rural areas, it has been re-weighted using data from the *Cambridge urban history of Britain* to accord with national rural, urban and semi-rural proportions of 80 per cent, 10 per cent and 10 per cent (Barron, 2000; A. Dyer, 2000; C. Dyer, 2000; Kermode, 2000). Thus, vills (a medieval term covering the local unit of tax assessment and payment) with more than 70 per cent of occupations in agriculture are treated as rural,

Table 9.02 *Sectoral distribution of the English labour-force in 1381 from the poll tax returns*

Sector	Weighted number of workers with known occupations		Allocated labourers with no stated occupations		Total workers		
	Males (no.)	Females (no.)	Males (no.)	Females (no.)	Males (no.)	Females (no.)	Males and females (no.)
Agriculture	14,351	1,467	2,526	288	16,877	1,755	
Industry	2,602	899	1,244	547	3,846	1,446	
Services	4,480	1,888	0	0	4,480	1,888	
Total	21,433	4,254	3,770	835	25,203	5,089	
	%	%	%	%	%	%	%
Agriculture	67.0	34.5	67.0	34.5	67.0	34.5	57.2
Industry	12.1	21.1	33.0	65.5	15.2	28.4	19.2
Services	20.9	44.4	0.0	0.0	17.8	37.1	23.6
Total	100.0	100.0	100.0	100.0	100.0	100.0	100.0

Sources and notes: Numbers of male and female workers are taken from Fenwick (1998, 2001, 2005). Workers with known occupations are allocated to agriculture, industry and services using Wrigley's (2006a) Primary–Secondary–Tertiary (PST) scheme, but with mining included in the industrial sector, as in Shaw-Taylor (2009a). Weights are derived from the *Cambridge urban history of Britain* as described in the text: urban 10%, semi-rural 10%, rural 80%. Areas with more than 70% of occupations in agriculture are classified as rural, cities as identified in A. Dyer (2000) are classified as urban, and the rest are semi-rural. Labourers are allocated between agriculture and non-agriculture in proportion to identified workers, but with all non-agricultural labourers allocated to industry. Females are assumed to account for 30 per cent of total employment, in line with Shaw-Taylor (2009a). Note that for total workers, the male and female percentages cannot be obtained by adding the numbers of workers in the upper panel, since females are assumed to have accounted for 30 per cent of the labour-force, rather than the 16.8 per cent recorded in the surviving poll tax returns.

towns with more than 2,000 inhabitants identified by Dyer (2000) are classified as urban, and the remainder are deemed to be semi-rural.

The sectoral distribution of the total labour-force in 1381 (Table 9.02) is obtained by combining the separate occupational break-downs for males and females. Females are assumed to have worked 30 per cent of the total number of days worked in the economy. This ratio is derived from mid-nineteenth-century data, where Shaw-Taylor (2009a) found a male participation rate of 97.1 per cent and a female participation rate of 43.0 per cent (i.e. equivalent to 70 per cent male and 30 female labour-force shares). Although Field and Erickson (2009) appear to suggest higher rates of female participation during the pre-modern period, it should be noted that they are referring to women active in the labour market, irrespective of how many days they actually worked. The proportion of days worked by women is nevertheless more relevant to the issue of labour productivity.

On a full-time equivalent basis, it seems highly unlikely that women could have worked much more than 30 per cent of total days worked, given the unequal distribution of child-rearing and household duties in pre-modern times. At the other end of the chronological spectrum, the poll tax returns suggest females accounted for just 16.8 per cent of the labour-force, which seems far too low. Fortunately, the results are not particularly sensitive to percentage differences of this magnitude. On the assumption that females accounted for 30 per cent of employment, around 60 per cent of the labour-force in 1381 was engaged in agriculture, while, of the remainder, slightly more were engaged in services than in industry. The equivalent shares, should females have accounted for as little as 16.8 per cent of employment, are 64 per cent agriculture, 15 per cent industry and 21 per cent services. This places a considerably lower share of the labour-force in agriculture during the late-medieval period than has hitherto been assumed, with Overton and Campbell (1996) and Allen (2000), for example, assuming shares in the range 75–80 per cent. It is, however, broadly consistent with the results of Clark (2013), derived by a different method from the 1379–81 poll tax returns.

The muster rolls or military surveys of 1522 are the next set of records with usable occupational information. Originally national in their coverage, disappointingly, only three extant returns record occupations systematically: those for Coventry (Hulton, 1999), representative of an urban environment; Babergh Hundred in Suffolk (Pound, 1986), a semi-rural environment; and Rutland (Cornwall, 1980), an example of a rural environment. Self-evidently, this is a smaller and geographically less comprehensive sample than the 1381 poll tax returns and is further handicapped by relating almost exclusively to males.

Table 9.03A shows the distribution of the labour-force in the three districts and in the sample as a whole. The weightings are taken from the *Cambridge urban history of Britain* and again assume rural, urban and semi-rural proportions respectively of 80 per cent, 10 per cent and 10 per cent (Barron, 2000; A. Dyer, 2000; C. Dyer, 2000; Kermode, 2000). As in the poll tax returns, the muster rolls contain a category of workers designated simply as 'labourers'. These comprise 25.9 per cent of those listed and in Table 9.03B are similarly assigned to agriculture and non-agriculture in proportion to the identified workers in these sectors, but with all non-agricultural labourers allocated to industry. Allocating the non-agricultural labourers in proportion to the shares of identified workers in industry and services would redistribute 2.8 per cent of the labour-force to services. The occupational estimates for females given in Table 9.03B depend upon two basic assumptions: first, that women worked 30 per cent of the total number of days worked in the economy and, second, that participation by female workers across sectors was proportionately the same as in 1381.

The final column of Table 9.03B combines the actual male and interpolated female data to provide an estimate of the total sectoral distribution of the labour-force. Around 56 per cent were still employed in agriculture, a proportion broadly in line with the findings of Clark and others (2012) based upon testamentary information for the mid-sixteenth century (Table 9.08C). Of the remaining workers, slightly more were now engaged in industry than in services.

Table 9.03 *Sectoral distribution of the English labour-force in 1522 from the muster rolls*

A.

Sector	Coventry (Urban) (10%)	Babergh (Semi-rural) (10%)	Rutland (rural) (80%)	Weighted number of male workers with known occupations	
	No.	No.	No.	No.	%
Agriculture	12	273	868	1,848	64.7
Industry	594	577	38	471	16.5
Services	143	133	218	537	18.8
TOTAL	749	983	1,124	2,856	100.0

B.

Sector	Weighted number of male workers with known occupations (from A)		Allocated male labourers with no stated occupations:		Total male workers		Total female workers		Weighted total workers
	No.	%	No.	%	No.	%	No.	%	%
Agriculture	1,848	64.7	644	64.7	2,492	64.7		34.5	55.6
Industry	471	16.5	352	35.3	823	21.4		28.4	23.5
Services	537	18.8	0	0	537	13.9		37.1	20.9
TOTAL	2,856	100.0	996	100.0	3,852	100.0		100.0	100.0

Sources and notes: Part A: Coventry: Hulton (1999); Babergh: Pound (1986); Rutland: Cornwall (1980). Workers with known occupations are allocated to agriculture, industry and services using Wrigley's (2006a) PST scheme, but with mining included in the industrial sector, as in Shaw-Taylor (2009a). Weights are derived from *The Cambridge urban history of Britain* as described in the text: Coventry (urban) 10%, Babergh (semi-rural) 10%, Rutland (rural) 80%. Part B: Labourers are allocated between agriculture and non-agriculture in proportion to identified workers, but with all non-agricultural labourers allocated to industry. The distribution of the female labour-force is assumed to be the same as in 1381 (Table 9.02), and females are assumed to account for 30 per cent of total employment, in line with Shaw-Taylor (2009a).

9.3.2   Labour-force shares 1688–1871

Recent work by Shaw-Taylor (2009a) and Shaw-Taylor and others (2010) has provided occupational estimates of the male labour-force *c*.1710, *c*.1755 and 1813–20 from large national samples of parish registers. Their figure of 43.0 per cent of males employed in agriculture *c*.1710 represents a dramatic decline from this study's estimate of 64.7 per cent in 1522 (Table 9.03) and also from the 59 per cent obtained from a sample of probate records by Clark and others (2012) for 1652–60 (Table 9.08B and C). Seemingly, there was little change in the share of the male labour-force in agriculture between 1710 and 1755, when Shaw-Taylor finds it was 44.0 per cent, but by 1813–20 the share had fallen to a securely documented 35.4 per cent.

Given the provisional nature of the results obtained by Shaw-Taylor and others (2010) from parish registers plus the need for data on females as well as males, in this study alternative occupational estimates have been derived for 1688, 1759 and 1801 from the social tables produced by Gregory King [1696], Joseph Massie [1760] and Patrick Colquhoun [1806] (Chapter 8, Section 8.3). As Maddison (2007: 252–84) notes, these writers had access to a rich array of data sources, including parish registers containing valuable information on occupations in association with demographic details of the life-cycle events of birth, marriage and death. They also had access to genealogical and heraldic information on high-status families, as well as detailed information on specific tax revenues. King [1696] tested his results by organising his own mini-censuses for Lichfield, Harfield and Buckfastleigh and just over a century later Colquhoun [1806] was able to use the first national population census as well as parliamentary surveys of paupers and taxation data on the richest families. The social tables produced by these pioneers of, in effect, national income accounting have been reworked on a consistent basis by Lindert and Williamson (1982) and Crafts (1985), but without making any explicit allowance for the different occupational structures of males and females. The latter omission is significant, since it is clear from the recent work of Shaw-Taylor (2009a) and Shaw-Taylor and others (2010) that the occupational distributions of 'families' in Colquhoun's, Massie's and King's social tables de facto correspond to those of males, and take little or no account of the contrasting occupational distributions of females. Obviously, allowance for this gender difference in occupations has to be made when assessing trends in total employment by sector.

Table 9.04 sets out King's social table for 1688. First, the basic data on the number of families in each occupational grouping are presented, as revised by Lindert and Williamson (1982). To King's total of 1,390,586 families, Crafts (1985: 14) recommends adding 10 per cent for domestic service. Since King's occupational distribution applies primarily to males, and around three-quarters of domestic servants were females, a more modest allowance of just 2.5 per cent has been made for domestic service. Following Crafts (1985: 14), the titled aristocracy and gentlemen (many of whom were active in government, administration and the law) plus vagrants are all classified as unoccupied, and, notwithstanding an amount of by-employment (above p. 345), the occupied labour-force is allocated unambiguously between agriculture, industry and services, as indicated in Table 9.04. Rather than allocate all unspecified labourers, cottagers and paupers to agriculture, as did Crafts (1985), 31.8 per cent have been apportioned to industry and the remaining 68.2 per cent to agriculture, in line with the corresponding ratio for 1522.

Next, female employment is allocated across sectors in line with the estimates for 1813–20 given by Shaw-Taylor (2009a). Again, in accordance with the situation at the beginning of the nineteenth century (Shaw-Taylor, 2009a), females are assumed to have accounted for 30 per cent of the total number of days worked in the economy. By 1851 Shaw-Taylor (2009a) finds that female labour-force participation had risen to 43.0 per cent but it then fell back to 35.1 per cent in 1911, at a time when the male participation rate was close to 100 per cent (equivalent to a decline in the female share of the labour-force from approximately 30 per cent to 25 per cent). Further research may uncover earlier fluctuations in female labour-force participation, but

Table 9.04 *Sectoral distribution of the English labour-force in 1688 from Gregory King's social table*

Sectors	Occupations	'Family' numbers (i.e. males)		Occupied	Labour-force shares (2, 3 and 4 as % of 7)		
		According to King[a]	Adjusted for labourers and servants[a]		Males	Females[e]	Total[f]
1. Unoccupied	High titles and gentlemen	19,626					
	Vagrants	23,489	43,115				
2. Agriculture	Agriculture	227,440	227,440	635,399	46.0	22.3	38.9
	Agricultural labourers[b]	Included in 5	407,959				
3. Industry	Industry and building	256,866	256,866	447,087	32.3	37.8	34.0
	Industrial labourers[c]	Included in 5	190,221				
4. Services	Commerce	128,025	128,025	299,750	21.7	39.9	27.2
	Professions	42,960	42,960				
	Military and maritime	94,000	94,000				
	Domestic servants[d]	Omitted	34,765				

Table 9.04 (cont.)

Sectors	Occupations	'Family' numbers (i.e. males)		Labour-force shares (2, 3 and 4 as % of 7)			
		According to King[a]	Adjusted for labourers and servants[a]	Occupied	Males	Females[e]	Total[f]
5. Labourers, Cottagers and Paupers		598,180					
6. TOTAL (1–5)		1,390,586	1,425,351				
7. TOTAL OCCUPIED (2–4)				1,382,236	100.0	100.0	100.0

Sources and notes: Derived from King [1696]; Lindert and Williamson (1982: 388); Crafts (1985: 13–15). [a] Assumed to apply to males only. [b] Estimated at 68.2% of the 598,180 'Labourers, cottagers and paupers'. [c] Estimated at 31.8% of the 598,180 'Labourers, cottagers and paupers'. [d] Male domestic servants are estimated at 2.5% of King's total families (6.). [e] Female labour is distributed across sectors in line with the 1813–20 shares from Shaw-Taylor (2009a). [f] Females are assumed to account for 30% of total employment, in line with Shaw-Taylor (2009a).

until such evidence is forthcoming, the female share of the labour-force is assumed to have been a constant 30 per cent before the mid-nineteenth century. This is consistent with the work of Humphries (2010: 107), who finds no evidence from a sample of autobiographies to support the idea of a change in women's aggregate participation rates during the eighteenth century, despite the large literature on the supposed effects of industrialisation on women's employment. Probably, too, any influence of temporal variations in the female participation rate upon sectoral labour productivity trends was dwarfed by the far greater gender differences in the sectoral distribution of employment, for which full allowance has been made.

For 1759, the basic 'family' (i.e. male) data for Joseph Massie's social table are set out in Table 9.05. For consistency, an allowance of 2.5 per cent is made for omitted male domestic servants, male labourers are divided between agriculture and industry in the ratio 68.2 to 31.8 and the 1813–20 employment distribution is again used to allocate females to sectors. Females are again assumed to have accounted for 30 per cent of the labour-force. Similar procedures are followed for 1801 using Colquhoun's [1806] social table (Table 9.06). Starting from the basic data on the number of 'families' (de facto males) in each occupational grouping, labourers with unspecified occupations and females are then allocated across sectors following the same procedures as for 1700 and 1759.

For the period 1813–71, Shaw-Taylor's (2009a) estimates of the sectoral labour-force shares are used. These are derived from Anglican parish registers for the period 1813–20 and from the population census data for the period 1851–71. Table 9.07 presents data for males, females and the total occupied labour-force. The results are very similar to the estimates of Mitchell (1988) for Great Britain, although, strictly speaking, the data refer solely to England and Wales. For 1851–71 the share of the labour-force in agriculture in England and Wales is very similar to Deane and Cole's (1967: 146) census-based estimate for Great Britain, while Mitchell (1988) offers comparable figures for the ratio of industrial to service-sector workers. Nevertheless, Mitchell's data

Table 9.05 *Sectoral distribution of the British labour-force in 1759 from Joseph Massie's social table*

Sectors	Occupations	'Family' numbers (i.e. males)		Occupied	Labour-force shares (2, 3 and 4 as % of 7)		
		According to Massie[a]	Adjusted for labourers and servants[a]		Males	Females[e]	Total[f]
1. Unoccupied	High titles and gentlemen	18,070	31,488				
	Vagrants	13,418					
2. Agriculture	Agriculture	379,008	379,008	664,692	43.0	22.3	36.8
	Agricultural labourers[b]	Included in 5	285,684				
3. Industry	Industry and building	366,252	366,252	499,460	32.3	37.8	33.9
	Industrial labourers[c]	Included in 5	133,208				
4. Services	Commerce	200,500	200,500	381,979	24.7	39.9	29.3
	Professions	57,000	57,000				
	Military and maritime	86,000	86,000				
	Domestic servants[d]	Omitted	38,479				

5. Labourers, cottagers and paupers	418,892			
6. TOTAL (1–5)	1,539,140	1,577,619		
7. TOTAL OCCUPIED (2–4)	1,546,131	100.0	100.0	100.0

Sources and notes: Derived from Massie [1760]; Lindert and Williamson (1982: 388); Crafts (1985: 13–15). [a] Assumed to apply to males only. [b] Estimated at 68.2% of the 418,892 'Labourers, cottagers and paupers'. [c] Estimated at 31.8% of the 418,892 'Labourers, cottagers and paupers'. [d] Male domestic servants are estimated at 2.5% of Massie's total families (6). [e] Female labour is distributed across sectors in line with the 1813–20 shares from Shaw-Taylor (2009a). [f] Females are assumed to account for 30% of total employment, in line with Shaw-Taylor (2009a).

Table 9.06 Sectoral distribution of the British labour-force in 1801/03 from Patrick Colquhoun's social table

Sectors	Occupations	'Family' numbers (i.e. males)		Labour-force shares (2, 3 and 4 as % of 7)			
		According to Colquhoun[a]	Adjusted for labourers and servants[a]	Occupied	Males	Females[e]	Total[f]
1. Unoccupied	High titles and gentlemen	27,203	206,921				
	Vagrants	179,718					
2. Agriculture	Agriculture	320,000	320,000	729,322	35.7	22.3	31.7
	Agricultural labourers[b]	Included in 5	409,322				
3. Industry	Industry and building	541,026	541,026	731,883	35.9	37.8	36.4
	Industrial labourers[c]	Included in 5	190,857				
4. Services	Commerce	205,800	205,800	579,816	28.4	39.9	31.9
	Professions	74,840	74,840				
	Military and maritime	244,348	244,348				
	Domestic servants[d]	Omitted	54,828				

5. Labourers, cottagers and paupers	600,179			
6. TOTAL (1–5)	2,193,114			
7. TOTAL OCCUPIED (2–4)	2,247,942	2,041,021	100.0	100.0	100.0	100.0

Sources and notes: Derived from Colquhoun (1806); Lindert and Williamson (1982: 388); Crafts (1985: 13–15). [a] Assumed to apply to males only. [b] Estimated at 68.2% of the 600,179 'Labourers, cottagers and paupers'. [c] Estimated at 31.8% of the 600,179 'Labourers, cottagers and paupers'. [d] Male domestic servants are estimated at 2.5% of Colquhoun's total families (6). [e] Female labour is distributed across sectors in line with the 1813–20 shares from Shaw-Taylor (2009a). [f] Females are assumed to account for 30% of total employment, in line with Shaw-Taylor (2009a).

understate female agricultural employment (Higgs, 1987), hence Shaw-Taylor's data for England and Wales are preferred. The latter fit better with trends in female as well as male employment. Plainly, by the early nineteenth century Britain was highly industrialised, with around 45 per cent of the labour-force in industry and less than a third of the labour-force in agriculture. Services accounted for the remaining 24 per cent of the workforce, the relatively substantial scale of this sector reflecting the by then highly commercialised and closely governed state of the British economy.

9.3.3   Long-run trends in labour-force shares

Table 9.01B summarises the individual occupational estimates set out in detail in Tables 9.02 to 9.07. Gregory King's social table for 1688 has been applied to 1700, since it is unlikely that the sectoral shares changed significantly between these two years, and following Deane and Cole (1962) and Crafts (1985), it is convenient to calculate growth rates of labour productivity for England before 1700 and Great Britain after 1700. These figures build upon the work of Shaw-Taylor and others (2010). The enduring differences between male and female participation in agriculture, industry and services, first documented in the 1381 poll tax returns and then, again, from 1813–20 in parish registers, are striking and emphasise the importance of factoring these contrasts into estimates of sectoral employment shares (Table 9.08A and B). Table 9.01B also highlights the scale of the structural shift away from agricultural employment which had already occurred before 1700 and the more modest scale of subsequent structural employment change between 1700 and 1871.

Shaw-Taylor and others (2010) find no further erosion of the proportion of the male labour-force engaged in agriculture between 1710 and 1755 (Table 9.08B) and comparison of King's social table for 1688 with Massie's for 1759 likewise reveals stability rather than change (Tables 9.06 and 9.07). Some time after 1755/9 the contraction of agriculture's share of male employment resumed and, on the evidence of Colquhoun's soundly based social table for 1801 and Shaw-Taylor and

Table 9.07 *Sectoral distribution of the English and Welsh labour-force in 1813–71 from Anglican parish registers*

Sector	1813–20 (%)			1851 (%)			1861 (%)			1871 (%)		
	Males	Females	Total	Males	Females	Total	Males	Females	Total	Males	Females	Total
Agriculture	35.4	22.3	31.4	27.2	15.6	23.5	24.4	12.6	20.6	19.8	11.2	16.9
Industry	47.4	37.8	44.5	50.1	36.4	45.7	49.6	38.3	45.9	52.6	35.8	47.1
Services	17.2	39.9	24.1	22.7	48.0	30.9	26.0	49.1	33.5	27.6	53.0	36.0
TOTAL	100.0	100.0	100.0	100.0	100.0	100.0	100.0	100.0	100.0	100.0	100.0	100.0

Source: Shaw-Taylor (2009a).

Table 9.08 Alternative estimates of the share of the English labour-force engaged in agriculture, 1381–1869 (%)

Years	A. This study			B. Shaw-Taylor			C. Clark (farming, fishing and forestry)		
	% males	% females	% total	% males	% females	% total	% males	% females	% total
1381	67.0	34.5	57.2				[a]61	[a]43	[a]56–59
1522	68.2	34.5	58.1						
1560–79							61		
1652–60							59		
1688	46.0	22.3	38.9						
1710				43.0					
1755				44.0					
1759	43.0	22.3	36.8						
1801	35.7	22.3	31.7						
1813–20				35.4	22.3	31.4			[b]42
1851	27.2	15.6	23.5	27.2	15.6	23.5			
1861	24.4	12.6	20.6	24.4	12.6	20.6			[c]20

Sources and notes: Part A: Tables 9.02 to 9.06; Part B: Shaw-Taylor (2009a); Shaw-Taylor and others (2010); Part C: [a]1379–81, Clark (2013: 9); 1560–79 and 1652–60, Clark and others (2012: 387); [b]1817 (includes coal miners and is equivalent to an *effective* share of 52 per cent), Clark (2010b) based on Shaw-Taylor and Wrigley (2008); [c]1860–69, Clark (2013: 6).

others' analysis of parish registers for 1813–20, by the opening decades of the nineteenth century it was down to 35 per cent. The close agreement between these two independently generated sets of estimates is reassuring and underscores just how far out of line is that of Clark (2010b) during this critical transitional period when industry finally emerged to become the single largest employer of labour. Yet, significant as these changes were, they are less dramatic than those suggested by earlier writers, including Deane and Cole (1967) and Crafts (1985), and were not as great as those that had already taken place during the early modern period, when the share in agriculture shrank from 60 to 40 per cent. The classic period of the industrial revolution, therefore, has to be seen less as a period of unusually rapid change in occupational structures and more as an era of mechanisation and technological transformation.

The results obtained from this study thus imply that the share of the labour-force employed in agriculture was already less than 60 per cent in 1381 and remained at more or less that same modest level in the 1520s. By the 1650s, if Clark and others' probate evidence for male testators can be relied upon (Table 9.08C), it had possibly slipped down to around 50 per cent and, following half a century of vigorous economic growth, King's social table and the parish register evidence agree that by 1688/1710 it had shrunk to less than 40 per cent. For the next half century further decline was arrested until the advent of the industrial revolution squeezed agriculture's share of employment further, so that by the opening decade of the nineteenth century only a third of the labour-force was working in agriculture and by 1851 this had reduced to less than a quarter as Britain became a nation of town-dwellers and factory workers. This chronology is naturally consistent with the trend in GDP per head outlined in Chapter 5 and reproduced in Figure 5.06 but also fits the independently estimated fivefold increase in the urbanisation ratio between the 1520s and 1801 (calculated for English towns with at least 5,000 inhabitants: Wrigley, 1985: 688). The occupational estimates of Shaw-Taylor (2009a) and Shaw-Taylor and others (2010) for 1710, 1755 and 1813–20 for men and women employed solely in agriculture are also reassuringly close. Sampling error, the inclusion of all primary-sector occupations (including mining) and the lack of adjustment for female agricultural workers explain why Clark's (2010a, 2010b) preferred figure of 42 per cent in c.1817 is misleading.

9.4 SECTORAL LABOUR PRODUCTIVITY

Table 9.01 summarises the sectoral output and labour-force shares established in Sections 9.2 and 9.3. These are then translated into the indexed trends in output and labour-force, taking due account of the potentially distorting effect of changes in relative prices, set out in Parts A and B of Table 9.09. Derivation of the sectoral output trends has already been discussed in Chapter 5. Some explanation is now necessary respecting the labour-force trends. The starting point is the population totals presented in Chapter 1. First, the raw totals of population have been apportioned between males and females on the assumption of a 49:51 split in favour of females, based on census evidence for the nineteenth century. Second, those below the age of 16 are considered not to have been part of the labour-force and that proportion is assumed to have been a constant 37.5 per cent, in line with the assumptions made for the poll tax data in Chapter 1 and based on evidence from Wrigley and Schofield (1989). Third, labour-force participation rates of 97.1 per cent for males and 43.0 per cent for females, estimated by Shaw-Taylor (2009a) for the mid-nineteenth century, are assumed to have been the norm in all earlier periods. These assumptions give the total labour-force at each benchmark date. These totals are then disaggregated by sector using the labour-force shares given in Tables 9.02 to 9.07 and summarised in Table 9.01B.

Despite the unavoidable inflexibility of several of these assumptions, the results set out in Table 9.09B, while inviting refinement, are credible. Between the benchmark dates 1381 and 1522 the labour-force declined slightly in agriculture and more markedly in services, broadly in line with population, but grew in industry as the fledgling English cloth industry began to prosper. After 1522, with the resumption of

Table 9.09 *Indexed trends in output, labour-force and output per worker, England 1381–1700 and Great Britain 1700–1851 (1700 = 100)*

Sector	1381	1522	1700	1759	1801	1851
A. Output						
Agriculture	50.9	51.3	100.0	159.2	227.0	328.3
Industry	18.9	27.6	100.0	144.7	275.2	1,206.3
Services	24.8	27.1	100.0	150.9	266.6	777.4
GDP	29.2	34.2	100.0	150.4	251.6	711.5
B. Labour-force						
Agriculture	68.7	64.7	100.0	114.2	137.1	188.2
Industry	26.3	31.3	100.0	120.3	180.3	428.0
Services	40.5	34.8	100.0	130.0	197.2	404.5
GDP	46.6	45.2	100.0	120.6	168.1	328.4
C. Output per worker						
Agriculture	74.2	79.2	100.0	139.5	165.6	174.4
Industry	71.8	88.4	100.0	120.3	152.7	281.9
Services	61.3	78.0	100.0	116.1	135.2	192.2
GDP	62.6	75.7	100.0	124.7	149.7	216.6

Sources and notes: Part A, output is derived from Appendix 5.3 (data are reported for 10-year averages). Part B, population is from Appendix 5.3, allocated as 51 per cent female and 49 per cent male before 1801; male and female proportions after 1801 are from Wrigley (2011). Population of working age is derived on the assumption of 37.5% below age 16. Labour-force derived on the assumption of a participation rate of 97.1% for males and 43.0% for females. Labour-force by sector is derived using the shares for appropriate years from Tables 9.02 to 9.07. Part C, derived by dividing Part A by Part B.

Before 1700, the estimates are derived from data referring only to the territory of England. An earlier version of this table in Broadberry and others (2013) contained some errors in the labour-force figures for 1851 in Part B, which also affected the labour productivity data for the same year in Part C and the labour productivity growth rates for 1700–1851.

population growth, the labour-force grew in all three sectors, but much less rapidly in agriculture than in services or industry, where it grew fastest. This pattern persisted after 1700 when, for a time, the service-sector labour-force grew faster than the industrial labour-force. The most dramatic changes, however, followed the industrial revolution: between 1759 and 1851, against an overall doubling of the labour-force, service-sector employment trebled and that of industry increased three-and-a-half-fold. Meanwhile, agricultural employment grew by just a third.

Dividing the output trends by the labour-force trends gives the trends in output per worker shown in Part C of Table 9.09. These, in turn, allow calculation of the annual growth rates in labour productivity set out in Table 9.10. As will be noted, labour productivity growth was consistently positive both in the economy as a whole and across all sectors throughout the period 1381–1851. It was rarely rapid and only in industry between 1801 and 1851 exceeded 1 per cent a year but, unsurprisingly, was more than three times faster after 1759 than before. Labour productivity growth was negligible in agriculture between 1381 and 1522 but significant in both industry and services as the foundations for England's later industrial rise were laid. Productivity growth slowed in both industry and services between 1522 and 1700, reflecting the labour-intensive rather than capital-intensive character of industry during this period and a continuing reliance upon hand tools and human energy, but grew in agriculture, in accordance with contemporary trends in urbanisation. Even when productivity growth accelerated across the economy between 1700 and 1759 agriculture continued to hold its own; indeed, its annual growth rate was more rapid than both industry and services. After 1759, however, during the classic period of agricultural revolution, productivity growth in agriculture appears to have slowed whereas that of services accelerated and productivity growth in industry, boosted by adoption of labour-saving technology and wider application of the division of labour, rose to an unprecedented rate of over 0.5 per cent per year. After 1801 labour productivity growth continued to accelerate in both industry and services but fell back in

Table 9.10 *Sectoral annual growth rates of output, labour-force and labour productivity, England 1381–1700 and Great Britain 1700–1851*

	Annual % growth											
	Agriculture			Industry			Services			GDP		
Period	Output	Labour-force	Labour productivity	Output	Labour-force	Labour productivity	Output	Labour-force	Labour productivity	Output	Labour-force	Labour productivity
1381–1522	0.01	−0.01	0.02	0.27	0.10	0.17	0.06	−0.16	0.23	0.11	−0.02	0.14
1522–1700	0.38	0.25	0.13	0.73	0.66	0.07	0.74	0.60	0.14	0.60	0.45	0.16
1700–1759	0.79	0.22	0.57	0.63	0.31	0.32	0.70	0.44	0.26	0.69	0.32	0.38
1759–1801	0.85	0.44	0.41	1.54	0.97	0.57	1.36	1.00	0.36	1.23	0.79	0.44
1801–1851	0.74	0.64	0.10	3.00	1.74	1.23	2.16	1.45	0.71	2.10	1.35	0.74
1381–1759	0.30	0.13	0.17	0.54	0.40	0.14	0.48	0.31	0.17	0.43	0.25	0.18
1759–1851	0.79	0.54	0.24	2.33	1.39	0.93	1.80	1.24	0.55	1.70	1.09	0.60

Source: Calculated from Table 9.09.

agriculture, where, although a wide range of labour-saving implements and machines were being adopted by farmers (Overton, 1996: 123–8), diminishing returns were possibly beginning to set in.

These results indicate that the agricultural innovations of the sixteenth and especially the seventeenth centuries (Jones, 1965; Kerridge, 1967; John 1976; Allen, 1992, 1999) were accompanied by improvements in labour productivity and, further, that this productivity growth in agriculture occurred ahead of that in industry and services. From this early beginning, agricultural labour productivity growth reached its peak during the first half of the eighteenth century, thereby allowing release of provisions, raw materials and labour to other sectors of the economy. So at this stage in the growth process agriculture was outperforming industry, as is implicit in the work of Crafts (1985). The constraints of organic farming systems and prevailing agrarian institutions nevertheless meant that faster rates of productivity growth were unattainable. In fact, from c.1760 labour productivity growth in agriculture slowed as industry entered its water-powered phase of mechanisation and thereby achieved faster growth rates than animal-powered agriculture had ever been able to deliver. The harnessing of steam power to manufacturing processes from the 1780s consolidated and reinforced these trends and elevated industrial labour productivity growth to new heights.

Meanwhile labour productivity growth in agriculture slowed to rates last seen before 1700. While the level of agricultural output rose to unprecedented heights in the first half of the nineteenth century (Table 3.16), it did so with declining growth rates of both output and labour productivity. The opposite applies to industry. With much of the structural shift of labour from agriculture to industry already achieved, industry's most revolutionary phase of output growth clearly owed almost as much to technologically generated productivity gains as to rapid expansion of the industrial labour-force (Table 9.10). Moreover, the latter was no longer contingent upon wholesale migration of labour from agriculture to industry since the industrial population was increasingly self-reproducing. That in turn involved transformations of public health and urban demography. In all these respects the results presented in this chapter invite a return to an earlier view of the industrial revolution with its emphasis upon productivity-enhancing technological innovation (Allen, 2009a).

9.5   CONCLUSIONS

The evidence presented in this chapter suggests that once female participation in the labour-force is taken into account the British economy emerges as less overwhelmingly agricultural during the late-medieval and early modern periods than previous writers have assumed, with the implication that industry and services were both more developed. There is no disagreement with Clark and others (2012) over the proportion of the labour-force employed in agriculture in both 1381 and 1522, nor necessarily with their estimates of agriculture's share of the male labour-force in the 1560s and 1650s. But whereas Clark (2013) detects no significant structural change before the late eighteenth century, the estimates presented here suggest that the critical occupational migration from agriculture to industry commenced some time after 1522 and had already made significant progress by 1700, leaving less scope for a dramatic shift of labour from agriculture to industry during the eighteenth and especially nine-teenth centuries. This is in line with the recent findings of Shaw-Taylor (2009a). Labour productivity growth was on average faster in agriculture than industry or services from 1522 to 1759; thereafter, it slowed and industry came rapidly to the fore as the most dynamic sector.

The once orthodox view that industry indeed exhibited the fastest growing productivity during the classic industrial revolution is thus reinstated, along with the idea that mechanisation based upon techno-logical advance delivered sustained productivity gains to Britain's expanding industrial labour-force. The fast commercialising service sec-tor made steadier but cumulatively impressive gains so that, notwith-standing the much-vaunted achievements of the agricultural revolution, whether measured by output, employment or labour productivity, agriculture was the slowest growing economic sector during 1759–1851 (Table 9.10). Until the industrial revolution this study suggests that agricultural labour productivity had been rising during much of the early modern period and especially during the early eighteenth century. During the first half of the nineteenth century domestic agricultural output continued to rise, but food imports became essential (Table 7.06), and the rate of growth in labour productivity slowed considerably.

The substantial shift of labour out of agriculture between 1522 and 1759 is consistent with the chronology of GDP-per-head growth reconstructed in Chapter 5. The country after all was becoming more urbanised and the disproportionate growth of London was acting as an 'engine of growth' (Wrigley, 1967). Agriculture was an early beneficiary of the capital's growing appetite for provisions and organic raw materials, as is now acknowledged in accounts which stress the drawn-out character of English agricultural progress (Wrigley, 2006b). The detailed work of Shaw-Taylor and others (2010) establishes the quantitative dimensions of the structural transformation of the labour-force which accompanied these early modern urban and agrarian developments. The reconstruction of British GDP from the output side in this study is also at variance with a Malthusian interpretation of the late-medieval and early modern British economy (Persson, 2008), insofar as from 1522 population, GDP per head (Figure 5.05) and labour productivity in all three economic sectors were trending upwards over time. Further research is needed on the issues of female labour-force participation and by-employment, but the broad trends of the long-run development of the British economy are now firmly established. In contrast to the post-Renaissance stagnation and decline experienced by Italy (Malanima: 2011), Britain belonged to an elite club of north-west European countries whose economies displayed considerable dynamism and growth from the sixteenth century to the point in the nineteenth century when modern economic growth began.

10 Britain in an international context

10.1 INTRODUCTION

How does Britain's experience of long-run economic growth and development, as revealed by the output-based estimation of GDP per head set out in Part I of this book, compare with that of other countries? Maddison's (2010) historical national income estimates show that by the middle of the nineteenth century Britain had become the most developed economy in the world, with higher output per head than any other country in Europe, Asia or the Americas. A majority of its population lived in towns, agriculture contributed less than a quarter of employment and a fifth of value-added output, after centuries of mercantilism it was trading across the world under the banner of free trade, and the value of that international commerce accounted for a fifth of national income and was rising. Demographic and economic growth were proceeding in tandem and thereby fulfilling one of Kuznets's (1966) key requirements of modern economic growth. Contrary to Malthus's gloomiest predictions, the population was not only growing but it was becoming richer. The Great Exhibition of 1851, conceived to make clear to the world Great Britain's role as industrial leader, could not have been better timed.

Eight centuries earlier, when William of Normandy had cast his covetous eyes upon the Crown of England, the country had been less a land of plenty than a kingdom with plenty of land. Its relatively sparse population of 1.7 million was overwhelmingly rural, towns were small and London alone had more than 10,000 inhabitants, commerce was limited and commercial institutions and infrastructure weakly developed, and exports were chiefly of unprocessed primary products, most notably wool and tin. England may have been resource-rich but its lack of development meant that its GDP per head was only a quarter what it would become in 1850. It was poorer than most of its immediate continental neighbours, significantly poorer than northern and central Italy, at that time Europe's economic leader, conspicuously poorer than the world's most successful economy, China under the Northern Song Dynasty (960–1127), and poorer than the core economies of the Roman Empire a millennium earlier under Augustus (Lo Cascio and Malanima, 2009). After four centuries of institutional, infrastructural and commercial development and at the time when the voyages of discovery were redefining the world, England remained a peripheral and relatively minor player in a Europe whose economic heavyweights remained northern and central Italy and the Low Countries. And when, in the sixteenth century, Italy's centuries old economic hegemony was challenged, it was by Holland not England.

England's progression from European laggard to European and global leader took three centuries and entailed a trebling of GDP per head at an average annual growth rate between 1550 and 1850 of over 0.3 per cent. This chapter examines the factors involved in bringing this transformation about. It involved a reversal of fortunes within Europe, sometimes known as the Little Divergence, as the once leading Italian economy stagnated and declined, a group of neighbouring economies clustered around the southern shores of the North Sea – Flanders, Brabant, Holland and England – displayed increasing dynamism, and Eastern Europe lagged ever further behind Western Europe. In terms of GDP per head, Holland had overtaken Italy by 1500; Britain then overtook Italy by 1700 and the Netherlands by 1800. Symbolically, financial leadership passed from Florence in the fourteenth century to Milan in the fifteenth, Antwerp in the sixteenth, Amsterdam in the seventeenth, and London in the eighteenth century. A second reversal of fortunes, generally known as the Great Divergence, occurred within Eurasia, as the economic fortunes of the once commercially pre-eminent Chinese economy waned, those of Japan waxed, but those of the rival maritime states of Western Europe rose to the fore. In the late thirteenth century it had been the fabled commercial wealth of Cathay and the luxury products of its skilled artisans that had lured the three mercantile Polos from Venice to China, whereas by the nineteenth century, such was the industrial power of Britain that it was Western manufactured goods that went East.

Most accounts of economic growth before 1870 rely on the picture painted by Maddison (2001, 2003, 2010). The scope of his great enterprise in quantitative economic history means that too few of his national income series are soundly based and, in fact, many of the pre-modern observations are artificially set at or close to $400 in 1990 international prices. This is equivalent to most people living at the World Bank's definition of poverty on $1 per day, or 'bare-bones subsistence', with any surpluses appropriated by a small rich elite. Table 10.01 sets out Maddison's estimates for the four European and three Asian countries upon which this chapter will focus. For Europe, the richest countries for both the middle ages (Italy and Spain) and for the early modern and modern periods (Holland and Britain) have been chosen. Similarly, the Asian trio encompass the most developed parts of East Asia in the early part of the second millennium (China) and in the modern period (Japan) as well as underdeveloped India. For all seven of these economies, and some others, economic historians have now

Table 10.01 *Maddison's estimates of GDP per head in Western Europe and Asia, 1000–1870 (Geary–Khamis 1990 international dollars)*

Date	UK	Netherlands	Italy	Spain	Japan	China	India
1000	400	425	450	450	425	466	450
1500	714	761	1,100	661	500	600	550
1600	974	1,381	1,100	853	520	600	550
1700	1,250	2,130	1,100	853	570	600	550
1820	1,706	1,838	1,117	1,008	669	600	533
1870	3,190	2,757	1,499	1,207	737	530	533

Sources and notes: Maddison (2010). The estimates are for countries within their modern boundaries; hence the United Kingdom (UK) rather than Great Britain or England, and the Netherlands rather than Holland.

been able to produce estimates of income per head in a national accounting framework, based on hard data, and a firmer picture has begun to emerge of the contours of long-run growth and development in both Europe and Asia. It is these new estimates which inform the review in Section 10.2 of the reversal of fortunes within Europe, in Section 10.3 of the Great Divergence within Eurasia, and in Section 10.4 underpin a brief overview of the factors behind Britain's rise to global economic leadership.

10.2 BRITAIN AND THE REVERSAL OF FORTUNES WITHIN EUROPE

Output-based historical national accounts are ideally constructed on a sectoral basis from detailed quantitative information on real outputs. In addition to the study of Britain, which has been documented in Part I, van Zanden and van Leeuwen (2012) have been able to build on decades of meticulous data gathering by generations of scholars working in well-stocked archives to produce a detailed set of historical national accounts for Holland. For other countries, where information is more limited or there has been less processing of existing data, Malanima (2011), Álvarez-Nogal and Prados de la Escosura (2013) and others have developed a short-cut method for reconstructing GDP. First, the economy is divided between agriculture and other activities. In the agricultural sector, output is estimated via a demand function, making use of data on population, real wage rates and the relative price of food, together with elasticities derived from later periods and the experience of other economies at comparable levels of development. Allowance is also made for international trade in food. For the non-agricultural sector, output is assumed to have moved in line with the urban population, but with some allowance made for rural industry and the phenomenon of agro-towns (urban settlements containing significant numbers of agricultural workers).

The new estimates for Italy, Spain, Holland and Britain presented in Table 10.02A revise upwards the level of GDP per head in late-medieval Western Europe, which turns out to have been

Table 10.02 *GDP per head in Western Europe and Asia, 730–1850 (Geary–Khamis 1990 international dollars)*

Date	A. Europe				B. Asia		
	England/GB	Holland/NL	Italy	Spain	Japan	China	India
725					551		
900					476		
980			c.1,000ᵃ				
1020						1,247	
1050						1,518	
1086	754					1,458	
1120						1,204	
1150					508	1,063	
1280	679			957ᵇ	552		
1300	755		1,482	957			
1348	777	876	1,376	1,030			
1400	1,090	1,245	1,601	885		960	
1450	1,055	1,432	1,668	889	552	983	
1500	1,114	1,483	1,403	889		1,127	
1570	1,143	1,783	1,337	990		968	
1600	1,123	2,372	1,244	944	605	977	682
1650	1,110	2,171	1,271	820	619		638
1700	1,563	2,403	1,350	880	597	841	622

Table 10.02 (*cont.*)

	A. Europe					B. Asia		
Date	England/GB	Holland/NL	Italy	Spain	Japan	China	India
1750	1,710	2,440	1,403	910	622	685	573
1800	2,080	1,752	1,244	962	703	597	569
1820	2,133	1,953	1,376	1,087			
1850	2,997	2,397	1,350	1,144	777	594	556

Sources and notes: Europe: England/Great Britain (GB): Appendix 5.3; Walker (2008); the data are for England before 1700 and GB from 1700 onwards; Holland/Netherlands (NL): van Zanden and van Leuwen (2012); the data are for Holland before 1800 and for the Netherlands from 1800 onwards; Italy: Malanima (2002: 450), Malanima (2011); Spain: Álvarez-Nogal and Prados de la Escosura (2013). Figures are for 10-year averages starting in the stated year (i.e. 1270–79, 1300–09 etc.) apart from 1348, which refers to the pre-Black Death years 1339–48. Asia: Japan: Basssino and others (2014); China: Broadberry and others (2014b); India: Broadberry and others (2014a); Chinese data are for 10-year averages starting in the stated year (i.e. 980–89, 1086–95, etc.), but data for Japan and India are only available for benchmark years.
[a] 1000 AD. [b] 1270 AD.

substantially richer than Maddison (2001) thought (Table 10.01). Accordingly, subsequent economic growth was more gradual, thereby extending back further in time the revisionist views of Crafts and Harley (1992), who revised downwards the British growth rate during the industrial revolution. Note that by 1300 incomes per head in Italy were almost double those of England and higher than those in Spain. By the mid-fourteenth century, Spain had a higher GDP per head than Holland, and Holland, by a small margin, led England. By 1500 Holland had overtaken Italy, and England overtaken Spain; and by 1700 Holland and England were both ahead of Italy and Spain. By 1800 the lead of these North Sea economies had widened further and incomes per head were 40–115 per cent higher in Britain and the Netherlands than in Italy and Spain. Over these five centuries economic leadership had passed from southern to northern Europe.

For Italy, England and Holland the Black Death of the mid-fourteenth century had been more of an economic boon than a misfortune, since in each case, once the initial hiatus had passed, their reduced populations enjoyed increased incomes per head (Table 10.02A). In contrast, Spain, the most thinly peopled of the four countries, experienced a loss of prosperity as its fragile pre-plague commercial economy proved unsustainable in the seriously underpopulated post-plague world. Nor was Italy's Renaissance prosperity founded upon more than an improved population–resource ratio, for Italian incomes per head rapidly regressed to pre-Black Death levels once population growth resumed after c.1450. In the economies of the southern North Sea region it was otherwise. England seems to have held onto most of its post-Black Death gains per head during the renewed population growth of the sixteenth century. Something similar appears to have happened in Flanders (Buyst, 2011) and until the 1570s neighbouring Brabant and its capital Antwerp were booming (Allen, 2001). Meanwhile, the Dutch economy had entered its Golden Age and by 1650 Dutch GDP per head was almost touching a historically unprecedented $2,500. Then, from the late seventeenth century, as the pace of progress slackened in Holland, so it increased in

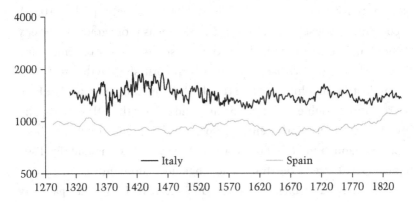

FIGURE 10.01 Real GDP per head in Italy and Spain 1270–1850 (Geary–Khamis 1990 international dollars, log scale). *Source:* Malanima (2011); Álvarez-Nogal and Prados de la Escosura (2013).

England and in the second half of the eighteenth century the reversal of fortunes within Europe culminated in the British industrial revolution.

Fluctuations in Italian and Spanish GDP per head are charted on an annual basis in Figure 10.01, and illustrate well the general pattern of pre-modern growth. The problem is not that there was no growth, but rather that periods of positive growth were followed by periods of absolute decline, or growth reversals, so that there was no general upward trend in GDP per head between the late thirteenth and the early nineteenth centuries. This pattern of fluctuations in economic prosperity without trend is what Le Roy Ladurie (1966) identified in Languedoc and termed *l'histoire immobile*, attributing much of its recurrent pattern of growth and decline to the episodic rise and fall of populations. In Britain it is a pattern more often described as Malthusian, with the periods of rising income per head usually associated with declining population and those of falling income per head with rising population (Postan, 1972: 27–40; Hatcher and Bailey, 2001: 21–65; Clark, 2007: 19–39).

Northern and central Italy appears to present an intriguing example of an economy which switched from a positive correlation between population and economic growth during its commercial revolution of the twelfth and thirteenth centuries to a negative correlation following progressive collapse of the underlying commercial preconditions for its earlier success from the late thirteenth century. Thus, Italian income per head rose following the Black Death to a temporal peak in the mid-fifteenth century when the population–resource balance was especially favourable, but fell back with the recovery of population from the mid-fifteenth century and continued to slide down until the population ceased growing in the seventeenth century. Even after the Black Death, Italy remained one of the most populous, commercialised and urbanised societies in Europe, which is why such an inverse relationship between population and GDP per head was able to exist. In far more thinly peopled and less urbanised Spain, however, the negative effects of the loss of population far outweighed any positive benefits to the survivors and in a striking inversion of the Malthusian rule, GDP per head declined with population following the Black Death and recovered with population from the late fifteenth century (Figure 10.01).

In fact, Álvarez-Nogal and Prados de la Escosura (2013) argue for two distinct epochs in pre-industrial Spain. In the first epoch, from the 1270s to the 1590s, sustained progress was interrupted by the Black Death and then resumed from the 1390s. At the beginning of this period, Spain was a relatively high-income society born of a generous land–labour ratio and a modest but developing commercial sector. When the Black Death struck, it had a negative effect on Spanish incomes, possibly in common with other thinly peopled and especially landlocked parts of Europe where it created problems of underpopulation. In this altered demographic environment established commercial networks and levels of specialisation proved unsustainable and the already sparse population experienced increased isolation, with the result that output per head fell. When renewed expansion occurred from the 1390s it was on the basis of wool, whose production was well suited to a land-abundant and labour-scarce society. As a high-value commodity in strong demand from European wool-textile manufacturers, the wool trade stimulated rebuilding of commercial networks both nationally and internationally. The renewal of population growth also helped. Consequently, by the end of the sixteenth century, real output per head was close to its pre-Black Death peak and Spain had built a colonial empire and become an economic centre connecting Europe and the New World.

Further progress was halted by a decline in wool exports from the 1570s, a contraction in the purchasing power of American silver from the early seventeenth century, and an inward reorientation of the Spanish economy. This profound crisis marks the onset of the second epoch, running from the 1600s to the 1800s. It began with incomes per head trending down once again as the rising costs of ruling and defending a far-flung empire put a strain on the fiscal system and the cities and as population pressure led inferior land to be brought into cultivation. Economic recovery only took place in the eighteenth century, and when, at the beginning of the nineteenth century, incomes per head again reached the level of the 1590s Spain no longer had an empire or was a vital link between Europe and the New World.

The cases of Britain and Holland are charted in Figure 10.02. In contrast to Italy and Spain, GDP per head displayed considerable long-term resilience in these two North Sea economies, despite substantial and occasionally severe growth reversals over short periods.

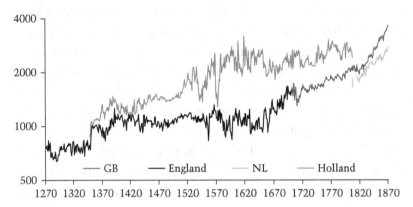

FIGURE 10.02 Real GDP per head in Britain and Holland, 1270–1870 (Geary–Khamis 1990 international dollars, log scale). *Source:* Appendix 5.3; van Zanden and van Leeuwen (2012).

Gains were incremental with the result that both were significantly richer by the end of the pre-industrial period than they had been on the eve of the Black Death, when two out of five English families were living below the poverty line. Britain, like Italy, therefore received a substantial boost to incomes per head from the mortality crisis of the mid-fourteenth century. Prolonged population decline is, however, rarely conducive to sustained economic growth and by the 1420s, as in Spain, demand had contracted to the point that economic activity was suffering. Henceforth, British GDP per head neither improved as the population shrank further, nor declined when the population grew again, as it did for most of the sixteenth and early seventeenth centuries. The negative effect of population growth on wage rates was countered by increasing industriousness on the part of workers, whose energies were readily absorbed by a greatly expanded industrial sector. Population growth finally levelled off from the mid-seventeenth century, resulting in a further step gain in GDP per head.

Dutch GDP per head also sagged in the second quarter of the fifteenth century when, in addition to a major downturn in international commerce, serious ecological problems beset the country. These forced a significant reorientation of the rural economy towards livestock production, increased dependence upon substantial grain imports paid for with exports of a range of manufactured goods, expansion of the urban sector and heavy investment in shipping, fishing and related maritime activities (van Bavel and van Zanden, 2004). These developments set in train processes of market integration, expanding international trade and shipping and rapid structural change which brought about a doubling of Dutch GDP per head in little more than a century and elevated the country's urbanisation ratio to an impressive 35 per cent (van Zanden and van Leeuwen, 2012). Amsterdam, in particular, grew from insignificance to become a major maritime metropolis and financial centre of 175,000 inhabitants.

The strong growth in the economy of the Duchy of Brabant before 1570, of Holland during its Golden Age from around 1570 to

1650 and then of England from the 1650s can all be linked to success in international trade. Economic historians have often pointed to long-distance trade as playing an important role in this post-1500 reversal of fortunes between the southern North Sea region and Mediterranean Europe and between the Atlantic-edge economies of Western Europe and continental interior economies of Eastern Europe. Capture by the Ottomans between 1453 and 1517 of virtually the whole of the lands formerly controlled by the Byzantine and Mamluk empires put an end to any prospect of European merchants trading directly and at low cost with the Arabian Sea and Indian Ocean, since all the key overland links between these two maritime orbits of exchange were now subject to monopoly franchises and tolls (Abu-Lughod, 1989). Finding and developing alternative maritime routes to Asia therefore became a European priority.

Since the late thirteenth century the Genoese had been exploring the alternative commercial potential of the Atlantic, including establishment of a direct maritime connection with the southern North Sea. Genoese backing was also fundamental to Portuguese exploration of the African coast. Bartolomeu Dias finally rounded the Cape of Good Hope in 1488 and between 1497 and 1499 Vasco da Gama made his celebrated return voyage from Lisbon to India. Meanwhile, the Genoese Cristoforo Colombo, sailing under Spanish colours, had reached the West Indies and Spanish conquest and colonisation of Central and most of South America swiftly followed. The effect of these discoveries was to redefine Europe's geocommercial location. Silks and ceramics from China, spices from India and gold, ivory and slaves from West Africa could all now be shipped directly to Europe and to the profit of Europeans. Sugar could be obtained from Madeira and the Caribbean, silver from South America and fish from the Grand Banks of Newfoundland, all in seemingly limitless quantities.

Given that the Genoese, Portuguese and Spanish had pioneered these overseas ventures, it might be expected that they would derive the greatest benefits from them. Certainly, Portugal and Spain acquired major overseas empires. Nevertheless, it was the ports of the southern North Sea – Antwerp, Amsterdam and London and their lesser satellites – that eventually drove the greater trade and won the larger commercial profits. Acemoglu and others (2005) explain the relative success of Holland and Britain (and failure of Portugal and Spain) through an interaction between Atlantic access and institutional constraints on executive power. In Holland and Britain, political checks on rulers were sufficient to ensure that they were unable to appropriate the bulk of the gains from trade, with the result that mercantile capitalism thrived. In Spain and Portugal, by contrast, rulers were politically sufficiently strong to exploit these opportunities themselves and prevent a strong merchant class from constraining their powers to appropriate.

Such a view is ostensibly in opposition to that of Epstein (2000), who argued that centralisation of state power and expansion of state capacity were fundamental to eliminating the coordination failures and multiple tolls that bedevilled commerce and inhibited greater market integration where state power was weak and fragmented. The two interpretations can be reconciled once it is recognised that a balance is needed between having a state that is strong enough to enforce property rights and reduce transaction costs but not so strong that it can appropriate all the gains from trade. Private enterprise had to be protected and allowed to flourish if expanding trade was to have the beneficial economic effects envisaged by Adam Smith [1776]. What was required was both the growth of state capacity (Epstein, 2000; O'Brien, 2011) and the constraint of the executive, as occurred in Holland following establishment of the Dutch Republic in 1581 and in England as was doubly confirmed by the outcome of the Civil War of 1642–51 and the Glorious Revolution of 1688 (North and Weingast, 1989; Acemoglu and others, 2005). Both countries thereby possessed constitutions which supported institutions conducive to economic growth and endowed them with a real commercial advantage over rival European states.

10.3 BRITAIN AND THE GREAT DIVERGENCE BETWEEN EUROPE AND ASIA

Historical output data are available in abundance for some Asian economies and some time periods, but work gathering and processing this material has so far been limited. Excepting periods of dynastic change, enough Chinese data are now available to allow construction of preliminary output estimates of GDP back to the high point represented by the Northern Song Dynasty (960–1127) (Broadberry and others, 2014b). Japanese GDP can also be reconstructed following the short-cut method used for Italy and Spain back to 1600 and then more intermittently for occasional benchmark years back to 730 (Bassino and others, 2014). Indian data are less abundant, and it has so far only been possible to produce estimates back to 1600 (Broadberry and others, 2014a). Apart from Abū 'l-Fazl's [1595] remarkable document, *The Ā' īn-i-Akbarī*, dating from the highpoint of the Mughal Empire, most of the information about India comes from the records of the European East India Companies and the British Raj. The results of these Asian historical national income reconstructions are presented in Table 10.02B.

These new estimates are again higher than those produced by Maddison (Table 10.01) but the scale of the upward revision is more modest than for Western Europe. Japan, for instance, apparently had very low levels of GDP per head of $500–$550 from the tenth to the fifteenth centuries but then experienced modest but steady growth at 0.06 per cent per annum through to the mid-nineteenth century, when it finally exceeded $700. Japan's more dynamic growth after the Meiji Restoration of 1868 thus built on this earlier progress. China's GDP per head, by contrast, was on a downward trajectory from its highpoint during the Northern Song Dynasty when it probably boasted the most productive economy in the world and very likely was twice as wealthy as Japan. By the early nineteenth century, however, Chinese output per head had halved, decline accelerating as contact with Europe intensified from 1700. On these estimates, Japan overtook China during the eighteenth century. Even at the height of the Mughal Empire under Akbar (r. 1556–1605), India was conspicuously less wealthy than either, with a GDP per head of less than $700 and therefore poorer than England under both William I (r. 1066–87) and Edward I (r. 1272–1307). After two centuries of continuous economic decline, its poverty was even more pronounced by the early nineteenth century.

Note that in Asia China's transition from economic leader to laggard echoed Italy's 'long decline of a leading economy' (Malanima, 2011). Like Italy, China had achieved striking commercial success at a remarkably early date but then found it progressively more difficult to maintain this high level of economic activity. Japan's trajectory, like England's, was the opposite. It began far poorer than the larger and more successful imperial China but by the nineteenth century, after centuries of slow but cumulative growth, was the richer of the two per head and the first Asian economy poised to make the transition to modern economic growth. In this respect, the GDP per head estimates in Table 10.02B suggest that a reversal of fortunes was emerging within Asia in parallel with that in Western Europe. A full understanding of the Great Divergence between Western Europe and East Asia thus requires sensitivity to both similarities and differences between the British and Japanese experience (Broadberry, 2014). This pair of small and insular economies at opposite ends of Eurasia made the transition to modern economic growth earlier than their continental neighbours, but with the crucial difference that Britain was decisively ahead of Japan. Once initiated, modern economic growth also spread more quickly from Britain to other Western European countries than from Japan to neighbouring Asian countries.

Parts A and B of Table 10.02 bring this comparison between Britain and Japan into sharper focus by aligning the GDP per head estimates for these four European and three Asian economies. Although Japan was following a similarly dynamic trajectory to the group of North Sea economies its GDP per head was at a much lower level and exhibited a slower rate of growth, so that it continued to fall behind the West until after the Meiji Restoration in 1868. After centuries of steady progress it also remained significantly poorer than Song Dynasty China. At the opening of the second millennium the latter had been more developed and prosperous than even the most developed part of Europe, namely the centre and north of Italy. Moreover, China was so vast, with a population more than double that of the whole of Europe, that the GDP per head of its richest provinces must have been significantly greater than the national average of around $1,250 and conceivably superior to even the wealthiest parts of late-medieval Europe: Tuscany, Lombardy and Flanders. This would have been the case if, for instance, incomes per head in the Yangzi Delta were around 50 per cent higher than those in China as a whole, which is broadly consistent with the scale of regional economic differences within China during the nineteenth century and in accord with the accounts given in the earlier, qualitative literature.

Whether or not the most developed parts of China were still ahead of the most developed part of Italy at the time that Niccolò, Maffeo and Marco Polo made their celebrated visit to the court of Emperor Kublai Khan between 1275 and 1292 is a moot point. Certainly, the three Venetians were greatly impressed by the sophistication and intensity of Chinese commercial activity and awed by the scale of Kublai's capital of Beijing, but China during the Mongol interlude was already past its Northern Song peak. By the fifteenth century, Renaissance Italy, with a GDP per head approaching $2,000, was certainly ahead. By the sixteenth century European economic leadership had passed to Holland, whose rate of growth during its early modern Golden Age was unprecedented, and there can be little doubt that the Great Divergence between an economically dynamic Western Europe and stagnating Eastern Asia was beginning to emerge. By the seventeenth century the discrepancy between the aggregates for China and the major North Sea region economies (Table 10.02) are too large to be bridged by regional variation and it is plain that the leading European economies and their most commercially developed regions were now decisively ahead of their Asian counterparts. In this context it is worth noting that Pomeranz (2011) has conceded that his earlier (2000) claim that the most advanced parts of China were on a par with those of Europe as late as 1800 was overstated, and that China had already fallen behind by 1700. Meanwhile, although Japan's slow growth rate was sufficient to enable it to catch up and overtake China, it was too slow to prevent it from falling even further behind Holland and Britain.

10.4 UNDERSTANDING BRITAIN'S RISE TO GLOBAL ECONOMIC HEGEMONY

A full explanation of Britain's unforeseeable transformation from an underdeveloped and overwhelmingly primary-producing economy on the commercial periphery of Europe, which was itself less developed than the most advanced provinces of Song China at the start of the second millennium, to a position of undisputed global economic leadership by the mid-nineteenth century is beyond the scope of this volume. Nevertheless, a few observations are in order as a focus for future research, now that the quantitative dimensions of comparative levels and growth rates of GDP per head have become clearer. Broadberry (2014) offers one approach to conceptualising British success, based on a combination of shocks and structural factors.

The single most obvious shock was the demographic disaster of the Black Death. It was universal in its impact but not in its socio-economic consequences. Southern England was one of a core group of populous and highly commercialised regions whose GDP per head was boosted by the sudden and lasting reduction in demographic pressure. Structural and institutional changes then set in train meant that these windfall gains were retained when the population finally began to recover from the late fifteenth century. The net effect of this unusual, prolonged and intrinsically non-Malthusian interlude was therefore to elevate economic productivity onto a higher plane.

Over a century later, military extension of Ottoman control of the whole of the eastern Mediterranean, opening of a direct sea route around Africa to India and beyond, and discovery of the New World collectively redefined Europe's geopolitical location and, for those of its states engaged in maritime commerce, shifted the comparative advantage between a Mediterranean and Atlantic-edge location. As long as the West relied upon the old overland routes across Egypt and Arabia to gain access to the East, few countries were strategically better placed to dominate that commerce than Italy. Once the Atlantic became the main highway to the Orient, as also to the newly discovered Americas and the rich fishing grounds off Newfoundland, the port cities of the southern North Sea, with their wealthy and populous hinterlands served by extensive waterway networks gained the commercial upper hand. Had trans-Eurasian trade continued to flow along the well-worn channels relied upon during Europe's earlier commercial revolution of the twelfth and thirteenth centuries (Lopez, 1976; Abu-Lughod, 1989) it is doubtful whether southern Europe would have stagnated and northern Europe prospered to the extent that they did from the sixteenth century onwards. The ability of economies to take advantage of the opportunities created by the Black Death and voyages of discovery was nevertheless contingent upon a number of structural factors, of which the most important were the composition of agriculture, nature of human fertility regimes, labour supply per head and the institutional framework within which entrepreneurial groups operated.

The substantial livestock component of northwest European agriculture was one ingredient of the region's relative economic success. Animals were indispensable for traction and haulage, their fibres and skins were vital industrial raw materials and their milk and meat essential sources of protein and kilocalories (Chapter 3). Animal production lent itself to specialisation by livestock type, age, gender and purpose and live animals and their products were more cheaply and easily transported and traded overland than grain (Overton and Campbell, 1992). Livestock production therefore helped broker commercial exchange. The heavy reliance upon working animals for ploughing, harrowing and carting also created the potential to achieve relatively high levels of agricultural labour productivity. In addition, constructing and maintaining implements, ploughs, harrows, livestock tackle, carts, byres, stables, sties and cotes and shoeing draft beasts created a great deal of skilled and semi-skilled ancillary employment and generated a constant demand for iron.

The mixed-farming systems of the southern North Sea region were therefore capital-intensive, with animals making up a large share of the capital stock, as well as highly intensive in the use of non-human energy. As Chapter 7 has shown, the diet they delivered may not have been particularly abundant in terms of kilocalories but it had a high value-added component, a modest degree of variety, and much of the food consumed was more processed than in other societies thus creating employment for millers, bakers and brewers (Allen, 2009a). Mills powered by wind or water and occasionally horses were in near-universal use from the thirteenth century and ensured that few communities could manage without practical knowledge and experience of cogs, gears and hydraulics. In due course these high-value-added, capital-intensive, non-human-energy-intensive techniques spread from agriculture to industry and services and, as structural change promoted the importance of industry and services, the countries of the North Sea region pulled ahead of Mediterranean Europe and Asia.

Northwest Europe's economic development was further helped by the fact that rates of population growth were rarely excessive. In England, for example, rates of growth in excess of 1 per cent a year were unusual until the final years of the eighteenth century. To be sure, there were long periods when high disease mortality sapped the population of its capacity to grow but this seems to have been reinforced by a low-fertility demographic regime which limited reproduction rates. Hajnal (1965) argued that female marriage took place at a later age and more women never married in northwest Europe than in the rest of the European continent and probably the whole of Asia. Although he originally called this the European Marriage Pattern, later work established that it applied only to the northwest. When, why and how this distinctive fertility pattern came into being has stimulated much debate and research. What is clear, however, is that by limiting births it effectively restrained reproduction rates from swamping the growth of GDP.

These patterns of late marriage and family limitation can be seen as one important aspect of the emergence of the Low Countries and Britain as high-wage economies. Smaller family sizes represented a shift from quantity to quality in reproduction since they made possible greater investment in human capital, with better-fed and better-educated workers commanding a higher wage in the labour market (Voigtländer and Voth, 2013). Societies practising this marriage pattern were therefore characterised by human- as well as physical-capital intensity (Baten and van Zanden, 2008). In the case of Holland, de Moor and van Zanden (2010) have also linked emergence of the Northwest European Marriage Pattern to increased female participation in the labour market, with many women working before marriage, which in turn reinforced later marriage and fewer children. Wherever these marriage patterns prevailed, high real wage rates tended to result. Allen (2001) has drawn attention to the reversal of fortunes in real wages between northwest Europe and the rest of the continent from c.1450 and emphasised its role in promoting adoption of capital-intensive technologies in the former. Broadberry and Gupta (2006) likewise highlight the wage-rate differences between northwest Europe and the largest Asian economies, where female marriage typically took place much earlier. The average age of brides was just 13.0 years in modern India, 18.6 in late Ming China and 16.0 among lower-class women in Qing China (Bhat and Halli, 1999: 137; Lee and Wang, 1999: 67; Guo, 2000: 217). This compares with an average female age at marriage of 25.4 years in early modern England (Wrigley and Schofield, 1989: 255). Japan constitutes an intermediate case and, intriguingly, followed a fertility regime closer to that of northwest Europe: brides in Tokugawa Japan had an average age of 22.1 years (Mosk, 1980: 476).

For Hayami (1977) the male and female workforce of Tokugawa Japan was nothing if not 'industrious'. With Tsubouchi (Hayami and Tsubouchi, 1990) he then generalised this work ethic to an East Asian industrious revolution, based on rice cultivation, which was seen as the basis of an alternative to Western capital-intensive industrialisation. This idea was picked up by Pomeranz (2000: 91–106), who argued for a Chinese industrious revolution. Yet Huang (2002) considers this to be a misinterpretation of what he calls 'involution', a term coined by Geertz (1963) to describe the progressive intensification of existing methods that characterised Indonesian agriculture. In Huang's view the high involvement of Chinese women in proto-industry arose from the inadequate size of many landholdings as a result of rural overpopulation. In effect, all household members were obliged to work hard simply to meet basic subsistence needs.

There was, of course, a large element of involution in Western Europe before the Black Death and later, as Chapter 6 has shown, when the increased labour supply per head to the market was in part a response to the rising cost of subsistence. Nevertheless, there is also a crucial demand side component to de Vries's (1994) notion of an industrious revolution, as applied to northwest Europe, that is lacking from Hayami's original concept as formulated with reference to Japan and East Asia. In the growing economies of northwest Europe from the sixteenth century many people by working harder were able to acquire more consumer goods. Moreover, as Weber (1930) recognised, this was legitimated by the emphasis of the new reformed Protestant religions upon the godliness of industriousness. In England, Allen and Weisdorf (2011) have shown that real-wage-rate differentials were such that urban and artisanal households were best placed to practise this 'virtue' of hard work. It was the expanding consumer demand of these increasingly numerous and industrious households that stimulated long-distance trade, manufacturing output and industrial innovation. Labour intensity may have increased in the short run, but improved incomes led to higher savings, providing funds for investment and thus increasing capital intensity in the long run. There was an element of this in Japan, where harder work also brought rising income and consumption per head. Maintaining this virtuous circle was nevertheless contingent upon the continued growth of GDP per head, which greater industriousness by itself could not sustain. It was industriousness in conjunction with other factors that made the difference and enabled certain European and Asian economies to out perform their neighbours and rivals.

The most obvious difference between China and Europe is that for much of their histories the former was a great empire and the latter a conglomeration of independent and rival states. Regional divergences within Europe therefore assumed a national dimension, with states differing institutionally in their constitutions, laws, religions and policies. This institutional diversity had its drawbacks, as emphasised by Epstein (2000), in terms of higher transaction costs and the preservation of privileges secured by vested interest groups, but did allow individual states to break away from the pack and forge their own economic paths. For Acemoglu and others (2005), what mattered was whether the ruling executive's power to appropriate economic surpluses to further its own political, military and vainglorious ends was counterbalanced by institutional constraints upon that power exercised by parliaments and other groups. It was this that determined the extent to which entrepreneurial groups were able to retain the profits of their enterprise and, therefore, the incentive structure within which merchants, financiers and industrialists operated.

Acemoglu and others (2005) argue that from c.1500 and especially 1581, constraints on Holland's ruling executive were sufficient to ensure that it was unable to act arbitrarily in its dealings with merchants. On the contrary, it recognised that its own fortunes were bound up with those of its mercantile classes. In England, the strength of parliamentary power, affirmed by military victory against the Crown in 1651 and constitutional victory against the monarchy in 1688, had a similar effect. The capacity of mercantile interests in both these countries to protect themselves against the potentially overmighty power of their ruling executives, combined with the ability, nonetheless, of their governments to raise taxes, expand state capacity and adopt measures that furthered market integration and national economic interests, meant that early modern Britain and Holland economically out performed Spain and Portugal, where far less favourable constitutional and institutional conditions applied (Karaman and Pamuk, 2010; van Zanden and others, 2012). The consequence in these institutionally advantaged northern states was greater market specialisation, a fuller division of labour, higher labour productivity and, thus, higher wages. Indeed, Allen (2009a) emphasises Britain's success in international trade as a key factor underpinning Britain's high wages and the incentives these gave to the introduction of capital-intensive technology during the period of the industrial revolution. Meanwhile, Italy remained fissured into an excessive number of petty polities and well exemplifies Epstein's (2000) strictures on the economic disadvantages of too great a fragmentation of state power and, in particular, the barriers this presented to fuller integration of markets and freer trade. It therefore reverted to a low-wage economy with earlier female marriage, higher fertility and lower human-capital formation than in the commercially dynamic economies of the southern North Sea region.

The reversal of fortunes within Europe and the Great Divergence between Europe and Asia emerged as the shocks of the Black Death, closure and restriction of the old overland trade routes by Mongols, Mamluks and Ottomans, and the opening up of the new seaways to Asia and the New World interacted with the structural factors outlined above. The repeated bouts of high plague mortality solved problems of overpopulation in countries like Italy and England while creating problems of underpopulation in countries like Spain. These population losses boosted GDP per head in the former but depressed it in the latter. Whereas Italy's peak in prosperity turned out to be transitory, England's gain in income proved enduring once its population began to grow again and Holland's kept growing as it overtook Italy to become the world's richest economy. Ottoman domination of all of the old trade routes that linked the commerce of the Mediterranean with that of the Arabian Sea and Indian Ocean meant that Italy was unable to recapture the international commercial success it had achieved during its high-medieval heyday. The North Sea economies, in contrast, were less directly affected by these political and military developments and

394 PART II ANALYSING ECONOMIC GROWTH

geographically better placed to take advantage of the new commercial opportunities opening within, across and beyond the Atlantic.

Although the Second Plague Pandemic is now known to have originated in or near the Qinghai Province of northwest China, the effects of the Black Death upon China and many other parts of East Asia remain unclear. Certainly, it is known that the disease did not reach Japan. Nevertheless, neither it nor the rest of eastern and south-eastern Asia escaped the consequences of concurrent changes in climate, as manifest in the altered timing, magnitude and reliability of the monsoons. The negative ecological consequences for the wet-rice-growing societies of China and Cambodia and beyond were considerable and in China the political instability thereby engendered helped bring down the Yuan Dynasty. The combination of environmental and political breakdown meant that East Asia in general and China in particular experienced major population losses at much the same time as Europe, if for largely different reasons (Brook, 2010). Unsurprisingly, this brought no observable GDP per head benefits to China, whose economy was already past the peak of prosperity achieved in the tenth and eleventh centuries under the Northern Song Dynasty. The Mongol conquests had destroyed the institutional framework that had underpinned these remarkably high incomes per head and dynastic breakdown in the fourteenth century proved similarly disruptive. Agricultural productivity was undermined and as populations and incomes per head shrank, markets contracted and specialisation and the division of labour diminished. In these respects, there is a strange parallel between China's experience and that of Spain.

At the end of the fourteenth century the foundation of the Ming Dynasty re-established stability but brought no complete return to the precocious prosperity of earlier centuries. Moreover, China was less keen on re-establishing commercial connections with Europe than Europe was with China. Whereas European states and rulers encouraged the voyages of discovery that led to establishment of the new maritime trade routes, China and Japan turned inwards. Although India remained open, it lacked state capacity, so this did not lead to Indian prosperity (Tashiro, 1982; Fairbank, 1992: 137–140; Parthasarathi, 2011; Prange, 2011). Within Europe news of both the new maritime routes and the New World spread fast but acting on that information and deriving sustained profits from these opportunities proved less easy, as Genoa, Portugal and Spain all discovered. Capital, mercantile enterprise, state backing, maritime knowledge and experience and buoyant domestic markets all proved to be key requirements for conducting overseas trade at this range with any prospect of economic success.

Among European states, the Dutch Republic and Britain evidently combined the ingredients of international commercial success in greater measure than most. Holland's small but modestly prosperous economy was already growing during the final quarter of the fifteenth century, as the hitherto leading Italian economy began to display the dwindling dynamism that would plague it for the next four centuries (van Bavel and van Zanden, 2004; Malanima, 2011). At the opening of the sixteenth century incomes per head were approximately $1,500 in both Italy and Holland; Italy's then slid down as Holland's increased (Table 10.02). In terms of the reversal of fortunes within Europe this was the pivotal point. Henceforth the economies of the southern North Sea region forged ahead, advantaged by their developed mixed- and livestock-farming systems, distinctive sociodemographic regimes, growing industriousness of their workforces and more equitable balances of power between the rulers and the ruled. Their high real wages demonstrated their growing economic strength. Economic leadership passed from the Duchy of Brabant in the early sixteenth century, to Holland during its sixteenth- and early-seventeenth-century Golden Age, and then England during the long period of efflorescence that culminated in its industrial revolution (Goldstone, 2002). Growth rates fluctuated and were rarely rapid but they were persistent and their cumulative effects considerable. By 1750 there is no reason to doubt that the Dutch Republic and Britain eclipsed all other Eurasian economies in GDP per head (Table 10.02). At that time the Netherlands was still ahead of Britain, as it had been for the previous 300 years; by the early nineteenth century, however, their positions had been reversed and Britain had moved in front.

Britain's rise from obscurity to global economic leadership can largely be understood as part of the southern North Sea region's transformation relative to the rest of Europe and Asia. A conjunction of geographical, historical, institutional and fortuitous circumstances worked to this region's advantage, more particularly after 1350 and especially 1500 than before. Given the clear economic lead that Holland had established over England as early as the late fifteenth century, which by 1600 had widened to the point where Holland was per head twice as rich as England (Figure 10.02), it is necessary to consider why it was eventually Britain rather than the Netherlands that first made the breakthrough to modern economic growth. Scale is part of the explanation. The Dutch Republic was a small country. This was probably a positive advantage in the context of the sixteenth century but in the altered circumstances of the eighteenth century meant that it lacked the large market needed to provide sufficient rewards for industrial innovation (Sullivan, 1989; Broadberry and Gupta, 2009). Britain, in contrast, had a national income almost four times larger and therefore a domestic market that could provide such rewards. The two countries' respective resource endowments also made a difference. Although both were high-wage economies, with a powerful incentive to substitute capital for labour, Britain had energy in greater abundance and at cheaper prices than Holland (Allen, 2009a: 33–42, 98–104). This applied both to water power and, of course, coal.

Holland's Golden Age had been founded primarily on the country's comparative advantage in services, especially finance, commerce and shipping. England's industrial revolution stemmed from its comparative advantage in manufacturing (Broadberry and others, 2012). Herein lay the critical difference between these two leading North Sea economies. Whereas both had high wages and therefore an incentive to invest in labour-saving machinery, only Britain combined high wages with cheap coal and substantial domestic and colonial markets. This conjuncture of advantages provided the incentive to develop and adopt the steam-powered machinery whose diffusion lies at the heart of many accounts of the industrial revolution.

10.5   CONCLUSIONS

Historically, the poorest and least-developed economies in which the vast majority of the population lived at a basic subsistence level typically had GDPs per head in the range $400–500 (1990 International): the equivalent of less than 1½ dollars a day. Of the four European and three Asian economies reviewed in this chapter, only eighth-century Japan was as impoverished as this (Table 10.02). England at its poorest, in 1086 following the Norman Conquest and c.1290 after two centuries of population growth and in the aftermath of a devastating panzootic of sheep, had a GDP per head 50 per cent greater of approximately $700–750. This was sufficient to support its ruling and landed elite in considerable affluence, fund construction of great cultural monuments, sustain a modest urban sector, and in normal years allow 60 per cent of the population to afford a respectability basket of consumables (Chapter 8). Japan remained poorer than Norman and pre-Black Death England until the nineteenth century, China declined to below this level from the late eighteenth century, and from 1600 to 1850 India never rose above it (Table 10.02). By this yardstick, much of Asia must have been poorer than most of Europe for the greater part of the last millennium, although there must have been numbers of other pre-industrial European economies that were no wealthier than England in 1086 and c.1290 but for which reliable historical national income estimates are not yet available.

To achieve a GDP per head of at least $1,000 required a higher level of commercial development and more favourable balance between population and resources. In the tenth and eleventh centuries, China under the Northern Song Dynasty, alone among the Asian economies considered here, reached this level of productivity and did so well ahead of any Western European economy. Eight centuries later Japan had not yet reached it and only broke through the $1,000 ceiling following the Meiji Restoration of 1868. In Europe, Italy was undoubtedly the first post-Roman economy with a GDP per head of at least $1,000, which it seems to have reached around the opening of the second millennium (Malanima, 2002: 450). At that time it headed Europe's economic league table but fell some way short of the standard set by Song China. Thereafter, even after centuries of post-medieval decline, Italian GDP per head never fell below this income threshold (Figure 10.01 and Table 10.02). Spain briefly touched it on the eve of the Black Death but did not regain it until the early nineteenth century (Figure 10.01). Holland and England only reached it with the help of the massive negative demographic shock ministered by the Black Death but then succeeded in averting any reversion to lower levels of GDP per head when in the sixteenth century their populations eventually began to recover to pre-Black Death levels (Figure 10.02). In fact, for generations and sometimes centuries at a time, this small group of commercially dynamic pre-industrial economies all managed to reconcile the maintenance and even improvement of incomes per head with population growth, since the rising returns to market integration and growth envisaged by Adam Smith trumped the diminishing returns to land predicted by Malthus.

Only the most developed pre-industrial economies, actively involved in international trade and commerce and with substantial industrial and service sectors, attained a GDP per head of $1,500 or more. None of the Asian economies that have been considered became this developed and rich before 1870, although it would be surprising if the most advanced provinces of eleventh-century Song China did not match this impressive level of prosperity. If so, their earliest and clearest counterpart in the West was the centre and north of Italy, whose GDP per head was probably elevated to $1,500–1,750 during the boom years of the Italian-led commercial revolution of the twelfth and thirteenth centuries. Flanders, too, which boasted an even higher urbanisation ratio by 1300 starting in 1000 from a lower base, may have been in the same league (Campbell, 2014). After the commercial, financial and demographic setbacks of the fourteenth century, Italy's

GDP per head was back at \$1,500–2,000 during the Renaissance, but this was a temporary respite and it then slid irrevocably downwards as the foundations upon which Italian commercial prosperity had been erected first weakened and then failed (Malanima, 2011). In northern Europe, however, there were clear signs of renewed dynamism in the Low Countries from the late fifteenth century, and by the late sixteenth century Holland had probably replaced Italy as one of only two or three European economies with a GDP per head of \$1,500 or greater and by the seventeenth century was very likely the first economy in the world in which it exceeded \$2,000. By this stage, however, diminishing returns were setting in and for the next 250 years the GDP per head of the Dutch Republic/Netherlands fluctuated around \$2,000–2,500. Holland remained highly prosperous, with a small agrarian sector, substantial service sector and high level of urbanisation, but its era of greatest dynamism and fastest growth was over (van Zanden and van Leeuwen, 2012).

Thus far, Song China, high-medieval Italy and Flanders and early modern Holland had all enjoyed economic Golden Ages, characterised by expanding populations, buoyant trade and commerce, state building and, for most households, a reasonably comfortable and secure living standard (Goldstone, 2002). None, however, had made the breakthrough to modern economic growth, with fast population growth, heavy investment in new technology, rapidly rising productivity, improving living standards, urbanisation and, in due course, diminishing inequality. Britain was the first country to so. It had been a rank outsider when the Domesday survey was compiled in 1086 but since the fifteenth century the odds of its doing so had been steadily shortening. By the eighteenth century it had overtaken declining Italy in income per head and, although still significantly poorer than Holland, now had the faster growing economy, with an annual growth rate 1650–1750 of 0.44 per cent compared with Holland's 0.12 per cent.

Since the mid-fourteenth century Britain's economy had been on an intermittently rising trend (Chapter 5). It had taken from the early fourteenth century to the late seventeenth century for its GDP per head to double from c.$750 to c.$1,500 but by 1850 it had doubled again, when Britain became the first country in history with a GDP per head of $3,000 and set to increase further (Table 10.02). Moreover, since c.1500 these advances in output per head had proceeded in tandem with the growth of population (Chapter 5). To be sure, there were short periods when the population grew faster than economic output, placing living standards under strain, and many passing episodes of crisis, when for one reason or another output failed and many households experienced great hardship. Certainly, in accordance with Malthusian theory, the adoption of improved technology and achievement of higher productivity allowed an enlarged population to be supported, but the inconvenient fact remains that from 1500 this was at little sacrifice of living standards and from 1650 was actually delivering improvements in living standards. *Contra* Clark (2007), this was an economy escaping from Malthusian constraints, not a Malthusian economy. Population growth was not negating economic growth and driving living standards down; rather, economic growth was sustaining population growth and incrementally elevating living standards to new levels. As prosperity grew, urbanisation increased, demographic susceptibility to harvest shortfalls diminished, and, for the time being, inequalities of wealth became more pronounced (Wrigley, 1985; Campbell and Ó Gráda, 2011; Chapter 8). In Asia, Japan would eventually go through a similar process of transformation but at the time of Britain's industrial revolution it remained a long way behind.

Comparison of Figures 10.01 and 10.02 suggests that the economies of the southern North Sea region should be seen as catching up on the richer Mediterranean economies of Italy and Spain between the Black Death of the mid-fourteenth century and the opening of new trade routes around 1500. After that, however, the North Sea area was forging ahead, led first, during the sixteenth and early seventeenth centuries, by Holland and then, from the late seventeenth century, by Britain. The transition to modern economic growth, when population, GDP and incomes per head were all rising together and doing so more or less continuously, did not occur until the industrial revolution in Britain. It then spread quickly to Britain's immediate European neighbours. Japan followed after a considerable delay; other Asian economies later still. There was nothing preordained about this breakthrough except that it sprang from processes of structural economic change, commercial specialisation and technological innovation whose origins should be seen as stretching back to the late-medieval period. That was when the cluster of small but intrinsically dynamic economies grouped around the southern shores of the North Sea entered a phase of persistent if not consistent growth based on production methods that were capital intensive, non-human-energy intensive and human-capital intensive. Workers responded to the new consumer goods that expanding trade and diversifying manufacturing were increasingly supplying with an industrious revolution (de Vries, 1994; Chapter 6). By working longer and harder, households increased their incomes and in due course accumulated the savings that helped finance the investments in physical and human capital that underpinned the economic transformation of the industrial revolution. The forging ahead occurred within an institutional framework provided by states whose ruling executives were strong enough to provide secure property rights but constitutionally constrained from acting arbitrarily towards the entrepreneurial classes and politically prevented from enriching themselves at the expense of private enterprise.

11 Epilogue: British economic growth, 1270–1870

11.1 INTRODUCTION

Between 1270 and 1870 Britain slowly progressed from the periphery of the European economy to centre-stage of an integrated world economy. In the process it escaped from Malthusian constraints and by the eighteenth century had successfully reconciled rising population with rising living standards. This final chapter reflects upon this protracted but profound economic transformation from the perspective of the national income estimates assembled in Part I and analysed in Part II of this book. Because Britain's economic rise did not unfold in isolation, account is taken of the broader comparative context provided by the national income reconstructions now available for several other Eurasian countries: Spain from 1282, Italy from 1310 and Holland from 1348, plus Japan from 725, China from 980 and India from 1600. All are output-based estimates but have been derived via a range of alternative approaches according to the nature of the available historical evidence. Several make ingenious use of real wage rates and urbanisation ratios (Malanima, 2011; Álvarez-Nogal and Prados de la Escosura, 2013), two economic indicators often used as surrogates for estimates of GDP per head. Only the GDP estimates for Holland, like these for Britain, have been made the hard way, by summing the weighted value-added outputs of the agricultural, industrial and service sectors and then dividing the results by estimates of total population obtained by reconciling time-series and cross-sectional demographic data. Methodologically, the British and Dutch national income estimates are therefore the most directly comparable. Each is free from overdependence upon any single or narrow range of data series and, instead, they encapsulate variations in the wide range of economic indicators, appropriately

402

weighted in line with their importance in overall economic activity, from which they have been reconstructed.

11.2   TRENDS IN POPULATION, GDP AND GDP PER HEAD

Figure 11.01 summarises the broad trends in population, real GDP and real GDP per head for England from 1270 to 1700 and Great Britain from 1700 to 1870, indexed on 1700 to provide a continuous series. Change over the course of these 600 years may have been slow but in magnitude its cumulative effects were impressive: population grew fivefold, GDP twenty-eight-fold and GDP per head by a factor of 5.7. Progress was episodic and five broad phases can be identified from the changing relationship between these three key variables. The first, when GDP per head was lowest, extended from the 1270s to outbreak of the Black Death in 1348; the second, when population fell and GDP per head made a step gain of one-third, from the Black Death to the

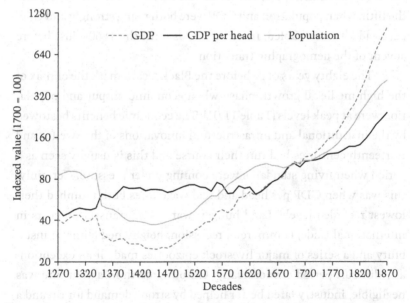

FIGURE 11.01 Real GDP, population and real GDP per head, England 1270–1700 and Great Britain 1700–1870 (averages per decade, log scale, 1700 = 100).
Source: Figure 5.05.

Table 11.01 *Mean annual growth rates of British agricultural,*
industrial and service-sector output at constant prices, real GDP,
population and real GDP per head, 1270–1870

Years	Mean annual growth rate (%)					
	Agriculture	Industry	Services	GDP	Population	GDP per head
1270s–1340s	0.09	0.27	0.25	0.11	0.11	0.00
1340s–1470s	−0.33	0.27	−0.46	−0.34	−0.53	0.20
1470s–1650s	0.43	0.64	0.69	0.56	0.52	0.04
1650s–1770s	0.51	0.75	0.73	0.66	0.22	0.44
1770s–1860s	0.95	2.35	1.88	1.80	1.15	0.64

Source: Calculated from Appendix 5.3.

1470s; the third, when population rose but GDP per head remained at
its post-Black Death level, from the 1470s until the end of the Civil
War in 1651; the fourth, when GDP per head grew by 90 per cent, from
the 1650s until the eve of the industrial revolution in the 1770s; and
the fifth, when population and GDP were both rising strongly and GDP
per head almost doubled, from the 1770s until the 1860s, just before
advent of the demographic transition.

The eighty years or so before the Black Death mark the climax of
the high-medieval growth phase when economic output and population were at peak levels (Table 11.01). The economic benefits bestowed
by the institutional and infrastructural innovations of the twelfth and
thirteenth centuries had run their course and this is usually seen as a
period when living standards were coming under pressure. Certainly,
this was when GDP per head and real wage rates both plumbed their
lowest recorded levels. Land hunger, war, rising transaction costs in
international trade, commercial recession, heightened climatic instability and a series of major livestock epizootics made it an exceptionally difficult period economically. Output growth in agriculture was
negligible, industry fared better helped by strong demand for tin and a
modest revival of cloth production, and services grew as state finances
and administration were placed on a war footing. Under these mostly

inauspicious economic and political circumstances, it was remarkable that, except in the short term, population, GDP and GDP per head did not in fact decline. Expansion had plainly come to an end but, despite a series of major negative shocks, contraction had not yet set in.

It took the massive death toll caused by the Black Death to break the economic stalemate and in 1348–9 transform the economic status quo. Population and GDP both shrank but, relieved of the heavy burden of poverty, GDP per head improved by 35 per cent. For the next hundred years or so processes of contraction, rationalisation and reorientation prevailed. Land and capital became cheaper but labour dearer; the old feudal institutions of serfdom and manorialism decayed and the population became freer and more mobile. Output of agriculture, industry and especially services all declined, but by less than population, as work and consumption patterns both changed. Once the initial post-plague boost to productivity had been delivered, however, and despite continuing improvements in real wage rates, further economic growth was not forthcoming and GDP per head stabilised at its new and improved level.

Towards the end of the fifteenth century the population began its long-delayed recovery and by the 1650s the demographic losses of the Black Death and its aftermath had been more than made good. During this early modern phase of expansion the growth of GDP more or less kept pace with that of population with the result that the gains in GDP per head achieved following the Black Death were largely retained. On the face of it this looks like expansion without growth but in reality the failure of rising population to depress GDP per head indicates that Malthusian constraints were weakening. This was achieved by, first, full adoption of the Northwest European Marriage Pattern and the restraints this placed upon fertility; second, structural economic change, as the industrial and services sectors expanded their shares of employment and output, to the benefit of productivity in agriculture; and, third, by an industrious revolution as workers increased the numbers of days worked in order to maintain household incomes. In the final decade of the sixteenth century when living standards again came under serious pressure government responded with major institutional innovations in welfare provision which henceforth helped the poor survive better through hard times and dampened down the mortality response to harvest failure. During this expansionist phase England began to exploit the commercial potential and fishing resources of the North Atlantic and by the early seventeenth century had established its first permanent American colonies. The latter, together with the Irish plantations, became the destination for increasing numbers of British emigrants and, therefore, an important demographic safety valve. Meanwhile, mounting political tensions between Crown and Parliament came to a head in the Civil Wars of 1642–51, from which Parliament emerged the victor.

English population growth, which had been slowing since the 1620s, finally ceased altogether in the 1650s, and for the next thirty years numbers sagged under the combined impact of emigration, metropolitan migration, reduced nuptiality and bouts of heavy disease mortality. GDP nevertheless continued to grow: between 1651 and 1700 agricultural output expanded by 14 per cent, industrial output by 38 per cent and service-sector output, boosted by external trade growing at over 1.0 per cent a year (calculated from Ormrod, 2003: 56–7), by 42 per cent. As a result, GDP per head registered its first sustained improvement since the second half of the fourteenth century, increasing at a yearly rate of 1.12 per cent between its Civil War minimum in 1650 and the beginning of the eighteenth century (Figure 11.01). The pace of structural change was quickening and by 1700 industry and services were employing over 60 per cent of the labour-force and the urban share of the population had expanded to 17 per cent of the total. Two-thirds of those living in towns with at least 5,000 inhabitants were Londoners and, with a population by 1700 of 575,000, the metropolis had become an even greater engine of growth (Wrigley, 1967, 1985). England, from 1707 united with Scotland, was now embarked upon its own commercial revolution and over the course of the next eighty years the economy advanced apace. For the first time, population, GDP and GDP per head were all rising together (Table 11.01) and the country was becoming more prosperous as well as more populous.

The period from the 1700s to 1770s constitutes a Smithian growth phase: population was growing at a little under 0.4 per cent, GDP at almost 0.6 per cent and GDP per head at 0.2 per cent. By its close England's population had increased to 7 millions, that of Great Britain to 8.7 millions, and GDP per head had risen by 17 per cent. The domestic market was expanding in size and spending power and English domestic exports were growing by 1.29 per cent (calculated from Ormrod, 2003: 56–7) so that overseas trade accounted for a larger share of national income at the end than beginning of this period. In return for the Indian calicoes and American sugar and tobacco craved by a British labour-force prepared to work harder in order to be able to afford them, British producers and traders delivered textiles and a widening range of the manufactured goods of which the American colonies in particular had urgent need, together with slaves from Africa. Trade and transport, financial services and government services all grew vigorously over these years (Tables 4.07 and 4.08). With so many expanding sources of demand opening – from proliferating numbers of town-dwellers, Londoners, miners and manufacturers, sailors and fishermen, carters, hauliers and travellers – the prospects for agricultural producers had never been as good. They responded with a sustained increase in output (Table 3.21) achieved by adopting more advanced and intensive methods of organic production. Agriculture's achievements took place across a broad front and involved making many interrelated and usually environmentally specific improvements to the overall technological complex at the level of individual farm enterprises. Much the same was true of the developments taking place elsewhere in the economy, where, endorsed by government, private enterprise was keeping output growing faster than population (Table 11.01).

In the final decades of the eighteenth century population growth accelerated and was growing faster than ever before. This might have jeopardised continuing economic growth except that GDP growth also accelerated so that GDP per head maintained its upward course. By the 1830s British GDP per head was growing at more than 1 per cent a year. Over these pivotal decades a new relationship was forged between population and resources by technological progress, adoption of the factory as the principal unit by which the factors of production were combined and harnessing of fossil fuels. Rising labour productivity constitutes the clearest symptom of the technological advances then taking place. Industry led the way. Industrial labour productivity growth had lagged behind that of agriculture during the hand-tools era from 1522 to 1759 when extensive use of draught animals had given agricultural labour the edge. Thereafter, once mechanised power was applied to more and more manufacturing processes, it was a different story and industry became the sector with the fastest growing labour productivity and the first in which it rose above 1.0 per cent a year (Table 9.10). Labour productivity growth in services followed that of industry but at a slower pace and from 1801 labour productivity growth in agriculture, still bound by organic rates of reproduction and animate sources of energy, lagged ever further behind. Living standards would have risen faster except that food remained dear and the cost of living high. By 1870, however, Britain was the richest country in the world and richer than any before.

11.3   GROWTH RATES

Switching attention from absolute levels of population, GDP and GDP per head to their respective annual growth rates offers a further perspective on the chronology of these developments. As will be observed from Figure 11.02, the 400 years from the mid-thirteenth to the mid-seventeenth century were characterised by a strong positive correlation between the growth rates of population and GDP but negative correlation between population and GDP per head. Throughout this long period, output per head fared worst when population growth was strongest, best when population growth was slowest, and best of all, as in the case of the second half of the fourteenth century, when the population was declining. With the sole

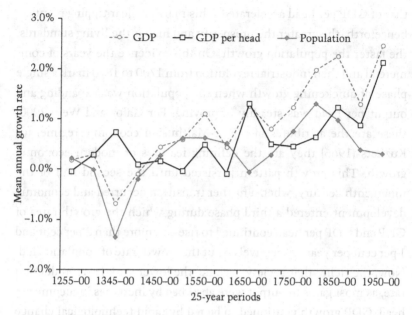

FIGURE 11.02 Annual percentage growth rates of British population, GDP and GDP per head, 1255–2000. *Source:* England 1270–1700 and Great Britain 1700–1870 calculated from Appendix 5.3; the United Kingdom 1870–2000 calculated from Maddison (2010).

exception of this plague-dominated half-century, annual growth rates of population, GDP and GDP per head mostly fluctuated within less than ±1.0 per cent. Negative growth rates were, however, rare after 1450 and at their lowest, in the case of GDP per head between 1500 and 1550, were a modest –0.14 per cent. From 1550 to 1650 the equivalent rate was 0.00 per cent, at a time when the population was growing by 0.59 per cent, which indicates that the English economy, in common with Holland but unlike most other economies at this time, was becoming more resilient at coping with increasing population numbers.

During the second half of the seventeenth century these long-established relationships between the growth rates of population, GDP and GDP per head began to shift more decisively (Table 11.01; Figure 11.02) as the growth rates of population and GDP diverged and that of GDP per head accelerated. This marks a clear tipping point as, henceforth, the greater the prosperity and higher the living standards, the faster the population growth. On this evidence the years of commercial and then industrial revolution from 1700 to 1850 mark a single phase of quickening growth when the population was expanding and output per head was steadily improving. For Galor and Weil (2000) these are the attributes of a post-Malthusian economic regime; for Kuznets (1966) they are the defining features of modern economic growth. This growth pattern persisted until the second half of the nineteenth century, when a further transition occurred and economic development entered a third phase during which the growth rates of GDP and GDP per head continued to rise – to more than 2 per cent and 1 per cent per year, respectively – but the growth rate of population fell. Now, the richer that society became, the lower sank its reproduction rate, as most gains in output were absorbed by increases in income per head. GDP growth continued to be fed by rapid technological change which, in turn, was sustained by greater investment in human-capital formation, but this rendered child-rearing far costlier so that, contrary to the situation before 1870, it was population growth and not economic growth that was squeezed.

11.4 STRUCTURAL CHANGE

The advances in GDP per head documented between 1270 and 1870 and, in particular, the country's growing ability to maintain GDP per head in the face of sustained population growth, was achieved in part by processes of structural economic change. This is implicit in the differential rates of sectoral output growth at constant prices summarised in Table 11.01, with industrial output growing fastest and agricultural output growing slowest from the 1450s to 1860s. It is explicit in the sectoral labour-force shares reconstructed in Figure 11.03. When female as well as male labour-force participation is taken into account, it emerges that by 1381 the industrial and service sectors already accounted for approximately 43 per cent of employment and the agricultural sector for barely 57 per cent. In 1522 these proportions

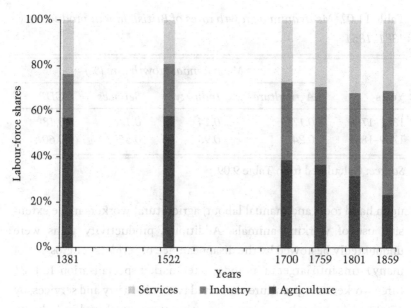

FIGURE 11.03 Sectoral shares in the labour-force, England 1381–1700 and Great Britain 1700–1851 (%). *Source:* Table 5.02.

remained broadly the same but by 1652–60 the probate records ana-lysed by Clark and others (2012) suggest that agriculture's share had reduced to 50 per cent and by 1700 it was down to less than 40 per cent. Meanwhile, industry's share of employment had expanded to 34 per cent and the service sector's to 27 per cent. These results extend the findings of Shaw-Taylor and Wrigley (2009) and demonstrate, first, that England's employment structure was diversified from a relatively early date, second, that much of the shift of labour from agriculture to industry and services had occurred well before the factory age and, third, that there was a marked quickening in the pace of structural change from the seventeenth century.

These changes in employment structure were only possible because labour employed in agriculture was becoming more produc-tive. As Table 11.02 indicates, labour was becoming more productive in all three sectors between 1381 and 1759 but was improving faster in agriculture than industry. Whereas industry remained heavily reliant

Table 11.02 *Mean annual growth rates of British labour productivity,*
1381–1851

	Mean annual growth rate (%)			
Years	Agriculture	Industry	Services	GDP
1381–1759	0.17	0.14	0.17	0.18
1759–1851	0.24	0.93	0.55	0.60

Source: Calculated from Table 9.09.

upon hand tools and manual labour, agricultural workers made extensive use of working animals. Additional productivity gains were
undoubtedly bestowed by the disappearance of serfdom, engrossing of
many farms into larger units and greater market specialisation. In 1381
three workers in agriculture supported two in industry and services; by
1700 two in agriculture were supporting three employed in industry
and services. The nature of industrial technology meant that at this
stage in the country's economic development continued growth of
industrial output was heavily dependent upon recruitment and
employment of an enlarged industrial workforce. From the eighteenth
century that changed as technological progress enabled mechanical
power to be applied to an ever-greater number of manufacturing processes. Between 1759 and 1851 labour productivity growth in industry
was substantially faster than that in either services or agriculture and
more than six times faster than it had been between 1381 and 1759.
Further, agriculture's continued reliance upon animate sources of
energy meant that its labour productivity was now the slowest growing. These developments highlight the importance of moderate rates of
labour productivity growth in agriculture from the seventeenth century in facilitating the shift of labour into industry and the major
contribution made by technologically induced gains in labour productivity to industrial output growth after 1759.

  The growing proportion living in towns is a further symptom of
the structural changes that were afoot during the centuries that

preceded the industrial revolution. In 1290 fewer than 5 per cent of England's population had lived in towns with at least 5,000 inhabitants, with Londoners accounting for just over a third of them, and in 1500 the urban share was scarcely greater although the proportion of Londoners had risen to over 40 per cent as London merchants tightened their grip upon the nation's commerce, to the lasting advantage of the metropolis and enervation of numbers of provincial towns (Wrigley, 1985: 688; Campbell, 2008: 908–11). By 1670, however, the urban share had increased to 13.5 per cent and London's dominance was overwhelming, for 70 per cent of these town-dwellers were Londoners. Growth of the capital as a centre of concentrated demand had become a powerful source of change within the economy, absorbing migrants, promoting agricultural specialisation across a widening hinterland, stimulating the Tyneside coal trade and promoting development of domestic trade and transport. The metropolis, in turn, benefited from the country's increasing success in the global economy, with London merchants in particular increasing their share of international trade in goods and in the services surrounding their distribution and finance. By 1670 London was poised to supersede Amsterdam as the greatest entrepôt of northern Europe. The crowning of Dutch stadtholder William of Orange as William III of England in 1688 further encouraged Dutch banks and trading houses to strengthen ties with London and the Glorious Revolution of that year cemented the political alliance between government and the English mercantile classes and their interests. During the eighteenth century, bolstered by the growth of government services, the capital continued to grow but so, too, did other towns and cities, so that by 1800 the urban share had risen to 27.5 per cent but London's share of the urban total had shrunk to 40 per cent. The late seventeenth century thus marks a watershed between one long era when urban growth was increasingly concentrated in London and the next when vigorous urban growth was becoming more general as economic growth began to flow in new directions.

11.5 WAGE RATES, WORK INTENSITY AND CONSUMPTION

The intermittently upward course of GDP per head between the Black Death and the industrial revolution provides a striking contrast to the chronology of building and farm labourers' daily real wage rates, which rose and fell in inverse relation to population. Whereas the former implies significant economic progress over this 500-year period, the latter provides a classic illustration of Malthus's iron law of wages. Figure 11.04 expresses labourers' daily real wage rates relative to GDP per head, the ratio between them rising when real wage rates gained relative to GDP per head and falling when GDP per head made the greater progress. Note that real wage rates improved by more than GDP per head during the labour-scarce years between the Black Death and the 1470s, when relative factor prices favoured labour over

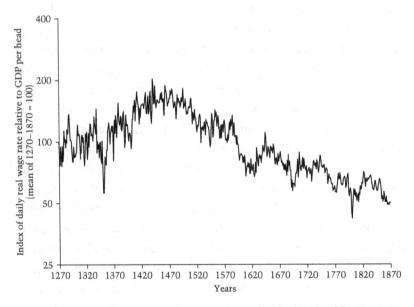

FIGURE 11.04 Index of daily real wage rates of unskilled building and farm labourers relative to GDP per head, 1250–1870 (log scale, mean of 1270–1870 = 100). *Sources:* combined wage-rate calculated from Munro (no date) and Clark (2005); GDP per head from Appendix 5.3.

land and capital. In contrast, GDP per head gained by more than real wage rates from the 1670s and especially the 1740s. Apart from the fact that labour gained value when it was scarce and lost value when it was abundant, these divergences are mostly to be explained by variations in the lengths of the working day and year. High daily real wage rates gave labourers the option of working less, which further reduced the supply of labour and placed additional upward pressure on wage rates. Low daily real wage rates, on the other hand, were an incentive to work harder which, in turn, further depressed the rate at which labour was remunerated. Working harder, of course, was contingent upon a commensurate increase in the demand for labour. Expansion of the textile industries from the late fifteenth century was in part founded upon the availability of a cheap and work-hungry labour-force.

Whereas fifteenth-century labourers could afford to work for less than half the days in the year and still meet their subsistence needs, early-nineteenth-century labourers were working a six-day week in order to do so. Since the Reformation there had been fewer public holidays to enjoy and as the economy became more commercialised many employers had imposed a tighter work discipline. Then, from the late seventeenth century, many labourers chose to work harder so as to be able to afford the sugar, tea, tobacco, spirits, calicoes and assorted manufactured goods that trade and industry were beginning to furnish (Table 7.05). By working harder in an era of falling daily real wage rates they maintained their household incomes and raised their consumption of material and non-material goods. As a result of this 'industrious revolution' (de Vries, 1994), it was household incomes that tracked GDP per head not real wage rates (Figure 6.07; Chapter 6). Where fifteenth-century labourers had chosen to work less and indulge in more non-market-based leisure activities, both secular and religious, their eighteenth-century counterparts, especially those employed in industry and/or living in towns (Allen and Weisdorf, 2011), preferred to work harder so that they could consume more market-based commodities. It was these decisions which in aggregate altered the relationship between real wage rates and GDP per head.

It might be expected that increased food consumption would have first claim upon any improvement in incomes, especially for workers living close to or below the poverty line. Yet as far as consumption per head of kilocalories was concerned, this appears not to have been the case until the second half of the nineteenth century. The problem was the limited capacity of domestic agriculture, which was the source of the bulk of all foodstuffs consumed, to deliver more kilocalories per head at an affordable price. Instead, as the estimates summarised in Table 11.03 indicate, the quantity of kilocalories consumed per head remained remarkably unvarying from the 1300s to the 1850s. Agriculture was mostly able to supply the minimum daily intake of 2,000 kilocalories per person required to enable the population to be able to work and reproduce but rarely much more. At times of acute population pressure, as in the early fourteenth century and mid-seventeenth century, even these minimum requirements were barely achieved and it was only when the opposite conditions prevailed, following the Black Death and, later, during the demographic lull of the late seventeenth century, that diets for a time became more abundant.

What changed over time, as incomes improved, was less the quantity than the form of kilocalories consumed. When they could afford to do so, consumers traded up to higher-quality foodstuffs that were more costly to produce. Typically, that meant eating more livestock products and consuming grain in more refined and highly processed forms. Thus, in the fifteenth century diets were more abundant, contained more dairy produce and meat and were more extravagant of grain kilocalories than had been the case in the 1300s or would again be the case in the 1650s. Similar shifts are apparent from the 1700s as GDP per head rose: from the 1750s diets had lower grain-extraction rates and contained more livestock products than at any time in the past. Potatoes, sugar, tea and tobacco were also being more widely consumed. Note, however, that by the end of the eighteenth century, as the population began to increase rapidly and the relative price of agricultural products rose steeply, it was only possible to maintain

Table 11.03 *Daily kilocalorie consumption per head of major arable crops and animal products in England, 1300s–1850s*

Decade	Population (1700 = 100)	GDP per head (1700 = 100)	Agricultural prices relative to industrial prices (1700 = 100)	Kilocalories per head (2,000 = 100)	Kcal from meat and dairy (%)	Grain extraction rate (%)	Kcal from imports (%)
1300s	90.8	47.9	111	102.8	6.4	54	
1350s	51.0	62.1	95				
1400s	39.5	68.7	80	115.3[a]	9.2[a]	49[a]	
1450s	37.1	66.8	75	108.8	12.1	48	
1500s	43.0	70.6	76				
1550s	60.0	65.2	91				
1600s	82.1	71.2	105	105.2	9.8	53	
1650s	102.9	69.7	111	97.3	8.7	52	
1700s	102.5	103.3	95	109.4	9.6	52	
1750s	119.7	113.0	116	105.2	15.2	43	-3.4
1800s	180.0	137.5	174	108.8	17.7	43	7.1
1850s	349.5	198.1	307	105.6	15.5	45	24.1

Sources and notes: Population and GDP per head from Chapter 5; Kilocalorie estimates derived from the agricultural output data in Chapter 3 using the assumptions set out in Chapter 7.
[a] The average of estimates for the 1380s and 1420s.

these improved dietary standards by expanding food imports. This was the rub, for high transport costs, in combination with the protection provided by the Corn Laws to British grain growers, priced mass food imports out of the British market and confronted consumers with ever-costlier calories supplied by a domestic agricultural sector able to reap high profits. This helps to explain one of the great paradoxes of the age, whereby GDP per head rose strongly but levels of kilocalorie consumption per head changed little (Table 11.03). The Corn Laws were repealed in 1846 at a time when trans-Atlantic shipping costs were starting to fall. In the 1840s, the imported proportion of kilocalories rose to 14 per cent, then to 24 per cent in the 1850s and 37 per cent in the 1860s (Table 7.06), when substantial deliveries of cheap North American grain finally began to drive British food prices down and allow consumers to raise their daily food intake. Until that belated internationalisation of food supplies, the price differential between foodstuffs and manufactured goods had become ever wider: cooking pots, knives and forks and plates all became cheaper but not the food that was eaten.

By the eighteenth century food supplies were bound by a land constraint from which technological advance and the harnessing of fossil fuels were increasingly liberating industrial output. Accordingly, food rose and manufactured goods fell in relative price, encouraging consumers to substitute away from food. Growth of consumption per head is therefore likely to show up more strongly in the non-food sector, especially in the material goods and valuations placed on those goods recorded in probate inventories. Given the high degree of positive skewness and inequality in the distribution of wealth, the median valuation provides the best measure of the path in average wealth at death. From the 1550s to 1630s GDP per head tended to sag and the median valuations given in probate inventories for a sample of five counties declined by an average of –0.34 per cent a year. Following the hiatus of the Civil War (1642–51) GDP per head rose by 0.45 per cent a year from the 1670s to 1740s and median probate valuations rose at the higher rate of 0.59 per cent (Table 11.04). Furthermore, the

Table 11.04 *Average annual growth rates of GDP per head and median probate-inventory valuations for five counties (Cornwall, Hertfordshire, Kent, Lincolnshire and Worcestershire), 1550s–1740s*

| | Mean value | | Mean decadal annual growth rates (%) | |
Decades	Real *GDP per head* (1700 = 100)	*Median real probate valuations (£)*	Real *GDP per head*	*Median real probate valuations (£)*
1550s–1590s	68	£11.09	–0.07	–0.14
1590s–1630s	68	£8.76	–0.04	–0.55
1660s–1700s	85	£15.66	0.76	0.42
1700s–1740s	105	£19.78	0.14	0.76

Sources: Calculated from Appendices 5.3 and 7.1.

data on individual consumer goods from Overton and others (2004) reveal a clear pattern of increased ownership of manufactured items in four main areas: furnishings; linen; goods concerned with heating, cooking and eating; and miscellaneous goods such as clocks, mirrors and books. By the 1750s relative prices were increasingly favouring expenditure upon commodities such as these over foodstuffs and this bias would become even more pronounced as mechanised methods of production increased the supply and lowered the unit costs of manufactured goods.

11.6   INCOME INEQUALITY

Until society became affluent, education and training universal, and in the twentieth century it became politically acceptable to adopt wealth redistribution measures, income inequality grew with prosperity. Between 1290 and 1688 GDP per head doubled and the Gini coefficient of the social distribution of income rose from 33 per cent to 49 per cent, at around which level it seems to have remained throughout the industrialising eighteenth century. This 50 per cent rise in the Gini coefficient between 1290 and 1688 indicates that the benefits of the nation's increased income were very unequally shared. A substantial group remained at the bottom of the social hierarchy, deficient in resources, skills and education, living in poverty and largely missing out on the fruits of economic growth. The existence of this group is not at issue; its size is. So, too is whether it expanded or contracted as the economy grew and GDP per head rose. Here, Allen (2009a) draws a useful distinction between those able to afford a respectability basket of consumption goods and those having to make shift with a cheaper and more basic bare-bones version of the same which nonetheless provided just sufficient kilocalories and protein, rent and clothing to satisfy the minimum subsistence requirements of a family comprising a husband and wife and two children. Since women and children required fewer kilocalories than a working adult male, a family is assumed to have required three baskets to survive. The poverty line is defined as the income required to afford the more desirable and generous respectability basket of consumables which enabled families to lead an economically more secure and socially less marginalised existence.

Table 11.05 sets out the costs of the family-sized bare-bones and respectability baskets relative to the annual earnings of a building labourer and building craftsman, if each obtained 200 days of paid work. Whereas labourers could always afford some version of the bare-bones basket, even craftsmen sometimes fell below the poverty line and were unable to afford the respectability basket. The incomes of each class of worker bought least in 1290 and most in 1522, although both were relatively well off in 1759. When times were hard and wage rates low, notably at the close of the thirteenth century, during the seventeenth century and, again, at the opening of the nineteenth century, it was only by working substantially more than 200 days a year that craftsmen could have elevated themselves above the poverty line and afforded the respectability consumption basket. The recurrent difficulty they experienced in earning enough to maintain a respectable living standard was compounded by the reduced premium their skills commanded from the sixteenth century and the rising cost of the contents of the respectability basket relative to that of the bare-bones

Table 11.05 *Wages and the affordability of the bare-bones and respectability baskets, 1290–1801/03*

Ratios	1290	1381	1522	1620	1688	1759	1801/3
Building labourer's wage to bare-bones basket	1.29	2.00	2.41	1.40	1.76	2.34	1.97
Building craftsman's wage to respectability basket	0.83	1.22	1.23	0.73	0.92	1.16	0.96
Skilled to unskilled wage	1.71	1.67	1.50	1.50	1.55	1.50	1.55
Respectability basket to bare-bones basket	2.67	2.74	2.96	2.89	2.96	3.02	3.17
% of families below the poverty line	41.2	22.1			24.2	13.7	19.9

Sources: Tables 8.01 and 8.07.

basket over the same period as better-quality and more highly processed foodstuffs became dearer. By 1801/03 the respectability basket was 7 per cent more expensive relative to the bare-bones basket than it had been in 1688 and 19 per cent more expensive than in 1290, when a craftsman's skill premium was highest (Table 11.05). Craftsmen who wished to maintain their families in a moderate degree of comfort therefore had little option but to work harder, provided that sufficient employment was available.

An alternative approach to this issue, which takes account of real as opposed to hypothetical earnings, entails assessing the costs of the two consumption baskets against estimates of family income derived from social tables for 1290, 1381, 1688, 1759 and 1801/03 cast within an accounting framework that ensures consistency with the national totals (the same social tables as those used to calculate the Gini coefficients). The results bear out the impression conveyed by Figure 11.04 that wage-earners, both skilled and unskilled, were offsetting deteriorating wage rates by lengthening the numbers of hours and days worked. At the price of less leisure, a growing proportion of families were able to maintain themselves above the poverty line (Table 11.05).

Unsurprisingly, poverty was greatest when GDP per head was lowest, at the end of the thirteenth century, when two out of five households, and probably a somewhat smaller proportion of individuals, were living below the poverty line. The proportion of poor families shrank dramatically following the Black Death but demographic recovery in the sixteenth and seventeenth centuries seems to have brought no return to the pre-Black Death situation. By 1688, by which time GDP per head had doubled, probably no more than one in four families and probably less than one in five individuals were living below the poverty line. By 1759 both proportions had probably reduced further until the profound social dislocations arising from enclosure, the engrossing of farms and decay of domestic industry caused poverty to rebound. Even so, by 1801/03 Colquhoun's exceptionally well-informed and reliable social table implies that four out of five families and maybe five out of six individuals were now living above the poverty line. This is consistent with a Gini coefficient fractionally lower than that for 1688 and indicates that economic growth, slowly but surely, was acting as a solvent upon the most abject forms of poverty. Further progress was contingent upon the extension of education and training to all from 1880 and improved welfare measures, including introduction of an old-age pension from 1908, that guaranteed a minimum living standard to the most vulnerable members of society.

11.7   BRITAIN IN COMPARATIVE PERSPECTIVE

Figure 11.05 places Britain's economic development in a wider European context. For all countries, levels of GDP per head have been converted to 1990 international dollars, which is convenient for making comparisons across space and time. For each country, GDP is measured in local currency, but converted to constant price terms by correcting for price changes over time with a 1990 base year. The conversion to a common currency involves comparison of local prices in 1990 with dollar prices in the same year, and a weighting scheme

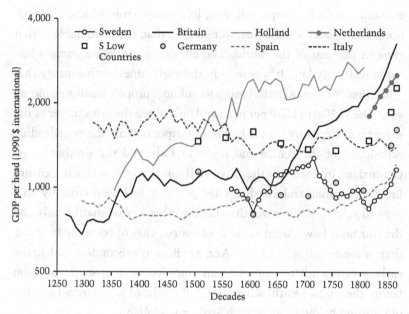

FIGURE 11.05 GDP per head in seven European countries, 1260s to 1860s ($ 1990 international; log scale). *Sources:* Britain, Appendix 5.3; Sweden, Southern Low Countries and Germany, Bolt and Zanden (2014); Holland/Netherlands (NL), van Zanden and van Leeuwen (2012); Italy, Malanima (2011); Spain, Álvarez-Nogal and Prados de la Escosura (2013).

based on international rather than just US patterns of consumption. For the purposes of this study, the levels of GDP per head for each country in 1850 have been taken from the study by Maddison (2010), who provided continuous time series to link up with the 1990 benchmarks. In interpreting these data, it is worth bearing in mind that in 1990, the World Bank poverty level for an individual was a dollar a day, or $365 a year, so that the minimum or 'bare-bones subsistence' level of GDP per head in 1990 international dollars is usually taken as $400, since even the poorest economies have a small elite with much higher levels of income.

Figure 11.05 reinforces the picture of uneven but sustained long-run growth and development which has emerged from reconstruction of Britain's historical national accounts from the output side. By the mid-nineteenth century Great Britain was clearly Europe's leading economy, with its people enjoying living standards which, although not high by today's standards, were higher than those available at that time in the rest of the world. The country's economic success had come relatively late. It was only in the early nineteenth century that it had finally overtaken the Dutch Republic (Europe's leading economy since the 1520s) in GDP per head and only since the last quarter of the seventeenth century that it had been outperforming the once-leading economies of the centre and north of Italy and the southern Low Countries. In fact, in the first half of the seventeenth century English, German and Swedish GDP per head had been virtually on a par and substantially lower than GDP per head of stagnating Italy and the southern Low Countries and, of course, that of booming Holland, then at the zenith of its Golden Age. Yet Britain's secondary rank in the early seventeenth century was an improvement upon its position before the Black Death, when its GDP per head was barely half that of Italy and below those of both Spain and Holland.

At the climax of Western Christendom's high-medieval commercial revolution in the mid-thirteenth century, when the first tentative estimates of England's national income can be made, there was almost nothing to indicate the prosperity that lay ahead or the reversal of fortunes that would eventually take place between Italy and England. At that time Italy was riding the crest of an economic wave and it was to Italy that England sent a growing proportion of its wool and tin and to which it looked as a source of exotic goods and credit. Nevertheless, the institutional and infrastructural foundations upon which England's later rise would be erected had already been laid in the form of developed factor and commodity markets and the first of the industries – textiles and tin – that would help make the country's fortune had begun to prosper. Then, in 1348–9, the Black Death provided a brutal solution to the acute congestion that had developed on the land with the result that England was one of several populous and commercialised economies left better off per head as a result of this demographic disaster. Demographic collapse elevated England's GDP per head above that of Spain and narrowed the gap between England

and Italy. By the mid-sixteenth century Italy's economic fortunes were plainly waning whereas England's were holding steady and the neighbouring economies of Flanders, Brabant and Holland were all prospering, as Europe's economic centre of gravity was permanently relocated from the Mediterranean to the southern North Sea region.

Holland was the economic success story of the sixteenth century. Its GDP per head grew from $1,400 in 1490 to $2,450 in 1600, when it was more than double that of England and Holland had become the richest country in Europe, and possibly the richest the world had ever seen. Successful pre-industrial economies rarely grew fast, yet Dutch economic growth averaged 0.52 per cent a year throughout the sixteenth century and for a time in the 1580s and 1590s was growing at well over 1.0 per cent (van Zanden and van Leeuwen, 2012). Moreover, in defiance of Malthusian logic, population growth during this Golden Age averaged 0.61 per cent, as workers from around the North Sea responded to the pull of the fast-expanding Dutch labour market. The runaway success of the Dutch economy left all others behind (Figure 11.05). Spain, now a great colonial power, had been unable to turn its vast New World wealth to economic advantage: it grew by just 0.13 per cent a year between 1500 and the 1590s, when a far-reaching crisis sent growth into reverse for the next hundred years (Álvarez-Nogal and Prados de la Escosura, 2013). Germany and Sweden, lacking Spain's colonial opportunities, were both per head significantly poorer by 1600 than they had been earlier in the century (Schön and Krantz, 2012; Bolt and van Zanden, 2014). England's singular achievement was to end the sixteenth century more populous but no less prosperous than it had begun the century, a situation that it was able to maintain until the middle of the following century.

By the early seventeenth century Holland was securely established as the maritime superpower of the age, with Amsterdam Europe's premier entrepôt and the Dutch East India Company the greatest European merchant company active in the Asian trade. Nevertheless, at this peak of prosperity Dutch GDP per head ceased to grow. Seemingly, there were inherent limits to the amount of

Smithian growth that specialisation and trade along Dutch lines could generate. Italy's commercial revolution of the twelfth and thirteenth centuries had come up against a similar ceiling. Rapid expansion of international trade and commerce had lifted the economies of both into a new league where the momentum of their success long maintained them, but once the initial commercial booms had run their courses further growth ceased to materialise (Malanima, 2011; van Zanden and van Leeuwen, 2012). In fact, the economies of Italy, Spain, the southern Low Countries, Holland and Germany all stagnated for much of the seventeenth century (Figure 11.05). Belligerent Sweden was the one conspicuous exception. Its sudden emergence as a great military power drove a war-fed economic boom which raised the country's GDP per head from barely $900 at the opening of the century to almost $1,200 by the 1660s (Schön and Krantz, 2012; Bolt and van Zanden, 2013). This, however, was at the price of devastating the Holy Roman Empire during the Thirty Years War (1618–48) and provided no secure foundation for enduring prosperity, as witnessed by the fact that most of these gains in GDP per head did not long outlast Sweden's military greatness (Figure 11.05).

Sweden's GDP per head held up until the end of the seventeenth century whereas that of Spain made no significant improvement and those of Holland, the southern Low Countries, Germany and Italy all drifted down. For most of Europe this was not a prosperous century. England was the sole conspicuous exception and it was following Parliament's victory in the Civil War and during the climatically unstable and politically troubled second half of the century that its take off to rising GDP per head began. For the next 150 years no other European economy could rival Britain's dynamism. The Dutch economy remained far ahead in terms of its level of GDP per head but was growing slowly at just half the speed of Britain. Growth in the southern Low Countries was slower still and Germany was little richer in 1800 than it had been in 1700. Spain registered no growth in the first half of the century but then grew at 0.19 per cent during the second half. In contrast, Italy's fortunes revived somewhat until 1760 but then slipped back again. Sweden fared worst of all and declined throughout the century. Britain alone, by finding effective institutional, technological and resource solutions to the problems that it encountered as it developed, was able to maintain and even improve the momentum of its growth into the nineteenth century, doing so irrespective of accelerating population growth. It was helped by its comparative advantage in industry and its novel success in transforming what began as a commercial revolution into an industrial revolution. Success begat success, and it helped that competition and market growth increased with the dawning of the free-trade era from the second quarter of the nineteenth century. From this time the institutions, technologies and economic structures of the industrial revolution spread rapidly beyond Britain so that other European economies began to experience rising prosperity. GDP per head turned decisively upwards in the southern Low Countries, Netherlands, Germany and Sweden from the 1820s, in Spain from the 1860s and, belatedly, in Italy from the 1870s, whose long post-Renaissance decline had finally come to an end (Figure 11.05). As had long been the case, however, growth remained strongest in the southern North Sea economies of Great Britain, the southern Low Countries, and the Netherlands, joined now by Germany.

While this great economic reversal had been taking place within Europe, an even greater divergence had opened between the economies of westernmost and easternmost Eurasia. At the opening of the second millennium, long before Europe's high-medieval commercial revolution, China under the Northern Song Dynasty had led the world in GDP per head. The trickle of European traders, travellers and missionaries who ventured to Cathay following the Mongol conquests of the thirteenth century were awed by the technological, commercial and administrative sophistication of the society they encountered, nowhere more so than in the Yangzi Delta. Yet at the height of its Renaissance prosperity GDP per head in Italy was probably at least as great as that of the most developed parts of China and from the sixteenth century, as European economic leadership passed to the southern North Sea region, China and the rest of Asia began to fall behind.

The era of European world hegemony had dawned. It was not just that Western Europe's growth performance was improving; it was also that China's was declining, to the extent that by 1750 Chinese GDP per head was no greater than that of England at the time that Marco, Niccolò and Maffeo Polo had travelled to the Chinese court of Kublai Khan (Table 10.02).

China's economic difficulties were not, however, shared by Japan, which constitutes Asia's great economic exception. Until 1600 Japanese GDP per head had remained low by Western European standards, at less than $600. Nonetheless, it had been trending slowly upwards since the tenth century so that by the late eighteenth century GDP per head in Japan was greater than that of China and in the nineteenth century this upward trend became more marked so that by 1850 Japanese exceeded Chinese GDP per head by a substantial margin (Table 10.02). This Asian reversal of fortunes thus mirrors that occurring in Europe at around the same time, with both adding complexity to comparisons of European and Asian economic development. In fact, the gradual rise of Japan, the first Asian economy to achieve modern economic growth, in some ways parallels that of Britain in Europe, although with the caveat that until the 1980s Britain remained decisively ahead. Both insular economies began to develop early but were long overshadowed by bigger and richer continental neighbours. Growth was slow and uneven but improvements in GDP per head were steadily consolidated and rarely for long reversed. In each case the breakthrough to sustained growth came relatively late and proved both transformative and enduring. Since the gestation of economic growth was protracted, the experience of each emphasises the importance of understanding the historical roots from which modern economic growth eventually emerged.

Bibliography

Abū 'l-Fazl [1595] (1927), *The Ā' īn-i-Akbarī*, trans. H. Blochman, Delhi: Low Price Publications.

Abu-Lughod, J.L. (1989), *Before European hegemony: the world system A.D. 1250–1350*, Oxford: Oxford University Press.

Acemoglu, D.; Johnson, S.; and Robinson, J. (2005), 'The rise of Europe: Atlantic trade, institutional change, and economic growth', *American Economic Review*, 95, 546–79.

Afton, B.; and Turner, M. E. (2000), 'The statistical base of agricultural performance in England and Wales, 1850–1914', 1755–2140 in E. J. T. Collins (ed.), *The agrarian history of England and Wales*, vol. VII, *1850–1950*, Cambridge: Cambridge University Press.

Agrarian history of England and Wales, 8 vols. (1967–2000), Cambridge: Cambridge University Press.

Agricultural Returns for Great Britain for 1871 (1871), British Parliamentary Papers LXIX, London: House of Commons.

Allen, M. (2001), 'The volume of the English currency, 1158–1470', *Economic History Review*, 54, 595–611.

 (2012), *Mints and money in medieval England*, Cambridge: Cambridge University Press.

Allen, R. C. (1988), 'Inferring yields from probate inventories', *Journal of Economic History*, 48, 117–25.

 (1992), *Enclosure and the yeoman: the agricultural development of the south midlands 1450–1850*, Oxford: Oxford University Press.

 (1994) 'Agriculture during the industrial revolution', 96–122 in R. Floud and D. McCloskey (eds.), *The economic history of Britain since 1700*, vol. I, *1700–1860*, 2nd edn, Cambridge: Cambridge University Press.

 (1999), 'Tracking the agricultural revolution in England', *Economic History Review*, 52, 209–25.

 (2000), 'Economic structure and agricultural productivity in Europe, 1300–1800', *European Review of Economic History*, 3, 1–25.

 (2001), 'The great divergence in European wages and prices from the middle ages to the First World War', *Explorations in Economic History*, 38, 411–47 (wages of labourers and craftsmen together with consumer price indices are available on the Global Prices and Incomes Database website at University of California, Davis: http://gpih.ucdavis.edu/Datafilelist.htm).

(2005) 'English and Welsh agriculture 1300–1850: output, inputs and income', unpublished paper presented at International Economic History Congress, Helsinki, Session 122, 'Progress, stasis, and crisis: demographic and economic developments in England and beyond, AD c.1000–c.1800', www.helsinki.fi/ie hc2006/papers3/Allen.pdf.

(2009a), *The British industrial revolution in global perspective*, Cambridge: Cambridge University Press.

(2009b), 'Engels' pause: technical change, capital accumulation, and inequality in the British industrial revolution', *Explorations in Economic History*, 46, 418–35.

(no date) 'Data: wages and price history', http://gpih.ucdavis.edu/Datafilelist.htm.

Allen, R. C.; and Weisdorf, J. (2011), 'Was there an "industrious revolution" before the industrial revolution? An empirical exercise for England, c. 1300–1830', *Economic History Review*, 64, 715–29.

Álvarez-Nogal, C.; and Prados de la Escosura, L. (2013), 'The rise and fall of Spain (1270–1850)', *Economic History Review*, 66, 1–37.

Angeles, L. (2008), 'GDP per capita or real wages? Making sense of conflicting views on pre-industrial Europe', *Explorations in Economic History*, 45, 147–63.

Anon. (1968), *A century of agricultural statistics: Great Britain 1866–1966*, London: HMSO.

Arkell, T. (2000), 'Interpreting probate inventories', 72–102 in T. Arkell, N. Evans and N. Goose (eds.), *When death do us part: understanding and interpreting the probate records of early modern England*, Oxford: Leopard's Head Press.

Ashton, T. S. (1948), *The industrial revolution*, London: Oxford University Press

Bailey, M. (1989), *A marginal economy? East-Anglian Breckland in the later middle ages*, Cambridge: Cambridge University Press.

Barron, C. M. (2000), 'London 1300–1540', 395–440 in D. M. Palliser (ed.), *The Cambridge urban history of Britain*, vol. I, *600–1540*, Cambridge: Cambridge University Press.

Bassino, J.-P.; Broadberry, S.; Fukao, K.; Gupta, B.; and Takashima, M. (2014), 'Japan and the Great Divergence, 725–1874', www2.lse.ac.uk/economicHistory/who sWho/profiles/sbroadberry.aspx

Baten, J.; and Zanden, J.-L. van (2008), 'Book production and the onset of modern economic growth', *Journal of Economic Growth*, 13, 217–35.

Bavel, B. van; and Zanden, J.-L. van (2004), 'The jump start of the Holland economy during the late medieval crisis, c.1350–c.1500', *Economic History Review*, 57, 503–32.

Bekar, C. T.; and Reed, C. G. (2013), 'Land markets and inequality: evidence from medieval England', *European Review of Economic History*, 17, 294–317.

Bennett, J. M. (1987), *Women in the medieval English countryside: gender and household in Brigstock before the plague*, Oxford: Oxford University Press.

Beresford, M. (1989), 'A review of historical research (to 1968)', 3–75 in M. Beresford and J. G. Hurst (eds.), *Deserted medieval villages*, Gloucester: Alan Sutton.

Beveridge, W. (1939), *Prices and wages in England from the twelfth to the nineteenth century*, vol. I, *Price tables: mercantile era*, London: Longmans, Green.

Bhat, P. N. M.; and Halli, S. S. (1999), 'Demography of bride prices and dowry: causes and consequences of the Indian marriage squeeze', *Population Studies*, 53, 129–48.

Biddick, K. (1989), *The other economy: pastoral husbandry on a medieval estate*, Berkeley: University of California Press.

Blanchard, I. S. W. (1974), 'Rejoinder: *stannator fabulosus*', *Agricultural History Review*, 22, 62–74.

(1978), 'Labour productivity and work psychology in the English mining industry, 1400–1600', *Economic History Review*, 31, 1–24.

(1996), *The middle ages: a concept too many?* Avonbridge: Newlees Press.

Bogart, D. (2005), 'Turnpike trusts and the transport revolution in eighteenth century England', *Explorations in Economic History*, 42, 479–508.

Bolt, J.; and Zanden, J.-L, van (2014), 'The Maddison project: collaborative research on historical national accounts', *Economic History Review*, 67, 627–51.

Bolton, J. L. (1980), *The medieval English economy, 1150–1500*, London: Dent.

Boserup, E, (1965), *The conditions of agricultural growth: the economics of agrarian change under population pressure*, London: Allen and Unwin.

(1981), *Population and technological change: a study in long-term trends*, Oxford: Blackwell.

Boulton, J. (2000), 'London 1540–1700', 315–46 in P. Clark (ed.), *The Cambridge urban history of Britain*, vol. II, *1540–1840*, Cambridge: Cambridge University Press.

Brenner, R. (1976), 'Agrarian class structure and economic development in pre-industrial Europe', *Past and Present*, 70, 30–75.

Bridbury, A. R. (1962), *Economic growth: England in the later middle ages*, London: Allen and Unwin.

Britnell, R. H. (2001), 'Specialization of work in England, 1100–1300', *Economic History Review*, 54, 1–16.

(2004), *Britain and Ireland 1050–1530: economy and society*, Oxford: Oxford University Press.

Britton, E. (1977), *The community of the vill: a study of family and village life in the fourteenth century*, Toronto: Macmillan.

Broadberry, S. N. (2014), 'Accounting for the Great Divergence', London School of Economics, www2.lse.ac.uk/economicHistory/whosWho/profiles/sbroadberry.aspx.

Broadberry, S. N.; and Gupta, B. (2006), 'The early modern Great Divergence: wages, prices and economic development in Europe and Asia, 1500–1800', *Economic History Review*, 59, 2–31.

(2009), 'Lancashire, India and shifting competitive advantage in cotton textiles, 1700–1850: the neglected role of factor prices', *Economic History Review*, 62, 279–305.

Broadberry, S. N.; Fremdling, R.; and Solar, P. (2010), 'Industry', 164–86 in S. N. Broadberry and K. H. O'Rourke (eds.), *The Cambridge economic history of modern Europe*, vol. I, *1700–1870*, Cambridge: Cambridge University Press.

Broadberry, S. N.; Leeuwen, B. van; and Zanden, J.-L. van (2012), 'Reversals of fortune: Holland, Britain and the rise of the North Sea area, 1270–1870', www2.lse.ac.uk/economicHistory/whosWho/profiles/sbroadberry.aspx.

Broadberry, S. N.; Campbell, B. M. S.; and Leeuwen, B. van (2013), 'When did Britain industrialise? The sectoral distribution of the labour force and labour productivity in Britain, 1381–1851', *Explorations in Economic History*, 50, 16–27.

Broadberry, S. N.; Custodis, J.; and Gupta, B. (2014a), 'India and the Great Divergence: an Anglo-Indian comparison of GDP per capita, 1600–1871', *Explorations in Economic History* (forthcoming).

Broadberry, S. N.; Guan, H.; and Li, D. (2014b), 'China, Europe and the Great Divergence: a study in historical national accounting', London School of Economics, www2.lse.ac.uk/economicHistory/whosWho/profiles/sbroadberry.aspx

Brook, T. (2010), *The troubled empire: China in the Yuan and Ming Dynasties*, Cambridge, Mass.: Harvard University Press.

Buyst, E. (2011), 'Towards estimates of long term growth in the southern Low Countries, c.1500–1846', unpublished paper presented at HI-POD Workshop *Quantifying long run economic development*, University of Warwick in Venice, Palazzo Pesaro Papafava.

Cameron, R. (1967), 'England, 1750–1844', 15–59 in R. Cameron (ed.), *Banking in the early stages of industrialization: a study in comparative economic history*, New York: Oxford University Press.

Campbell, B. M. S. (1980), 'Population change and the genesis of commonfields on a Norfolk manor', *Economic History Review*, 33, 174–92.

(1981), 'The population of early Tudor England: a re-evaluation of the 1522 Muster Returns and 1524 and 1525 Lay Subsidies', *Journal of Historical Geography*, 7, 145–54.

(1984), 'Population pressure, inheritance, and the land market in a fourteenth-century peasant community', 87–134 in R. M. Smith (ed.), *Land, kinship and lifecycle*, Cambridge: Cambridge University Press.

(1995), 'Measuring the commercialisation of seigneurial agriculture c.1300', 132–93 in R. H. Britnell and B. M. S. Campbell (eds.), *A commercialising economy: England 1086 to c.1300*, Manchester: Manchester University Press.

(1997), 'Economic rent and the intensification of English agriculture, 1086–1350', 225–50 in G. Astill and J. Langdon (eds.), *Medieval farming and technology: the impact of agricultural change in northwest Europe*, Leiden: Brill.

(2000), *English seigniorial agriculture, 1250–1450*, Cambridge: Cambridge University Press.

(2005), 'The agrarian problem in the early fourteenth century', *Past and Present*, 188, 3–70.

(2007), *Three centuries of English crop yields, 1211–1491*, www.cropyields.ac.uk.

(2008), 'Benchmarking medieval economic development: England, Wales, Scotland, and Ireland, c.1290', *Economic History Review*, 61, 896–945.

(2009), 'Four famines and a pestilence: harvest, price, and wage variations in England, thirteenth to nineteenth centuries', 23–56 in B. Liljewall, I. A. Flygare, U. Lange, L. Ljunggren and J. Söderberg (eds.), *Agrarhistoria på många sätt; 28 studier om manniskan och jorden. Festskrift till Janken Myrdal på hans 60-årsdag (Agrarian history many ways: 28 studies on humans and the land, Festschrift to Janken Myrdal 2009)*, Stockholm: KSLAB.

(2010), 'Nature as historical protagonist: environment and society in pre-industrial England', *Economic History Review*, 63, 281–314.

(2011), 'Panzootics, pandemics and climatic anomalies in the fourteenth century', 177–215 in B. Herrmann (ed.), *Beiträge zum göttinger umwelthistorischen Kolloquium 2010–2011*, Göttingen: Universitätsverlag Göttingen.

(2012), 'Grain yields on English demesnes after the Black Death', 121–74 in M. Bailey and S. H. Rigby (eds.), *Town and countryside in the age of the Black Death: essays in honour of John Hatcher*, Turnhout: Brepols.

(2014), 'National incomes and economic growth in pre-industrial Europe: insights from recent research', *Quaestiones Medii Aevi Novae*, 18, 167–96.

Campbell, B. M. S.; and Bartley, K. C. (2006), *England on the eve of the Black Death: an atlas of lay lordship, land and wealth, 1300–49*, Manchester: Manchester University Press.

Campbell, B. M. S.; and Ó Gráda, C. (2011), 'Harvest shortfalls, grain prices, and famines in pre-industrial England', *Journal of Economic History*, 71, 859–86.

Campbell, B.M.S.; and Overton, M. (1993), 'A new perspective on medieval and early modern agriculture: six centuries of Norfolk farming, c.1250–c.1850', *Past and Present*, 141, 38–105.

Campbell, B. M. S.; Galloway, J. A.; Keene, D. J.; and Murphy, M. (1993), *A medieval capital and its grain supply: agrarian production and distribution in the London region, c.1300*, No place: Historical Geography Research Group.

Campbell, B. M. S.; Bartley, K. C.; and Power, J. P. (1996), 'The demesne-farming systems of post Black Death England: a classification', *Agricultural History Review*, 44, 131–79.

Cantor, L. M. (1982), 'Introduction: the English medieval landscape', 17–24 in L. Cantor (ed.), *The English medieval landscape*, London: Croom Helm.

Carus-Wilson, E. M. (1941), 'An industrial revolution of the thirteenth century', *Economic History Review*, 1st series, 11, 39–60.

(1952), 'The woollen industry', 355–428 in M. M. Postan and E. W. Rich (eds.), *The Cambridge economic history of Europe*, vol. II, *Trade and industry in the middle ages*, Cambridge: Cambridge University Press.

Carus-Wilson, E. M.; and Coleman, O. (1963), *England's export trade, 1275–1547*, Oxford: Clarendon Press.

Chartres, J. A. (1985), 'The marketing of agricultural produce', 406–502 in J. Thirsk (ed.), *The agrarian history of England and Wales*, vol. V, *1640–1750*, Part II, *Agrarian change*, Cambridge: Cambridge University Press.

Cherry, J. (1994), 'Leather', 295–318 in J. Blair and N. Ramsay (eds.), *English medieval industries: craftsmen, techniques, products*, London: Hambledon.

Clark, C. (1951), *The conditions of economic progress*, 2nd edn, London: Macmillan.

Clark, G. (1991), 'Labour productivity in English agriculture, 1300–1860', 211–35 in B. M. S Campbell and M. Overton (eds.), *Land, labour and livestock: historical studies in European agricultural productivity*, Manchester: Manchester University Press.

(2004), 'The price history of English agriculture, 1209–1914', *Research in Economic History*, 22, 41–125.

(2005), 'The condition of the working-class in England, 1209–2004', *Journal of Political Economy*, 113, 1307–40.

(2006), *English prices and wages, 1209–1914*, Global Price and Income History Group, University of California, Davis, http://gpih.ucdavis.edu/Datafilelist. htm.

(2007a), 'The long march of history: farm wages, population and economic growth, England 1209–1869', *Economic History Review*, 60, 97–135.

(2007b), *A farewell to alms: a brief economic history of the world*, Princeton: Princeton University Press.

(2010a), 'The macroeconomic aggregates for England, 1209–1869', *Research in Economic History*, 27, 51–140.

(2010b), '1381 and the Malthus delusion', MPRA Paper 25466, http://mpra.ub.uni-muenchen.de/id/eprint/25466

(2011), 'Major growth or Malthusian stagnation? Farming in England 1209–1869', unpublished working paper, University of California at Davis.

(2013), '1381 and the Malthus delusion', *Explorations in Economic History*, 50, 4–15.

(2014), 'What were the British earnings and prices then? (new series)', *Measuring Worth*: www.measuringworth.com/ukearncpi/

Clark, G.; and Jacks, D. (2007), 'Coal and the industrial revolution, 1700–1860', *European Review of Economic History*, 11, 39–72.

Clark, G.; and Werf, Y. van der (1998), 'Work in progress? The industrious revolution', *Journal of Economic History*, 58, 830–43.

Clark, G.; Huberman, M.; and Lindert, P. H. (1995), 'A British food puzzle, 1770–1850', *Economic History Review*, 48, 215–37.

Clark, G.; Cummins, J.; and Smith, B. (2012), 'Malthus, wages, and preindustrial growth', *Journal of Economic History*, 72, 364–92.

Clark, P. (1976), 'The ownership of books in England, 1560–1640: the example of some Kentish townsfolk', 95–111 in L. Stone (ed.), *Schooling and society: studies in the history of education*, Baltimore: Johns Hopkins University Press.

Clark, P. (ed.) (2000), *The Cambridge urban history of Britain*, vol. II, *1540–1840*, Cambridge: Cambridge University Press.

Clarkson, L. A. (1966), 'The leather crafts in Tudor and Stuart England', *Agricultural History Review*, 14, 25–39.

(1989), 'The manufacture of leather', 466–85 in G. E. Mingay (ed.), *The agrarian history of England and Wales*, vol. VI, *1750–1850*, Cambridge: Cambridge University Press.

Clay, C. G. A. (1984), *Economic expansion and social change: England 1500–1700*, vol. II, *Industry, trade and government*, Cambridge: Cambridge University Press.

Cohn, S. K. Jr. (2007), 'After the Black Death: labour legislation and attitudes towards labour in late-medieval Western Europe', *Economic History Review*, 60, 457–85.

Coleman, D. C. (1977), *The economy of England, 1450–1750*, Oxford: Oxford University Press.

Colquhoun, P. (1806), *A treatise on indigence; exhibiting a general view of the national resources for productive labour; with propositions for ameliorating* the condition of the poor, and improving the moral habits and increasing the comforts of the labouring people, particularly the rising generation; by regulations of political economy, calculated to prevent poverty from descending into indigence, to produce sobriety and industry, to reduce the parochial rates of the kingdom, and generally to promote the happiness and security of the community at large, by the diminution of moral and penal offences, and the future prevention of crimes, London: J. Hatchard.

Connell, B.; Jones, A. G.; Redfern, R.; and Walker, D. (2012), *A bioarchaeological study of medieval burials on the site of St Mary Spital: excavations at Spitalfields Market, London E1, 1991–2007*, London: Museum of London Archaeology.

Coppock, J. T. (1984), 'Mapping the agricultural returns: a neglected tool of historical geography', 8–55 in M. Reed (ed.), *Discovering past landscapes*, London: Croom Helm.

Cornwall, J. (1970), 'English population in the early sixteenth century', *Economic History Review*, 23, 32–44.

   ed. (1980), *The county community under Henry VIII: the military survey, 1522 and the lay subsidy, 1524–5*, Oakham: Rutland Record Society.

Crafts, N. F. R. (1976), 'English economic growth in the eighteenth century: a re-examination of Deane and Cole's estimates', *Economic History Review*, 29, 226–35.

   (1985), *British economic growth during the industrial revolution*, Oxford: Oxford University Press.

   (1989), 'British industrialization in an international context', *Journal of Interdisciplinary History*, 19, 415–28.

   (2004), 'Steam as a general purpose technology: a growth accounting perspective', *Economic Journal*, 114, 338–51.

Crafts, N. F. R.; and Harley, C. K. (1992), 'Output growth and the British industrial revolution: a restatement of the Crafts–Harley view', *Economic History Review*, 45, 703–70.

Crafts, N. F. R.; Leybourne, S. J.; and Mills, T. C. (1989), 'Trends and cycles in British industrial production, 1700–1913', *Journal of the Royal Statistical Society, Series A*, 152, 43–60.

Cressy, D. (1980), *Literacy and the social order: reading and writing in Tudor and Stuart England*, Cambridge: Cambridge University Press.

Darby, H. C. (1977), *Domesday England*, Cambridge: Cambridge University Press.

Davies, R. S. W.; and Pollard, S. (1988), 'The iron industry, 1750–1850', 73–104 in C. H. Feinstein and S. Pollard (eds.), *Studies in capital formation in the United Kingdom, 1750–1920*, Oxford: Clarendon Press.

Davis, R. (1954), 'English foreign trade, 1660–1700', *Economic History Review*, 7, 150–66.

(1962), *The rise of the English shipping industry in the seventeenth and eighteenth centuries*, London: Macmillan.

(1973), *English overseas trade, 1500–1700*, London: Macmillan.

Deane, P.; and Cole, W. A. (1962), *British economic growth, 1688–1959: trends and structure*, Cambridge: Cambridge University Press.

(1967), *British economic growth, 1688–1959: trends and structure*, 2nd Edn, Cambridge: Cambridge University Press.

Deaton, A.; and Muellbauer, J. (1980), *Economics and consumer behaviour*, Cambridge: Cambridge University Press.

DeWindt, E. B. (1972), *Land and people in Holywell-Cum-Needingworth: structures of tenure and patterns of social organization in an east midlands village, 1252–1457*, Toronto: Pontifical Institute of Mediaeval Studies.

Dittmar, J. (2011), 'Information technology and economic change: the impact of the printing press', *Quarterly Journal of Economics*, 126, 1133–72.

Dodds, B. (2004), 'Estimating arable output using Durham Priory tithe receipts, 1341–1450', *Economic History Review*, 57, 245–85.

(2007), *Peasants and production in the medieval North-East: the evidence from tithes 1270–1536*, Woodbridge: Boydell and Brewer.

Dyer, A. (2000), 'Appendix: ranking lists of English medieval towns', 747–70 in D. M. Palliser (ed.), *The Cambridge urban history of Britain*, vol. I, 600–1540, Cambridge: Cambridge University Press.

Dyer, C. C. (1982), 'Deserted medieval villages in the west midlands', *Economic History Review*, 35, 19–34.

(1988), 'Changes in diet in the late middle ages: the case of harvest workers', *Agricultural History Review*, 36, 21–38.

(1989), *Standards of living in the later middle ages: social change in England c.1200–1520*, Cambridge: Cambridge University Press.

(2000), 'Small towns 1270–1540', 505–37 in D. M. Palliser (ed.), *The Cambridge urban history of Britain*, vol. I, 600–1540, Cambridge: Cambridge University Press.

(2012), 'Poverty and its relief in late medieval England', *Past and Present*, 216, 41–78.

Ecclestone, M. J. (1996), 'Dairy production on the Glastonbury Abbey demesnes 1258–1334', unpublished M.A. dissertation, University of Bristol.

Ellison, T. [1886] (1968), *The cotton trade of Great Britain*, reprint of original edition, New York: Augustus Kelly.

Epstein, S. R. (2000), *Freedom and growth: the rise of states and markets in Europe, 1300–1750*, London: Routledge.

Fairbank, J. K. (1992), *China: a new history*, Cambridge, Mass.: Harvard University Press.

Farmer, D. L. (1988), 'Prices and wages', 715–817 in H. E. Hallam (ed.), *The agrarian history of England and Wales*, vol. II, *1042–1350*, Cambridge: Cambridge University Press.

(1991), 'Prices and wages, 1350–1500', 431–525 in E. Miller (ed.), *The agrarian history of England and Wales*, vol. III, *1348–1500*, Cambridge: Cambridge University Press.

Farnie, D. A. (2003), 'Cotton, 1780–1914', 721–60 in D. Jenkins (ed.), *The Cambridge history of Western textiles*, Cambridge: Cambridge University Press.

Feinstein, C. H. (1972), *National income, expenditure and output of the United Kingdom, 1855–1965*, Cambridge: Cambridge University Press.

(1978), 'Capital formation in Great Britain', 28–96 in P. Mathias and M. M. Postan (eds.), *The Cambridge economic history of Europe*, vol. VII, *The industrial economies: capital, labour and enterprise*, Part I, *Britain, France, Germany and Scandinavia*, Cambridge: Cambridge University Press.

(1988), 'National statistics, 1760–1920: sources and methods of estimation for domestic reproducible fixed assets, stocks and works in progress, overseas assets, and land', 257–471 in C. H. Feinstein and S. Pollard (eds.), *Studies in capital formation in the United Kingdom, 1750–1920*, Oxford: Clarendon Press.

(1995), 'Changes in nominal wages, the cost of living and real wages in the United Kingdom over two centuries, 1780–1990', 3–36 in P. Scholliers and V. Zamagni (eds.), *Labour's reward: real wages and economic change in nineteenth- and twentieth-century Europe*, Aldershot: Elgar.

Fenwick, C. C., ed. (1998), *The poll taxes of 1377, 1379 and 1381*, Part 1, *Bedfordshire – Leicestershire*, Oxford: British Academy and Oxford University Press.

ed. (2001), *The poll taxes of 1377, 1379 and 1381*, Part 2, *Lincolnshire – Westmorland*, Oxford: British Academy and Oxford University Press.

ed. (2005), *The poll taxes of 1377, 1379 and 1381*, Part 3, *Wiltshire – Yorkshire*, Oxford: British Academy and Oxford University Press.

Field, J.; and Erickson, A. (2009), 'Prospects and preliminary work on female occupational structure in England from 1500 to the national census', Occupations Project Paper 18, Cambridge: Cambridge Group for the History of Population and Social Structure, www.geog.cam.ac.uk/research/projects/occupations/abstracts/.

Fisher, F. J. (1935), 'The development of the London food market, 1540–1640', *Economic History Review*, 1st series, 5, 46–54.

(1940), 'Commercial trends and policy in sixteenth-century England', *Economic History Review*, 1st series, 10, 95–117.

(1948), 'The development of London as a centre of conspicuous consumption in the sixteenth and seventeenth century', *Transactions of the Royal Historical Society*, 4th series, 30, 37–50.

(1950), 'London's export trade in the early seventeenth century', *Economic History Review*, 3, 151–61.

Flinn, M. W. (1958), 'The growth of the English iron industry, 1660–1760', *Economic History Review*, 11, 144–53.

(1984), *The history of the British coal industry*, vol. II, *1700–1830: The industrial revolution*, Oxford: Clarendon Press.

Floud, R.; Fogel, R. W.; Harris, B.; and Hong, S. C. (2011), *The changing body: health, nutrition, and human development in the Western world since 1700*, Cambridge: Cambridge University Press.

Floud, R.; Wachter, K.; and Gregory, A. (1990), *Height, health and history: nutritional status in the United Kingdom, 1750–1980*, Cambridge: Cambridge University Press.

Fussell, G. E. (1963), 'The evolution of farm dairy machinery in England', *Agricultural History*, 37, 217–24.

Galor, O.; and Weil, D. N. (2000), 'Population, technology, and growth: from Malthusian stagnation to the demographic transition and beyond', *American Economic Review*, 90, 806–28.

Geertz, C. (1963), *Agricultural involution: the processes of ecological change in Indonesia*, Berkeley: University of California Press.

Ginarlis, J.; and Pollard, S. (1988), 'Roads and waterways', 182–224 in C. H. Feinstein and S. Pollard (eds.), *Studies in capital formation in the United Kingdom, 1750–1920*, Oxford: Oxford University Press.

Glennie, P. (1991), 'Measuring crop yields in early modern England', 255–83 in B. M. S. Campbell and M. Overton (eds.), *Land, labour and livestock: historical studies in European agricultural productivity*, Manchester: Manchester University Press.

Goldberg, P. J. P. (1990), 'Urban identity and the poll taxes of 1377, 1379, and 1381', *Economic History Review*, 43, 194–216.

Goldstone, J. A. (2002), 'Efflorescences and economic growth in world history: rethinking the "rise of the West" and the industrial revolution', *Journal of World History*, 13, 323–89.

Goose, N.; and Evans, N. (2000), 'Wills as an historical source', 38–71 in T. Arkell, N. Evans and N. Goose (eds.), *When death do us part: understanding and interpreting the probate records of early modern England*, Oxford: Leopard's Head Press.

Gottfried, R. S. (1978), *Epidemic disease in fifteenth century England: the medical response and the demographic consequences*, Leicester: Leicester University Press.

Gourvish, T. R.; and Wilson, R. G. (1994), *The British brewing industry, 1830–1980*, Cambridge: Cambridge University Press.

Grigg, D. (1989), *English agriculture: an historical perspective*, Oxford: Blackwell.

Grove, J. (2004), *Little Ice Ages, ancient and modern*, vol. II, 2nd edn, London: Routledge.

Guo, S. (2000), *Ethics and life: marriage behaviours in Qing Dynasty China*, Hong Kong: The Commercial Press.

Hajnal, J. (1965), 'European marriage patterns in perspective', 101–43 in D. V. Glass and D. E. C. Eversley (eds.), *Population in history: essays in historical demography*, London: Edward Arnold.

Hall, P., ed. (1966), *Von Thünen's isolated state: an English edition of* Der isolierte Staat *by Johann Heinrich von Thünen*, trans. C. M. Wartengerg, London: Pergamon.

Hallam, H. E. (1988), 'Population movements in England, 1086–1350', 508–93 in H. E Hallam (ed.), *The agrarian history of England and Wales*, vol. II, *1042–1350*, Cambridge: Cambridge University Press.

Hammersley, G. (1973), 'The charcoal iron industry and its fuel, 1540–1750', *Economic History Review*, 26, 593–613.

Hanawalt, B. A. (1979), *Crime and conflict in English communities, 1300–1348*, Cambridge, Mass.: Harvard University Press.

Harley, C. K. (1982), 'British industrialization before 1841: evidence of slower growth during the industrial revolution', *Journal of Economic History*, 42, 267–89.

(1988), 'Ocean freight rates and productivity, 1740–1913: the primacy of mechanical invention reaffirmed', *Journal of Economic History*, 48, 851–76.

(1998), 'Cotton textile prices and the industrial revolution', *Economic History Review*, 61, 49–83.

Harvey, B. (1993), *Living and dying in England, 1100–1540: the monastic experience*, Oxford: Oxford University Press.

Harvey, S. (1988), 'Domesday England', 45–136 in H. E. Hallam (ed.), *The agrarian history of England and Wales*, vol. II, *1042–1350*, Cambridge: Cambridge University Press.

Hatcher, J. (1973), *English tin production and trade before 1550*, Oxford: Clarendon Press.

(1977), *Plague, population and the English economy, 1348–1530*, London: Macmillan.

(1986), 'Mortality in the fifteenth century: some new evidence', *Economic History Review*, 39, 19–38.

(1993), *The history of the British coal industry*, vol. I, *Before 1700: towards the age of coal*, Oxford: Oxford University Press.

(1994), 'England in the aftermath of the Black Death', *Past and Present* 144, 3–35.

(2002), 'The great slump of the mid-fifteenth century', 237–72 in R. H. Britnell and J. Hatcher (eds.), *Progress and problems in medieval England: essays in honour of Edward Miller*, Cambridge: Cambridge University Press.

(2011), 'Unreal wages: long run living standards and the "golden age" of the fifteenth century?', 1–24 in B. Dodds and C. D. Liddy (eds.), *Commercial activity, markets and entrepreneurs in the middle ages: essays in honour of Richard Britnell*, Woodbridge: Boydell.

Hatcher, J.; and Bailey, M. (2001), *Modelling the middle ages: the history and theory of England's economic development*, Oxford: Oxford University Press.

Hatcher, J.; and Barker, T. C. (1974), *A history of English pewter*, London: Longman.

Hatcher, J.; Piper, A. J.; and Stone, D. (2006), 'Monastic mortality: Durham Priory, 1395–1529', *Economic History Review*, 59, 667–87.

Hayami, A. (1967), 'Keizai Shakai no Seiretsu to sono Tokushitsu (The emergence of the economic society and its characteristics)', 3–18 in S. K. Gakkai (ed.), *Atarashii Edo Jidaizo o Motomete (In search of the historical image of the Edo period)*, Tokyo: Toyo Keizai Shinposha.

Hayami, A.; and Tsubouchi, Y., eds. (1990), *Economic and demographic development in rice producing societies: some aspects of East Asian economic history (1500–1900)*, Leuven: Leuven University Press.

Hersh, J.; and Voth, H.-J. (2009), 'Sweet diversity: colonial goods and the rise of European living standards after 1492', CEPR Discussion Paper DP7386. Available at SSRN: http://ssrn.com/abstract=1462015.

Higgs, E. (1987), 'Women, occupations and work in the nineteenth century censuses', *History Workshop Journal*, 23, 59–80.

Hindle, S. (2004), *On the parish? The micro-politics of poor relief in rural England c.1550–1750*, Oxford: Clarendon Press.

(2008), 'Dearth and the English revolution: the harvest crisis of 1647–50', *Economic History Review*, 61 S1, 64–98.

Hoffman, P. T.; Jacks, D.; Levin, P. A.; and Lindert, P. H. (2002), 'Real inequality in Europe since 1500', *Journal of Economic History*, 62, 322–55.

Hoffmann, W. G. (1955), *British industry 1700–1950*, Oxford: Blackwell.

Holderness, B. A. (1989), 'Prices, productivity, and output', 84–189 in G. E. Mingay (ed.), *The agrarian history of England and Wales*, vol. VI, *1750–1850*, Cambridge: Cambridge University Press.

Hollingsworth, T. H. (1969), *Historical demography*, London: Hodder and Stoughton.

Homer, R. F. (1991), 'Tin, lead and pewter', 57–80 in J. Blair and N. Ramsay (eds.), *English medieval industries: craftsmen, techniques, products*, London: Continuum International Publishing Group.

Horrell, S.; Humphries, J.; and Weale, M. (1994), 'An input–output table for 1841', *Economic History Review*, 47, 545–66.

Houstan, R. A. (1982), 'The development of literacy: northern England, 1640–1750', *Economic History Review*, 35, 199–216.

Huang, P. C. C. (2002), 'Development or involution in eighteenth-century Britain and China? A review of Kenneth Pomeranz's "The Great Divergence: China, Europe and the making of the modern world economy"', *Journal of Asian Studies*, 61, 501–38.

Hulton, M. H. M., ed. (1999), *Coventry and its people in the 1520s*, Stratford-upon-Avon: The Dugdale Society.

Humphries, J. (2010), *Childhood and child labour in the British industrial revolution*, Cambridge: Cambridge University Press.

Hyde, C. K. (1977), *Technological change and the British iron industry, 1700–1870*, Princeton: Princeton University Press.

James, M. K.; and Veale, E. M. (1971), *Studies in the medieval wine trade*, Oxford: Clarendon Press.

John, A. H. (1976), 'English agricultural improvements and grain exports, 1660–1765', 45–67 in, D. C. Coleman and A. H. John (eds), *Trade, government and economy in pre-industrial England*, London: Weidenfeld and Nicolson.

(1989), 'Statistical appendix', 972–1155 in G. E. Mingay (ed.), *The agrarian history of England and Wales*, vol. VI, *1750–1850*, Cambridge, Cambridge University Press.

Jones, E. L. (1965), 'Agriculture and economic growth in England, 1660–1750: agricultural change', *Journal of Economic History*, 25, 1–18.

Kain, R. J. P. (1986), *An atlas and index of the tithe files of mid-nineteenth century England and Wales*, Cambridge: Cambridge University Press.

Kanzaka, J. (2002), 'Villein rents in thirteenth–century England: an analysis of the Hundred Rolls of 1279–80', *Economic History Review*, 55, 593–618.

Karaman, K. K.; and Pamuk, S. (2010), 'Ottoman state finances in European perspective, 1500–1914', *Journal of Economic History*, 70, 593–629.

Kelly, M.; and Ó Gráda, C. (2012), 'The *preventive check* in medieval and preindustrial England', *Journal of Economic History*, 72, 1015–35.

(2013), '*Numerare est errare*: agricultural output and food supply in England before and during the industrial revolution', *Journal of Economic History*, 73, 1132–63.

Kermode, J. (2000), 'The greater towns', 441–65 in D. M. Palliser (ed.), *The Cambridge urban history of Britain*, vol. I, *600–1540*, Cambridge: Cambridge University Press.

Kerridge, E. (1967), *The agricultural revolution*, London: George Allen and Unwin.

(1985), *Textile manufactures in early modern England*, Manchester: Manchester University Press.

King, G. [1696] (1936), 'Natural and political observations and conclusions upon the state and condition of England', 11–56 in G. E. Barnett (ed.), *Two tracts by Gregory King*, Baltimore: Johns Hopkins University Press.

King, P. (2005), 'The production and consumption of bar iron in early modern England and Wales', *Economic History Review*, 58, 1–33.

Kitsikopoulos, H. (2012), 'Epilogue', 330–60 in H. Kitsikopoulos (ed.), *Agrarian change and crisis in Europe, 1200–1500*, London: Routledge.

Komlos, J. (1993), 'The secular trend in the biological standard of living in the United Kingdom, 1730–1860', *Economic History Review*, 46, 115–44.

(1998), 'Shrinking in a growing economy? The mystery of physical stature during the industrial revolution', *Journal of Economic History*, 58, 779–802.

Kussmaul, A. (1990), *A general view of the rural economy of England, 1538–1840*, Cambridge: Cambridge University Press.

Kuznets, S. (1955), 'Economic growth and income inequality', *American Economic Review*, 45, 1–28.

(1966), *Modern economic growth: rate, structure and spread*, New Haven: Yale University Press.

Langdon, J. (1982), 'The economics of horses and oxen in medieval England', *Agricultural History Review*, 30, 31–40.

(1986), *Horses, oxen and technological innovation: the use of draught animals in English farming from 1066 to 1500*, Cambridge: Cambridge University Press.

Langton, J.; and Hoppe, G. (1983), *Town and country in the development of early modern Western Europe*, Historical Geography Research Series 11, Norwich: Geo Books.

Le Roy Ladurie, E. (1966), *Les Paysans de Languedoc*, Paris: S. E. V. P. E. N. English edition (1974), *The peasants of Languedoc*, trans. J. Day, Urbana: University of Illinois Press.

Lee, C. H. (1986), *The British economy since 1700: a macroeconomic perspective*, Cambridge: Cambridge University Press.

Lee, J. Z.; and Wang, F. (1999), *One quarter of humanity: Malthusian mythology and Chinese realities*, Cambridge, Mass.: Harvard University Press.

Lee, R. D. (1985), 'Inverse projection and back projection: a critical appraisal, and comparative results for England, 1539 to 1871, *Population Studies*, 39, 233–48.

Leunig, T. (2011), 'Measuring economic performance and social progress', *European Review of Economic History*, 15, 357–63.

Lennard, R. V. (1959), *Rural England 1986 to 1135: a study of social and agrarian conditions*, Oxford: Clarendon Press.

Letters, S. (2005), *Gazetteer of markets and fairs in England and Wales to 1516*, London: Centre for Metropolitan History, www.british-history.ac.uk/source.a spx?pubid=272.

Lewis, G. R. (1908), *The stannaries: a study of the medieval tin miners of Cornwall and Devon*, Cambridge, Mass.: Harvard University Press.

Lindert, P. H.; and Williamson, J. G. (1982), 'Revising England's social tables 1688–1913', *Explorations in Economic History*, 19, 385–408.

Livi-Bacci, M. (1991), *Population and nutrition: an essay on European demographic history*, trans. T. Croft-Murray and C. Ipsen, Cambridge: Cambridge University Press.

Lloyd, T. H. (1977), *The English wool trade in the middle ages*, Cambridge: Cambridge University Press.

Lo Cascio, E., and Malanima, P. (2009), 'GDP in pre-modern agrarian economies (1–1820 AD): a revision of the estimates', *Rivista di storia economica*, 25, 391–420.

Lopez, R. S. (1976), *The commercial revolution of the middle ages, 950–1350*, Cambridge: Cambridge University Press.

Maddison, A. (2001), *The world economy: a millennial perspective*, Paris: Organisation for Economic Co-operation and Development.

(2003), *The world economy: historical statistics*, Paris: Organisation for Economic Co-operation and Development.

(2007), *Contours of the world economy, 1–2030 AD: essays in macro-economic history*, Oxford: Oxford University Press.

(2010), 'Statistics on world population, GDP and per capita GDP, 1–2008 AD', Groningen Growth and Development Centre, www.ggdc.net/MADDISON/ori index.htm

Maitland, F. W. (1897), *Domesday Book and beyond: three essays in the early history of England*, Cambridge: Cambridge University Press.

Malanima, P. (2002), *L'economia italiana: dalla crescita medievale alla crescita contemporanea*, Bologna: Il Mulino.

(2011), 'The long decline of a leading economy: GDP in central and northern Italy, 1300–1913', *European Review of Economic History*, 15, 169–219.

Malthus, T. R. [1798] (1970), *An essay on the principle of population, as it affects the future improvement of society with remarks on the speculations of Mr Godwin, M. Condorcet, and other writers*, Harmondsworth: Penguin.

[1803] (1992), *An essay on the principle of population: or, a view of its past and present effects on human happiness: with an inquiry into our prospects respecting the future removal or mitigation of the evils which it occasions*, 2nd edn, ed. D. Winch and P. James, Cambridge, Cambridge University Press.

Marshall, E. J. P.; Wade, P. M.; and Clare, P. (1978), 'Land drainage channels in England and Wales', *Geographical Journal*, 144, 254–63.

Massie, J. [1760] (2010), *A computation of the money that hath been exorbitantly raised upon the people of Great Britain by the sugar-planters, in one year, from January 1759 to January 1760; shewing how much money a family of each rank, degree or class hath lost by that rapacious monopoly having continued so long after I laid it open, in my state of the British sugar-colony trade, which was published last winter*, London: The Making of the Modern World, Gale, Cengage Learning.

Mathias, P. (1959), *The brewing industry in England, 1700–1830*, Cambridge: Cambridge University Press.

Mayhew, N. J. (1995a), 'Modelling medieval monetisation', 55–77 in R. H. Britnell and B. M. S. Campbell (eds.), *A commercialising economy: England 1086 to c.1300*, Manchester: Manchester University Press.

(1995b), 'Population, money supply, and the velocity of circulation in England, 1300–1700', *Economic History Review*, 48, 238–57.

(2009), 'Money supply and GDP in England 1085–1700', unpublished paper presented at Session E4, 15th World Economic History Congress, Utrecht.

McCance, R. A.; and Widdowson, E. M. (1960), *The composition of foods*, Medical Research Council Special Report Series, 297 (3rd revised edn of Special Report No. 235), London: HMSO.

McIntosh, M. K. (1986), *Autonomy and community: the royal manor of Havering, 1200–1500*, Cambridge: Cambridge University Press.

(2012), *Poor relief in England, 1350–1600*, Cambridge: Cambridge University Press.

Milanovic, B.; Lindert, P. H.; and Williamson J. G. (2007), *Measuring ancient inequality*, National Bureau of Economic Research, working paper 13550, www.nber. org/papers/w13550; Washington, D.C.: World Bank, https://openknowledge.wor ldbank.org/handle/10986/7630.

Mitchell, B. R. (1988), *British historical statistics*, Cambridge: Cambridge University Press.

Mokyr, J. (1990), *The lever of riches: technological creativity and economic progress*, Oxford: Oxford University Press.

Mokyr, J.; and Voth, H. J. (2010), 'Understanding growth in Europe, 1700–1870: theory and evidence', 7–42 in S. N. Broadberry and K. O'Rourke (eds.), *The Cambridge economic history of modern Europe*, vol. I, 1700–1870, Cambridge: Cambridge University Press.

Moor, T. de; and Zanden, J. L. van (2010), 'Girl power: the European marriage pattern and labour markets in the North Sea region in the late medieval and early modern period', *Economic History Review*, 63, 1–33.

Morris, R. (1979), *Cathedrals and abbeys of England and Wales: the building church, 600–1540*, London: Dent.

Mosk, C. (1980), 'Nuptiality in Meiji Japan', *Journal of Social History*, 13, 474–89.

Muldrew, C. (2011), *Food, energy and the creation of industriousness: work and material culture in agrarian England, 1550–1780*, Cambridge: Cambridge University Press.

Munro, J. H. (1999), 'The "industrial crisis" of the English textile towns, 1290–1330', 103–41 in M. Prestwich, R. H. Britnell and R. Frame (eds.), *Thirteenth-century England VII: proceedings of the Durham conference*, Woodbridge: Boydell and Brewer.

(2004), 'Medieval woollens: the Western European woollen industries and their struggle for international markets, c. 1000–1500', 228–324 in D. Jenkins (ed.), *The Cambridge history of Western textiles*, Cambridge: Cambridge University Press.

(no date), 'The Phelps Brown and Hopkins "basket of consumables" commodity price series and craftsmen's wage series, 1264–1700: revised by John H. Munro', www.economics.utoronto.ca/munro5/ResearchData.html.

Musson, A. E. (1976), 'Industrial motive power in the United Kingdom, 1800–70', *Economic History Review*, 29, 415–39.

(1978), *The growth of British industry*, London: Batsford.

Neal, L. (1990), *The rise of financial capitalism: international capital markets in the Age of Reason*, Cambridge: Cambridge University Press.

Nef, J. U. (1932), *The rise of the British coal industry*, vol. II, London: Routledge and Kegan Paul.

(1934), 'The progress of technology and the growth of large-scale industry in Great Britain, 1540–1640', *Economic History Review*, 1st series, 5, 3–24.

North, D. C.; and Weingast, B. R. (1989), 'Constitutions and commitment: the evolution of institutions governing public choice in seventeenth-century England,' *Journal of Economic History*, 49, 803–32.

O'Brien, P. K. (1982), 'European economic development: the contribution of the periphery', *Economic History Review*, 35, 1–18.

(2011), 'The nature and historical evolution of an exceptional fiscal state and its possible significance for the precocious commercialization and industrialization of the British economy from Cromwell to Nelson', *Economic History Review*, 64, 408–46.

O'Brien, P. K.; and Hunt, P. A. (1999), 'England, 1485–1815', 53–100 in R. Bonney (ed.), *The rise of the fiscal state in Europe, c. 1200–1850*, Oxford: Oxford University Press.

Oeppen, J. (1993), 'Back projection and inverse projection: members of a wider class of constrained projection models', *Population Studies*, 47, 245–67.

Oldland, J. (2013), 'Wool and cloth production in late medieval and early Tudor England', *Economic History Review*, 67, 25–47.

Ormrod, D. (2003), *The rise of commercial empires: England and the Netherlands in the age of mercantilism, 1650–1770*, Cambridge: Cambridge University Press.

Ormrod, W. M. (1990), *The regin of Edward III: crown and political society in England, 1327–1377*, New Haven: Yale University Press.

Orwin, C. S.; and Whetham, E. H. (1971) *History of British agriculture, 1846–1914*, 2nd edn, Newton Abbot: David and Charles.

Outhwaite, R. B. (1986), 'Progress and backwardness in English agriculture, 1500–1650', *Economic History Review*, 39, 1–18.

Overton, M. (1979), 'Estimating crop yields from probate inventories: an example from East Anglia, 1585–1735', *Journal of Economic History*, 39, 363–78.

(1984), 'Probate inventories and the reconstruction of agrarian landscapes', 167–94 in M. Reed (ed.), *Discovering past landscapes*, London: Croom Helm.

(1985), 'The diffusion of agricultural innovations in early modern England: turnips and clover in Norfolk and Suffolk 1580–1740', *Transactions of the Institute of British Geographers*, new series, 10, 205–21.

(1986), 'Agriculture', 34–53 in J. Langton and R. J. Morris (eds.), *Atlas of industrializing Britain 1780–1914*, London: Methuen.

(1990), 'Re-estimating crop yields from probate inventories: a comment', *Journal of Economic History*, 50, 931–35.

(1991), 'The determinants of crop yields in early modern England', 284–322 in B. M. S. Campbell and M. Overton (eds.), *Land, labour and livestock: historical studies in European agricultural productivity*, Manchester: Manchester University Press.

(1996), *Agricultural revolution in England: the transformation of the agrarian economy 1500–1850*, Cambridge: Cambridge University Press.

(2000), 'Prices from probate inventories', 120–43 in T. Arkell, N. Evans and N. Goose (eds.), *When death do us part: understanding and interpreting the probate records of early modern England*, Oxford: Leopard's Head Press.

(2006), 'Household wealth, indebtedness, and economic growth in early modern England', Open Research Exeter, http://hdl.handle.net/10036/4073.

Overton, M.; and Campbell, B. M. S. (1992), 'Norfolk livestock farming 1250–1740: a comparative study of manorial accounts and probate inventories', *Journal of Historical Geography*, 18, 377–96.

(1996), 'Production et productivité dans l'agriculture anglais, 1086–1871', *Histoire et Mesure*, 11, 255–97.

(1999), 'Statistics of production and productivity in English agriculture, 1086–1871', 189–208 in B. J. P. van Bavel and E. Thoen (eds.), *Land productivity* and agro-systems in the North Sea area (middle ages – twentieth century): elements for comparison, Turnhout: Brepols.

Overton, M.; Whittle, J.; Dean, D.; and Hann, A. (2004), *Production and consumption in English households, 1600–1750*, London: Routledge.

Parker, G. (2013), *Global crisis: war, climate change and catastrophe in the seventeenth century*, New Haven: Yale University Press.

Parthasarathi, P. (2011), *Why Europe grew rich and Asia did not: global economic divergence, 1600–1850*, Cambridge: Cambridge University Press.

Pearson, R. (2004), *Insuring the industrial revolution: fire insurance in Great Britain, 1700–1850*, Aldershot: Ashgate.

Perren, R. (1975), 'The meat and livestock trade in Britain, 1850–70', *Economic History Review*, 28, 385–400.

Persson, K. G. (2008), 'The Malthus delusion', *European Review of Economic History*, 12, 165–73.

(2010), *An economic history of Europe, 600 to the present*, Cambridge: Cambridge University Press.

Phelps Brown, H.; and Hopkins, S. V. (1955), 'Seven centuries of building wages', *Economica*, 22, 195–206.

(1956), 'Seven centuries of the prices of consumables, compared with builders' wage-rates', *Economica*, 23, 296–314.

Phillips, A. D. M. (1989), *The underdraining of farmland in England during the nineteenth century*, Cambridge: Cambridge University Press.

Platt, C. (1994), *The great rebuildings of Tudor and Stuart England*, London: University College London Press.

Pollard, S. (1980), 'A new estimate of British coal production, 1750–1850', *Economic History Review*, 33, 212–35.

Pomeranz, K. (2000), *The Great Divergence: China, Europe, and the making of the modern world economy*, Princeton: Princeton University Press.

(2011), 'Ten years after: responses and reconsiderations', *Historically Speaking*, 12, 20–5, https://muse.jhu.edu/login%3Fauth=0&type=summary&url=/journals/historically_speaking/v012/12.4.coclanis.html

Poos, L. (1991), *A rural society after the Black Death: Essex, 1350–1525*, Cambridge: Cambridge University Press.

Postan, M. M. (1962), 'Village livestock in the thirteenth century', *Economic History Review*, 15, 219–49.

(1966), 'Medieval agrarian society in its prime: England', 549–632 in M. M. Postan (ed.), *The Cambridge economic history of Europe*, vol. I, *The agrarian life of the middle ages*, 2nd edn, Cambridge: Cambridge University Press.

(1972), *The medieval economy and society: an economic history of Britain in the middle ages*, London: Weidenfeld and Nicolson.

Pound, J., ed. (1986), *The military survey of 1522 for Babergh Hundred*, Woodbridge: Suffolk Records Society and Boydell Press.

Power, J. P.; and Campbell, B. M. S. (1992), 'Cluster analysis and the classification of medieval demesne-farming systems', *Transactions of the Institute of British Geographers*, 17, 227–45.

Prange, S. (2011), 'A trade of no dishonor: piracy, commerce, and community in the western Indian Ocean, twelfth to sixteenth century', *American Historical Review*, 116, 1269–93.

Pressnell, L. S. (1956), *Country banking in the industrial revolution*, Oxford: Clarendon Press.

Prest, A. R. (1954), *Consumers' expenditure in the United Kingdom, 1900–1919*, Cambridge: Cambridge University Press.

Prince, H. C. (1980), *Parks in England*, Shalfleet: Pinhorns.

(1989), 'The changing rural landscape, 1750–1850', 7–83 in G. E. Mingay (ed.), *The agrarian history of England and Wales, VI, 1750–1850*, Cambridge: Cambridge University Press.

Rackham, O. (1980), *Ancient woodland*, London: Edward Arnold.

Raftis, J. A (1974), *Warboys: two hundred years in the life of a mediaeval village*, Toronto: Pontifical Institute of Mediaeval Studies.

(1990), *Early Tudor Godmanchester: survivals and new arrivals*, Toronto: Pontifical Institute of Mediaeval Studies.

Ramsey, P. H., ed. (1971), *The price revolution in sixteenth-century England*, London: Methuen.

Razi, Z. (1980), *Life, marriage and death in a medieval parish: economy, society and demography in Halesowen, 1270–1400*, Cambridge: Cambridge University Press.

Reid, D. A. (1976), 'The decline of Saint Monday 1766–1876', *Past and Present*, 71, 76–101.

Riden, P. (1977), 'The output of the British iron industry before 1870', *Economic History Review*, 30, 442–59.

Rigby, S. H. (2010), 'Urban population in late medieval England: the evidence of the lay subsidies', *Economic History Review*, 63, 393–417.

Rowntree, B. S. (1901), *Poverty: a study of town life*, London: Macmillan.

Russell, J. C. (1948), *British medieval population*, Albuquerque: University of New Mexico Press.

Saito, O. (2010), 'By-employment and historical occupational structures in comparative perspective', unpublished paper presented at the Annual Conference of the Economic History Society, University of Durham.

Sapoznik, A. (2013), 'The productivity of peasant agriculture: Oakington, Cambridgeshire, 1360–1399', *Economic History Review*, 66, 518–44.

Schofield, P. R. (1997), 'Dearth, debt and the local land market in a late thirteenth-century village community'. *Agricultural History Review*, 45, 1–17.

Schofield, R. S. (1973), 'Dimensions of illiteracy, 1750–1850', *Explorations in Economic History*, 10, 437–44.

(1994), 'British population change, 1700–1871', 60–95 in R. Floud and D. N. McCloskey (eds.), *The economic history of Britain since 1700*, vol. I, *1700–1860*, 2nd edn, Cambridge: Cambridge University Press.

Schön, L.; and Krantz, O. (2012), 'The Swedish economy in the early modern period: constructing historical national accounts', *European Review of Economic History*, 16, 529–49.

Schubert, H. R. (1957), *History of the British iron and steel industry from c. 450 BC to AD 1775*, London: Routledge and Kegan Paul.

Schumpeter, E. B. (1960), *English overseas trade statistics, 1697–1808*, Oxford: Clarendon Press.

Seebohm, F. (1883), *The English village community examined in its relations to the manorial and tribal systems and to the common or open field system of husbandry, an essay in economic history*, London: Longmans Green.

Shaw-Taylor, L. (2009a), 'The occupational structure of England and Wales, c.1750–1911', Occupations Project Paper 19, Cambridge: Cambridge Group for the History of Population and Social Structure, www.geog.cam.ac.uk/research/projects/occupations/abstracts/.

(2009b), 'The nature and scale of the cottage economy', Occupations Project Paper 15, Cambridge: Cambridge Group for the History of Population and Social Structure, www.hpss.geog.cam.ac.uk/research/projects/occupations/abstracts/.

Shaw-Taylor, L.; and Wrigley, E. A. (2008), 'The occupational structure of England c.1750–1871: a preliminary report', Cambridge: Cambridge Group for the History of Population and Social Structure.

Shaw-Taylor, L.; Wrigley, E. A.; Kitson, P.; Davies, R.; Newton, G.; and Satchell, M. (2010), 'The occupational structure of England, c.1710–1871', Occupations Project Paper 22, Cambridge: Cambridge Group for the History of Population and Social Structure, www.geog.cam.ac.uk/research/projects/occupations/abstracts/.

Slack, P. (1988), *Poverty and policy in Tudor and Stuart England*, London: Longman.

(1990), *The English poor law, 1531–1782*, Basingstoke: Macmillan.

Slavin, P. (2008), 'Feeding the brethren: grain provisioning of Norwich Cathedral Priory, c.1280–1370', unpublished PhD thesis, University of Toronto.

(2009), 'Chicken husbandry in late-medieval eastern England: c.1250–1400', *Anthropozoologica*, 44, 35–56.

(2010), 'Goose management and rearing in late medieval eastern England, c.1250–1400', *Agricultural History Review*, 58, 1–29.

Smith, A. [1776] (1880), *The wealth of nations*, vol. I, Oxford: Clarendon Press.

Smith, R. M. (1979), 'Some reflections on the evidence for the origins of the "European marriage pattern" in England', *Sociological Review Monograph*, 28, 74–112.

(1988), 'Human resources', 188–212 in G. Astill and A. Grant (eds.), *The country-side of medieval England*, Oxford: Blackwell.

(2012), 'Measuring adult mortality in an age of plague: England, 1349–1540', 43–85 in M. Bailey and S. H. Rigby (eds.), *Town and countryside in the age of the Black Death: essays in honour of John Hatcher*, Turnhout: Brepols.

Snooks, G. D. (1995), 'The dynamic role of the market in the Anglo-Norman econ-omy and beyond, 1086–1300', 27–54 in R. H. Britnell and B. M. S. Campbell (eds.), *A commercialising economy: England 1086 to c.1300*, Manchester: Manchester University Press.

Spufford, M. (1984), *The great reclothing of rural England: petty chapmen and their wares in the seventeenth century*, London: Hambledon Press.

Stephenson, M. J. (1988), 'Wool yields in the medieval economy', *Economic History Review*, 61, 368–91.

Stone, D. J. (2006), 'The consumption of field crops in late medieval England', 11–26 in C. M. Woolgar, D. Serjeantson and A. Waldron (eds.), *Food in medieval England: diet and nutrition*, Oxford: Oxford University Press.

Stone, L. (1949), 'Elizabethan overseas trade', *Economic History Review*, 2, 30–58.

Sullivan, R. J. (1989), 'England's "Age of Invention": the acceleration of patents and patentable invention during the industrial revolution', *Explorations in Economic History*, 26, 424–52.

Supple, B. E. (1964), *Commercial crisis and change in England, 1600–1642: a study in the instability of a mercantile economy*, Cambridge: Cambridge University Press.

Tashiro, K. (1982), 'Foreign relations during the Edo period: Sakoku re-examined', *Journal of Japanese Studies*, 8, 283–306.

Thirsk, J. (1985), 'Agricultural policy: public debate and legislation', 298–388 in J. Thirsk (ed.), *The agrarian history of England and Wales*, vol. V, *1640–1750*, Part II, *Agrarian change*, Cambridge: Cambridge University Press.

Thompson, F. M. L. (1976), 'Nineteenth-century horse sense', *Economic History Review*, 29, 60–81.

(1983), 'Horses and hay in Britain, 1830–1918', 50–72 in F. M. L. Thompson (ed.), *Horses in European economic history: a preliminary canter*, Reading: British Agricultural History Society.

Thorold Rogers, J. E. (1866–1902), *A history of agriculture and prices in England*, vols. I–VI, Oxford: Clarendon Press.

Thorpe, W. A. (1961), *English glass*, 3rd edn, London: A. and C. Black.

Thrupp, S. L. (1965), 'The problem of replacement rates in late medieval English population', *Economic History Review*, 18, 101–19.

Titow, J. Z. (1961), 'Some evidence of thirteenth-century population growth', *Economic History Review*, 14, 218–24.

Tunzelmann, G. N. von (1978), *Steam power and British industrialisation to 1860*, Oxford: Oxford University Press.

Turner, M. E. (1981), 'Arable in England and Wales: estimates from the 1801 crop return', *Journal of Historical Geography*, 7, 291–302.

(1998), 'Counting sheep: waking up to new estimates of livestock numbers in England', *Agricultural History Review*, 46, 142–61.

Turner, M. E.; Beckett, J. V.; and Afton, B. (2001), *Farm production in England 1700–1914*, Oxford: Oxford University Press.

Vancouver, C. (1808), *General view of agriculture of the county of Devon: drawn up for the consideration of the Board of Agriculture*, London: Richard Phillips.

Voigtländer, N.; and Voth, H.-J. (2013), 'How the West "invented" fertility restriction', *American Economic Review*, 103, 2227–64.

Voth, H.-J. (1998), 'Time and work in eighteenth-century London', *Journal of Economic History*, 58, 29–58.

(2001), 'The longest years: new estimates of labor input in England, 1760–1830', *Journal of Economic History*, 61, 1065–82.

(2004), 'Living standards and the urban environment', 268–94 in R. Floud and P. Johnson (eds.), *The Cambridge economic history of modern Britain*, vol. I, *Industrialisation, 1700–1860*, Cambridge: Cambridge University Press.

Vries, J. de (1984), *European urbanization 1500–1800*, London: Methuen.

(1994), 'The industrial revolution and the industrious revolution', *Journal of Economic History*, 54, 249–70.

(2008), *The industrious revolution: consumer behavior and the household economy, 1650 to the present*, Cambridge: Cambridge University Press.

Walker, J. T. (2008), 'National income in Domesday England', Discussion Paper em-dp2008-67, Henley Business School, University of Reading.

Wallerstein, I. (1980), *The modern world-system*, vol. II, *Mercantilism and the consolidation of the European world-economy, 1600–1750*, London: Academic Press.

Weatherill, L. (1983), 'The growth of the pottery industry in England, 1660–1815', *Post Medieval Archaeology*, 17, 15–46.

(1988), *Consumer behaviour and material culture in Britain, 1660–1760*, London: Routledge.

Weber, M. (1930), *The protestant ethic and the spirit of capitalism*, London: Allen and Unwin.

Weir, D. R. (1998), 'Malthus's theory of population', 290–93 in J. Eatwell and M. Milgate (eds.), *The new Palgrave: a dictionary of economics*, London: Macmillan.

Williamson, T. (2010), 'The origins of "champion" landscapes in midland England: new evidence from Northamptonshire', unpublished paper presented at the conference 'Rural history 2010', University of Sussex, 13 September 2010.

Woolgar, C. M.; Serjeantson, D.; and Waldron, T. (2006), 'Introduction', 1–8 in C. M. Woolgar, D. Serjeantson and T. Waldron (eds.), *Food in medieval England: diet and nutrition*, Oxford: Oxford University Press.

Wrigley, E. A. (1967), 'A simple model of London's importance in changing English society and economy 1650–1750', *Past and Present*, 37, 44–70.

(1985), 'Urban growth and agricultural change: England and the Continent in the early modern period', *Journal of Interdisciplinary History*, 15, 683–728.

(2000), 'The divergence of England: the growth of the English economy in the seventeenth and eighteenth centuries', *Transactions of the Royal Historical Society*, 6th series, 10, 117–41.

(2004), *Poverty, progress and population*, Cambridge: Cambridge University Press.

(2006a), 'Categorising occupations: the primary, secondary, tertiary (PST) system', Department of Geography, University of Cambridge, www.geog.cam.ac.uk/res earch/projects/occupations/categorisation/.

(2006b), 'The transition to an advanced organic economy: half a millennium of English agriculture', *Economic History Review* 59, 435–80.

(2009), 'Rickman revisited: the population growth rates of English counties in the early modern period', *Economic History Review*, 62, 711–35.

(2011), *The early English censuses*, British Academy Records of Social and Economic History, Oxford: Oxford University Press.

Wrigley, E. A.; and Schofield, R. S. (1989), *The population history of England, 1541–1871: a reconstruction*, revised edn, Cambridge: Cambridge University Press.

Wrigley, E. A.; Davies, R. S.; Oeppen, J. E.; and Schofield, R. S. (1997), *English population history from family reconstitution, 1580–1837*, Cambridge: Cambridge University Press.

Young, C. R. (1979), *The royal forests of medieval England*, Philadelphia: University of Pennsylvania Press.

Zanden, J.-L. van (1995), 'Tracing the beginning of the Kuznets curve: Western Europe during the early modern period', *Economic History Review*, 48, 643–64.

(2009), *The long road to the industrial revolution: the European economy in a global perspective, 1000–1800*, Leiden: Brill.

Zanden, J.-L van; and Leeuwen, B. van (2012), 'Persistent but not consistent: the growth of national income in Holland 1347–1807', *Explorations in Economic History*, 49, 119–30.

Zanden, J.-L. van; Buringh, E.; and Bosker, M. (2012), 'The rise and decline of European parliaments, 1188–1789', *Economic History Review*, 65, 835–61.

Index

Printed in the United States
By Bookmasters